A. G.
DANIELLS

ADVENTIST PIONEER SERIES
George R. Knight, Series Editor

Published volumes:
James White: Innovator and Overcomer,
by Gerald Wheeler

Joseph Bates: The Real Founder of Seventh-day Adventism,
by George R. Knight

W. W. Prescott: Forgotten Giant of Adventism's Second Generation,
by Gilbert M. Valentine

John Harvey Kellogg, M.D.: Pioneering Health Reformer,
by Richard W. Schwarz

E. J. Waggoner: From the Physician of Good News to the Agent of Division,
by Woodrow W. Whidden II

Lewis C. Sheafe: Apostle to Black America,
by Douglas Morgan

A. T. Jones: Point Man on Adventism's Charismatic Frontier,
by George R. Knight

J. N. Loughborough: The Last of the Adventist Pioneers,
by Brian E. Stayer

Uriah Smith: Apologist and Biblical Commentator,
by Gary Land

A. G. DANIELLS

Shaper of Twentieth-Century Adventism

BENJAMIN McARTHUR

Pacific Press®
Publishing Association
Nampa, Idaho | Oshawa, Ontario, Canada
www.pacificpress.com

Cover design by Steve Lanto
Inside design by Trent Truman

The author assumes full responsibility for the accuracy of all facts and quotations as cited in this book.

You can obtain additional copies of this book by calling toll-free 1-800-765-6955 or by visiting http://www.adventistbookcenter.com.

Library of Congress Cataloging-in-Publication Data:
McArthur, Ben, 1951–
A.G. Daniells : shaper of twentieth-century Adventism / Ben McArthur.
pages cm
ISBN 978-0-8163-5880-9 (hard cover)
1. Daniells, Arthur G. (Arthur Grosvenor), 1858–1935. 2. Seventh-day Adventists—United States—Biography. 3. Adventists—United States—Biography. I. Title.
BX6193.D3M33 2016
286.7092—dc23
[B]
2015031358

November 2015

Contents

FOREWORD

Arthur G. Daniells served as General Conference president longer than any other person. Yet *A. G. Daniells: Shaper of Twentieth-Century Adventism* is the first full biography of his life.

The twenty-one years (1901–1922) Daniells led the denomination were some of the most tempestuous in its history. One only has to think of the schism led by John Harvey Kellogg, the apostasies of A. T. Jones and E. J. Waggoner, the theological crisis over the sanctuary doctrine fomented by A. F. Ballenger, the struggle over the meaning of "the daily" in Daniel 8, the vigorous debates over Turkey and the "Eastern Question," and probing discussion regarding the role of Ellen White and the nature of her authority to realize some of the currents that threatened to divide the denomination from the inside. But to those issues and problems must be added those crises brought to it from the larger culture—especially the growing struggle between modernism and fundamentalism and the crisis of World War I, during which Adventism was for the first time divided by warring nations. All of those things provided a backdrop for the administration of Daniells.

But there were other pressing dynamics. Perhaps the most important was the need to reorganize the church to meet the needs of the twentieth century and the denomination's recently recognized worldwide mission. And then there was the challenge in the last years of his administration of being the first General Conference president to lead the church without the presence of a living prophet.

Such circumstances called for a leader of extraordinary vision, energy, and dedication. Adventism found such a person in Arthur G. Daniells. Beginning with his leadership in restructuring the denomination in 1901 and 1903, Daniells did more than any other person to shape the denomination for its dynamic journey through the twentieth century.

The good news is that Daniells has found the biographer he deserves in Ben McArthur, professor of history at Southern Adventist University.

Holding a PhD in American history from the University of Chicago, McArthur is no stranger to the field of biography. His latest book, *The Man Who Was Rip Van Winkle: Joseph Jefferson and Nineteenth-Century American Theatre* (Yale, 2007), and his role as an associate editor of Oxford's influential twenty-four-volume *American National Biography* have certified him as an experienced hand in the art of biography. The present book builds upon those skills.

A. G. Daniells is the tenth volume in an unprecedented series on Adventist biography. Thus far the series has seen treatments of James White, Joseph Bates, W. W. Prescott, John Harvey Kellogg, E. J. Waggoner, Lewis C. Sheafe, A. T. Jones, John Loughborough, and Uriah Smith. Scheduled future volumes include S. N. Haskell, Ellen G. White, W. C. White, J. N. Andrews, G. I. Butler, and D. M. Canright. And these contributions are merely the beginning of the titles projected for the Adventist Pioneer Series, which will eventually include more than thirty volumes. Each book will focus on the individual's major contributions to the church and will be written by a person well versed in his or her topic.

It should be noted that *A. G. Daniells* is the first book in the Pioneer Series to be published by Pacific Press. Daniells would have liked that. He favored Pacific Press during his lifetime and stipulated on his death bed that his last book, *The Abiding Gift of Prophecy*, should go to that publisher. Meanwhile, it is quite fitting that the last volume in the series to be published by the Review and Herald was *Uriah Smith*. After all, Smith had spent his entire career employed by the Review.

We are indebted to Ben McArthur for enabling us to better understand the life of Arthur G. Daniells and his contributions to the church that he dedicated his life to serving. I trust that the reading of this book will be a fascinating and profitable journey.

George R. Knight
Series editor
Rogue River, Oregon

Introduction

Arthur Grosvenor Daniells was Seventh-day Adventism's greatest administrator. That claim might at first appear as faint praise, lacking the inspirational drama that the founders' stories possess or the aura of danger some missionary narratives provide. Nonetheless, A. G. Daniells's return to America in 1900 came at a moment when his beloved church was at a turning point. Adventism needed his gifts of leadership. The year he was chosen to head the General Conference, 1901, church and nation found themselves entering a new century that heralded a new world. America had just become a player on the world's stage in Cuba and the Philippines (empire and missions often went hand in hand). Transportation and communication had been revolutionized by technology; the world was shrinking. Furthermore, America was becoming predominantly urban, a social change that presented cultural challenges to traditional Christian witness. New ways of thinking were demanded if Adventism was to fulfill its commission to take an end-time gospel to the world.

What qualities enabled Daniells to lead his church in these momentous times? Certainly not flash of personality nor brilliance. Although he carried himself with dignity and looked every inch of his five-feet-eleven frame a General Conference president, Daniells could not be described as a man of charisma or eloquence, great learning or towering intellect. Rather, in the manner of many effective administrators, he possessed quiet, often underappreciated qualities: a capacity for work, the hard unrelenting labor of chairing endless committees, attending to a daily stack of correspondence, traveling by train across the country and by steamship across oceans; the ability to discern danger or opportunity in situations where others might see only confusion; the maturity to let others rail at him without responding in kind; a self-confidence tempered by an awareness of his limitations and need for advice; and above all, a commitment to his vision of an Adventist presence throughout the world.

Daniells possessed the Midwestern small-town roots so typical of many American leaders in his day. He knew farm work. He completed only one year of higher education. He married the proverbial girl next door. After a stint of teaching, he felt called to the ministry. His introduction to tent evangelism in Texas was followed by a brief but influential time assisting James and Ellen White in that state. Successful evangelism back in Iowa led to a request from the General Conference to missionary work in New Zealand. From there he crossed the Tasman Sea for new challenges in Australia, where he enjoyed a rapid rise to administrative prominence. Most significantly, he developed an intimate working relationship with Ellen White and her son Willie. The prophet would serve as mentor, confidante, and prod to Daniells for much of his presidential career.

His accession to leadership came within a few months of President Theodore Roosevelt's. The two men could hardly be more different, yet both put a stamp on their respective presidencies that would forever change their offices. But where Roosevelt served seven and a half years, Daniells enjoyed (if that is the appropriate term) twenty-one years at the helm. Never one to shy away from the responsibilities of leadership, Daniells comported himself much as an executive of a modern corporation. This was unavoidable in an organization that spanned the world, operated scores of institutions, and had a budget in the millions of dollars. Decisions made, precedents set, budgets allocated, personnel appointed, and goals envisioned over those two decades created the modern Adventist Church.

One thinks of Daniells most often as the man who helped design, then institute, the sweeping structural reforms of 1901 and 1903. He influenced the general shape of the denomination for that century and beyond. Reorganization offered the clearest example of how bureaucratization affected the church. Like in government and business, expanding religious denominations required multilevel, specialized administration. Successful oversight of these modern organizations required leaders with particular talents. And Daniells seemed preternaturally gifted in these arts.

This development was more striking in Adventism than in most other Protestant denominations, because the church still benefitted from the counsel of its prophet. Ellen White, cofounder of the church, was well into her eighth decade when Daniells assumed leadership. She would live another fourteen years, roughly ten of which she actively participated in church affairs. Daniells had to negotiate the transition from charismatic to bureaucratic leadership within Adventism.

The change went smoothly for the most part, facilitated by the close relationship between White and Daniells. When issues arose, the younger man nearly always deferred to White's judgment. But on occasion, Daniells felt that he had a clearer picture of church affairs and sought to persuade her of his conviction (often through her son Willie). Nor was Daniells a leader reluctant to express opinions or be hesitant in decision making. It should not be surprising, then, that Ellen White sometimes commented disapprovingly of "kingly power" exercised in the church. But if friction occasionally arose between the two, it never seriously threatened a rupture. Daniells held a staunch loyalty to White's prophetic office. Despite this record, Daniells found himself increasingly under suspicion of being insufficiently supportive, even of doubting her writings. His controversial non-reelection to the presidential office in 1922 was engineered by an ugly campaign against his reputation.

Daniells knew serious disputes, most famously with Adventism's most prominent public figure, Dr. John Harvey Kellogg. Within two years of Daniells's accession to the presidency, Kellogg turned on him for failing to support the medical work at the level of funding the doctor desired. The alienation was prolonged, and it ended badly. If bruised, Daniells emerged from the struggle in a strong administrative position. He also demonstrated the support for the medical arm of the church by aiding the establishment of a new medical training school in Loma Linda, California.

But Daniells's legacy is not defined by conflict. Rather, it lies in three convictions that he championed during or after his presidency. First, in championing the bold vision of Adventism to take the three angels' messages to the world. He did so first as a missionary in his own right and then as the ultimate administrative sponsor of Adventist mission's outreach. He traveled thousands of miles outside of America to examine mission outposts firsthand. These trips were fatiguing, but Daniells's enthusiasm transcended the weariness. Even on his tenth visit to Europe, in 1910, he could testify that it "has given me a new vision of our work, and with it has come a new life and joy and delight in the work." Second, in affirming the ministry of Ellen White, an effort climaxed by his book *The Abiding Gift of Prophecy* (finished literally on his death bed). And third, in seeking to communicate his conviction that the Adventist ministry must both improve its professionalism and better communicate to members in the pew the glorious truth of righteousness by faith.[1]

A. G. Daniells generated thousands of letters and scores of *Review and Herald* articles during his long tenure as president. He also received thousands of letters from church workers around the world. The modern historian re-creating his career benefits from this rich trove of material. But virtually all of this concerns Daniells in his official capacity. The private man, the husband and father, is harder to discern. Apart from occasional comments to his colleagues on matters of family or health, Daniells drew a veil about his personal life. His reticence was partly a reflection of his own nineteenth-century notions of propriety. But more important, it bespoke his "all-business" approach to his work. As fully as Daniells devoted himself to the affairs of the church, he always knew much more needed to be done. Time was short. Resources were limited. He must keep about his Father's business.

In sum, this consummate administrator, this man of committees and budgets, was also a man of passion. The exhausting pace of his work, the blows to his health, found no reward in wealth. Daniells endured these difficulties only because of his conviction in heart and mind that Adventism had a message the world must hear.

---

[1] AGD to WCW, June 23, 1911, EGWE.

Acknowledgments

A recital of individuals who assisted this biography should begin by thanking those who previously wrote on Arthur Daniells's career. The earliest work on his life was intended to inspire Adventist youth. May Cole Kuhn, a General Conference employee, authored *Leader of Men: The Life of Arthur G. Daniells* (1946). The first scholarly study of Daniells, focusing on his preparation for leadership, was penned by John J. Robertson, *A. G. Daniells: The Making of a General Conference President, 1901* (1977). In recent years, Gilbert Valentine has written two books, *W. W. Prescott: Forgotten Giant of Adventism's Second Generation* (2005) and *The Prophet and the Presidents* (2011) that include extensive material on Daniells's presidency.

As with most research projects, librarians and archivists were essential to my progress. I began my research at the Center for Adventist Research at Andrews University, where Merlin Burt, Jim Ford, and their staff assisted my work. Jim Nix and Tim Poirier at the Ellen G. White Estate in Silver Spring, Maryland, provided me generous access to their materials over several visits. Likewise, Alfredo Vergel, archivist at the Ellen White Research Center at Southwestern Adventist University, provided ready assistance. Dick Schaefer and Seth Bates of Loma Linda University's Heritage Research Center responded promptly to several requests I made and provided details regarding Daniells's work on the Board of the College of Medical Evangelists. The bulk of my research occurred at the General Conference Office of Archives, Statistics, and Research. Through the years, several of its archivists assisted me, first Bert Haloviak, then David Trim and Ben Baker (who was especially helpful in locating illustrations for the book). I would be remiss not to mention the staff at Southern Adventist University's McKee Library, whose efficient interlibrary loan department aided my work.

Many other individuals deserve thanks for various contributions. I appreciate George Knight's extending me the invitation to take on the A. G.

Daniells project. Further, George read chapters as they were completed and kept me on target. Russell Staples, who likewise read chapters in draft, was particularly helpful on the history of Adventist missions. Brian Strayer not only read each chapter but gave each a thorough copyediting. Doug Morgan shared research materials that were essential for my chapter on Lewis Sheafe. Eric Anderson and the Walter C. Utt Center at Pacific Union College provided a wonderful environment and time to advance this project during my half year there. Jan Paulson provided useful reflections on the nature of being a General Conference president. Thanks also to Floyd Greenleaf, Bill Kilgore, Ron Numbers, Gil Valentine, Michael Campbell, and the staff members of the Fayette County, Iowa, genealogical society, who helped along the way.

Thanks go, finally, to Southern Adventist University for financial support through faculty research grants and professional development funds, which have allowed numerous trips to archives and for release time to complete the manuscript.

—Ben McArthur
Southern Adventist University

Abbreviations

AGD	Arthur G. Daniells
ASTR	General Conference Office of Archives, Statistics, and Records
CAR	Center for Adventist Research, Andrews University
Echo	*Bible Echo and Signs of the Times*
EGW	Ellen G. White
EGWE	Ellen G. White Estate
GCB	*General Conference Bulletin*
GCCMin	General Conference Committee Minutes
GCPL	General Conference Presidential Letterbooks
LLUASP	Loma Linda University Department of Archives and Special Collections
RH	*Review and Herald*
SWAU	Southwestern Adventist University
WCW	William C. White

A. G. Daniells

Chapter I

IOWA BEGINNINGS

Arthur Grosvenor Daniells was a child of the Midwest. He was born on September 28, 1858, in West Union, Iowa, and grew up in the midst of the rolling hills of the northeastern portion of that state. The town was scarcely beyond its frontier days in his youth. The first rough-hewn cabin in what became the seat of Fayette County went up a decade earlier. The entire state had been Indian territory just twenty-five years previously, and tales of attacks still pervaded local folklore. Wolves continued to plague the area during his childhood.[1]

Arthur was born to Thomas Grosvenor Daniells, a stonemason born in Vermont, and Mary McQuillan Daniells, who was born in Illinois. Mary was orphaned as a girl, and at some point made her way to West Union, where she met her future husband. It is not clear why they placed themselves in this outpost of an expanding America. Perhaps Thomas found ready market for his construction skills. He was already fifty-three when their first child, Arthur, was born. Mary was but twenty-three when she became a mother. The thirty years difference in their ages was not so unusual at a time when a wife's death often occasioned a widower's remarrying someone much his junior.[2]

Iowa was staunch Union country when the Civil War came in 1861. The state contributed more soldiers per capita than any other. Patriotic fever burned hot even among the area's older men. In late 1862, a group of Iowans petitioned the War Department to form a regiment of men too old for normal enlistment. The Thirty-seventh Iowa Volunteer Infantry was styled "the Graybeards," the only such regiment on either side composed entirely of men over forty-five years of age. Thomas Daniells could not resist the opportunity of a lifetime, so he joined up in December of 1862. He entered service as an officer, first lieutenant of Company K.

Since most low-level officers were elected by their men, his selection suggests that he was deemed a man of ability and leadership.

Too old for the rigors of campaigning, the Graybeard regiment understood it would be limited to garrison and guard duty. This it did at various locations in the St. Louis area during the first half of 1863 before crossing the Mississippi to Alton, Illinois, where the regiment took up duty guarding Confederate prisoners at the large facility there. This was a grim place. It had among the highest mortality rate of any Union prison. Overcrowding exacerbated the dysentery, smallpox, pneumonia, and other contagions that were chronic wherever soldiers gathered in large numbers. Thomas Daniells shared the fate of many prisoners. He died in October of 1863 at age fifty-eight.[3]

Mary Daniells was now a widow, with not only Arthur but also twins, Charles and Jessie, three years younger. She struggled to keep the family together in a humble three-room house by doing laundry and whatever other work was available. Nonetheless, she lacked the means to support her young family. She had to place her children in an orphanage established by the government for just such circumstances. Arthur had lost not only his father, but temporarily, his mother as well.

Better times returned when Arthur's mother in 1867 married a prosperous farmer in West Union named Rememberence Lippincott. The material comfort of the family improved immediately. Under his stepfather's tutelage, Arthur, now nine, learned the hard facts about farm work: up before dawn to milk and clean stalls. The yearly cycle brought a variety of other labors. Spring ushered in maple sugar season; summer was a round of plowing and seeding; then harvest in the fall. Work lightened between November and March, during which time some schooling was accomplished. It is clear from Daniells's later comments that his stepfather was a demanding taskmaster. Lippincott, who was elderly by the time Arthur was in his mid-teens, had fallen victim to opium addiction (a not uncommon affliction in that age of no controlled substances and where few medicines existed for the accumulated pains of old age). Consequently, he relied heavily on Arthur to do the farm work.[4]

If Arthur learned useful habits of work that later served him well, his childhood also marked him in less favorable ways. In his early career, he struggled with a stammer that handicapped his public speaking. The common psychological origins of the condition are well understood. Stresses in childhood, particularly a family loss or dramatic change in family circumstances, can trigger the problem. Arthur qualified on several counts. His was a difficult childhood.

Arthur also attempted to impose order on the memory of his unsettled childhood. He did so through a selective account of his father's occupation. Daniells's associates always understood that his father was a physician. At Daniells's 1935 memorial service, for example, assembled church leaders heard that Thomas Grosvenor Daniells was a "physician and a surgeon," who had graduated from the University of Vermont. In fact, there is no record of his attending the university. And the 1860 census recorded that he was a stonemason.[5]

How do we account for his son's story to the contrary? It should be remembered that this was an age when the threshold for becoming a physician was low. Standards at medical schools were abysmal, competing theories of treatment fragmented the profession, and states lacked strong certifying boards. It is believable that Thomas may have practiced the healing arts on the side. As gruesome as it sounds, skills in dressing rock may have been good preparation for the surgical techniques of the day. He may also have told his family and others that he was a college man. On the Midwest frontier, who would check? But one must also ponder the possibility that Arthur may have sought to cultivate the public memory of his natural father as a professional. A "physician" (and an officer in the war at that) was his true father; not the hard-driving, tiller-of-the-soil stepfather. An embellished pedigree might have been thought to enhance Daniells's fitness for leadership. The psychological forces affecting a son who lost his father in early childhood can only be imagined.[6]

How did the Daniells family encounter Adventism? In the big picture, it was part of the young church's (the denomination had been formally organized in 1863) new emphasis on evangelism. Once the Shut Door belief, which had dampened evangelistic enthusiasm, had finally been laid to rest by the mid-1850s, energetic efforts to take the Advent gospel to broad swaths of the Midwest began in earnest. Iowa had proven fertile soil for the church, though its beginnings were rather backhanded. Two of the church's stalwarts, John Nevins Andrews and John Loughborough, left the East—and the ministry—in the mid-1850s to seek a living wage in Waukon, Iowa. James and Ellen White's dash by sled across an imperfectly frozen Mississippi River in 1856 to reenlist their talents would become part of Adventist legend. A renewed Adventist community began taking the message in traditional tent meetings across rural eastern Iowa. Over the following two decades, a virtual who's who of Adventist preachers and leaders would labor there: the above-mentioned Andrews and Loughborough, Merritt Cornell, J. H. Waggoner, Dudley M. Canright (whose aggressive efforts resulted in eight new churches), and George I. Butler. Indeed, Iowa would be among the first group of state conferences organized in the early 1860s.[7]

West Union, roughly thirty-five miles southwest of Waukon, was among the first Iowa communities to come within the Adventist orbit. This was due in part to the efforts of one of the most remarkable lay evangelists in Adventist history, Dan Shireman. Shireman was orphaned as a young boy and grew up homeless and impoverished. He learned skills as a carpenter and mason, moved to Iowa, and accepted the Sabbath message in 1858. He then proceeded to devote a long life to spreading the gospel in every free moment. His devotion (and poverty) led him in 1861 to walk eighty miles both ways from West Union to Marion in order to attend a meeting. He became a regular correspondent to the *Review and Herald,* sharing with its readers for some five decades reports of his lay efforts. Indeed, Ellen White would publicly commend Shireman's labors as a model of lay evangelism. M. E. Cornell followed with a series of evangelistic meetings at West Union in 1863, and then B. F. Snook (later one of Adventism's famous apostates) established a church there with Mary Daniells as a charter member. Having been a devout Methodist, Mary embraced Adventism about the time of her husband's death and the temporary surrendering of her children to the orphanage. No doubt she found the Advent message a special consolation during these trials. When the children returned to live with her, Arthur followed his mother's leading and was baptized at age ten by conference president G. I. Butler. Adventism appeared to have bit deep in young Arthur. Years later he recalled his first camp meeting at age twelve. Among others, James and Ellen White attended. "Their sermons filled me with deep remorse for my sins, and yet led me to hope in God for salvation." Although he experienced those moments of doubt or apathy common to growing Christians, his devotion to the church persisted through the rest of his life.[8]

The Adventism his family experienced in post–Civil War Iowa would be very different than that of later decades. Church membership was then spread thin across the landscape, with few paid clergy to nurture faith. Reports in the *Review and Herald* from the Iowa field draw a portrait of small Adventist communities that looked largely to themselves for sustenance. E. P. Wilkins, a veteran of the Millerite disappointment, wrote from West Union of his solitary persistence in evangelism: "I have been very lonely here in Iowa," he admitted. "I have visited from house to house with the paper [the *Review*] in my hand, endeavoring to do what little good I could. . . . Some have been reclaimed from a backslidden state, and embraced the Sabbath." His efforts paid off as the West Union company expanded. Gathering sometimes in meeting houses but often in members' homes, the small flocks looked forward to Quarterly Meetings, when they would often gather with neighboring churches from Waukon, Elgin, and other nearby congregations for worship and celebrating the ordinances. Often, conference officials such as Butler and Daniel T. Bordeau would join them, providing reassurance to the local congregations that they were not orphans but part of the larger Adventist fellowship. By 1871, Iowa was the third largest conference, surpassed only by Michigan and Wisconsin.[9]

But the Iowa Conference, earlier in the 1860s, had also seen the earliest important offshoot movement in the denomination's short history. B. F. Snook and W. H. Brinkerhoff, first president and secretary respectively of the conference, made public their disenchantment with the prophetic claims of Ellen White. Snook and Brinkerhoff soon resigned their posts and became the core of the faction called the Marion party. On the other hand, G. I. Butler, who became conference president, cast the mold for the strong church leader of that era: actively promoting evangelism; scouting the field for new ministerial talent; inquiring after and, if necessary, disciplining backsliders. He apparently succeeded in retaining the confidence of most Iowa believers in Ellen White, at least measured by the wide adoption of White's dress reform by women in West Union and Waukon.[10]

Thus, Arthur spent his early and mid-teenage years in a round of laborious farm work overlaid by participation in a religious community that would have set him apart from most others in his West Union circles. Whether he felt a sense of difference—with pride or regret—we do not know. His mother's firm commitment to Adventism probably precluded his imagining anything else.

Daniells later credited his youthful experience on the farm with imparting a sound work ethic. Here Daniells's memory serves him well; he would become known as a terrifically hard worker. But it is also clear that there was tension between himself and his stepfather. At age sixteen, he essentially ran away from home, complaining to his mother that he was "learning nothing and getting no place." With his mother's blessing and scarcely more than the clothes on his back, Arthur entered the world, determined to get an education. It was common in those decades for a young man of seventeen to seek his way in the world. Daniells did not venture far, rooming with an area doctor (and doing chores for his keep) while he attended a normal school. He aspired to be a teacher. The bar for teaching was then quite low; a smattering of advanced work often sufficed. It became nearly a rite of passage for young people to devote a year to instructing children at a country school (as a year's service as a student missionary would be for later generations).[11]

INTO ADULTHOOD

Just turning seventeen in the fall of 1875, Arthur G. Daniells (probably with his mother's encouragement) determined to take a more ambitious step in his education. The establishment of Battle Creek College the previous year opened up new possibilities for Adventist youth. Daniells found 266 other students joining him on campus. He had modest savings, enhanced a bit by the government pension he received because of his father's death (which his stepfather had previously been appropriating). Not ample, but a sufficient start. Daniells's aspirations were not unusual for Iowa. It is a measure of the growth of the local Adventist community and of the hunger of young, rural Adventists for a college education that five others from West Union and Waukon joined him in the journey to Battle Creek.[12]

The Battle Creek College of the mid-1870s was a fitful establishment. It was founded upon earlier, short-lived schools in Battle Creek. Sidney Brownsberger served as president. Only thirty and sporting a University of Michigan degree, he steeped the institution in the classical curriculum then dominant across higher education. That Adventist leaders wanted a college speaks to the young denomination's felt need for educated ministers and teachers and to the confidence in its ability to staff and financially support such an institution. The confidence was only partly justified, as future financial struggles would show. Further, the proper educational blueprint remained a matter for debate.[13]

Though styled a college, like many such institutions of the nineteenth century, much of Battle Creek College's classwork was more properly secondary level. This was unavoidable, since secondary education was still a luxury enjoyed by few young Americans. Daniells never received a high school diploma (though his attendance at a normal school was a partial substitute). At the college, students chose among several curricular tracks. A classical track, involving intensive immersion in Latin and Greek; a theology track; a normal track—the most popular—a less demanding curriculum preparing students to enter the public school teaching ranks; and an English track. Arthur chose the latter, for which he would have studied in his first year algebra, physiology, history, rhetoric, and biology. Oddly, there were no required Bible courses for students in most of the curricula. This absence may not have been from oversight. Battle Creek, like nearly all religious colleges of that time, downplayed denominational identity. An early college catalogue notes that its doors were open "to all worthy persons desiring an education," and that it was to be an aim of instructors to "discountenance in students the spirit of sectarian exclusiveness."[14]

College founders had not considered the housing of students from afar to be a cause of great concern; they would board with local families. Arthur found himself in the home of young president Brownsberger. Sharing the same house was another West Union native, Mary Hoyt. Although Arthur soon took up residence elsewhere, his friendship with Mary blossomed through the school term. He also worked in G. H. Bell's garden and took "plunged baths" in the Kalamazoo River with friends. But these activities were not at the expense of his studies. It was clear even at this stage that whatever A. G. Daniells took up, he did so with energy and purpose. This trait could be to his detriment. Back at West Union the following summer and working on a farm, he labored so intensely that he suffered a heat stroke that included a seizure. Then back at Battle Creek for the fall session of 1876 (this time with his twin siblings in tow, who at fourteen illustrate the range of ages at the institution), the chronic headaches and fainting spells continued. He left school and entered the Battle Creek Sanitarium. Despite ministrations from John Harvey Kellogg, he showed little improvement. Kellogg despaired of any full recovery.

Thus, Arthur went back to Iowa, not to return to Battle Creek until 1900, when, so to speak, he returned in triumph after nearly a decade and a half of outstanding church service in New Zealand and Australia. His Battle Creek College experience certainly served him better than it did his brother. "Although I was blest in the Battle Creek school my brother went to ruin," Daniells told a colleague a quarter century later. "He became an infidel and a drunkard."[15]

If Arthur Daniells never earned a degree, he nonetheless took away from Battle Creek a notable consolation prize: Mary Ellen Hoyt. Mary was the daughter of Nason and Mariam Hoyt, a farm couple who had immigrated to Iowa from Canada in the mid-1850s. Her father, a veteran of the 1844 disappointment, joined the Adventist Church following the same Cornell evangelistic series that Arthur's mother had, perhaps the result of the same evangelistic effort. Mary stayed in Battle Creek when Arthur returned to West Union, and the two maintained an active correspondence. But he reported distressing news. His stepfather's scoldings set off his recurring fits. Mary became so worried that after several months she likewise returned to Iowa.[16]

Mary hoped to nurse him to health but found him in worse condition than she had expected. Arthur's mother was not doing well herself and could provide only limited care for her son. What to do? They had talked of marriage after completing college but now decided on an immediate wedding. Only that way could Mary devote full time to Arthur. Who knew how long they had together.[17]

Thus, on Thanksgiving Day 1876, Mary's twenty-second birthday, they wed. Arthur had just turned eighteen (at a time when the average age for American males at first marriage was over twenty-five). With no Adventist pastor available nearby, a United Brethren minister performed the service before a church full of relatives. If Mary's family had anything to say about it, the knot would never have been tied. Her father thought it odd to link herself to a poor, sick boy four years her junior. Her mother told her flatly not to ask her consent. And her relatives openly scoffed at her decision. But Mary persisted in a decision that resulted in a marriage of nearly sixty years, enabled her to see the world, and later made her the first lady of the Seventh-day Adventist Church.[18]

Although young and sickly, Arthur seemed to possess a maturity beyond his years. In a sense, the preternaturally serious Daniells was never young. If any eighteen-year-old was ready for early marriage, it was him. At twenty-two, Mary was already a year older than the average American bride at that time. No doubt she felt ready for her own home. One might also speculate about the influence of Arthur's long-departed father, who was well into late middle age when Arthur was born and died but five years later. Did Arthur, at some subconscious level (and especially in light of his recent illness) determine to get on with adulthood and parenthood before the uncertainties of life overtook him?

Although lacking any formal training, Mary served as Arthur's nurse, utilizing the water treatments (and even some electric therapy) popular in the day. They began to sell books together. Mary then returned to teaching in country schools, which she had done for several years before attending college (not unusual in that age). Arthur continued colporteuring for a time but then decided to try his hand at teaching when winter came. He faced a hurdle, though. Having so little advanced education, he could not obtain even the lowest level teaching certificate. Only when Mary's brother, the county superintendent of schools, intervened was a license obtained. They landed jobs at country schools four miles apart. Renting a room in a farmhouse for seventy-five cents a month, they experienced the hardships common to young couples of that age. On Fridays, they closed their schools early and took their horse and buggy the fourteen miles to her father's house, often singing hymns along the way.[19]

What would Arthur Daniells have experienced as teacher of a one-room school in the 1870s? We have no firsthand testimony from him. But he labored in a state where local control of schools was a defining feature. This also meant that the length of school terms often was determined by abundance of the harvest. Daniells worked in a rural culture where hard work and striving were axiomatic. One imagines that his discipline and intelligence would make him a successful teacher, though what his interpersonal skills were with children remains anyone's guess. Certainly, he, like all other teachers of that age, did not have to compete with television or video games for the attention of students. Curriculum centered on the basics, the "three Rs," with particular emphasis on spelling. Recitation was the lackluster backbone of instruction, but pedagogy was spiced up with debates, orations, spelldowns, and arithmetic competitions.[20]

For the fall of 1878, the Daniellses obtained a new position in a town. Arthur was to serve as principal as well as an upper-grade teacher, with Mary handling the lower grades. As it turned out, it never happened.

Accounts differ regarding Daniells's decision to enter the ministry. The early book on his life credited an inspirational series of meetings held by E. W. Farnsworth, newly chosen Iowa Conference president. These, said author May Kuhn, first got Arthur thinking about a ministerial career. Then, as he later testified, while walking to his normal school class, a sort of Damascus road experience occurred. He heard a voice tell him, "Go work today in My vineyard." It was not a change of career he agreed to easily; only after retreating to a straw stack for an intense season of prayer did he surrender to the call.[21]

But Mary Daniells, late in her life, gave an account that, if not completely incompatible with the above, at least added a new dynamic. She stated that it was she herself who encouraged a resistant Arthur to consider the ministry even before Farnsworth put out his call for Iowa youth to take up the Lord's work. Mary said she took her advocacy a step further, buttonholing Farnsworth and promoting her young husband. But the conference president demurred; he would offer no encouragement (probably because of Arthur's stammer). Farnsworth repeated his skepticism over several days. The conference committee even refused Daniells's offer to assist a traveling evangelist in Iowa (that the conference was running five tents that year and needed help suggests how deeply ran suspicion of Daniells's fitness). Doubts about the divine origin of his call must certainly have afflicted him. Thus, A. G. Daniells's ministerial career nearly ended before it started. Farnsworth certainly never envisioned the apparently limited young Iowan as General Conference president material. Even his wife later admitted that she "didn't dream he would make a talented worker," but simply an "earnest, good worker."[22]

A second chance came when R. M. Kilgore, who had left Iowa for Texas, gave him a chance to prove himself. Kilgore, who rose from private to captain in the Union army during the Civil War, would have preferred to stay in Iowa, but when implored by church leaders to consider moving his family to Texas, he showed himself still the good soldier. This was unorganized territory, with a scattering of believers. Kilgore's task was first to bring unity to an evidently fractious collection of believers, then to champion evangelism, and finally to organize a conference. He did so with unflagging energy and disregard for storms and flooding, religious opposition, and even several threats to his life. He labored in Texas for eight years, leaving a conference of some eight hundred members when he left.[23]

At their own expense, Mary and Arthur traveled to Texas toward the end of June 1878 to sign on with Kilgore. He would be Kilgore's new tent master, a task often assigned to young ministerial interns. This was strenuous work. Tents were large and cumbersome, and the fight against mildew was unending. Worse, a summer did not pass without a storm felling tents and ripping canvas. Arthur and Mary essentially camped out for months, living in a small tent pitched on plowed ground. Their only furniture were boards nailed together for a table and bench and a wooden frame for straw ticks. Mary did the cooking over an outdoor pit. Their tent tore easily in the unceasing Texas wind, and the pitiless summer sun threatened to give Arthur another sunstroke.[24]

Kilgore's and Daniells's work centered on the Plano-Dallas-Cleburne axis, an area of farms, ranches, and small towns. The team traveled about the region holding tent efforts of up to two months in duration. These were aimed at both the small band of Adventist believers scattered about the large area and at prospective converts. Typically, as with the effort in Rockwall County (Daniells's initial Texas experience), tracts on the Sabbath doctrine were widely scattered about the region to stir up interest. Local Protestant ministers often fulminated against the Sabbatarians, but this only served to heighten interest. Kilgore was not one to duck such challenges. He engaged in doctrinal disputes with relish.[25]

Daniells, though, continued to struggle with his stammer and acute discomfort in public speaking. But Kilgore, a rigorous taskmaster, was in this matter patient and encouraging to his charge. His assurance that Daniells would overcome his handicap instilled confidence in the fledgling preacher. Further, when Arthur later held his own meetings, Mary provided unsparing tutoring. His preaching voice, gentle and slow, was unsuited for the sawdust trail. The couple devised a system whereby, when his voice began to die down, Mary, sitting immediately in front of him, would give an unobtrusive hand signal to raise his pitch. She also recorded his grammatical errors and verbal tics for future correction. Ultimately, A. G. Daniells would become an effective, forceful, if not necessarily eloquent public speaker.[26]

The Texas camp meeting in early August posed different sorts of challenges to Daniells. He had to find a way to help the 125 to 150 attendees cope with the midsummer Texas heat. His answer was to construct an arbor on the south side of the ample twenty-eight-by-seventy-feet main tent, a haven from the unrelenting great-plains sun. In the fall, during meetings in Plano, Daniells had a chance to see his mentor Kilgore handle the local clergy's "holy war against the new evangelist," as a local newspaper described it. The paper admitted that the Adventists were "having a good hearing from our best citizens." Mary had a gratifying experience, one that bore fruit in later years. The first effort the Daniellses were involved in, held in Rockwall, Texas, apparently had no success. At its conclusion, with Kilgore away, Mary befriended two young men recently moved to the area. She gave them Bible studies, and they embraced the Advent message. But the full reach of her efforts would only be clear late in Daniells's career.[27]

In the midst of the itinerant tent evangelism, Arthur and Mary Daniells got a sudden reassignment. In November of 1878 James and Ellen White took up temporary residence in Denison, Texas, just south of the Red River boundary of Texas and Oklahoma. James White, his health sadly taxed by the unremitting pace of his work, needed to get away from Battle Creek. Northern Texas filled that bill nicely. Kilgore lent Arthur to the Whites to serve as secretary and general assistant. Mary, who had been teaching at a local school, took up cooking duties and copying Ellen White's writings.[28]

Not a great deal is known about the few months the Daniellses served the Whites. We do know that Mary helped restore James's strength through a regular diet of venison. Arthur served as James's amanuensis and valet. White would walk the floor dictating articles to Daniells, who scrawled them as best he could in longhand. Daniells also accompanied White on outings, driving the team of horses for him. Among the details remembered by Mary is an important first for her husband: In the evenings Arthur walked four miles to a country schoolhouse, where he held his first solo evangelistic efforts. In true Adventist fashion, the inaugural sermon concerned Daniel 2. Baptisms ensued from his meetings, and a new Adventist family became local pillars of the faith.[29]

We also know something of the Whites' perspective on their time in Texas from a candid letter Ellen White penned a few months after they moved out of state. She considered the Texas sojourn an unmitigated disaster. "I have no faith that it was our duty to go there when we did. It looks to me as though our time was lost." Not only were results meager but local newspapers were harsh. "I have no desire to know anything more of southern chivalry," she wrote with a tinge of sarcasm. Just as bad, she was embarrassed by the behavior of James. Her husband's penchant for entrepreneurship was indulged fully during these months—buffalo skins, brooms, and notably mules, which could be had cheap in Texas and sold dear in Colorado. In the young Daniells, James White had someone who could be tasked with rounding up a herd of mules who escaped from a corral. But James's ambitions could make him difficult, and for this his wife had to apologize. "I hope you will not have a very unfavorable impression of my husband," she wrote from South Dakota. "He was surfeited while in Texas with the cares of business which he should never have had." Ellen assured them that James was now "not the same man he was in Texas. He is more gentle, subdued, courteous, and kind." She went on to express her fondness for the Daniellses. "I love you both and earnestly desire to see you." Arthur Daniells's response a few months later was a model of graciousness. "I have all confidence in him," Daniells proclaimed of James. "I am sorry I did not do more for him last winter." He hastened to add that Mary had no hard feelings toward Elder White. This brief encounter was enough to lay a foundation of amity and trust between the Daniellses and the soon-to-be widowed Ellen White, upon which their close association in Australia twelve years later was built.[30]

When the Whites left for Colorado, Daniells found himself partnered with R. M. Kilgore's brother, Scott, in north Texas evangelism. Scott, Daniells soon learned, was a pale imitation of his stout-hearted brother. After some time with him on the evangelistic trail, Daniells had had enough. He penned a letter to the Whites, bitterly complaining of Scott's behavior and why he felt he must leave.[31]

The Daniellses' Texas sojourn, an exhilarating if stressful introduction to church work, was largely a volunteer endeavor. The Texas Conference, as R. M. Kilgore admitted, had "an empty treasury." So they received only sustenance pay. At some point the couple decided Mary would return to her parents in Iowa while Arthur ventured into colporteuring (they had money for only one train ticket to Iowa). For some months he accompanied a blind Adventist named Baylor across the Texas plains, offering the public an inspirational brochure on the latter's life. Daniells learned lessons only acquired through days of trudging door to door. Still, he must have been relieved when G. I. Butler, Iowa Conference president, called him to be a minister in his home state.[32]

IOWA EVANGELISM

Daniells returned to a thriving state. Iowa's booming population would reach the two million mark by the middle of the decade (a population considerably greater than its neighboring states to the north, west, or southwest). The Hawkeye state's largely farming inhabitants were dispersed across ninety-nine counties, hundreds of small communities, and innumerable farmsteads. Evangelism required frequent use of Iowa's extensive train network, but also a horse and buggy for more local travel.

Iowa Adventism enjoyed similar prosperity. Ever since the arrival of Adventism at Waukon twenty-five years earlier, Iowa had been a center of the church's Midwestern efforts. By 1880 the conference had just over twelve hundred members, slightly more than Minnesota and far more than other immediate states to the south or west. Indeed, Iowa was something of a repository of leaders and members who furthered the gospel in surrounding states. George I. Butler, for example, alternated between Iowa Conference and General Conference presidencies, an indication of the state's prominence.[33]

As a hub of late-century Adventism, Iowa provides a window into the nature of the denomination. Several characteristics stand out. First, Adventism was a collection of scores of small churches, fifty-eight in 1880. To this must be added scattered believers who lacked a church but, if at least two families shared the Sabbath message, might gather in one another's homes. Overwhelmingly, the Iowa Conference was peopled by new members. Many were of native American stock, but significant numbers also came from the abundant German, Swedish, and Danish immigration to the state.[34]

Daniells was a five-dollar-a-week licensed minister in the Iowa Conference. He was not a "pastor." Adventism did not have pastors in the modern sense of the word. Early Adventism was an evangelistic machine; all efforts, lay and ministerial, were directed toward proselytism. It could hardly have been any other way. The conviction of a soon Second Coming remained strong. Thus, to be a minister meant not an assignment to nurture one or several congregations but to work as an itinerant, holding tent meetings across the state. He also trained young Bible workers in techniques of holding Bible studies.[35]

The clearest window into the life of a Midwestern evangelist of this time comes from the memoirs of W. B. Hill, who labored for years in southern Minnesota. Hill tells a story of remarkable dedication; he persevered through hardships of travel, severe weather, and the death of two children from diphtheria. Evangelism was highly doctrinal, distinguishing Adventism from other denominations, particularly through the fourth commandment. Hill's favorite rhetorical device (especially when a clergyman was present) was to ask his hearers to stand if they believed in the Ten Commandments. Naturally, any attending clergymen would be embarrassed not to stand; but if he did, Hill would inquire why he did not keep the Sabbath. This good-natured yet confrontational style marked Adventist proselytism.[36]

One can get a sense of Daniells's early career through the reports he sent to the *Review and Herald*. His first reported meetings, appropriately, were near West Union. Over the next few years he went on (usually accompanied by another minister) to hold meetings in Sumner, Correctionville, Hazleton, Odebolt, Elgin, Battle Creek, and other small (and still small) communities. These efforts could last up to seven weeks. At Correctionville, for example, Daniells shared with readers the results of a six-week effort. "Interest and attendance were good from the beginning until the close. At our closing service the tent was filled with attentive hearers. We . . . would have remained longer, but we were obliged to move the tent to the Smithland camp-meeting. . . . We preached forty-seven sermons, sold $15.27 worth of books, and obtained one yearly and fifty monthly subscriptions for the *Signs*. Fourteen signed the covenant, five of whom had previously kept the Sabbath. We organized a Sabbath-school and established regular Sabbath meetings." This constituted a successful effort.[37]

But things did not always go smoothly. Spring and summer storms were perpetual threats to the canvas tents. Human opposition was even more difficult. Daniells's reports are filled with accounts of overt resistence from local clergy who were angry over what they saw as sheep stealing by an alien belief. Daniells was occasionally called on to debate doctrine (normally the Sabbath). Although ministers were advised to avoid public debates if possible, fleeing the field was not advised. Indeed, the Adventist pioneers seemed to relish battle. In Battle Creek, Iowa, Daniells and a local pastor dedicated two hours a night for four consecutive nights on the topic. On rare occasions a local pastor showed support, as did the Congregational minister in Correctionville, who attended Daniells's meetings, once even giving the opening prayer.[38]

During these early years Daniells also wore an organizational hat. He headed up one of Iowa's thirteen Tract and Missionary Society districts. The "T. and M." societies, as they were often called, were the organizational legacy of a group of four Massachusetts women who, in the late 1860s, met regularly in the home of Mary and Stephen Haskell. Their interest in lay evangelism led to an ambitious program of tract distribution. Stephen Haskell caught a vision for the larger church. He organized the first Tract and Missionary Society in 1870, dividing the New England Conference into districts to facilitate efforts. Haskell, supported by James White, went on to promote similar societies throughout the country. Headed locally by ministers, these T. and M. societies became the backbone lay movement to advance the Adventist message.[39]

The tracts were distributed freely, but the sale of Adventist books and periodicals was another key component of missionary advance. Daniells was a tireless promoter of Adventist literature. He frequently reported the value of the books he had sold. The work of the colporteur was regarded as frontline efforts for the church. The colporteur "should be kind and courteous," instructed Stephen Haskell in 1880, "always affable and never taking offense." Subscriptions to the *Signs of the Times* were encouraged. The publication of *Thoughts on Daniel and the Revelation* led to a particularly focused effort. Daniells both exhorted and organized Iowa colleagues to "circulate this most excellent work."[40]

By all appearances, A. G. Daniells made a smooth transition into the ministry. Dedicated, with an unflagging work ethic, he fit comfortably into the Iowa landscape in which he had grown up. Daniells proved himself sufficiently well so that in Iowa's spring camp meeting of 1882 he was ordained to the ministry.[41]

Nonetheless, all was not well with Iowa Adventism. In the early morning hours of October 23, 1879 (the anniversary of a devastating night thirty-five years earlier), Ellen White experienced God's presence. Testimony No. 29 delivered a graphic vision of God's judging some people who had been "traitors to their holy trust." The testimony decried the neglect in "getting our publications before the public," the inadequacy of the ministry, and the spiritual lethargy at Battle Creek College. But for the Adventist community in Iowa the testimony had particular punch, for White singled out "The Cause in Iowa" for particular comment.[42]

What and from whom White had heard talk about the state of Iowan Adventism is not known. A couple of things, however, are clear. She saw problems among the young ministers of the state (this just before Daniells returned to Iowa); and certain of the young men had been seriously misbehaving while at Battle Creek College. The fruits of this behavior not only compromised Iowa evangelism but also besmirched the reputation of the young Michigan college (whose very real problems would lead in just two years to its temporary closing). In the common manner of her testimonies, Mrs. White singled out individuals for reproof. "Brother F is not fitted for his work. He has nearly everything to learn. His character is defective." Collectively, matters added up to a crisis of leadership. "We have a dwarfed and defective ministry. . . . Not having experimental godliness themselves, how can they lead the people to that Fountain with which they themselves are unacquainted?" Worrisome to her as well were attitudes toward her writings. "A prevailing skepticism is continually increasing in reference to the *Testimonies* of the Spirit of God."[43]

Iowa leaders might have wondered at the intensity of the criticism, given the healthy growth of the conference. In 1879, the state's T. and M. Society had, next to mother conference Michigan, by far the largest membership in America and the most cash received (though not always near the top in quantity of material distributed). Still, Iowa leaders took her criticism to heart. A directive went out to tract society leaders, instructing each one to "see that every family and scattered member in his district has Testimony No. 29."[44]

If overall numbers were comparatively impressive, the decline of churches in northern Iowa, particularly the landmark congregation at Waukon, was disturbing. Nothing could be done about members moving away, but leaders recognized a broader problem. Dudley M. Canright, then a shining light of Adventism, stated it plainly: It was one thing to plant a church; it was "quite another thing to water it and cultivate it." Some churches in Iowa had not benefitted from preaching for two years. This would be addressed over the following decades, as the church embraced a more pastoral model for the ministry.[45]

But for the moment, evangelism ruled. Local members were expected to gather on Sabbath and worship—in the manner of New Testament churches—on their own. The Bible and Adventist literature would suffice for study. Four times a year, local churches held quarterly meetings; occasionally a conference minister would be present to preside over celebration of the ordinances. These were to be occasions of reaffirmation to the cause. Annually, a conference camp meeting provided opportunity to gather and gain a sense of comradeship and collective strength. For a provincial church these occasions were very important, and members were always encouraged to attend. "Let this be the largest meeting of Sabbath-keepers ever held in the State of Iowa," conference president George I. Butler exhorted in 1881. This particular camp meeting, held as usual in centrally located Des Moines, was highlighted by the unexpected appearance of the Whites. To have in one's presence a person acknowledged to be a modern prophet of God must have been a glorious experience to most, fearful perhaps to others. Yet even a prophet could not forestall a terrific hail and rain storm the very afternoon she was scheduled to speak, nearly tearing down the tent and postponing the meeting.[46]

PREPARING FOR A LARGER STAGE

In sum, the Adventist Church for which A. G. Daniells labored so tirelessly during the 1880s was one utterly confident of its message and mission. It held the truth about the Sabbath, Christ's heavenly work, and the nearness of the end. It was charged with alerting the entire world to these truths. This self-assurance was empowering. The message energized capable individuals to create an organizational framework that, while not perfect, was nonetheless impressively effective. It enabled laymen and evangelists to spread the Advent truth across vast swaths of the American Midwest.

This achievement came at some cost. The call from leadership to unremitting labor on everyone's part, though intended to inspire, at times passed over into hectoring. "A fearful responsibility rests upon those who have received the light of present truth," Stephen Haskell lectured in the

Review, a sentiment that in untold variations appeared again and again in church publications—and doubtless in camp meeting addresses. A sense that no amount of effort was ever quite enough contributed to a bickering leadership and a pervasive undertow of guilt.[47]

The still-young church also preached a gospel message that was light on the gospel. One can find messages of assurance and hope in the *Review*, but they are obscured by what leaders considered the church's real task of the remnant: to correct doctrine and lifestyle. Evangelists, after all, preached to a largely Christian Iowa audience. It was a matter of convincing Lutherans, Disciples of Christ, or Methodists of new light on a few key issues. Conversion stories focused not on an abiding sense of salvation and acceptance but on promise to put away tobacco and other vices, and especially on embrace of a Saturday Sabbath. Adventist evangelism also developed a culture of counting. Conference reports to the *Review* quantified book sales, pages of pamphlets distributed, letters written, families visited, members added. A fondness for statistics reflected a need to objectify the progress of the kingdom. There was a dry literalism about Adventist teaching well-suited to agricultural life. Sturdy yeoman, bound to the demands of planting and harvest, responded less to emotional matters of spirit than to solid matters of doctrinal fact.

This quality of Adventism, which Ellen White repeatedly decried, received a severe challenge at the landmark Minneapolis General Conference Session in 1888. The meaning of the contentious two-week session has been long debated. It seems fair to say, though, that Ellet J. Waggoner's sermons on the law in Galatians prompted a reconsideration of the balance between law and grace within Adventism.[48]

Daniells would not witness these struggles, however. Iowa seemed a state that Adventists went out from. Some went out from Adventism altogether. Its Marion Party was among the first major offshoots of the church in the 1860s. D. M. Canright, who became the denomination's most infamous apostate, was preparing to debate the president of Drake University in Des Moines in 1886 when he finally decided he could support Adventist beliefs no longer. A. G. Daniells, on the other hand, left Iowa that same year on quite different terms. After seven years in the state, and just as he and Mary established a city mission in Des Moines, he received a call from the General Conference to travel halfway around the world to New Zealand. As Daniells recounted to the General Conference sessions in 1901 and 1922 (the years he was first elected and then not returned to the presidency), it was a very difficult decision. His first reaction was begrudging. He knew nothing of New Zealand or the South Pacific. Then, after an intense season of prayer in a haymow, he became persuaded that God indeed was making the call. He wrote another letter to Battle Creek accepting the invitation, but this time with enthusiasm. "I cut the tethering line," he said. In his mind, he and Mary were heading for the South Pacific, never to return. A decisive man, A. G. Daniells had made his decision. His mother supported his course of action, despite knowing she might never see him again. In early October 1886 the Daniellses headed by train to San Francisco, where on October 24 they boarded a steamer bound for New Zealand. Not yet thirty years old, Arthur Daniells was to be a missionary.[49]

---

[1] Information on his Iowa community found in *The History of Fayette County, Iowa* (Chicago: Western Historical Company, 1878).

[2] United States Census, 1860. I'm indebted to the Fayette County Historical and Genealogical Society staff for providing information on Daniells's family. Mary Daniells's obituary (written by her son Arthur) is found in *RH*, February 23, 1922, p. 22.

[3] Guy E. Logan, *Roster and Record of Iowa Troops in the Rebellion*, vol. 5, http://iagenweb.org/civilwar/books/logan/mil706.htm.

[4] Everett N. Dick, "Arthur G. Daniells, Organizer," *Youth's Instructor*, Oct. 24, 1944, 4.

[5] Percy T. Magan, "Life Sketch of Arthur Grosvenor Daniells," *RH,* April 18, 1935, 1. Regarding Thomas Daniells's nonattendance at the University of Vermont, phone conversation with reference librarian, University of Vermont Special Collections, May 23, 2007.

[6] On medical training in the antebellum era, see Ronald Numbers, "The Rise and Fall of the American Medical Profession," in Nathan O. Hatch, ed., *The Professions in American History* (Notre Dame, IN: University of Notre Dame Press, 1988), 52–54.

[7] This story is well told in Richard W. Schwarz and Floyd Greenleaf's *Light Bearers: A History of the Seventh-day Adventist Church,* rev. ed. (Nampa, ID: Pacific Press®, 2000), 85–87.

[8] Information on Shireman found in Bert Haloviak, "The Orphan, the Angel, and the Long Walk," *RH,* May 31, 1990, 19, 20. In *RH,* April 9, 1861, 167, Shireman tells of his Iowa walk. Mary Daniells's obituary, *RH*, February 23, 1922, 23. AGD to "Brethren and Sisters," May 16, 1904, ASTR. An alternative story of her conversion is told by May Cole Kuhn in *Leader of Men: The Life of Arthur G. Daniells* (Takoma Park, MD: Review and Herald®, 1946), 18. In this version, a neighbor (apparently influenced by Shireman), in an old-fashioned act of personal evangelism, lent her a copy of J. N. Andrews's *A History of*

the Sabbath. Despite her Methodist friends' disappointment and her husband's disapproval (Rememberence never accepted her new faith, casting a pall over the family's religious life), Mary embraced Adventism. However, the version told by Mary seems close to the truth.

[9] *RH*, November 6, 1860, 199; March 29, 1860, 151; October 6, 1863, 151; August 14, 1866, 84. Description of the early days of the church's work in Iowa can be found in Emmett K. Vande Vere, *Rugged Heart: The Story of George I. Butler* (Nashville, TN: Southern Publishing Association, 1979), 18–28.

[10] Vande Vere, *Rugged Heart*, 18–28; on dress reform adoption, see *RH*, July 9, 1867, 60.

[11] Dick, "Arthur G. Daniells," 4.

[12] Kuhn, *Leader of Men*, 27, 28; Emmett K. Vande Vere, *The Wisdom Seekers* (Nashville, TN: Southern Publishing Association, 1972), 33.

[13] Information on Battle Creek College found in Vande Vere, *The Wisdom Seekers*. For a more recent and detailed history of Andrews University, including its origin in Battle Creek, see Meredith Jones-Gray, *As We Set Forth: Battle Creek College & Emmanuel Missionary College* (Berrien Springs, MI: Andrews University Press, 2002).

[14] Despite claims to the contrary by his earliest biographer, Daniells did not finish high school. Fayette County had no high school–level work until the 1890s. My thanks to the Fayette County (Iowa) Historical Society for information on local public education. *Second Annual Catalogue of Officers and Students of the Battle Creek College* (1875), 30, 20; *Third Annual Catalogue of Officers and Students of the Battle Creek College* (1876), 10.

[15] Kuhn, *Leader of Men*, 27–29; on Daniells's student life, see George B. Avery, diary, vol. 10, CAR; AGD to "Brother" Colcord, January 16, 1900, CAR. Daniells also told Colcord that his half brother who attended Healdsburg "was not benefitted by the school." In late life, Mary Daniells wrote a reminiscence of her husband's early life that includes the Battle Creek incidents ("Story of the Early Life of A. G. Daniells"). Unpublished, it is in the General Conference Office of Archives, Statistics, and Records.

[16] Clippings regarding the Hoyt family courtesy of the Fayette County Historical and Genealogical Society; Mary Daniells, "Story of the Early Life"; *RH*, November 11, 1890, 14.

[17] Mary Daniells, "Story of Early Life."

[18] *West Union Gazette*, May 5, 1883; April 11, 1896. Clippings regarding the Hoyt family courtesy of the Fayette County Historical and Genealogical Society.

[19] Dick, "Arthur G. Daniells," 12; Mary Daniells, "Story of Early Life."

[20] Information on nineteenth-century schooling found in Wayne E. Fuller, *The Old Country School: The Story of Rural Education in the Middle West* (Chicago: University of Chicago Press, 1982).

[21] Kuhn, *Leader of Men*, 29, 30. This dramatic account may have been encouraged by the young audience Kuhn wrote for.

[22] Mary Daniells, "Story of Early Life."

[23] *RH*, March 29, 1877, 104; June 7, 1877, 182; September 6, 1877, 86; September 20, 1877, 102; October 25, 1877, 131; a short sketch of his life is found in *RH*, August 1, 1912, 13.

[24] In his early days in Texas, Kilgore had put out a plea to church members via the *Review* for funds to purchase a tent. *RH*, May 24, 1877, 166; June 14, 1877, 190; July 11,

1878, 23; Mary Daniells, "Story of Early Life."

[25] *RH*, August 1, 1878, 46.

[26] Kuhn, *Leader of Men*, 32, 33; Mary Daniells, "Story of Early Life."

[27] *RH*, August 29, 1878, 79; November 7, 1878, 150; May 8, 1930, 24.

[28] Arthur L. White, *Ellen G. White: The Lonely Years, 1876–1891* (Washington, DC: Review and Herald®, 1984), 106, 107.

[29] "Report of [1919] Bible Conference," transcript, July 16, 943, 944; July 30, 1920, ASTR; Mary Daniells, "Story of Early Life."

[30] EGW to Arthur and Mary Daniells, July 17, 1879, CAR; Gerald Wheeler, *James White: Innovator and Overcomer* (Hagerstown, MD: Review and Herald®, 2003), 204, 205; AGD to EGW, October 22, 1879, Ellen G. White Research Center, SWAU.

[31] AGD to EGW, October 22, 1879.

[32] Kuhn, *Leader of Men*, 35; *RH*, October 9, 1879, 127.

[33] Vande Vere, *Rugged Heart*, 46.

[34] Evangelistic work among immigrants was often noted in the *Review and Herald* column entitled "Progress of the Cause." See, for example, *RH,* April 22, 1880, 269, and June 24, 1884, 411, on work with Swedes and Germans.

[35] Mary Daniells, "Story of Early Life." Bert Haloviak provides a fine sense of the ministry in this age in "Longing for the Pastorate: Ministry in 19th Century Adventism," unpublished paper, http://www.camelbackchurch.net/assets/391783.

[36] W. B. Hill, *Experiences of a Pioneer Evangelist of the Northwest* (published by author, 1902).

[37] *RH*, September 11, 1883, 588.

[38] *RH*, May 6, 1884, 301; March 20, 1883, 188; July 31, 1883, 493.

[39] Schwarz and Greenleaf, *Light Bearers,* 147, 148; *RH*, May 27, 1880, 344.

[40] Stephen Haskell, "Hints to Colporteurs," *RH*, January 8, 1880, 27; E. W. Farnsworth, "Intelligent Canvassers," *RH*, October 10, 1882, 634; AGD, "To 'Thoughts' Canvassers in Iowa," *RH*, October 13, 1885, 638.

[41] *RH*, June 13, 1882, 377.

[42] Ellen G. White, *Testimonies for the Church* (Mountain View, CA: Pacific Press®, 1948 [first published in 1880]), 4:384–522.

[43] Ibid., 430–441.

[44] Church statistics found in *RH*, Supplement, August 21, 1879, 3; January 1, 1880, 12.

[45] *RH*, April 1, 1880, 220; D. M. Canright, "Planting and Watering Churches," *RH*, August 9, 1881, 99; Haloviak, "Longing for the Pastorate."

[46] *RH*, May 17, 1881, 313; June 21, 1881, 393.

[47] Haskell, "Our Work," *RH,* Supplement, August 21, 1879, 1.

[48] George Knight, *From 1888 to Apostasy: The Case of A. T. Jones* (Hagerstown, MD: Review and Herald®, 1987) provides an insightful discussion of Minneapolis.

[49] The General Conference had first extended the call to Iowa Conference president E. A. Farnsworth, but he felt the job too big for one couple. Church leaders felt they could not afford to send two pairs, however, and then turned to the less experienced Daniellses.

Mary Daniells, "Story of Early Life"; *RH*, October 5, 1886, 624; January 4, 1887, 12; Dick, "Arthur G. Daniells," 4; *The Seventh-day Adventist Year Book* (Battle Creek, MI: Review and Herald®, 1887), 135; *GCB*, Extra No. 2, April 4, 1901, 49; *RH*, June 5, 1922, 20–26.

CHAPTER II

TO THE ANTIPODES

The Daniellses' passage aboard the steamship *Alameda* may have lacked the romance of sailing on the earlier clipper ships, but it had the advantage of speed. After a one-day stop in Hawaii, where they met the entirety of Hawaiian Adventists, Arthur and Mary resumed their 8,800-mile journey across the Pacific to Auckland, New Zealand. It was a pleasant voyage, a time of enforced leisure for one who scarcely knew the meaning of that term.[1]

What had leaders seen in Daniells that caused them to entrust the New Zealand field to him? To begin with, General Conference president George Butler knew Daniells from Iowa. Butler thought highly of him, seeing in his protégé one who possessed maturity and absolute dedication to the Adventist cause. Butler was not wrong. Daniells was seemingly "born old," preternaturally serious and devoted to work. The young denomination struggled to develop high-caliber ministers; in Daniells they recognized the genuine article. Evangelism already defined him. And in Mary, Daniells had a wife willing to leave her people for a distant posting.

And why New Zealand? Because the indefatigable Stephen Haskell had the year before introduced Adventism to that land. A promising reception of the Advent message prompted leadership to send a follow-up evangelist. Daniells's journey was part of a great impetus for Adventist mission work during the latter decades of the nineteenth century, sparked by John Nevins Andrews's voyage to Europe in 1874. Ellen White herself in 1885 went to Europe for two years. The same year Daniells reached New Zealand, John Tay visited Pitcairn Island, with famous results. Indeed, Adventist mission pioneers reflected American Protestantism's great age of world missions.[2]

What of the New Zealand the Daniellses encountered? European settlement dated back to the late 1700s, as an offshoot of the new Australian colony (it remained a British colony into the twentieth century). New Zealand's two large islands offered a generally mild though wet climate and rugged volcanic landscapes of breathtaking beauty. The beauty came with a cost. Just a few months prior to the Daniellses' disembarking, a huge eruption on the North Island's Mount Tarawera buried two native villages, rattled windows in Auckland, and altered the local landscape. Colonial New Zealand grew slowly. By the 1880s, European (largely English and Scottish) settlers still numbered under six hundred thousand, some in towns but more scattered about rural areas. However, the 1880s were a time of economic depression in the islands, resulting for a time in out-migration. The long-term situation was even grim for the Maoris, who, in the manner of natives everywhere, gave way before the European invasion. At first, the Maoris had stoutly resisted. When Daniells arrived, the savage Maori wars were still a vivid memory to North Islanders.[3]

A. G. Daniells's efforts in New Zealand were greatly aided by Haskell's previous visit. Haskell had encountered in Auckland a young Edward Hare, who in turn introduced him to his father, Joseph Hare, an educated Irish immigrant. His embrace of the Adventist message, and patriarchal influence over his family, provided a stout Adventist presence from the start. The Hares became the "first family" of Australasian Adventism. Another son, Robert, would assume a leading evangelistic role after two years of ministerial preparation at Healdsburg College in California (Robert's son Eric would later become the proverbial storyteller of Adventist missions).[4]

Daniells also benefited from a society composed of many young immigrants, and as often the case, containing religious "seekers." Traditional religious attachments were weakened in the uprooting process, and as immigrants planted a new society they exhibited an openness to new religious organizations.[5]

The Daniellses' arrival at Auckland in mid-November was marred by an unexpected tariff on the tent they brought with them. Daniells's request for more funds from church leaders back home brought a quick rebuke from George Butler, who decried his spendthrift ways (though he did send $300). An offended Daniells determined never to ask American leadership for another dime.[6]

Relations with New Zealand Adventists were better. Making contact with Edward Hare, Daniells soon set off to Kaeo, near the northern tip of New Zealand, where the center of New Zealand Adventism revolved about the residence of Hare's father. This was not simply a social call. In his typically businesslike fashion, Daniells hit the ground running with a two-week series of meetings and formal organization of the colony's first Adventist congregation. He reported to American readers of the *Review* that his New Zealand friends were "reasonable, common-sense people" who would do "all they can to make the work self-supporting." Daniells's efforts resulted in fifteen baptisms, including a Maori woman, the first native to embrace Adventism. Her tattooed face, Daniells noted, bore "the marks of the darkness from which God has delivered her."[7]

The young Adventist community in Kaeo was anxious to do things the proper way. Daniells instructed them in how to conduct church and Sabbath school services, how to organize a Tract and Missionary Society, and how to figure tithe. Daniells must have felt a bit like the apostle Paul, tutoring converts in the details of their new faith. The care with which the American pattern of organization was replicated elsewhere suggests a church that had come to a secure sense of itself.[8]

With a beachhead secured, it was back to Auckland. New Zealand's largest city, with more than sixty thousand people, Auckland held great promise in Daniells's eyes. It had been the capital city from the colony's founding in 1840 until 1865, when it lost the governing seat to more centrally located Wellington. Auckland's thriving port, ties with Australia, and trade with the Maoris continued to drive growth. Thus, in the austral summer Daniells undertook a tent meeting (utilizing the fifty-foot tent brought from America) that ran some ninety days with more than a hundred sermons. He did not intend so protracted a series. But attendance kept rising, abetted by the delightfully temperate weather of that clime. Twenty-five to thirty people began to keep the Sabbath, many of these, Daniells was pleased to note, being heads of household. Local ministers, who thought the novelty of a tent meeting would soon fade, began to worry as the weeks progressed. Daniells even invited a minister to speak on the "Lord's day," a tactic that led a half-dozen people to accept the Sabbath after hearing both sides. Not only Saturday but also Sunday services were offered, the latter accommodation proving popular. Evening meetings continued, though the chilly dampness of winter and lack of heating source in the church kept many people at home.[9]

Early success meant church building, and the small congregation moved forward enthusiastically. Daniells's efforts climaxed in mid-October 1887 with sixty-seven people gathering to formally organize the Ponsonby church in Auckland. Lacking satisfactory local waters, a baptistry was installed and put to use. Some were elderly people, lifelong Christians who had known only sprinkling in their childhood. A younger businessman, Daniells proudly noted, took a "bold stand for the truth." An "energetic, self-made man," he dissolved his partnership once convicted of the Advent message and entered the canvassing work.[10]

In Daniells's mind a new church meant the beginning of evangelism, not its end. More tent meetings were scheduled to begin after the Christmas holiday. This time the tent was raised near the public hospital. Although he remained the primary speaker in new efforts, the church's tract and missionary society drew members into the work. An ambitious mail campaign sought to distribute tracts widely throughout the area. Colporteurs, organized in groups of two to five, continued to be recruited to take Adventist books systematically throughout the land. Daniells oversaw an orderly approach to evangelism in New Zealand. In retrospect, we see the birth of an administrator.[11]

Daniells cannot be considered an innovative public speaker. But he showed willingness to try new topics in his addresses, such as the lectures on health he delivered during these years. This endeavor owed much to Dr. John Harvey Kellogg's work. Daniells testified to his reliance on a series of Kellogg's "fine charts on anatomy, physiology, and hygiene" for visual aids. The heart of Daniells's health lectures concerned temperance. "Our position as a people on the temperance question has made us many friends," Daniells asserted. He was gratified that many pledged to eschew tobacco, and "whole families [had] banished tea from their tables." "I am sorry that I have not in the past used this important means of doing good," Daniells wrote. Once enthused, he prepared talks for a series on "The Human Body" for the *Bible Echo and Signs of the Times* in Australia. Essentially a gloss of Kellogg's work, Daniells reviewed basic systems of the body, such as skeletal, nervous, and circulatory, with admonitions on how to keep them healthy.[12]

The presentations on health helped to build bridges with the community. Daniells's evangelistic meetings, as he happily reported, also benefited from generally favorable local press. Why a little-known religious group led by a Yankee should find favor—or at least tolerance—in a quite conventional society is not readily explained. Perhaps it was the very novelty of tent-meeting evangelism that caught the editors' fancy. Perhaps it was the latitudinarian and fair-minded spirit of the late British Empire. Further, a prohibition movement became a powerful political force during the 1880s, which Daniells's views naturally complemented. Less clear are the effects of the chronic economic problems plaguing the islands. A long-term drop in prices of rural products and a mounting public debt depressed growth. That hard times might have actually helped aid the Adventist message cannot be discounted.[13]

With the Auckland church well established, Daniells prepared to move to Napier, on the southeastern coast of the North Island. One senses that Daniells took little time to enjoy the fragrance of the azaleas and camellias that bloomed across the island. Time was short; workers were few; much remained to be done.

But in August 1888, before he began a new series of meetings, Daniells made his first trip across twelve hundred miles of the Tasman Sea to take part in the organization of an Australian conference. The ship called at several New Zealand ports along the way, so he had an opportunity to scout out future meeting sites, including Wellington, where Adventist work had yet to begin. Then it was on to the two major cities of the South Island, Christchurch and Dunedin. Only one Adventist colporteur had yet ventured to the island, whose colonial society had been shaped by the gold rush two decades earlier and now by fleece more literal than golden. Daniells was tearfully received by the one family in Christchurch that had accepted the Sabbath through reading *Thoughts on Daniel and the Revelation*. Further south, at Dunedin, no work had begun; indeed, the largely Scottish immigrant community would never be as receptive to the Adventist message. "My heart was made inexpressibly sad," Daniells reflected, "as I looked over this field, and realized how powerless we are to reach the people now."[14]

Arriving finally at Melbourne, whose four hundred thousand people made it the largest city in the Southern Hemisphere, Daniells was immediately impressed. "It is one of the most stirring, wonderful places it has been my privilege to visit," he testified. He saw the city at its scrubbed best, with a Centennial Exhibition then being held, celebrating a hundred years of English presence on the continent. Melbourne was also the center of Adventist work in Australia. Its society, according to another Adventist visitor from America, G. C. Tenney, had the "spirit of progress" congenial to his countrymen.[15]

Just three years after the coming of Adventism to the continent, a full-fledged conference would take form. Australia (including Tasmania) counted only 335 Sabbath keepers, but they were deemed enough to assume self-governing, self-supporting form. The gathering of twenty-six delegates (twenty-two of whom were laypeople) was facilitated by the reduced train fares for the national exhibition. They organized not only a conference but also a Sabbath School Association and a Tract and Missionary Society. Their publication, the *Bible Echo*, had been conveying the Advent message two years already. Delegates acknowledged "the past kindness of the American brethren," Daniells noted with satisfaction, but the time had come to organize and thus "relieve American churches from further expense and anxiety." Nonetheless, recognizing a dearth of local administrative experience, the newly arrived minister from America, George Tenney, was elected president.[16]

Arthur Daniells could not know that in a few years he would administer the Australian Conference. For the moment, both he and Mary returned to New Zealand and to an extended series of meetings in Napier. He could hardly have chosen a more scenic spot than the beautiful Hawkes Bay region, with its ocean-side setting and sunny, Mediterranean-like climate. More to the point, the heavily Methodist population of the northern region proved receptive to the Advent message. The ground had been prepared for Daniells and assistant evangelist Robert Hare by young Auckland church members, who covered the region with Adventist literature. The meetings were well chronicled by local newspapers and thus provide a clear window into the nature of that day's evangelism.[17]

Daniells pitched the "calico tent" near the center of a town. Mary did her best to keep house in an adjoining twenty-one-by-fourteen-foot tent, fitted with a wooden floor, carpeted, and divided by curtains into five rooms. Townspeople were promised that the "sentimentalism so often cultivated in evangelistic meetings" would not be present; instead, a sterner "Thus said the Lord" would mark the preaching. Nor was there to be any special "ism"; teachings were to be pure first-century gospel, "without any recourse to nineteenth-century emendations, interpolations, or 'improvements' of any kind." But it was not all prose. Singing had its place, by choir and congregation, accompanied by the organ. The series opening on October 28 must have gratified Daniells, as the three hundred seats were insufficient for the overflow crowd.[18]

The evangelistic series unfolded with a logic that has changed little over the decades. Daniells began by reviewing evidence for the reliability of the Bible, then proceeded to the prophecies of Daniel, the place of the papacy in prophecy, the sanctuary, the Ten Commandments, and the Sabbath (perhaps not as free of sectarian doctrine as had been promised). Daniells found opportunity in early November to strike a responsive chord with his English colonials. In the city's Theatre Royal he gave a special address, "What is Protestantism?" Attended enthusiastically by the town's Orangemen, the occasion commemorated the two-hundredth anniversary of William of Orange's landing in England, an event revered by British Protestants as a blow against the revival of "popery" in that country. Naturally, Daniells found this an opportune moment to remind his listeners of Rome's dangers, even worrying aloud about encroachments of Romanism in America.[19]

Interest among Napier residents continued strong through the weeks, even during some nights of stormy weather. Robert Hare occasionally relieved Daniells, preparing for the time when he would head out alone on the sawdust trail. Hare preached on the topic returned to most often, the Sabbath. More so even than the Second Coming, Adventist evangelism found its distinctive voice in proclaiming the immutability of God's prescribed day of rest.[20]

But health was another "entering wedge." In the midst of the series Daniells presented "Health, or Cause and Cure of Indigestion," complete with large diagrams showing the body's organs and the nutritional values of various foods. More delicately, Daniells later dealt with "Social Purity, or How to Maintain all the Power of Body and Mind." Held in the Athenian Hall, this was open only to men (who still overflowed the room). Daniells spoke as plainly as Victorian propriety allowed of the "vices which sap the health and manliness of youth," and which must be foresworn if the "nobility of true manhood" is to be attained.[21]

Daniells recognized that he did not labor in a pagan mission field. Rather, as the apostles preached first to the Jews, pioneer Adventist missions worked among historically Christian European peoples. The goal was to bring Christians into an expanded truth. But nineteenth-century New Zealand contained many biblically literate Christians assured of their own truth. They were prepared to take on Daniells in the public forums of the pulpit or the newspaper column.

The most contentious debate arose after an initial cordiality. J. Edwards, a Methodist pastor who had assisted Daniells with opening prayer or a hymn in early meetings, suddenly turned hostile. In a series of lengthy letters to the local paper editor (who finally appealed to writers to "study brevity"), Edwards excoriated Daniells for his assumption of infallibility in biblical interpretation. "He cannot err, he cannot be deceived." Further, Edwards (claiming to be speaking for other town ministers) objected to the Adventist suggestion that all churches save their own are "fast ripening for everlasting destruction." Daniells responded with an offer to meet Edwards "in the open field and there test the strength of our positions in dignified debate." That did not happen. But neutral observers who weighed in on the discussion came to Daniells's defense. "An Infidel," claiming to have "no dog in the hunt," noted that local church leaders had no answer to Daniells's contention that the fourth commandment claimed their allegiance. The local churches were "either densely ignorant or else easy-going hypocrites." "Fair Play" challenged Edwards to accept Daniells's offer for an open debate. Having studied some of the Adventist positions, he thought "another Luther's day" might be coming.[22]

Debate also raged over the less orthodox issue of spiritualism. The later nineteenth century witnessed great interest in the phenomenon, when even tough-minded scientists such as William James thought the subject worth investigating. Obviously, its belief challenged Adventist notions of conditional immortality and could not be allowed to pass. Daniells provoked response in some Napierites with multiple lectures intending to "unmask Spiritualism." In a letter signed by "Spiritualist," one local implored Daniells to be fair to his beliefs and not simply demolish straw men arguments. An "Enquirer" questioned after the lecture whether Daniells's skeptical question, "Can a man think without a brain?" was necessarily true. He went on to relate the tale of a man whose amputated leg, when subjected to heat or stabs, gave pain to the man, suggesting the existence of a "spirit leg" more real than flesh and blood. Two correspondents were surprised that Daniells admitted the truth of much spiritualist communication (attributing it to evil angels rather than to deceased human contact) but asked how he could "be so certain that it is all diabolical agency?"[23]

If Daniells, according to some, acquitted himself admirably in his lectures, there were at least two occasions when the limitations of his education became clear. One concerned the perennial challenge of explaining how a seventh-day Sabbath should be figured in a round world. Just a few years earlier, in 1884, delegates from twenty-five nations had gathered in Washington, D.C., for the International Meridian Conference. It sought to establish a prime meridian and thus a globally accepted solar day. The uniformity took some time to accomplish. In 1888 it was still possible, as one traveled west, to find oneself traveling from Saturday to Sunday and back to Saturday again. The new week began in New Zealand before any other major population center in the world. But other islands of the western Pacific adopted Saturdays or Sundays independently. Who was to say, one writer asked, which are keeping the correct Sabbath? "Is it not absurd to make a matter of conscience, and stake one's salvation, on what at best is a purely human and conventional, and therefore exceedingly fallible and clumsy argument?" Daniells sidestepped this thorny problem but did score a point by asking how observing Sunday solved the dilemma.[24]

Daniells stumbled more badly in a scientific assertion he made when discussing the resurrection of the dead. Evidently concerned to show that the corporeal substance of the dead is preserved in the earth, he asserted that vegetable matter does not absorb decayed elements of human bodies. The basis of his idea is unknown, but W. H. Neal publically called him on this scientific gaffe. Daniells, it would seem, needed more tutorials from Dr. Kellogg.[25]

Controversy was inevitable, of course. Adventist proselytizing posed too great a challenge to the religious status quo not to arouse resistance. But Daniells's and Hare's success in Napier was striking. After five months' work (some of which took place in the Theatre Royal), fifty-five people signed the covenant "to keep the commandments of the decalogue and the faith of Jesus." A Sabbath School (with more than a hundred members) and a tract society followed. Stories of converts taking brave stands for the Sabbath at their jobs encouraged all. Daniells was particularly pleased at the number of young people attracted. Three young men decamped to Battle Creek College for further study.[26]

By May 1889, three New Zealand churches appeared to thrive: Kaeo, Auckland, and Napier, with a collective membership of above one-hundred fifty. The logic of Adventist development demanded that a local conference be formed. Thus, late that month an organizational meeting in Auckland replicated what their Australian cousins had done a half year earlier. Again, American missionaries provided the leadership: Daniells (elected president); M. C. Israel (then working in Tasmania); and E. M. Morrison (recently arrived from the States to coordinate publications). Given this, it is not surprising that organization closely followed American patterns and that the gathering saw fit to give a vote of thanks to the brethren in America. This moment represented a triumph for Arthur Daniells. A modern essay on the beginning of Adventism in New Zealand notes, "It is difficult to exaggerate the effects of the work of A. G. Daniells."[27]

Still, his final months in the North Island were marked by reduced success, criticism, and illness. After Napier, Hare took a tent to Gisborne, while Daniells took another to Wellington. The latter city, conveniently located near the South Island, seemed the right choice as a center of Adventist work in the colony. But Wellingtonians proved cooler to the Advent message, and though a church was founded there, Daniells could not replicate the earlier successes in Auckland and Napier. Further, he and his wife came under criticism from fellow believers. The problem apparently was rooted in jealousy that Mary Daniells felt toward the younger daughters of Joseph Hare, who stayed for a time with the Daniellses. Mary, who in Ellen White's words, had "not always the oil of the grace of God," stirred up resentment among the close-knit New Zealand Adventist community by her treatment of the girls. But Arthur also had failings. Although effective as an evangelistic preacher, he failed to understand the importance of home visitation. As he moved on to new locales, in the manner of evangelists, he sometimes left behind young groups of believers not yet capable of sustaining themselves. Thus, the Auckland church, thriving when Daniells left, reduced to about half in succeeding years. In fairness to Daniells, this inattention to congregational nurture characterized the church more broadly.[28]

Compounding all other problems, Daniells was bedeviled by recurring pain. During the Napier effort, facial neuralgia had forced him to cease work for a time. The illness (attributed—as always—to overwork) would finally contribute to his leaving the New Zealand field in March 1891 for what he hoped would be the healing dry heat of Australia. "We have sustained quite a loss in the removal of Elder Daniells to Australia," one of his colleagues wrote. There is little doubt about the truth of that statement. Daniells's work, if imperfect, laid the foundations upon which a New Zealand church was built long after he was gone.[29]

NEW HORIZONS IN AUSTRALIA

The Daniellses' arrival in Sydney joined them to an Australian Adventist community that had grown, if not flourished, in the six years since eleven Adventist pioneers landed there in 1885. Stephen Haskell and his fellow workers found a land in the midst of peaceful political evolution toward becoming a federation of states within the British Commonwealth, a status culminated in 1901. A country characterized by its broad vistas, exotic wildlife, and ranches, Australia was also well on its way to replicating the modern urban, industrial society of its European colonizers. Both Sydney and Melbourne had several hundred thousand people in their metropolitan area by 1890, and factory work began to employ large numbers of people. Anxious to efface the "convict stain" of the colonies' founding, middle-class Australians embraced proprieties of Victorian culture. Formal gardens, concert halls, and other accoutrements of civilized life marked the large cities. The 1880s in particular was a decade of national self-congratulation as people reflected on their progress of a century.[30]

Religion, too, was thriving. The self-assured British colonial culture of the late Victorian years was congenial to Protestant Christianity. Though the Church of England was preeminent, religious liberty was secure, and members of a variety of denominations freely worshiped. Beautiful churches dotted the urban landscape. Thus, Adventists arrived at an opportune moment to persuade Australians of present truth. The only clouds on the horizon were a looming economic recession in the country and the encroaching ethic of pleasure, abetted by a shorter workweek and more leisure time. In the long run, the appeals of secularism would prove the greatest challenge to Christianity.[31]

The young Sydney Adventist community numbered about thirty when Daniells arrived. They welcomed his addition, one who at age thirty-one could be counted a veteran of the gospel. He and his associate mounted a standard tent meeting series in the suburbs (center-of-town locations being difficult to procure). They did not go well. Part of the problem lay in a lack of effective speakers. But Daniells also concluded that tent meetings were simply not to the taste of Sydney residents. "The people are too English," he wrote General Conference president Ole Olsen. Like Londoners, they avoided tents but would attend meetings in public halls, especially lectures on temperance. A later Sydney effort suffered additional complications of a flu epidemic that virtually brought the meetings to an end.[32]

Daniells next spent a month at Ballarat, northwest of Melbourne. Founded at the epicenter of Australia's gold strike in the early 1850s, Ballarat had a well-earned reputation for typical gold rush excess. By 1890 the city had transcended its origins to become an important urban center in Victoria. Daniells's task was to revive its foundering Adventist church, which he found in "cold, backslidden condition." One brother was " 'off' on the tithing and Testimonies, and others were formal." Rather than reiterate doctrine, Daniells went back to the gospel basics: that Christ is "to dwell in their hearts by faith; that when there, Christ will cause them not only to desire but to do God's will." He witnessed a successful revival. "You should hear their testimonies now," he wrote Stephen Haskell, "they have something fresh to tell."[33]

Australian church headquarters were in Melbourne, capital of the Victoria colony, where Adventist work had begun on the continent. Early church workers met fierce opposition from local Protestant ministers, suspicious of Adventist theology (sales of Uriah Smith's *Thoughts on Daniel and the Revelation*, with its heterodox Arian Christology, did not help). But, as Haskell observed, Melbourne was something of an American city, bustling and receptive to those ideas that seem to have made America thrive. It was also a city of readers, congenial to Adventists' great emphasis on literature evangelism.[34]

The biggest event in the life of the young Australian Adventist church was the arrival of Ellen White and her son William in late 1891. Their coming was voluntary, but to Ellen White, also somewhat coerced. Perhaps unhappy with their prophet's criticisms of their spiritual leadership, General Conference brethren, through the agency of the Foreign Mission Board, officially encouraged the White family to undertake an extended visit to Australia. Desiring rather to spend her time at home on her writings, White nonetheless consented, convinced that God had a purpose for her in furthering the Advent message in a new land. Her party left San Francisco harbor in mid-November and arrived in early December.[35]

The Daniellses were part of the entourage welcoming the Whites at the dock. They were taken by phaeton through the beautiful garden parks of Sydney to the Daniellses' rented house. Ellen White approved of their "plain, simply furnished, but comfortable home" that seemed "in accordance with our faith." Mary prepared a "wholesome, well prepared breakfast," White wrote her son Edson, after which the local canvassers and Bible workers gathered about for worship. "It was very touching to hear Elder Daniells tell how different ones were awakened to inquiry in regard to the truth." It was an affectionate, even intimate beginning to her Australian ministry.[36]

Unfortunately, the feelings would soon turn warm in less pleasant ways. The Whites had arrived just before the annual Australian conference meeting. The first and well-loved president, George Tenney, needed relief to focus efforts on his greater strengths of writing and editing the *Bible Echo*. But who to replace him? The leadership pool was very small, and the leading candidates were American—which was the problem. A tender national pride was offended by the dominant, pushy Yankees. None of the potential candidates "was competent for the situation," Ellen White told the nominating committee, "but we must have a president." With this underwhelming endorsement, she put forth Daniells's name, not so much for his New Zealand administrative credentials but because he seemed best able to provide the pastoral leadership the young local churches needed. Daniells, if not ideal, stood "in the best place spiritually of any of them," better fitted than "any other man in Australia." There was resistance on the committee, but he was finally appointed.[37]

Leadership selection was not the only cause of tension. One reason Ellen White initially balked at visiting Australia was her fear that she must bring a message of rebuke. She delivered such a message during the conference session. While the delegates and other attendees heard a sermon on Romans in the upstairs hall, below in the *Echo* office White spoke to the conference ministers. Mentioning individuals by name, she pointedly told them how "the Lord had shown me their dangers." As George Tenney candidly admitted to the *Review* readership in America, the testimonies "were not of a nature calculated to flatter our vanity, or to encourage a self-satisfied spirit." The assembled workers at first could scarcely believe the solemn words applied to them. "It was something different from what we had expected to hear." But the half-hour session had its desired effect. Confessions abounded. Robert Hare admitted that "he had been envious and jealous of Brother Daniells." Steed, Curtis, Tenney, all offered up *mea culpas*. Over the course of several hours, as White recounted, "The brethren confessed to one another and fell on one another's necks, weeping and asking forgiveness."[38]

The Australian Conference, numbering only 550 (but which had grown by 17 percent the previous year), was still family-sized, but it spread over broad reaches of the southern and eastern portions of the continent, plus Tasmania and missions in the scattered islands of Polynesia. To accomplish the ambitious goal of reaching Australia's three-plus million people with the gospel would require feats of organization. Fortunately, that was something Adventist pioneers did well. In this, the third general meeting of the conference, three key resolutions were passed, both premised on the assumption that Australia would be the center for Adventist work in the East Asian/Western Pacific region. First, given the openness of many people to Bible study in Australia's cities, workers must be trained for home visitation. Second, "that a few men of devotion, energy, and piety" should be identified and put to colporteuring. Third, given the increasing demand for educated workers and the inconvenience of traveling to Healdsburg or Battle Creek, that a school needed to be established for Australasia. These resolutions would shape much of Daniells's agenda for the next eight years.[39]

Among Daniells's initial tasks was to visit existing churches and spiritually renew members (putting to practice what Ellen White had urged). When ministers were devoted to evangelism rather than the pastoral care of congregations, spiritual lethargy could easily set in among members.

In late January, as Daniells traveled the five hundred miles northwest to Adelaide, a refreshing rain brought relief from the searing summer heat. Adelaide, the capital of South Australia, was a city of some fifty thousand people. Its cleanliness, broad streets, orchards, and gardens pleased Daniells. He was also "profoundly impressed with a sense of the need for more heart-work" among the church members. "Heart-work" to Daniells was evidenced by good works, especially evangelism. "We call ourselves Christians; but do we follow Christ in the path of self-denial and earnest labor for the redemption of man?" In particular, he detected a neglect in visiting "the sick, lonely, and oppressed ones." Daniells, displaying his administrative gift, organized the city into districts, doling out responsibility among members to visit at least once a month.[40]

But at the close of the year, having become familiar with much of the Australian church, Daniells expressed private concerns to Ellen White. "They can't truly repent of sin. They do not die to self. They cherish their darling idols." Adventist leaders, he continued, must work "to get them to see the sinfulness of sin and to hunger and thirst after righteousness." People needed "Bible study and secret prayer. I know for a fact that the masses of our people are strangers to real Bible study and communion with God."[41]

Daniells's comments reflected a still-young man, perhaps marked by perfectionist tendencies, who struggled to accept the imperfections of others. Ellen White, rarely shy herself about voicing need for a demonstrated faith, nonetheless sought to temper Daniells's negativity. "You may be inclined to look upon the dark side too much. . . . Do not strike a single discouraging note. . . . Let there be no reason for complaint that you are severe, and thus discourage souls." Such severity stirred resentment. Further, as W. C. White perceived, the Australian membership continued to chafe under what they felt was a leadership forced on them, one which, unlike Tenney's, did not appreciate their colonial ways. The Americans expected native members to quietly follow their lead; Australians believed their own people were not given "their proper place in the work." Fortunately, Daniells's administrative learning curve was steep, and within a year W. C. White reported "a growing feeling of confidence in the cause."[42]

It is very possible that Arthur Daniells's initial difficulty was not simply inexperience or perfectionism. He frequently felt bad physically. The same neuralgia that plagued him in New Zealand visited him in Australia.

Some temporary relief was gained by wrapping wet cloths around his head and laying them on his spine while he lay in bed. But not until the summer of 1893 was the true culprit identified: decayed teeth. "Getting one pulled and another filled has helped immensely," Mary told Ellen White. He felt good for the first time in years. Perhaps inspired by his example, Ellen White, then in New Zealand and suffering from toothaches, had her last eight teeth pulled (without benefit of anesthesia). Their experiences are reminders of how pioneers persevered in the face of chronic aches and pains.[43]

Daniells, years later as General Conference president, usefully called upon his early struggles as administrator. When consoling H. W. Cottrell in 1910 following his ouster as Pacific Union president, Daniells reflected on his own experience. "It seemed as though I could never get hold of administrative work," he confessed. "Many, many times I was overwhelmed with discouragement and decided in my own mind that I could never succeed in Conference management." He recalled how Willie White and he occasionally had unsettling differences on policy matters. Adding to his discouragement were the "sharp reproof[s]" from the prophet that were "not pleasant to the natural heart." But he accepted them and "inch by inch" worked his way into his work. One might partially discount Daniells's recollections as efforts at heartening Cottrell. But as evidence above suggests, however talented Daniells may have been, he was not exempt from learning hard administrative lessons.[44]

LITERATURE EVANGELISM

Daniells presided over an engine of evangelism that rested on two pillars: distribution of Adventist literature and public tent efforts. And of these two, literature evangelism was probably the most far-reaching. Indeed, the publishing and distribution system developed in the 1870s represented one of the great organizational triumphs of the Adventist Church. The conference tract societies effectively turned laypeople into an army of promoters of the Advent message. This in turn led to establishing two new presses, Pacific Press (1874) and Southern Publishing (1901), whose demand for a product to sell encouraged Ellen White and her assistants to refashion many of her letters and articles in best-selling books and then provided an outlet for later generations of Adventist writers.[45]

Daniells's early career in Iowa included overseeing the state tract society. He believed fervently in the vital role of literature evangelism. Now he led an Australian publishing work already well established but which needed encouragement. Two of the original five Adventist missionaries to the southern continent came directly from the publishing work. Within weeks of their arrival, a monthly, the *Bible Echo and Signs of the Times,* appeared. In 1889 it changed to a twice-a-month format. The editors explicitly sought to "place it in the very forefront of religious family journals." Although it was clearly an Adventist paper, with theological and prophetic distinctives featured, much of its pages contained general pieces on biblical themes, current events and history, short stories, anecdotes, and bits of personal wisdom that could appeal to an array of religious readers. Following Daniells's suggestion, a major circulation drive was mounted. The paper proved to be an invaluable evangelistic resource. Many embraced the Sabbath message solely through its reading.[46]

Although American tracts and books were available for sale, Aussies' desire to produce their own materials led to expanding the small press into a full-fledged commercial operation during the 1890s. Echo Publishing in Melbourne quickly earned an enviable reputation in the country, taking on commercial jobs, including becoming the official publisher for the governor. Even during the early depression years of the early 1890s, profits from sales of books (particularly Uriah Smith's venerable *Thoughts on Daniel and the Revelation*) helped carry other expenses. But as with the press in Battle Creek, growth was complicated by uneven business decisions, personal disputes, and wavering spiritual commitment, inviting intervention by Ellen White. Employees at the press were "working at cross purposes with each other," she wrote soon after her arrival. Experienced workers did not mentor the new, and the latter made mistakes out of fear of asking for help and thus revealing their ignorance. White also made quite specific recommendations about business practices.[47]

Daniells helped bring to the South Pacific region a form of maritime evangelism used profitably by Adventists in other parts of the world. A "ship mission" started in Sydney in 1892, involved gathering evangelistic material and putting them aboard ships for foreign calls. Such nautical broadcasting was obviously diffused. But the method was not simply casting bread upon the waters and hoping for the best. Contact information was provided, and interests were followed up with further correspondence.[48]

As the national depression deepened in 1893, the impact on the press was unavoidable. Although the press continued to expand during the decade, Daniells and W. C. White (General Conference District Superintendent and thus Daniells's superior) found themselves facing difficult decisions about how to reduce a wash of red ink. Some periodicals were cut (though not the big-expense item, the *Bible Echo*). Personnel cuts seemed inevitable: whatever could help achieve a balanced bottom line. Although earlier a voice of financial prudence, Ellen White in the mid-1890s warned against cutting that might compromise the church's mission. Her counsel was most striking in 1896, when fierce competition made outside work unprofitable. Daniells, thinking of mission as much as finances, decided to pare back commercial jobs, which implied that two experienced hands, brethren Miller and Woods, who volunteered to leave the Echo employ, be allowed to quietly go. Ellen White objected, replying in no uncertain terms, "Hold on to your educated workers." That the two men were already negotiating to purchase a press of their own and set up a business that might be yet another competitor made their loss even more problematic. If finances were an acute problem, White suggested, pressmen should be temporarily willing to work for less. "My husband and I worked on this principle," she testified (it is not apparent that such sacrifice was imposed).[49]

Troubles at the Echo office resembled those that at various times afflicted Review and Herald Publishing in Battle Creek and Pacific Press in California. They required technically skilled workers and adept business people to make them successful. But dedication to business success sometimes threatened consecration to the Advent cause. "No one who is an unbeliever should be permanently employed," White counseled Daniells. But he had difficulty addressing the printing press's problems, and firing workers was not an easy task. "Daniells made a mistake when he left matters in such a crisis at North Fitzroy," White complained to church leaders. The man later known for his tough-minded decisiveness had to learn that trait.[50]

Despite travails in the office, literature evangelism went on: book sales, periodical subscriptions, tract distributions, supplemented by visits to the home by colporteurs—a one-two punch of the pen and personal contact. It was a strategy that enjoyed modest but steady success, tempered by apathy on the part of many Australians and by overt hostility from some religious leaders of other denominations. The evangelistic formula had been developed in the United States and seemed equally suited to the British Commonwealth lands. It was so well oiled an engine (if underpowered by a lack of funds) that when Stephen McCullagh apostatized in 1897, one of his charges against Ellen White was that she sought to establish a school not to train people for the ministry but "to educate canvassers to sell your books." The charge was unfair. But McCullagh might have been thinking about the three-week workshop for canvassers Daniells held in Sydney. Workers were drilled in the art of sales and equipped to press *The Great Controversy* into the hands of the public. Daniells was pleased to tell White that hundreds of copies had been sold in the past year. Nonetheless, he admitted that many of the salesmen "had but very little idea of what the book really contains."[51]

RELIGIOUS LIBERTY ISSUES

The Adventist Church in Australia enjoyed essentially the same civil liberties as it did in America. Separation of church and state was accomplished everywhere by the 1880s save Western Australia. Still, threats of a breached wall troubled Adventists down under as it did American leaders that same decade and over much the same issues. The last two decades of that century witnessed concerted efforts by Australia's Protestant churches to kindle a fire under what they detected to be a waning national spirituality. This included new attention to traditional revivalism (and conversely, to discourage interest in nontraditional sects such as Adventism). But it also meant a spirited effort to protect the Sunday Sabbath from profanation and seek official recognition in the new constitution that Australia was a Christian land.[52]

As mentioned, the dynamic of church-state relations in the emerging Australian nation of the 1890s resembled very closely what was happening in America. In both places the twin forces of urbanization and industrialization encouraged a more secular, pleasure-seeking social ethic. The influence of churches over individual behavior seemed to be slipping. In particular, reverence for the Sabbath appeared to be waning. Consequently, interdenominational alliances formed as political lobbies for enforcement of existing Sabbatarian laws or enactment of new ones.

This began in Australia in the 1880s and continued into the next decade, with organizations such as the Lord's Day Observance Society agitating for the closing of Sunday amusements, public transport, and refraining from most secular labor. In 1894, two Adventist men were sentenced to the stocks because of their Sunday work. Adventist prophetic interpretation viewed these efforts as clear signs of imminent persecution, not to be embraced as harbingers of the world's end but to be fought in order to extend the ability to spread the gospel.

In truth, Australian society had moved even further down the path of secularism than had America. The neo-Puritan ordinances were not likely to be embraced by most Aussie citizens or politicians. But Adventist leaders could take no chances. "Our attention has been called to the image of the beast that is formed in this country," Daniells wrote General Conference president O. A. Olsen in 1893. "We feel that we have not done what we should in enlightening the people of Aust. on the question of church and state." Thus, Daniells (ably assisted by W. A. Colcord when he arrived from America) mounted efforts on behalf of religious liberty fully as strenuous as A. T. Jones and his cohorts did across the Pacific. He edited a new journal, the *Australian Sentinel and Herald of Liberty*, that broadcast the dangers of church-state union. Protest meetings were organized at the Parramatta Town Hall after the above-mentioned arrests, and the Australian dailies expressed outrage at the treatment.[53]

Religious liberty concerns arose again a few years later during the drafting of Australia's new federal constitution. This time religionists sought to affirm in the constitution the dominion's acknowledgment of God. Further, anticipating the American religious right of the later twentieth century, church leaders sought the collective political clout of their members to influence members of parliament and turn out those who would not cooperate. Daniells's blood was up. He wrote Ellen White an agitated letter seeking her blessing for a campaign. "Do you not think that we ought to make earnest efforts to place the principles taught by our Saviour on church and state before the people? . . . It seems to me that the question before the people is whether they will form an image to the beast or not." Finding no objections from her, Daniells and other Adventist leaders sprang into action with a full-court press of editorials, briefings for political leaders, and distribution of tracts on the subject.

"I am not fitted to do very good work in these lines," Daniells modestly told readers of the *Review*, but if able "I would feel it my duty to give myself almost entirely to religious liberty work during this time." In response to a massive petition campaign to establish a "Christian" Australia, Daniells spearheaded a counterpetition, getting some thirteen thousand to sign in the Melbourne area. He penned an exhortatory letter to church members, telling them they stood in a position similar to Americans at the time of the Constitutional Convention (though Daniells's grasp of American history was rather muddled, he got the big picture right). "Let all our own people sign the petitions. Then canvass your neighbours." A later non-Adventist historian admired the efforts of the small band. "There was about the Adventist campaign a professionalism, an efficient adjustment of small means to large ends. . . . For a church that so vigorously and with such determination believed in the separation of Church and State, the Adventists played politics very well."[54]

ADMINISTRATIVE CHALLENGES

The Adventist work in Australia had begun in a time of booming prosperity. But its institutional consolidation, especially attempts to establish a school, played out against a severe, protracted economic depression. The bursting of the speculative bubble brought the usual assortment of woes: declining land values, joblessness, increased demands for welfare. Labor-management conflict, perhaps even more bitter than that in America, was marked by torchlight protest marches and violence both threatened and realized.[55]

The depressed economy posed continual challenges to church leadership. On a personal level, Ellen White struggled to pay the bills for her household. In evangelism, the depression discouraged potential converts from risking their precious jobs by taking a stand on the Sabbath. Hard times also affected the publishing work (as already noted). Members, disproportionately urban tradesmen, struggled to pay a faithful tithe. Dr. Merritt Kellogg, who journeyed to Melbourne from California, was tasked by Daniells with identifying those who were not fulfilling their financial duty and personally appeal to them. He "manifests a rare lot of common sense in his manner of working," Daniells told Ellen White.[56]

Finances were just a part of the problems A.G. Daniells faced as president of the Australian Conference. Given the thin talent pool to draw on (and few workers had much beyond a rudimentary education), it fell to him to be the pastor-in-chief for the Australian churches, responsible for their spiritual nurture. In 1893 he held a set of revival meetings among a new church company at Parramatta that needed a reassuring hand, lest things "would go to pieces." Daniells understood that the moment called not for doctrinal reinforcement but on "the spiritual upbuilding of the individual members." He held prayer meetings for workers at the occasionally troubled Echo office. But attempting to be *über*pastor was an impossibly large task, especially given the myriad other duties that fell to him. In a sense, Daniells was a victim of his own competence and hard work; he would be given or would assume responsibility because he would see things through and in a proper way. (In this he resembled that other great executive of Adventist history, James White.) "I have urged forward Elder Daniells to take considerable responsibility," W. C. White told a colleague. "He feels deeply the burden of any work he undertakes, he is prompt and thorough in business matters, and is not afraid to ask people for money."[57]

Nor was he shy about confronting time-consuming personnel issues. A vexing situation came up when colporteur A. S. Hickox jumped from Australia to New Zealand without authorization. He had been given what was considered prime selling territory in the Riverina region of southwest New South Wales, a thriving agricultural area. As a young worker with a family, Hickox struggled to make ends meet. Daniells had advanced conference money to him and had been, Hickox testified, "kind to me more times than you can remember." Thus, when he suddenly decamped for New Zealand, loan unrepaid, Daniells's kind feelings were tested. "I can hardly see how you could cooly pack up your things and leave our field without obtaining our consent," he scolded. To Hickox's complaint that the weather was hot, Daniells had no patience. Other people there work and cope with conditions, he pointed out. Even so, Daniells continued, good territory might have been provided elsewhere in Australia. To make things "right with our Master and with each other we should retrace our steps." This comment, similar to what he made to Miller and Woods when they left the press, revealed a weakness Daniells had for turning comparatively minor transgressions into issues of salvation. "I have felt their (Miller and Woods) salvation depended" on their returning to the

Echo office, he wrote Hickox, a statement both theologically suspect and administratively inappropriate.[58]

A more serious personnel matter occurred in 1897. It began with the conversion of a Methodist minister in Hobart who essentially read his way into Adventism. The possibilities of a seminary-trained pastor publically changing allegiances was exciting. "I could not suppress the tears when he told me this," Daniells confessed to Ellen White. "I believe that the country will be stirred." The pastor, C. F. Hawkins, asked Daniells in July 1896 if he could find a position with the Adventists. This was readily granted, and Hawkins appeared to easily fit into his new denominational home. He was teamed with veteran minister Stephen McCullagh for an Adelaide tent effort in spring 1897 when trouble began.[59]

Both men brought issues to the table. McCullagh and his wife had a long relationship with Ellen White that had been marked by both warmth and remonstrance. In the months leading up to the apostasy, White had sent pointed testimonies to them both, questioning their commitment and their child rearing. This did not sit well with either. For his part, Hawkins's Wesleyan tradition predisposed him to enthusiasm for the holiness teachings then coming into vogue. In a short article for the *Echo* just weeks before his departure, Hawkins called for a more definite assurance of the indwelling Holy Spirit. The two men reinforced their individual doubts about Adventism and in particular about White's status as prophet. It came as a major shock to the close-knit Australian Adventist community when the men shut down their meetings and submitted their resignations. Worse, McCullagh and his wife went from house to house "filling the ears of the people with wicked misrepresentations of yourself [White] and work. It is shocking." The Adelaide church was thrown into turmoil.[60]

For Daniells this was the most severe challenge he had yet faced as administrator. He and Colcord immediately went to Adelaide to steady upset members. "The public are shocked and our church was in chaos on our arrival," Daniells reported to White. Some newer members were "carried away." Daniells labored unsuccessfully with the two apostate pastors. "This is my first experience in deep seated rebellion," he lamented. "It is awful." That Stephen Haskell and George Starr were also soon dispatched to Adelaide bespoke the sense of crisis the church felt. Daniells spent three weeks in the city and sent White a thorough briefing of the situation. The two men's preaching a gospel of holiness and perfection found a sympathetic response among listeners. More insidiously, they propagated rumors of corruption in church headquarters, and by speaking out against health reform, Daniells added, "they encouraged the people to gratify their appetites and to feel that they were free from the galling yoke of self control." Hawkins and McCullagh evidently felt they would take most of the local church with them. But they overplayed their cards when they publically doubted White's prophetic office. Rather than strengthening their influence, their attacks on White began to drive members the other way.[61]

A. G. Daniells found the Hawkins-McCullagh experience both chastening and educative. Events in Adelaide served as a cautionary tale. They caused him to redouble his personal commitments, to appreciate as never before "the importance of thoroughness in everything": repentance, conversion, union with Christ. Reform must begin with the ministers, and that meant—in an admirable moment of candor—"the place for it to begin is with myself." In fairness, this shared introspection was not unusual for Daniells. His letters to Ellen White are filled with confessions of weakness and renewed determination for his spiritual life. He also would restate his commitment to her testimonies. No one could accuse Arthur Daniells of living the unexamined life.[62]

DANIELLS AND ELLEN WHITE

Daniells's years in Australia nearly paralleled those of the Whites' sojourn there. They arrived about nine months after he did and likewise left Australia a few months after Arthur and Mary departed for America. Daniells's relationship with both Whites were among the most important of his career. W. C. (Willie) White, first as district superintendent for the General Conference and then as the first Australian Union Conference president, was Daniells's supervisor. Despite occasional irritations (prompted by White's unsure administrative grasp and financial ineptness), they forged a close and effective working relationship. Willie also served as advisor and gatekeeper for his mother; appeals for his mother's support often went through him. The friendship forged in Australia between the two men would continue importantly when they both returned to America.[63]

Arthur and Mary Daniells had of course known Ellen White since the early days of their marriage. The friendship renewed on new terms: Ellen had lost her husband, and Arthur had become a leading figure of the Adventist effort in Australia. What remained the same was White's prophetic authority. For the remainder of her life (until 1915) her gift would be to Daniells a source of advice, correction, reassurance, and support. In a particularly revealing moment, Daniells wrote her recalling the time in Texas when he and Mary had lived with the Whites. It seemed the most "like having a mother" that he had felt since he was small.[64]

This is not to say that their relationship was always cordial. Arthur Daniells was a man born to lead. He could be abrupt. His eye on mission often superseded concern for the personal feelings of his associates. Ellen White, likewise, was not one to spare feelings in her testimonies. Her letters of counsel generally went to the point, not bothering to couch exhortations in soft, indirect language.

Considering Daniells's reputation for imperiousness ("Be careful how you denounce those whom you should only pity and comfort and help," she counseled), his general meekness before Ellen White is noteworthy. He seemed genuinely anxious for her advice and approval. "I may say that I am glad to receive any words of warning you may have for me," he penned in 1893. "I know very well that my labors are defective and many times I fear that they are well nigh useless, but I desire to know where the fault is and correct it as far as it is possible." His ready contrition on most occasions might be attributed to his still being a relatively inexperienced administrator; his confident years lay ahead. Although he could be short with other workers, when called to task by White he revealed a streak of self-doubt others might not have seen. On one occasion he failed to respond to a letter of reproof, finally admitting the reasons for his avoidance. "I have been tempted to feel that you have little confidence in me, and that any thing I might say would lead to more severe criticism." Although he said he had read this testimony repeatedly and prayerfully, there were parts he still did "not yet understand" (and perhaps did not intend to follow). Even mothers can meet resistance from their sons.[65]

Ellen White spent nearly a year in New Zealand in 1893. After having traveled about the country some months, she raised by letter another issue that must have touched a nerve with Daniells. As mentioned above, during his years there he had failed to really get to know the people, instead choosing to have his wife or others give Bible studies. White pointed out that there was no substitute for home visitation as a means of bonding with the people. "You can never supply this by proxy," she observed. That Daniells had experienced serious though unspecified difficulty is clear. When a delegation of church leaders prepared to travel to New Zealand from Australia, it was decided that Daniells should not accompany them on account of resentments felt by residents there. As usual, he was contrite, claiming to have reflected on his failures in New Zealand and improved his efforts on the continent. Daniells received the reprimand from Ellen White with his usual meekness. He assured her that he had felt the same failure to make personal contact while in New Zealand and had worked hard to remedy that lack. When laboring in Ballarat, Melbourne, Geelong, and Sandhurst, he visited every Sabbath-keeping family of the area.[66]

Ellen White's testimonies to leaders extended to their wives. In the confined social world of Adventist Australian missions, it was inevitable that personalities would clash. Mary Daniells and Mrs. L. J. Rousseau formed a twosome critical of Mrs. George Starr (both being of other mission families from America). This tempest in a teapot remains unimportant except as it led to contention among the workers that threatened to compromise the work. Thus, White weighed in with a series of long, chastening letters stating that Mary had "indulged in evil thinking and evil speaking." Not only had she and Mrs. Rousseau wronged Mrs. Starr, but they had been guilty during camp-meeting sessions of "sitting inside or outside the tent, with some unimportant, common work. . . . These practices belittle the sacredness of the work." In a manner of speaking, they had fallen into a "Martha complex." Both needed to possess "the spirit of Mary" sitting "at the feet of Jesus."[67]

There was another aspect to White's reproval of Mary. "You do not realize the influence your words exert upon your husband's mind. Through defective spiritual eyesight you may, both now and in the future, make mistakes which will result in giving your husband a wrong impression in regard to persons and things." White was very concerned about the influences of church leaders' wives. She felt that George Butler had fallen victim to the same wifely influence as had A. G. Daniells. If the women were not exactly Lady Macbeth in their malevolence, still they banefully influenced their husbands' decisions. For Mary, in particular, White warned of an "idolatrous love" and "sickly sentimentalism" toward her husband. White appears to have been on the mark here, for decades later Mary would be remembered for her jealous protectiveness of her husband's right to lead.[68]

But the prophet's admonitions raise an intriguing question. Her warnings about wifely influence on one level supported Victorian assumptions about the quite separate spheres of husband and wife. Mary's attempts at influence represented a violation of that code. But to what degree did White, perhaps at an unconscious level, see herself in Mrs. Daniells or Mrs. Butler? The interaction of the Whites (when James was still living) was occasionally a tug of war, made no easier by Ellen being a prophet and her husband being the church's titular leader (and man of great will). White may have seen in these other women tensions never successfully resolved in her own marriage.

CAMP MEETINGS

The evolution of the Australian Adventist church resembled developments in California in the 1870s. "Missionaries" from the East converted West Coat believers in several regions. A handful of local churches then gathered to form a conference, which sponsored camp meetings yearly. A publishing house followed, to provide tract and book support. Sanitariums added the health message. Finally, a college offered advanced training for ministers and teachers. The same pattern was followed down under. And in both places the presence of Ellen White was formative. In one instance, though, Australia pioneered an organizational level that traveled the other way across the Pacific to profoundly shape the American church: the union conference. This important innovation (credited to Willie White) will be a topic for the next chapter. But the camp meeting and formation of Avondale deserve present attention as illustrations of A. G. Daniells's administrative leadership.

The camp meeting, so vital an institution in the United States, took a few years to get established in Australia. Several things held up its quick adoption. Setting them up was costly, and as Willie White admitted, "Times were hard, and most of our people were poor." The practice was unknown in the country. How would it be received? Even the acquisition of suitable tents posed a difficulty (workers finally made their own). Thus, not until the summer of 1894 was a camp meeting attempted, at Middle Brighton near Melbourne. Ellen White issued an urgent appeal to members to drop everything and attend. Although leaders expected a modest turnout and set up only thirty-five family tents, to their delight some five hundred people gathered. Many were church members, but even more gratifying were those who came with slight knowledge of Adventism. Perhaps the very novelty drew them. In any event, Willie White told American readers that the event "marked a new era" in Australian Adventism. The enthusiasm of members and the apparently unprejudiced interest of others inspired a redoubling of energies. General Conference president O. A. Olsen was present to witness the success and take back to America happy accounts. For Daniells, who presided over the occasion, it was both a "continuous strain" and a triumph.[69]

In the following years, more camp meetings would be held, again near Melbourne; in North Fitzroy (near Sydney); in Hobart, Tasmania; in Brisbane; in Adelaide, and other locations. Five were held in 1896 alone. The Brisbane effort at Woolloongabba in 1898 was impressive, considering the local church had only some hundred members. It benefited from the Australian public's love of the novel meetings and also from the local tram company's free publicity (in return, of course, for capacity business). The effort reaped about fifty new members, enough to start up a church near the campgrounds.[70]

The Australian approach to camp meetings was more ambitiously evangelistic than its America cousin. It began with a special edition of the *Bible Echo* distributed by colporteurs, who visited every family in the area, introducing the public to Adventism. Following the camp meetings a group of workers stayed by, sometimes for months, working the leads. After one camp meeting in Melbourne, three churches were established. Daniells found himself mystified by the dynamics of camp meetings. Many who displayed great attentiveness during them lost all interest afterwards; others "who paid but little attention to the camp meeting have since become aroused." He concluded that influence of the meetings was often slow working rather than immediate; one must measure results not by what "we see on the ground during the meeting or at its close" but in the longer run. Daniells may not have fully appreciated the implications of joining the Advent movement for his largely working-class urban audiences, where a six-day workweek (with Sunday off) posed a serious hurdle for converts.[71]

Daniells (at least in his mind) had the planning of camp meetings down to a science. He gave detailed advice to fellow workers on successful meetings. There must be no confusion. A bell ringer should herald the movements of the day. Chorister and choir, ushers, tent master, camp treasurer, reporter, and advertising agent, sanitary pastoral committees: all must be appointed to their given duty if organization is to be attained.[72]

A moment in the planning of a new camp meeting location illustrates Daniells's ongoing reliance on Ellen White. He wrote in 1897 asking her advice about some property they were considering as a permanent camp meeting site near Melbourne. "I wish if you have any light with reference to Melbourne that you would send it to us that we may know how to move in the counsel of God." She responded simply: "Follow your convictions." This vote of confidence must have been gratifying. Despite Daniells's usual posture of take-charge self-assurance, there remained some nagging self-doubt seeking reassurance.[73]

AVONDALE

By the 1890s the Adventist denomination had become a firm believer in the value of higher education. Indeed, Ellen White and her son had been sent by the General Conference to Australia in part to help establish a school. Harvard College was founded just six years after the Puritans landed in Massachusetts; Adventist leaders in Australia nearly equaled that mark.[74]

In June 1892 Daniells posted a notice in the *Echo* stating the church's readiness to get into the education business. "Teachers are about to sail direct from our American colleges," he noted, underlying the urgency of getting on with plans. Temporary facilities were being sought near Melbourne, still the center of Australian Adventism. The school would be targeted at both young people, for whom "a liberal education in the useful branches of secular studies" as well as a grounding "in the science of godliness" would be provided, and at older workers, who needed tutoring in the essentials of the Adventist faith and in practical skills for colporteuring and Bible studies. A special issue of the *Echo* was dedicated to the enterprise, featuring a long exhortation by Ellen White, a shorter one by Daniells, and a prospectus for the school. The Australian Bible School opened its doors on August 24, 1892, a boarding school set in a pleasant neighborhood. Substantial structures were rented, ample enough to house up to thirty people. A faculty of five gathered under the leadership of L. J. Rousseau, along with his wife newly arrived from America. The school geared up to instruct a wide age range of students, but as it turned out nearly all of the twenty-four students were adults wanting more training for their church work. Clearly more work remained to convince members of the desirability of sending their children to Christian schools.[75]

Rather soon, Daniells and other leaders determined that Melbourne would not be the permanent site of the school. It's winter climate, mild by the standards he knew in Iowa, was nonetheless harsher than in other parts of the continent. Particularly as the school was to become a center of learning for Polynesian workers, a more salubrious clime was needed. A committee on location considered Adelaide to the west, but no adequate facilities were located. Then attention turned toward Sydney, which provided the answer. The planting of a new school, along with the founding of the "health home" and later a health foods factory, marked an important shift eastward for the locus of Australian Adventism.[76]

But where exactly? Sydney continued to be a very difficult area for the Adventist message to penetrate. Yet Ellen White had moved to New South Wales, and a consensus developed that the school should be in the region. Further, Ellen White's ideas about the desirability of rural locales for schools influenced leaders to envision purchase of a large tract of land for a farm as well as a school. The discovery and eventual purchase of the 1,500-acre Brettville estate between Cooranbong and Dora Creek, seventy-six miles north of Sydney, has become central to the collective memory of Australian Adventism. Willie White was part of the group that originally spotted it in April 1894; but many other leaders, including Daniells and Ellen White, looked it over. Despite expert warnings about its poor soil and concern that conference impoverishment would preclude its purchase, Ellen White gave the site her blessing. Arrangements for the purchase began to go forward; surveys were done. But the Foreign Mission Board in America, fearing that a bargain price for subpar land was no bargain, counseled them to look elsewhere. Daniells and Rousseau, despite knowing of White's vision on the matter, concurred. The search, it seemed, must resume. But the influence of the sexagenarian prophet was not to be denied. She continued in her insistence that God wanted them to have this property. "Is there not a God in Israel, that ye have turned to the god of Ekron," she lectured her son and Daniells over their resistance to the site. In the end, she wore them down. Cooranbong it would be.[77]

Difficult though the decision to purchase the land had been, it only hinted at the struggles to establish Avondale, as it was named, as a viable institution. As ever, money remained a challenge. The ferocious national depression continued to plague the small Adventist community's ability to put legs under its dreams. But leaders moved forward, inspired by Ellen White's unflagging confidence and excitement in the project. She backed up her exhortations with money, investing her own funds and borrowing against future royalties. She also received a gift and a loan from members of the Wessels family in South Africa (enriched by discovery of diamonds on their property). She made it plain to Daniells that while the medical and health work should pay their own way, the school should "receive our first attention financially." For Daniells, who bore much of the responsibility for making a success of the school, the mid and late 1890s posed constant worry. He had, for example, to implore the help of the General Conference to demand that the Echo and other Australian organizations pay the school the funds due it. (At one point, students, upon entering the school, were asked if they could contribute a bit more than their tuition.) Further, Daniells prevailed upon the conference committee to take the daring step of directing tithe money to the school. Realizing the unprecedented nature of the act, he solicited Stephen Haskell's and Ellen White's support. His logic was that six months of schooling would create better workers for the ministry. White responded in no uncertain terms. "I have had special instruction from the Lord that the tithe is for a special purpose," namely the support of the ministry. "There will always be a temptation to divert the tithe money to other channels," she continued, but such must be avoided. Daniells meekly submitted. "This is the first time I have ever given my consent to use the tithes for any other purpose, and I did this because of the great needs of the School," he explained in self-defense.[78]

Not just finances but the educational program of Avondale had to be determined. A somewhat premature attempt to open a manual training department (preceding construction of any buildings) was made in 1895. Although students proved useful for landscape labor, a school could hardly be said to exist. Plans for a spring 1896 opening came and went, complicated by building delays, legal title issues, and as always, finances.

Daniells helped work through these problems. But clarity of educational purpose awaited the arrival of William Warren Prescott from America.

Prescott, three years Daniells's senior, stands as one of Adventism's most influential educators, administrators, and theologians of the decades on either side of 1900. A well-educated New Englander, Prescott brought finely honed skills of analysis and articulation to church leadership. Nonetheless, he had occasions of conflict with church brethren. Contretemps with faculty over the proper course for Battle Creek College curriculum in the mid-1890s contributed to his decision to undertake a round-the-world tour on behalf of the General Conference. His nearly twelve-month stay in Australia not only proved a welcome respite from a clutch of difficulties back in America, it also served to forge an important and enduring friendship between two men emerging as key leaders in the church.[79]

Prescott's sojourn in Australia proved to have important theological implications for Adventism. Arianism (the belief that Christ was a created Being and not equal to God the Father) had dominated Adventist theology from the church's beginnings. But Prescott's study (especially of the book of John) had moved him toward a Trinitarian theology. Ellen White heard him preach his Christocentric message and was impressed. Prescott's influence on White and his editorial assistance with *The Desire of Ages* (then in preparation) significantly moved her toward the Trinitarianism that would ultimately become Adventist doctrine. But Prescott was not the only one influencing White's theology. Daniells, who embraced Prescott's Christology, through his own study came to embrace a personalized Holy Spirit. Adventist theologians (including Ellen White) had traditionally viewed the Holy Spirit as an impersonal force rather than a being. But Daniells influenced a circle of Australian ministers in the view gaining currency in contemporary Protestant thought. Shortly thereafter, White, for the first time in print referred to the Holy Spirit as "He." Thus began a transition in her reference to the third member of the Godhead—and perhaps Daniells's most significant theological influence on the church's prophet.[80]

Prescott's primary purpose in his Australian visit was not theological, however, but educational. If he struggled to earn acceptance for his reforms in Battle Creek, he found a ready reception at Avondale. The institution must have a new name, he insisted, Avondale School for Christian Workers, clarifying exactly what the institution purported to do: prepare people for church work.

Delayed by a year, Avondale opened in late April 1897. Daniells was nervous. He had heard of only a few students planning to come. A quick-thinking member suggested that local churches be solicited to sponsor students from their church, which brought gratifying results. Its six staff members welcomed ten students. A modest beginning, to be sure. But by early June nearly fifty students had made their way to Cooranbong. They lived in campus rooms, partly from necessity and partly to "form habits of order, neatness, and Christian courtesy" through uplifting association. Students were taught habits of work through campus responsibilities. Under leadership of the venerable Stephen Haskell, not only Bible study but also rhetoric, speech, handwriting, church history, physiology, and "Bible hygiene" graced the curriculum. Teacher preparation courses were available, as well as music and rudimentary business instruction. Hard times persisted for Avondale. But it would endure as the focal institution of the Adventist Church in Australia.[81]

WRAPPING UP HIS STAY

What sort of a leader was Arthur Grosvenor Daniells in his early years? He was, in many regards, the model administrator. His learning curve remained steep, but he seemed to take naturally to leadership. There were no details too small for his attention. Problems were approached methodically. When "vile smells from drains of the surrounding outhouses" made church service in North Fitzroy unbearable during the summer, he took systematic action to remedy the problem. He regularly shared with Ellen White the flow of decisions he faced: camp meetings to organize; ministers to assign and advise; new churches to support. All this took place within a prevailing assumption that the world's end was near. This conviction colored all plans, lent urgency to actions, and perhaps even contributed to the stridency that occasionally crept into Daniells's relationships.[82]

But a gentler, more vulnerable side of Daniells appeared too. He understood his tendencies. He knew he could be overbearing. He suffered discouragement about the slow pace of the cause. He shared introspective reflections with others. "I was brought up in the message from a little boy," he confided to General Conference president O. A. Olsen, "and I never knew what it was to change my religious views. For that reason I have never been able to fully sympathize with people who having accepted the third angel's message, say that the Bible has become a new book to them." Still, Daniells admitted to having a new grasp of the gospel as the message of the Minneapolis convention of 1888 made its way across the seas to his post in New Zealand. A. T. Jones and E. J. Waggoner's appeal to ministers "to lay aside their prejudice and drink these things in" [righteousness by faith] seemed to Daniells the most natural thing in the world. "I was so interested in these studies that I sat up late at night studying them, and I got up long before daylight to study these." During his stay in Australia, Prescott's pastoral influence on Daniells seems to have been profound. Daniells began haunting secondhand bookstores in search of devotional and theological works. "He hardly seems to me like the same man now," Prescott confided to Willie White.[83]

Arthur and Mary Daniells stored up a lifetime of memories and friendships in Australia. One of their closest, enduring for decades, was forged with Edwin R. Palmer and his wife. Palmer, who came to Australia as a young worker and rose to be appointed president of Avondale, would go on to become one of the most important figures in Adventist publishing history (head of Review and Herald Publishing for years). Decades later, they would reminisce about their time together. He recalled "the pleasure Mary and I experienced in having you in our home, the journeys we made to second-hand stores to find a bed, table, chairs, etc." and "the happy three months we lived together in that beautiful villa on Northcote Hill."[84]

By early March, Arthur and Mary Daniells had been away from the United States some fourteen years. It was time to touch home base. The Daniellses arrived as a couple but left as a family. In 1896 they adopted a two-week-old boy, whom they named Grosvenor. He would be their only child. Mary and young Grosvenor left in March to visit family in America. Arthur stayed just two weeks longer, long enough to attend conference meetings in Geelong. But that was not the only reason he did not accompany his family. He was heading west across the Indian Ocean to attend to vexing church business in South Africa. From there, plans were unsettled. He was wanted in England to consult on church growth. But should he then go directly to America, or return first to Australia and then head east to San Francisco and on to Battle Creek, nearer the time of the spring 1901 General Conference Session? Given the persistent talk of administrative reorganization, this promised to be important, and the leader of the Australian church (since 1897, when he replaced Willie White as president of the Australasian Union Conference) needed to attend. He would return as someone already identified by others as a strong leader. Olsen, who saw Daniells's work firsthand, enthused to Prescott that the General Conference Committee had few on it equal to Daniells. "He is a good speaker, he is a careful manager; he has order and neatness in his work."[85]

In any event, Daniells did not intend a permanent goodbye to his Austral home. He fully expected to return, whether within a few months or, if he traveled directly to America, another year. Daniells relished laboring on the mission field's front lines; indeed, he encouraged E. R. Palmer, who wished to return to America, to stay down under. "Iowa has a hundred workers," he argued, "Kansas the same." Rather than "sending our men back to the rear let us strengthen them at the front." During his trip to America Daniells hoped to locate "at least one promising young man for each of the seven colonies" (which he hoped their home conference would sponsor). "Unless the Lord over rules it I shall return with my family to work on in Australia," Daniells wrote on his passage home. "I feel keener on this point than when I left."[86]

What did Arthur Daniells take away from his years in Australia? Obviously, a wealth of administrative experience as conference and then union conference president. He oversaw educational, medical, publishing, and evangelistic enterprises. The parochial Midwesterner learned, too, how things operated in another land. He dealt with the thorny problems of theological controversy and apostasy among his ministers. By his own testimony, he grew in his personal religious experience and in his confidence in the counsel of Ellen White. All of these lessons were more important than he then knew. Looking from our modern perspective, we sense poignancy in Daniells's love for his Australian efforts that were about to conclude. The brethren, he would learn a year later, wanted his services put to the use of the world church.

---

[1] *RH*, January 4, 1887, 12; *Echo*, December 1886, 192.

[2] Schwarz and Greenleaf, *Light Bearers*, 207–215. Sydney Ahlstrom provides an overview of the broader American mission movement in his *A Religious History of the American People* (New Haven, CT: Yale University Press, 1972), 864–866.

[3] On New Zealand's history, see Keith Sinclair, *A History of New Zealand* (London: Oxford University Press, 1961); William Pember Reeves, *The Long White Cloud, Ao Tea Roa*, 3rd ed. (Reading, England: Senate Pub., 1998 [1924]), 39.

[4] Ross Goldstone, "New Zealand," in *Seventh-day Adventists in the South Pacific, 1885–1985*, ed. Noel Clapham (Warburton, Australia: Signs Publishing, n.d.), 18–33; *Echo,* August 1888, 120; Ella M. Robinson tells in dramatic fashion the story of Haskell's conversion of the Hare family in *S. N. Haskell, Man of Action* (Washington, DC: Review and Herald®, 1967), 79–87.

[5] L. Fraser Jackson, "The Spread of a Religious Innovation: Examples in New Zealand 1885–1916," in *Symposium on Adventist History in the South Pacific: 1885–1918*, ed. Arthur Ferch (Wahroonga, Australia: South Pacific Division of Seventh-day Adventists, 1986), 105.

[6] Kuhn, *Leader of Men*, 40.

[7] *RH*, January 4, 1887, 12; January 18, 1887, 42; February 8, 1887, 91. Daniells wrote a feature for the *Review and Herald* (August 4, 1891, 4) about the beginnings of Christian missions among the Maori.

[8] *RH,* February 8, 1887, 91.

[9] *RH,* May 3, 1887, 284; June 28, 1887, 411; *Echo,* April 1887, 64; May 1887, 75; June 1887, 91; *RH,* September 20, 1887, 603.

[10] *RH,* November 8, 1887, 699; *Echo*, September 1887, 144; December 1887, 187.

[11] Goldstone, "New Zealand," 21; *Echo*, October 1887, 155; February 1888, 28; *RH*, September 20, 1887, 603.

[12] *Echo*, April 1887, 64; October 1887, 155; December 1887, 188; January 1888, 14; February 1888, 30; April 1888, 62.

[13] *Echo*, April 1884, 64; Reeves, *Long White Cloud*, 242, 243, 266–268.

[14] *Echo*, October 1888, 154.

[15] Ibid.; *RH*, September 18, 1888, 603.

[16] *Echo*, October 1888, 152, 154.

[17] *RH*, September 18, 1888, 603; Goldstone, "New Zealand," 21; entries from the *The Daily Telegraph* and *Hawkes Bay Herald* dealing with the Adventist evangelistic series in Napier have been conveniently transcribed and are held in the Loma Linda University Department of Archives and Special Collections (LLUASP).

[18] *Daily Telegraph,* October 27, 1888; October 29, 1888; *Hawks Bay Herald*, October 26, 1888.

[19] *Daily Telegraph*, November 5, 1888; *Hawkes Bay Herald*, November 5, 1888.

[20] *Daily Telegraph*, November 19, 1888.

[21] *Daily Telegraph*, November 21, 1888; December 18, 1888; *Hawkes Bay Herald*, December 17, 1888.

[22] *Hawkes Bay Herald*, November 30, 1888; December 5, 1888; December 1, 1888; December 3, 1888; December 6, 1888.

[23] *Hawkes Bay Herald*, January 23, 1889; January 28, 1889; January 29, 1889.

[24] *Hawkes Bay Herald*, November 22, 1888; November 24, 1888; November 23, 1888.

[25] *Hawkes Bay Herald*, November 27, 1888; November 28, 1888.

[26] *Daily Telegraph*, June 22, 1889; June 27, 1889; *RH*, September 24, 1889, 603; *Echo*, September 1, 1889, 268.

[27] *Echo*, August 1, 1889, 236; Goldstone, "New Zealand," 21.

[28] EGW to "Sister [Mary] Daniells," September 19, 1892; EGW to A. G. and Mary Daniells, April 1890, both in CAR; Gilbert Valentine, "A. G. Daniells as Evangelist and Administrator and the Development of Conference Organization in Australia, 1886–1901," paper presented to the South Pacific Division Centennial Symposium on Adventist History, Monash University, Melbourne, October 23, 1985, 4, copy in ASTR.

[29] Goldstone, "New Zealand," 21; *Echo*, April 15, 1889, 128; April 1, 1891, 112; *RH*, June 17, 1890, 379; May 26, 1891, 331.

[30] Manning Clark, *A History of Australia*, 6 vols. (Melbourne, Australia: Melbourne University Press, 1999) provides a highly detailed history of the country during this age.

[31] Walter Phillips, "The Religious Climate in Australia at the Time of the Arrival of the Seventh-day Adventist Pioneers," in *Symposium on Adventist History*, ed. Ferch, 11–15.

[32] *Echo*, May 1, 1891, 144; December 1, 1891, 864; AGD to O. A. Olsen, May 14, 1893.

[33] AGD to Stephen Haskell, August 3, 1891, CAR-AU.

[34] Gary D. Krause, "The Growth of the Seventh-day Adventist Church in Sydney and Melbourne: 1885–1918," in *Symposium on Adventist History*, 118–120.

[35] Arthur L. White, *Ellen G. White: The Australian Years, 1891–1900* (Hagerstown, MD: Review and Herald®, 1983), 13–21. The unofficial encouragement of Ellen White to go to Australia is explained by Jerry Moon in his *W. C. White and Ellen G. White: The Relationship Between the Prophet and Her Son,* Andrews University Seminary Doctoral Dissertation Series, vol. 19 (Berrien Springs, MI: Andrews University Press, 1993), 88–91.

[36] EGW to Edson and Emma White, December 7, 1891 [letter begun that date, finished some days later], CAR; *Echo*, January 1, 1892, 9.

[37] Valentine, "A. G. Daniells," 12, 13; A. L. White, *The Australian Years*, 28.

[38] A. L. White, *The Australian Years*, 25, 26; *RH*, March 8, 1892, 152.

[39] *Echo*, January 15, 1892, 28; *RH*, March 8, 1892, 152.

[40] *Echo*, March 15, 1892, 92.

[41] AGD to EGW, December 30, 1892, CAR.

[42] EGW to AGD, January 30, 1893, CAR. For an astute discussion of these problems, see Gilbert M. Valentine's *The Prophet and the Presidents* (Nampa, ID: Pacific Press®, 2011), 212, 213.

[43] Mary Daniells to EGW, April 26, 1893; Mary Daniells to EGW, June 26, 1893, CAR; A. L. White, *EGW: The Australian Years*, 98.

[44] AGD to W. H. Cottrell, March 15, 1910, ASTR.

[45] My discussion of the publishing history relies heavily on Donald R. McAdams,

"Pacific Press Versus Review and Herald: The Rise of Territorial Monopolies," *Spectrum* 8 (August 1977): 11–21.

[46] Donald Hansen, "The Adventist Press," in *Seventh-day Adventists in the South Pacific, 1885–1985*, ed. Clapham, 58–62; *Echo*, January 1, 1892, 8; December 29, 1896, 832; *RH*, March 8, 1892, 152.

[47] Hansen, "The Adventist Press," 61, 62; A. L. White, *The Australian Years*, 27.

[48] Valentine, "A. G. Daniells," 5.

[49] Moon, *W. C. White*, 188–192; EGW to AGD and W. A. Colcord, June 1, 1896; AGD to EGW, June 2, 1896; AGD to EGW, June 3, 1896, CAR; Milton R. Hook, "The Inter-Relationship Between A. G. Daniells and E. G. White During Their Years in Australasia," in *Symposium on Adventist History*, 97, 98. A concerted effort by Daniells failed to woo Miller and Woods back. Six months later, and only after White directly appealed to the men, did they return to the Echo office.

[50] EGW to AGD, September 20, 1896, CAR.

[51] A. L. White, *The Australian Years*, 282; AGD to EGW, June 26, 1893, CAR.

[52] Donald E. Hansen, "The Seventh-day Adventist Church and Religious Liberty," in *Symposium on Adventist History*, 30–39, provides an excellent discussion of Adventist religious liberty efforts in Australia.

[53] Hansen, "The Seventh-day Adventist Church and Religious Liberty," 33–35; AGD to O. A. Olsen, May 14, 1893, CAR.

[54] AGD to EGW, April 27, 1897, CAR; *RH*, June 22, 1897, 395; AGD to EGW, September 23, 1897 and AGD to "Brethren and Sisters," March 19, 1897, both in CAR; Hansen, "The Seventh-day Adventist Church and Religious Liberty," 36.

[55] Alwyn Fraser, "The Australian 1890s," in *The World of Ellen G. White*, ed. Gary Land (Washington, DC: Review and Herald®, 1987), 227–243.

[56] Ibid., 233; AGD to EGW, June 26, 1894; October 10, 1893, CAR.

[57] AGD to EGW, April 26, 1893; March 4, 1893, CAR; Valentine, "A. G. Daniells," 78.

[58] Extracts of letters written by A. S. Hickox to A. G. Daniells, July 11, 1896; AGD to A. S. Hickox, January 15, 1897; AGD to EGW, April 18, 1897, CAR.

[59] AGD to EGW, July 15, 1896; July 18, 1896, CAR; *Echo*, March 1, 1897, 72.

[60] Arthur White describes this incident in detail in *EGW: The Australian Years*, 275–286.

[61] AGD to EGW, March 29, 1897; April 15, 1897, CAR.

[62] AGD to EGW, April 15, 1897.

[63] Jerry Moon's *W. C. White and Ellen G. White* elaborates on Daniells's and Willie's relationship; Valentine's "A. G. Daniells" and Hook's "The Inter-Relationship Between Daniells and White" are even more detailed on Daniells's administrative relationship with the Whites during the Australia years.

[64] AGD to EGW, November 7, 1892, CAR.

[65] AGD to EGW, March 3, 1896; EGW to AGD, March 12, 1897, CAR.

[66] Hook, "Inter-Relationship Between Daniells and White," 95; AGD to EGW, June 26, 1893, CAR.

[67] EGW to AGD, March 23, 1894 and April 4, 1894, both in CAR.

[68] EGW to Brother and Sister Daniells, March 6, 1894; Hook, "Inter-Relationship Between Daniels and White," 98.

[69] A fine overview of the subject is found in S. Ross Goldstone, "Adventist Camp Meetings—A Church Growth Strategy: 1893–1918," in *Symposium on Adventist History*; Elaine Fletcher, "Public Evangelism," in *Seventh-day Adventists in the South Pacific, 1885–1985*, 44; *RH*, March 6, 1894, 152; June 19, 1894, 396; *Echo*, December 8, 1893, 386, 387. Arthur White gives a vivid description of the camp meeting in *EGW: The Australian Years*, 113–118.

[70] *RH*, December 29, 1896, 832; Ronald Lawson, *Brisbane in the 1890s: A Study in an Australian Urban Society* (Brisbane, Australia: University of Queensland Press, 1973), 273, 274.

[71] AGD to EGW, March 8, 1896, CAR; Lawson, *Brisbane in the 1890s*, 274.

[72] AGD to Brother Starr, January 10, 1900, CAR.

[73] AGD to EGW, September 25, 1897; EGW to AGD, September 28, 1897, CAR.

[74] The beginnings of Adventist education in Australia are recounted by A. L. White, *The Australian Years*, 42–45.

[75] *Echo*, June 15, 1892, 192; Supplement, September 1, 1892; Ellen White, *Life Sketches* (Mountain View, CA: Pacific Press®, 1915), 333–336.

[76] A. L. White, *The Australian Years*, 45.

[77] Ibid., 146–161, 177; Daniells reviewed the Avondale siting incident in detail to attendees of the Colorado camp meeting in 1906 ("Question-Box Service on the Spirit of Prophecy," August 29, 1906, EGWE) as well as devoting a chapter to his work with Ellen White in *The Abiding Gift of Prophecy* (1935).

[78] A. L. White, *The Australian Years*, 215, 216, 181; EGW to AGD, August 31, 1897; June 3, 1898; June 13, 1898; March 16, 1897; AGD to EGW, March 19, 1897, CAR.

[79] Prescott's life has been ably told by Gilbert Valentine in *W. W. Prescott: Forgotten Giant of Adventism's Second Generation* (Hagerstown, MD: Review and Herald®, 2005). See especially chapter 8.

[80] Gilbert Valentine describes these theological changes in "Clearer Views of Jesus and the Doctrine of the Trinity in the Seventh-day Adventist Church," *Spectrum* 42 (Winter 2014): 68–71.

[81] A. L. White, *The Australian Years*, 296–303; *Echo*, April 5, 1897, 109; *Union Conference Record*, January–February 1898, 9, 10.

[82] AGD to EGW, April 7, 1895; April 5, 1895, CAR.

[83] AGD to O. A. Olsen, May 14, 1893, CAR; AGD in "Report of [1919] Bible Conference," transcript, July 3, 163, ASTR; Valentine, "A. G. Daniells," 9; Prescott quoted in Valentine, *W. W. Prescott*, 117.

[84] E. R. Palmer to AGD, August 22, 1928; AGD to E. R. Palmer, October 28, 1928, ASTR.

[85] *Union Conference Record*, April 1, 1900, 15; AGD to George I. Butler, July 25, 1901, ASTR; AGD to WCW, March 7, 1900, CAR. Olsen quoted in Valentine, "A. G. Daniells," 30;

Valentine, *The Prophet and the Presidents*, 177.

[86] AGD to E. R. Palmer, June 10, 1900, CAR.

Chapter III

A "PUBLIC MAN": DANIELLS AND THE REORGANIZATION OF 1901

Arthur Daniells booked passage on the steamer *Persic* for his journey to South Africa. He first had a five-day sail from Melbourne to Albany, on Australia's southwest coast, then two and a half weeks across the expanse of the Indian Ocean to Cape Town. The *Persic*, as he detailed to a colleague back in Australia, was 550 feet long, displaced 12,000 tons, and carried more than 300 passengers, plus 15,000 tons of cargo. The cargo included 180 horses destined for the British war effort in South Africa. The ship's size (the fourth-largest steamer in the world, he boasted) was more than just a curiosity. Its heft gave it more stability as it cut through the water. This, combined with calm weather, meant that Daniells (highly prone to seasickness) enjoyed a bearable trip. "I do not know that I ever enjoyed a month more in my life," he enthused to Willie White. It was not just his calm stomach. The enforced quiet of the cruise provided Daniells something he rarely knew: sustained time for reflection. "I have truly 'come aside and rested awhile.' "[1]

Daniells was accompanied by John Wessels, a South African whose Adventist family's money had helped found Avondale. The previous year, John had settled with his family near Sydney and had quickly become a figure of significance in the Australian Adventist Church. He was named to the union conference executive committee, the board of Avondale, and chair of the Sanitarium Board. Wessels returned with Daniells to visit his native land because the Adventist work in South Africa now faced a crisis. The South African church was still quite young. Adventist literature had been brought in the 1870s by an American miner who sought his luck in the Kimberley diamond rush. The seeds he scattered led to the conversion of a handful of Sabbathkeepers. Independently, Pieter Wessels found in Scripture that the seventh day was the Sabbath. He discovered the like-minded believers, and together they made an appeal to the American Adventist Church to send evangelists. Thus, in 1887 a group of four Adventist workers and their wives, led by D. A. Robinson, arrived. Several churches were subsequently formed, and in 1892 a conference organized. As in Australia, a prospering British colony in Africa was congenial to the growth of Adventism.[2]

But two things set South African Adventism apart from its Austral cousin. First, it had to deal with the uneasy relationship of English and Dutch settlers. And second, the church was early shaped by the mixed blessing of the wealth of the Wessels family

The Dutch and English had by turn controlled the beautiful and strategically located lands at the tip of Africa. Throughout the nineteenth century, British settlers, aided by their home government, steadily increased their control of various regions in southern Africa, including the Cape Colony and Natal. But Dutch migrations into what became the Orange Free State and Transvaal regions proved a formidable challenge to English control. A workable detente between the two largely Protestant groups was maintained until an 1886 gold strike in the Transvaal led to the founding of what would become the country's largest city, Johannesburg, and fueling fierce conflict between newly arriving English and the locally dominant Afrikaaner majority. The upshot was the Second Boer War (1899–1902).

Daniells's arrival at Cape Town in the spring of 1900 put him not in a war zone (which was further north) but in the midst of a staging area. Fifty to seventy transports were anchored in Cape Town's Table Bay. They unloaded soldiers, mules, ammunition—all the accoutrements of war. Daniells visited a huge British war hospital that accommodated six thousand soldiers. The military presence formed an interesting backdrop to his visit, but the war prevented his traveling about the country as he had hoped.[3]

Adventism's beginnings in South Africa witnessed cooperation and surface amicability between the Dutch and English colonists. Most of the Dutch Adventists did not join the war effort, Daniells initially noted, but instead abandoned their homes and traveled south to the Cape. But he shortly modified his opinion. There were more sympathizers with the Boer rebellion than he had realized, including the influential Wessels family. Further, there was a cleavage in the church (which still numbered fewer than five hundred) more serious than he had realized. Trouble stemmed in part from the failure of the American church to provide Dutch-speaking workers from the beginning. As in Australia, the American missionaries assumed a superiority to the Dutch that rankled. Perceived support of the English war efforts by Americans made matters worse. Tensions rose to the point that the year after Daniells's visit, Pastor Hubertus Elffers led his Dutch congregation to break with the organized Adventist church.[4]

The tensions between the Wessels family and the Adventist Church organization proved even more consequential. From its Millerite beginnings, Adventism had been a movement of the economically modest. It claimed no members who could truly be termed wealthy. That changed suddenly in the early 1890s. Prosperous Dutch farmer and family patriarch Johannes Wessels, whose son Pieter had introduced the Sabbath to this Dutch Reformed family, had the good fortune to have diamonds discovered on his farm in the Kimberley district. He sold the farm to the De Beers mining concern for a fortune.

Immediately, the young South African church found a patron. Moreover, several of the Wessels sons attended college in the United States, where John Harvey Kellogg and other Battle Creek leaders inspired them with the possibilities of institution building. Thus, not only churches but also a school, orphanage, and publishing house were planted. And the crown jewel of them all, Claremont Sanitarium, was built in a Cape Town suburb in 1897, with more than half its funding from the Wessels family. This state-of-the-art facility was closely modeled after the Battle Creek Sanitarium. American and Australian church leaders were both excited by the potential support of this South African family for their own ambitions. These were encouraged by "Mother" Wessels' visit to Australia in 1894 and her munificent contribution for the founding of the Avondale school. Ellen White prevailed upon son John to move to Australia in 1899 and participate in the church's growth.[5]

But even with the considerable resources of the Wessels family behind it, the South African church's institutional eyes were larger than its pocketbook. Its school was fully staffed. And little expense was spared in the outfitting of Claremont Sanitarium, situated six miles south of Cape Town in a valley that commanded a beautiful view of Table Mountain. An English commentator on the Boer War gave the sanitarium high marks (a wing was devoted to treating British officers). But expenditures for first-class facilities were quickly driving the conference toward bankruptcy. The plague of debt did not reflect unique mismanagement; indeed, it was more the denominational norm, replicated in Denmark, Australia, and the United States. The first generation of Adventist institution builders were driven by grand visions that too often were unmatched by business savvy.[6]

A. G. Daniells journeyed to South Africa for two reasons. First, to help church leaders deal with the acute financial distress. And second, to seek to protect Australia's investment in the Wessels family. Daniells worried from the beginning that John Wessels's return to his home spelled trouble (as did Ellen White, who urged Daniells to accompany Wessels home). The Wesselses were the largest creditors of the Claremont Sanitarium, and John had received a cable from home that his investments were threatened and he should return. The problem was partly of his own making, since he had spent lavishly on the facility. But he could not have helped the impact of the Boer War on the sanitarium.[7]

The leisurely water passage to South Africa gave Daniells repeated opportunities to cultivate John's loyalty to the Adventist enterprise in Australia. Daniells brought with him copies of Ellen White's many letters to various members of the Wessels family. He pored over them, developing a line of argument to use with John. He succeeded in getting John to read portions as well (something members of his family later resisted doing). He gave his own witness to the salutary effect of White's testimonies on himself. But Wessels parried Daniells's efforts to commit him to returning to Australia. He was determined to salvage his investment in the Claremont Sanitarium. A likewise determined Daniells came to see that the chances of keeping the Wesselses' pocketbook in the fold were slipping away. "I am satisfied that John has been misleading us all the while he has been in Australia," he wrote W. C. White. But Daniells did not then know the close relationship that had developed between Wessels and Kellogg (Wessels and a brother had attended college at Battle Creek). The doctor would continue to drive a wedge between Wessels and denominational leadership.[8]

Daniells had better luck with other aspects of his Africa trip, as, for example, in evangelism. He spoke many times to both church workers and the general public. "My rest and Bible study on the boat seem to have [given] me fresh life. . . . I have not met with more anxious, intelligent hearers any where." There was also an element of vacation to his trip; he saw a new part of the world, one of great beauty.[9]

But the administrative instincts could not be long suppressed. Financial problems were too many, answers too few. It appeared that the sanitarium trustees would have no alternative to turning the institution over to the Wessels family, who were themselves both trustees and creditors. Talk of selling it to the English government as a military hospital came to nothing. An attempted audience with Cecil Rhodes to ask for his help failed. Daniells, the Whites, Adventist leaders in general—all were dealing with something new to them: rich and independent-minded members, who offered the prospect of significant institutional support but on their own terms. It should not be surprising that church leaders lacked adroitness at this new game, especially when the wily Kellogg was whispering in the Wesselses' ears. Daniells's primary tactic was use of the testimonies. He gathered Mother Wessels and her son-in-law together "and read portions and laboured with them. I spent three hours in their room." But to no lasting effect. "I am sick at heart," he told Willie, "The way matters stand with the family now it seems that there is little prospect of getting money from here for our building" [Australian sanitarium].[10]

Daniells turned the screws even harder on Wessels brothers Henry and John. He came perilously close to claiming divine sanction for his advice to Henry. After a long period of prayer, Daniells testified, "I feel more certain than ever that it is not God's will that the Wessels family should take over the property or the management of the institution." After paraphrasing White's earlier testimony about the gift God gave the Wesselses, he appealed to their ability to "stand before the people of this sin cursed land as trophies of the grace." Yet, he continued, "the Lord has not had his way. His plans have been defeated by the perverse will of man. . . . It is a terrible thing to fight against God." One is tempted to think that Daniells modeled his letter after the testimonies of Ellen White. After such an appeal to heavenly authority, it seemed anticlimactic for him to then reassure Henry that his family would not lose one penny by leaving that money in the Sanitarium.[11]

A modern reader sees manipulation in this letter. But it was unconscious manipulation, for Daniells was sincere in his beliefs. Had he read more closely White's major appeal in 1897 for John Wessels to come to Australia, he would have noticed that she took pains to point out that her wish for him to help their work was her own, not spurred by any light from Heaven. Whether this distinction was an oversight by Daniells or an intentional misreading, we cannot know.[12]

No single explanation of the brouhaha is possible. As in most human conflict, motives that may not be clear even to participants come into play. Perceived slights, imperfect communication, unrecognized self-interest, family dynamics—these all contributed, no doubt. Church leaders confronted a handful of Wesselses, each with his or her own views that in turn contended against or reinforced one another's. Compounding these were problems of culture and language between the American missionaries and the Dutch South Africans. By way of his back-channel contacts in Australia, Daniells had heard that John Wessels had been offended several times while there. Apparently his wealth led Australian brethren to assume that he would without complaint pick up expenses as they arose. And there was likely the well-earned suspicion of the rich that those about them are scheming for their wealth. In any event, John wrote to his mother that Australia was not the hospitable clime he had supposed; no further support should be forthcoming. And as for the Claremont Sanitarium dispute, lawyers were being summoned. From his perspective, Daniells could view John's cooling ardor only as repudiation of divine mission. "I try to show them how unsafe it is to go against the counsel of God, and that they ought not to dare to do as they are doing now."[13]

However, Ellen White cast less blame on John or his brothers than on American Adventist leaders. The Wesselses' visit to Battle Creek, she felt, was the source of more mischief than good, as they were plied with prideful tours of Adventist institutions there. She was even more blunt with church leaders in South Africa. "These brothers [Wesselses] have invested their means in buildings and in various ways to sustain the work, and what use have you tried to make of them? . . . Much more might have been done than has been done to bind them up with the work." White and Daniells both sensed a looming missed opportunity with the Wessels family—and time proved them right. In retrospect, this confrontation proved an eerie foreshadowing of what Daniells faced in the next few years: an even more contentious struggle with a powerful Adventist leader over control of the mother sanitarium in Battle Creek.[14]

TO EUROPE AND HOME

Daniells spent a month and a half in South Africa. He concluded that church efforts there "must be entirely reorganized." That would be for another day, however. He had already become a figure of note in a worldwide church that was searching for strong, effective leadership. The Advent work in England and the northern European nations now needed his counsel. Thus, he managed to secure an "indulgence passage" on a British transport ship returning to England in mid-June. He again found himself fortunate in inexpensive fare and a smooth passage.[15]

Daniells had scarcely disembarked at Southampton when W. W. Prescott solicited him to travel to the first German Adventist camp meeting. The landmark ten-day gathering in Friedensau, Germany, represented the largest collection of Adventists ever assembled in Europe up to that point and drew an array of notable American denominational leaders: O. A. Olsen, J. N. Loughborough, and J. H. Waggoner. In the usual manner of Adventist plantings, this center of the two-thousand-member German Adventist Church boasted a clutch of institutions: a school, a sanitarium, and a health foods factory. The orderly ways of Teutonic Adventists pleased Daniells. "The ministers," he complimented, "are a clean, intelligent, healthy-looking lot of men."[16]

Daniells could not say the same for former General Conference president O. A. Olsen, who seemed "broken in health and confused in mind." Olsen had pushed himself to the breaking point, and, being a Scandinavian, he poured himself into the northern European work with especial energy. "Unless he obtains rest, he will not be able hold out much longer," Daniells warned. But scheduled trips with European leader L. R. Conradi to Russia, the Balkan states, Turkey, and then on to Scandinavia promised no surcease.[17]

Daniells focused his energies in England, however. He spent time conferring with Prescott, persuading him to put away discouragement with his failed administrative reform efforts and renew the fight for change at the spring 1901 General Conference. He visited the various church companies in London, along with its sanitarium and food companies. He then journeyed to Birmingham, where a camp meeting along the lines of those in Australia was planned. He brought with him experience of successful Australian efforts, which he hoped to replicate there. But it was not to be. Terrific winds and nearly weeklong rains severely hampered the meetings and damaged the tents and chairs.[18]

In response to requests from Adventist leaders, Daniells made one more swing through the Continent. He went first to a camp meeting in Basel, Switzerland. He then joined Conradi (who, among other things, pioneered Adventism in Germany) for a tour of workers and congregations there. Daniells particularly enjoyed the opportunity to visit Eisenach, Erfurt, and Wittenberg, shrines of the Reformation. A brief swing through Norway, Sweden, and Denmark rounded out the closest thing to a Grand Tour of Europe Daniells ever knew. But Daniells was never really a tourist. As his letters convey, he was constantly ruminating over mission. And the next General Conference in 1901 would be an event that could profoundly advance missions. He could not bear to miss the fall planning sessions for that event.[19]

For this reason (and at the urging of others), Daniells left Liverpool on September 22, 1900, to cross the North Atlantic. It had been nearly fourteen years since he and Mary had left San Francisco for New Zealand. Not once in those years had he returned stateside. One can only imagine the knot of emotions as he stood on deck when the ship passed by the Statue of Liberty, still new enough (having been dedicated just two days after the Daniellses left America in October of 1886) to lack its familiar green patina. Mary and young Grosvenor came east to meet him.

He had little time for celebration or sightseeing. The very day he arrived he attended an Atlantic Conference annual session and found himself embroiled in a contentious affair. The *Review and Herald* reported obscurely of a "victory." But Daniells's candor with Ellen White bespoke troubles. E. E. Franke, a pioneer evangelist in New York City, verbally attacked conference president A. E. Place. It was a knockdown affair that lasted from nine in the morning until late afternoon, with Franke threatening to take the Gotham churches with him. "At times he acted like a mad man, accusing Bro. Place of lying, deceit, etc. I was horrified at the proceedings, for I had never seen any thing like it among our people before." Daniells feared for the future of the

New York church and was further dismayed by Franke's use of White's testimonies "as a club." Franke's insurgency was repelled, however, and Place reelected. The following month the General Conference Committee would point the vexatious Franke to other fields. And Daniells made a sufficiently positive impression on Atlantic Conference leadership that they asked the General Conference to permit his return to "labor in the interests of the New York church."[20]

Daniells could not avoid getting sucked into domestic church politics, but his heart was far away. He carried a profound burden for the worldwide dissemination of the three angels' messages. "The masses have not heard a word about the message. . . . As I look upon these whole nations for whom we have not yet begun to work scarcely, and then see how many workers we have employed in little conferences in the states and the money we are paying them to try to keep up the courage of faltering churches, my heart burns within me." Arthur Grosvenor Daniells's gift to the Adventist Church was his wedding of missionary passion to organizational genius. He returned to the United States with a vision of the "big picture," and through two decades of administrative oversight he never lost sight that goal.[21]

Daniells's first report to Ellen White (who, along with Willie, returned from Australia via San Francisco) told of a dire need for reorganization abroad. "In all my travels since leaving you I have seen every where the tendency to narrow down to the limits of our human capacity, instead of broadening out according to the greatness of the Lord's power. . . . Unless there is a decided change in our plans to give this message to the world I do not see how any of us who are now living can expect to see it close up in our day." The European work, especially, seemed constricted. France, Italy, Spain, Portugal—the major Catholic nations remained virtually unentered.[22]

The 1901 General Conference Session would not convene for nearly six months. During the interim, Daniells kept busy with travels, essentially taking the temperature of the American church. In late October he attended his first General Conference Committee meeting in Battle Creek. When he had left America in 1886, he was a junior evangelist/pastor; he returned as a senior figure, highly respected as an administrator and through his close association with the Whites. He arrived in Battle Creek in late October in time to hear the General Conference's leadership's struggles with the "Holy Flesh" outbreak in Indiana. This early dalliance with Pentecostalism (then just a few years old in America) stressed the indwelling power of the Holy Spirit and a vividly expressed religious experience. But to Adventist leaders, who had long before given up the exuberance of the early Advent movement for a more controlled religiosity, the baptism of the Holy Spirit remained a low priority, indeed dangerous for the behavioral excesses it could prompt. The Committee willingly accepted the resignation of Indiana Conference president R. S. Donnell, a defender and facilitator of the zealotry.[23]

Daniells next ventured across the continent to Northern California for a reunion with the Whites. In an age when most Americans infrequently ventured far from home, these three stood out as world travelers. Daniells, the small-town boy from Iowa, must at times have marveled at the path of his life. In a sense, his growing cosmopolitanism reflected that of the Adventist Church's, which moved from a narrow American base to world aspirations. Daniells bespoke this international focus in his describing to the Whites the financial straits of the sanitarium in Copenhagen. The American church, he felt, should step forward to save a foreign cousin, as it had other struggling institutions across the globe. Daniells recognized that he had "no authority" to take action in the United States; he could only urge. That limitation would be removed in only a few months.[24]

While in California he helped conduct two weeks of revival meetings at the Pacific Press in Oakland. The younger workers were bedeviled by the temptation of magazine fiction, Daniells fretted. They can't find time to read Adventist literature yet "can read the light, fictitious stories that are printed in the magazines." He devised a pledge that a gratifying number signed, eschewing this temptation. The concern with fiction, which vexed Ellen White perhaps even more than Daniells, can only be understood when one recalls the central place religious literature held in Adventist culture. A competitor with the allure of sensational fiction comprised a serious threat indeed.[25]

Thus, Daniells did much more than simply mark time until the spring General Conference. He made a circuit of the central California church and then envisioned ambitious travel plans to Portland and Walla Walla. He also authored a brief manuscript on canvassing for the American literature evangelists. He hoped Pacific Press would issue it as an inexpensive pamphlet. Not stopping here in his enthusiasm for the literature effort, Daniells also advised Willie White on his mother's preparation of Testimony No. 34. Section 5, they agreed, would deal with canvassing. Further, Daniells advised White on what this section might contain: an exhortation on the value of canvassing, while his pamphlet would concern practical matters.[26]

Given Daniells's ambitious travels in Europe and America, involvement in the operation of the denomination, and close connections with its prophet and her influential son, an onlooker might be excused for thinking he was running for elective office. Certainly his behavior bore the marks of what a politician ambitious for high office would do. In fact, rumors already swirled around the denomination about Daniells's future, driven largely by the Kellogg faction. John Wessels, visiting America at this same time, reported to Kellogg that an Australian scheme was afoot to install Daniells (with Willie White as a top aid). Given Daniells's activities of the past half year and travels with Wessels, the story had plausibility. In this notion of a conspiracy to install Daniells, one detects the seeds of his and Kellogg's later alienation being planted.[27]

What was incumbent General Conference president George Irwin thinking about these developments? He had been worried that a coup had been planned for the 1901 session even before Daniells returned from overseas. Daniells had to reassure him that nothing was afoot. "I am astonished at what is being said with reference to the Australian scheme to turn you out of office and put me in your place." "I am sure," Daniells went on, "that Sister White is as innocent as a little child of any scheming or hidden plans." The denominational rumor mill made Daniells anxious about "how to conduct myself" in America. But, he concluded to Irwin, "as we are public men I suppose we must expect these things." If Daniells reflected further on the matter, he should have realized that the presence of both of the Whites with him in Australia, his clearly rising star, and John Wessels's reports on Australian affairs gave Irwin some reason for his worry. Indeed, the Australian influence would soon be seen in the organizational reform. And Daniells, of course, would become the new leader.[28]

For all of this, there was no conspiracy. Daniells was not, in the manner of Julius Caesar, returning from Gaul to claim a crown. His ambitions were not of this sort. Power was for him a means to an end, and that end was the furtherance of the Advent gospel. Daniells came to America assuming he would return to Australia. That rumors of an Australian putsch circulated in Battle Creek suggests the unsettled state of administrative affairs in 1900. The growing Adventist Church was struggling to create a structure sufficient for its size and ambition. Doctrinal dispute dating to 1888 nurtured suspicions. And as it turned out, things would get worse before they got better.

HEADING TO GENERAL CONFERENCE

In 1901, the worldwide Seventh-day Adventist Church claimed a membership of 78,000. The vast majority of these resided in the United States. But the world church was growing, particularly in Europe and Australia, with at least a presence in all the major countries of the world (the Islamic lands excepted). It was a remarkable accomplishment for a group that had only sent out its first missionary in 1874.[29]

But growth was outstripping the organizational structure established at the church's founding in 1863. The state (or multistate) conference model that reported to a General Conference in Battle Creek headed by a president and executive committee worked well during the initial years. As new tasks were added in publishing, health, and religious liberty, a series of freestanding associations were formed. These included the Tract and Missionary Society, Health and Temperance Association, Religious Liberty Association, Foreign Missions Board, and John Harvey Kellogg's International Medical Missionary and Benevolent Association, among others. Additionally, in the fifteen years preceding the 1901 General Conference Session, twelve publishing houses, seventeen educational institutions, and fourteen medical centers were established. These organizations' independence (even though their boards were frequently composed of a sort of interlocking directorate of leaders) was an invitation to confused and overlapping effort.[30]

Nonetheless, organizations will usually muddle along in familiar ruts unless outside pressures force change. Through the mid-1890s the church seemed to be moving ahead handsomely. Missionaries were being dispatched abroad, and the American homeland witnessed the great age of educational institution founding. But the economic depression beginning in 1893 ultimately caught up with the church, and later years of that decade saw slowdown and even reversal of activities. The financial state of the church in the later 1890s nearly defies belief. The church treasury ended the 1898 year with scarcely sixty-one dollars in the bank and hundreds of thousands in debts. Daniells would inherit a church that was some twenty thousand dollars behind in salary to its workers. Part of the problem was overly ambitious institutional growth, especially in education and health facilities. And part of the problem lay with quibbling, contentious managers in Battle Creek, whose sense of institutional judgment—or even blatant self-interest—compromised progress. The surprise is not that Adventist leaders were capable of behaving badly, but that the international church continued its growth despite all. Still, an efficient, well-articulated church structure was clearly needed; there was little debate about that. But what would such a structure look like?[31]

A step toward change occurred at the General Conference session in 1888 when the U.S. and Canada were divided into four districts (made six in 1889), with various members of the General Conference Executive Committee given oversight of each. But they did not truly administer these districts; the main thrust of the change was to provide better information to various locales of General Conference decisions.

But problems in the church were not simply from confusing lines of oversight or responsibility. They also had to do with personalities. The acrimony from the 1888 Minneapolis conference never fully subsided. A. T. Jones and E. J. Waggoner's message found sympathetic ears in such influential leaders as Prescott and Ellen White. But the latter's support only resulted in their accepting a sort of voluntary exile to distant mission posts in the 1890s. George I. Butler, General Conference president through most of the 1880s, was a man of willful self-confidence. Aided by influential *Review and Herald* editor Uriah Smith and other Battle Creek church notables, Butler frustrated White and the small group of would-be reformers. When Butler resigned in 1888, O. A. Olsen took over leadership. Although prone to exhausting overwork, Olsen was a more pliable individual, less sure of himself. But the heart of the problem from Ellen White's viewpoint—a small group of leaders who dictated church affairs—persisted. White's dismay with the situation found vent in a stream of withering comment. "The whole body is sick because of mismanagement and miscalculation," she wrote. "A few minds in Battle Creek are not to be in power to manage everything in connection with our work," she commented later. White took Butler to the metaphorical woodshed on many occasions. "Let no man feel that his position as president either of the General Conference or of a state conference clothes him with a power over the conscience of others," she scolded. "Kingly power" was White's favorite term for authoritarian behavior in Battle Creek. The expression may strike modern readers as extreme. How regal could plain Midwesterners such as Butler or George Irwin really be? Could they really push the levers of authority to attain their ends?[32]

White's language was pure Victorian rhetoric: direct, uncompromising, often hyperbolic. Unconsciously, no doubt, she also partook of the language of the era's political reform. The age's titans of industry were described in similar terms. Carnegie and Rockefeller may have lacked titles of nobility, one contemporary fellow reformer wrote, but the "kingly power remain[s]." The parallel is telling, because in this phase of her life Ellen White was devoted to reforming the Adventist Church. She partook of a larger American reform impulse to disperse great centers of power. The Adventist church structure in one sense replicated the "interlocking directorates" so common at the highest levels of American business. Bankers and industrialists grew familiar in ways that thwarted competition (and frequently innovation) as they sat around inlaid mahogany tables in boardrooms. Similarly, a relative handful of leaders dominated Adventist church societies and associations. J. N. Loughborough, to give just one example, served in 1891 as superintendent of District 3, vice president of the General Conference Association (the legal, property-owning body of the church), a member of the Board of Foreign Missions, and president of the Illinois Conference. His situation was not unusual. To make matter worse, from White's and others' perspective, this power was centralized in hands dedicated to preserving the theological and administrative status quo.[33]

As the new century dawned in 1901, America got a new leader and a new spirit. William McKinley's assassination at Buffalo's Pan-American Exposition that fall elevated Vice President Theodore Roosevelt to the presidency. The office would be transformed, and America found a new spring to its step. His reputation as a trustbuster might have been exaggerated, but there is no question that the comfortable business class found its old ways being challenged. The Adventist Church in 1901, in a manner of speaking, found its trustbusters as well. Ellen White and son Willie, along with Waggoner, Jones, Prescott, and Daniells, were determined to topple the tightly held control of power in Battle Creek. It would not be coincidental that this group was composed of people from outside Battle Creek (some, indeed, from outside North America). They were not bound to the current structure of authority.

And yet the term "revolutionaries" hardly fits this group. Like the political reformers of the Progressive Era, White and Daniells et al sought not the overthrow of the system but its better functioning. The survival of American capitalism, democracy—or in this case, the Adventist Church—required drastic change. For Daniells and the Whites, the ability of institutional Adventism to accomplish its gospel mission demanded a more democratic and ably run church polity. Resembling American political reform, too, was the fact that the Adventist reforming coalition did not comprise people of like mind. Only after the conclusion of the spring General Conference session did it become apparent that Jones's and Waggoner's agenda was quite different than that of the others.

As with most notable political or institutional reforms, earlier efforts had been made. Calls for change from Jones, Prescott, and Waggoner went forward at the 1897 and 1899 sessions. Obviously, neither the Whites nor Daniells were then present to assist change. Frustration with the status quo grew over the next two years. The outliers, who had innovated change in Australia, felt it most. "It will be a great calamity," Daniells wrote Willie White the previous August, "to have this Conference go through as the last one did." To prevent that dead end, he urged White to get to Battle Creek or some other place where they could meet well before the session started. "It would be a most dangerous thing for us all to come to that meeting without a good and clear understanding regarding its object and how to secure the very best results." The methodical Daniells was never one to approach an important meeting unprepared.[34]

What made Daniells or the Whites confident that they had a better organizational idea? It was their experience in Australia. The creation of the Australasian Union Conference in 1894 was the first joining of local Adventist conferences under a new type of intermediary umbrella structure. It simultaneously provided for greater centralization and democratization. Information and directions from the General Conference would flow down to the local conferences (several in Australia, one in New Zealand) through the union conference. But it also allowed for decision-making more attuned to its region. It appeared to be a winning formula. There was a sense of auspiciousness about its contrivance even at the time. O. A. Olsen came from America to preside over the business meeting where the enabling vote was taken. A. G. Daniells, the administrative craftsman, wrote the constitution. But W. C. White, then superintendent of the Australasian Field, claims title as father of the union conference structure, the man who conceived and pushed for its adoption. As actual administrator, however, he had serious deficiencies, which even he recognized. Thus, the 1897 General Conference Session appointed Daniells as Australian Union Conference president. (White formally became his mother's assistant, a task he retained for the subsequent eighteen years of her life.)[35]

There is a temptation to cast the multiyear struggle for administrative reform in terms of progressives and reactionaries. But in truth, the reformers had sometimes been timid. Although Daniells and White get credit for advancing church organization, they were not always in the lead. A less-well-remembered leader in South Africa, A. T. Robinson, actually devised the conference department structure. When he suggested it for the Australia field, White and Daniells resisted (the latter terming it "anarchy" and "confusion"). The larger church committee championed the change over their objections (an unusual inversion of the usual pattern). With some significant modifications because of growth, the Adventist Church's organization in 1900 continued what had been set in the early 1860s. Adventist institutional culture had quickly become tradition-bound, endowing its way of doing things with a nearly divine sanction. "Over and over again," Ellen White chided, "men have said, 'The voice of the Conference is the voice of God; therefore everything must be referred to the Conference.' " Such presumption is perhaps not surprising for a movement that emphasized the pattern of the ancient Jewish temple service and believed that a heavenly prototype continued to operate. Also, there was no notion that church members comprised a constituency that should elect delegates to oversee church polity. The Advent movement, like ancient Israel, had been shaped by a handful of strong figures, and belief that a relative few should guide church affairs died hard. It took both influential reformers and a broadening perception that current structure was inadequate to get over the hump of inertia.[36]

Fortunately, Ellen White was part of the reforming group. As will be seen, her strong voice facilitated change. That support was necessary but not sufficient for success. Her advocacy did not predetermine victory. When one recalls the protracted struggle after 1888—even with White's strong support—to make righteousness by faith the linchpin of Adventism, one realizes that many voices shaped the course of the church. To White's oracular contribution was added the tactical and strategic vision of her son and Arthur Daniells. Even incumbent George Irwin, concerned though he was of plans to unseat him, recognized the need and helped work for change.[37]

The General Conference Committee, the executive body of the church, met in late March 1901 to set the agenda for the session and name working committees. Daniells was originally given chairmanship of the Plans and Resolutions Committee. But his evident heart for the ministry caused him to be moved to chairmanship of the Pastoral Committee (foreshadowing his major contributions to ministerial training in the 1920s). Daniells, showing no signs of shyness or deference to older leadership, intervened on behalf of Professor J. L. Shaw of South Africa in order that he be granted credentials as a delegate at large. With the adjournment of the General Conference Committee on April 1, the momentous General Conference Session of 1901 was ready to begin.[38]

BEGINNING OF A NEW ERA

Originally, the 1901 General Conference was to be held in Oakland and in February. Delayed and moved to the more centrally located Battle Creek, the session came to order on April 2 in the Battle Creek Tabernacle. Daniells's influence was apparent even before the session convened, as part of the three-person program committee. Apprehension about the session troubled church leaders, according to *Review* editor A. T. Jones. "From rumors that thickly flew across the horizon of every part of the field," Jones wrote, "hardly a delegate appeared at this session who did not anticipate worry, and even disaster more or less serious. . . . Whispers of disintegration were borne from ear to ear." Prone to hyperbole, Jones nonetheless sensed the unease of delegates over an unclear organizational future. Daniells himself testified that the conference opened "with gloomy forebodings."[39]

The session officially convened on a Tuesday at 9:00 A.M., but momentum for reform began the night before in the college library. Ellen White, who had not attended a General Conference session for a decade, was present (the delay in opening the session was for her convenience). It is not clear whose idea her pre-session address was. Perhaps her long absence made leaders nostalgic to revisit earlier years when God's prophet delivered timely testimonies. Now, surrounded by a group of Adventism's most influential leaders, White delivered a pointed address calling for organizational change. It was a heartfelt message by an individual who recognized the propitiousness of the moment. Leaders appeared to welcome her testimony. In any event, her talk marked a moment when Adventist institutional life was put irretrievably on a path to change.[40]

She emphasized several points. First, the time for change was long overdue. "God forbid, brethren, that this Conference should close . . . with the same management, the same tone, the same order." "For the past fifteen years wrong decisions have been made; and now God calls for a change." Second, she repeated her frequent admonition that tightly held power must be relaxed. "There are to be no kings in our work, no man who will put out his hand and say to God's workman, 'You cannot go there. We will not support you if you go there.' " She called instead for a more democratic polity. "There must be a committee, not composed of half a dozen men, but of representatives from all lines of our work." Third, she made it clear that not only ought there to be new forms of administration but that current leadership must be replaced. "God desires the committees which have been handling the same things for so long to be relieved of their command." But fourth, she desired that these changes not occur because she was advocating them. "Do not refer to what Sister White has said," she commanded, "do not quote my words again as long as you live until you can obey the Bible." The needed reforms, she felt, should be implemented because they were obvious and biblically based, not simply to indulge an aging prophet.

Ellen White made a final point: support for John Harvey Kellogg and medical missionary work. She couched this in a more general call for church unity (relations of clergy and medical worker were already showing strain). "God wants his workers to stand shoulder to shoulder with Dr. Kellogg." White apologized to him that she might "have written to you too strongly," and she was relieved that he had not "sunk into despair." Indeed, Kellogg's work offered opportunity to reach "the higher classes," for which the church should be grateful. White's endorsement of Kellogg rings poignant when one recalls the bitter disputes into which Daniells and Kellogg would soon fall.

The following day the thirty-fourth General Conference session convened. Delegates numbered 216 (twelve were women, including Ellen White). The meetings went on for three weeks, from April 2 to April 23. Moreover, a publisher's convention preceded the full sessions. This may seem brutally protracted, but when one recalls the travails of travel (even in 1901) and the still distant reality of long-distance telephone service, it is understandable why leaders sought to get much accomplished when they were together. And, as with modern General Conference sessions, visitors swarmed Battle Creek in what approached an Adventist Hegira. Indeed, 1901 witnessed the largest gathering yet seen, estimated at 1,500.[41]

George Irwin, current General Conference president, presided over the initial gathering at 9:00 A.M. on April 2. These were business meetings to be sure, largely devoted to review of accomplishments and planning for the future. But they were also occasions for collective worship and renewal of faith in the church's world mission. A hymn opened the day, followed by a reading of the 106th Psalm by J. N. Loughborough and prayer by Stephen Haskell. These two great workhorses of Adventism bestowed a legitimacy on the meetings that few others could.[42]

Among the first orders of business (after taking the roll of delegates) was the acceptance of new conferences into fellowship. The Adventist Church was on the march. Daniells had the privilege of moving the acceptance of two new conferences, the South Australian and Queensland. But the size of these infant conferences—211 members in the first, 270 in the second—conveys not only the modest scale of the church but also something of the heartfelt confidence in local organization that led them to approve this step.[43]

George A. Irwin delivered what proved to be his final presidential address. Prayer sessions, hymns, and reports of church progress followed, the staple of all sessions. But the delegates had also to get to business. And Ellen White helped to focus minds when on the first day she delivered a pointed address. It echoed her talk to leaders the previous evening. She spoke of the urgency of the moment; what had long been debated must now be accomplished. She imbued administrative change with divine sanction. "God wants the world to see that business can be carried on in accordance with the principles that mark the character of God in Christ." And the heart of these godly principles? Shared leadership. "There are to be more than one or two or three men to consider the whole vast field." White did not name names, but she spoke bluntly. "Men that have long stood in positions of trust while disregarding the light that God has given, are not to be depended upon. God wants them to be removed." White's longstanding complaints about "kingly power" were about to bear fruit.[44]

With a prophet's public blessing, the reform leaders wasted no time. When Irwin asked the delegates how they wished to proceed, Daniells seized the initiative. He reported to the assembly on the previous night's meeting of notables, where after White's address the group (informally chaired by Daniells) decided that a change in conference procedures was needed. In short, he moved a complete suspension of normal rules. A "General Committee" would be appointed to draft a new church organization that would be presented to the full assembly. The make-up of this powerful ad hoc group naturally provoked discussion. Daniells proposed that it be a sizable group composed of heads of all conferences and institutions, plus notables such as A. T. Jones, Prescott, Loughborough, and Haskell. Prescott, however, worried that this group was simply the current church leadership in a new setting. How would fresh thinking emerge from them (himself included)? Instead, he suggested, let delegates from the eight world districts choose their own representatives. Daniells admitted that the usual leaders would make up the committee but felt this would not be a problem. The reorganizational effort, he memorably observed, "is not a condemnation of *men* as men; but of *methods* and *principles* which must be swept away." In words that must have reassured many officials, he stated that the session is "not called upon to sweep away every man who has held a position during the last two years; but we are to sweep away every wrong principle under which we have been working." Prescott was satisfied. When E. J. Waggoner sought to slow down what he may have perceived to be a runaway convention by keeping power in the full body of delegates, Ellen White responded pointedly: "I want every one to be careful how he throws in a block—'Not now, wait, wait, wait, wait.' We want to know what the right thing is, and move right away." Willie White then called for a season of prayer, which occurred. After a few other details were addressed, a unanimous vote carried Daniells's plan.[45]

Thus a process for remaking church structure was born. Large (some seventy-five members) and including virtually every figure of note in the church, this group's wishes would clearly be imprinted on the entire gathering. No records survive of the Committee's internal deliberations. But beginning on the session's second day, Daniells began making regular reports to the assembled delegates.[46]

It quickly became clear that the Australian Union Conference was the organizational model for change. Delegates wanted to know more, so yet again A. G. Daniells was the man of the hour. On Friday, the fourth day of the conference, he delivered an extensive and candid account of its formation. Part geography lesson, part review of Adventist missions, part tutorial on organization building, Daniells's lecture was masterful. He told a story of efforts to carry the Adventist message with few workers and limited resources to a huge English-speaking colony. Early attempts to replicate the American organizational model further stretched human resources. To the Australian Conference was added a freestanding Tract and Missionary Society and a Sabbath School Association. Then came pressure from America to add a Religious Liberty Association (these being the years when the American church faced major church-state issues). At this point, the Australian church said "enough." There simply was not sufficient leadership in Australia for so many entities. Instead, a simple expedient was taken: all the associations were wrapped into the conference as departments. No more independent, potentially overlapping, and even competitive boards. Better coordination resulted. Greater efficiency was achieved, as more workers could be devoted to the field.[47]

When came the next step of forming a union conference composed of various local conferences, the same organizational plan was carried through. A union conference committee became the chief oversight body. It brought together not only conference presidents but also representatives of every branch of work—from publishing to education to medical—and key lay people as well. It became the pattern for later union committees.

General Conference session delegates from the United States (who comprised the greatest number by far), accustomed to the unwieldy jerry-built administrative structure of their country, must has been astonished by Daniells's description. When he finished, they quickly threw questions his way. Who pays workers, the local conferences or the union? (Local conferences.) Do tithes go to a general treasury at the union? (Yes.) Do medical workers receive any support from tithe? (Yes, when they need it.) The latter question was part of a larger discussion of the relationship of the medical work to the organized church. "We have no separate medical organization," Daniells announced. Physicians were members of the union conference committee, and they held licenses to preach. Daniells was describing an integration of minister and physician that was never realized in the United States. Indeed, at this moment he could not have known just how vexing this relationship would be to him over the next few years.

Daniells's immediate concern at the session was presiding over a supersized committee that sought to reshape the administrative skeleton of the church. How such a group of strong-willed leaders managed to overcome institutional and personal self-interest could only be accomplished, they would insist, by their constant appeal to prayer. Indeed, this was one of those too-rare moments in Adventist history when shared institutional vision became embodied in radically new practice. This must be counted among A. G. Daniells's greatest accomplishments. The ability to labor through endless detail, amendment, objection, and even occasional obfuscation by apprehensive colleagues, is not the stuff of heroic legend. But it enabled progress in the bureaucratically structured organizations of the twentieth century. And at these tasks, Daniells was a master.

The new church structure took definition bit by bit as Daniells brought in reports for discussion and approval by the full session. Change started with a direct borrowing from the Australian model: formation of union conferences (and in as expeditious a manner as possible). These intermediary organizations between local conferences and the General Conference were to be a means of removing much decision-making from the "kings" in Battle Creek and placing it in regional hands. In drafting union conference constitutions best suited to their needs, the Committee on Organization invited three delegates from each district to join them in the process (enlarging the committee even more!).[48]

A few days later, Daniells brought more of reorganization to the delegates. It represented a complete rethinking of church structure. The General Conference Committee would become the expanded heart of the church. It would "take the place of all the present boards and committees" (except those which were "essential legal corporations"—an important exception). No more Tract and Missionary societies, Sabbath School societies, or Religious Liberty Association. These would become "departments" under direction of the General Conference Committee, which would be partially composed of heads of the various departments. But, objected a delegate, what of the Foreign Mission Board? This organization was deemed by many as crucial to the church's work. Daniells hedged. The consummate committee man that he was, he understood the need to couch delicate issues in terms that would not threaten the larger goals. The Foreign Mission Board, he confessed, was "not fully discussed." Further, it was a legal corporation (an "essential" legal corporation), and thus the present motion spared it. Moreover, the Medical Missionary Board, with its legal oversight of much property, was without question going to remain independent.[49]

The General Conference Committee would be expanded from fifteen to twenty-five members. Each union conference president (eight at that time) would be a member, together with representatives from educational and publishing fields, six members selected by the Medical Missionary Association (a measure of the power of Kellogg and the medical arm of the church, which employed more people than did the General Conference), and five members to be chosen "with special reference to their ability to foster and develop a true evangelical spirit." But what of various nationalities, some quickly asked. Should not they get a representative? And what of the Sabbath School work, or Tract Society, or foreign missionary laborers? Surely they must merit a special voice. To these objections Prescott responded that the Bible gives an answer: "Neither barbarian, nor Scythian, bond nor free, Jew nor Greek; ye are all one in Christ Jesus." Prescott was invoking a model of virtual representation. But some delegates were no more convinced by that argument than American colonists had been when the British made the same point. Only when E. J. Waggoner pointed out the difficulty of deciding which of the many nationalities should have a delegate (would the Turks and Armenians both get a voice, or only large groups such as the Germans?) that the illogic of this objection was grasped. Still, the full session of delegates balked at voting Daniells's motion after just an hour's discussion. Instead, they voted unanimously that no action be taken until the proposals were printed and distributed to allow for more reflection on the changes.[50]

But this maneuver scarcely slowed the runaway express that reform had become. An overhaul of church administrative structure, voiced at biannual General Conference sessions from 1897 onward, now had overwhelming momentum. If Ellen White had stoked the boiler at the session's beginning, Daniells sat in the engineer's seat thereafter, guiding the process down the tracks. His skill at knowing when to apply brakes (rarely) or add more steam was masterful. When the time came to vote on the amended church constitution, it was passed without discussion.[51]

What was the heart of the change in church structure? As other church historians have noted, there was an interesting mix of increased centralization of power with dispersal of authority. The displacement of the various freestanding societies and associations by departments clearly meant more power for the General Conference than before. But (in theory) there would be no president to exercise strong executive authority. Instead, the enlarged General Conference Committee would wield power, serving as an executive committee between General Conference sessions. No president was elected by delegates; instead, the twenty-five-member executive committee would elect its own chair and other officers. This change of procedure and nomenclature aroused little debate at the time. But it would soon prove to be highly divisive, as the chair of the enlarged executive committee exercised powers that appeared very presidential (even "kingly").[52]

A more important barometer of democratizing change were the new union conferences, six in all, understood as being closer and thus more responsive to the needs of their region. Decision-making would be dispersed. Additionally, union conference presidents would now be elected by their members rather than being appointees of Battle Creek, as was the case in the previous district system. Further, educational and other institutions that had belonged to the General Conference or various auxiliaries were to be transferred to union ownership. There was, in short, more empowerment of local Adventist constituencies. The colleges in particular, most of which had been established in the 1890s, became focal points of member pride and ownership.

To understand reorganization in purely structural terms would be to miss the theological passion that underlay it. For Jones and Waggoner, still yoked together in reform, there was a vital need for the church to devise a church organization reflective of God's desires. They sought a New Testament model for organization, built upon each individual's relationship to God. Theirs was an extreme ecclesiology, with echoes of Roger Williams's similarly extreme doctrines. Reorganization was not about "organization" but about people, Jones insisted. Only as each Adventist was "reorganized" and "renewed" could the church move forward. Likewise, Jones's egalitarian view of church gave short shrift to human claims for authority. Since Christ was head of the church, Jones preached in his opening night sermon, there should be no president presuming to that role. "Position never gives authority," he proclaimed. Daniells, in the enthusiasm of the moment and no doubt welcoming any reforming help he could get, thought Jones's sermon "grand." But he would learn by 1902 that Jones and Waggoner underpinned reorganization in ways incompatible with his own.[53]

Daniells (along with Ellen and Willie White) approached reorganization pragmatically. It was a means to an end. And that end was the more effective spreading of the gospel. Church organization was evaluated with this overriding end in mind. In his devotional talk (the very morning of Jones's later address), Daniells poured forth his soul. He may not have been running for the presidency, but his address surely went far in persuading delegates that here was a man with a deep burden for God's work. His theme, quite simply, was "our field and its needs." The man whose previous fourteen years had been spent abroad knew a world that was hungry for the gospel. Church organization should be evaluated by one criterion: How well did it help support missions? He was hopeful that plans for reorganization might "sweep out the unnecessary wheels, take off the unnecessary cranks in the machinery, and simplify the whole thing." The goal was to reduce "friction" and get the energies of men away from "running [the] machinery" to work on the front lines of mission.[54]

By any reasonable measure, the 1901 reorganization of the Seventh-day Adventist Church was a success. For more than a century the new organizational structure has guided the church. It has shown remarkable flexibility, bridging an age of the typewriter, railroads, and telegraphic communications with that of computers, jet travel, and texting. Its resilience and utility lay in the fine balance its creators achieved between centralized and dispersed administrative authority. New efficiencies created by advances in transportation and communication—and unceasing pressures on budgets—will likely lead to overhaul of the 1901 system in the near future. When that day comes, it will not diminish the legacy of A. G. Daniells. As long as change was in the service of mission, he would embrace it warmly.

A "PROGRESSIVE" ERA

The reorganization of the Seventh-day Adventist Church was driven by internal church dynamics that required change and by leaders astute enough to grasp the situation. But almost certainly unrecognized by Daniells and his colleagues, the 1901 General Conference Session also reflected larger social developments in America. It has long been understood by historians that the late nineteenth and early twentieth centuries witnessed a "search for order." That is, the largely local and rather unsystematically formed social and business landscape was rapidly evolving into carefully structured organizations that were often state-wide or even national in scope. The 1901 General Conference, in other words, offers a nearly perfect case study of the larger trends toward rationalized bureaucratization occurring in American society. "We ought to simplify our machinery for transacting our business," Daniells advised. "It seems to many that we have multiplied organizations and boards and institutions. . . . Multiplying boards of two or three or four men to run the particular lines of work does not necessarily or naturally increase the efficiency of our management." Daniells's statement shows why the "Progressive Era" (as the early twentieth century is often called) is as appropriate a term for Adventist history as for anything happening in American government or business.[55]

Developments within church organization bespoke something even larger and more abstract. German sociologist Max Weber, a contemporary of Ellen White and Daniells, provided insights into the nature of modern society, which help illuminate Adventism (though Weber was almost certainly unknown to church leaders of that day). Weber identified what he termed "charismatic" leadership. The term in this usage does not imply speaking in tongues. Rather, "charisma" in its sociological meaning signifies that an individual exercises power because he or she possesses a special gift—a heavenly gift, if you will—that is acknowledged by his or her followers. This gift obligates followers to pay special deference to the leader. Adventism was profoundly shaped by the charismatic leadership of Ellen White. Her status as a prophet within the Adventist Church fit Weber's definition well.[56]

But inherent in charismatic leadership is the problem of its continuation after the figure is gone. This is accomplished, Weber explains, through the "routinization" of charisma. By this he means that a power, which by its nature is mysterious, highly personal, and nearly unbounded, becomes rationalized within a bureaucratic structure. Although there are significant differences between Weber's analysis of typical charismatic leaders and White's place within Adventism, developments at the 1901 General Conference represented an important step in the routinization of White's charisma. It was a consequence, clearly, of the onward march of bureaucratization in the church. Important institutional decisions, strongly influenced by James and Ellen White from the movement's beginning until the early 1880s, were now a function of committee action.

The prophet's influence was never effaced, to be sure. Through her writings she has continued to shape church culture long after her death. But White's charisma, to some degree always mediated through a male, now became an adjunct of a committee of males. The clearest indication of this process came with Daniells's repeated invocation of White's support for reorganization. He testified of her endorsing reform earlier in Australia and now for the entire church. "I esteem it a privilege to state to the delegates here what I have frequently heard Sister White say" (this in regard church organization). Daniells thus appropriated charisma in the service of bureaucratic ends. But Weber would not have anticipated that a charismatic figure such as White would have participated so willingly in this process of appropriation. It was White, after all, who endured the hardship of long travel to attend the General Conference session and urge change. No one can accuse Ellen White of seeking to maintain the tight administrative control over her church that contemporary Mary Baker Eddy exercised. White's primary concern was always for the well-being of the Advent movement.[57]

The 1901 General Conference will always be known for its refashioning church organization. The reorganization was perhaps the most significant action ever accomplished by a General Conference in session. But delegates also accomplished other noteworthy things. The southern states, in which organized Adventist work had started just a decade earlier, had been a financial drain on the larger church. But they were enjoying membership growth, had formed state conferences the previous summer, and now their delegates supported the idea of a union conference. In theory the new conferences would be self-supporting—even returning tithe to the General Conference. But they represented the poorest (by far) region of America. Thus, their delegates requested extended General Conference financial support. How would the hard-strapped church respond? Daniells displayed a generous spirit. He encouraged the step of conference formation, and he pledged to stand by the nascent organization "even if it should take more money." There was also a vote to move Battle Creek College to the rural location of Berrien Springs. Money issues, naturally, loomed large. One matter very close to Daniells's heart concerned support for the struggling institutions in Scandinavia, the Skodsborg Sanitarium in Denmark, and the Christiana publishing house in Norway. Their finances were desperate. To risk a large appropriation for them seemed to many throwing good money after bad. But in the midst of the debate, Daniells, who had visited there in the previous year, rose and delivered one of his most impassioned addresses. He drew heavily on his experiences in New Zealand, when things often looked equally bleak. He told a dramatic story of a sailor who leapt into the bay to save a woman whose horse-drawn cab had run off the wharf. Someone had to help. It is God's principle, Daniells moralized, that when someone is in peril, others must help. After much discussion, a special offering on June 1 for these sister institutions in Scandinavia was approved.[58]

On April 18, with the new organization approved, the General Conference Committee convened under the new dispensation. The first order of business was choosing its chair (effectively the new president). John Harvey Kellogg nominated Arthur Grosvenor Daniells, a motion seconded by A. T. Jones. This act by the two most mercurial figures in the church seemed to promise harmony going forward. But events of the next few years instead rendered their action among the most ironic of Adventist history.[59]

---

[1] AGD to "Dear Brother," April 3, 1900; AGD to WCW, April 25, 1900, CAR.

[2] Schwarz and Greenleaf, *Light Bearers*, 217, 218. The early work in South Africa was almost exclusively among the European population.

[3] AGD to WCW, May 4, 1900, CAR.

[4] AGD to WCW, May 18 addendum to May 4, 1900, letter. Jeff Crocombe provides the best account of Dutch-English tensions in his unpublished paper, "Hubertus Elffers (1858–1931) and the Dutch-English Tensions in the Developing South African Seventh-day Adventist Church," presented at the Association of Seventh-day Adventist Historians meetings, March 25–28, 2010, at Washington Adventist University, Takoma Park, Maryland, available at http://www.sdahistorians.org/uploads/1/2/3/6/12365223/CrocombeJ_Elffers_Final.pdf.

[5] A. L. White, *The Australian Years*, 180, 181, 269, 331, 332; Jean Cripps, "Journey Into Yesterday," *Trans-African Division Outlook*, June 15, 1971, 5–8.

[6] Daniells, with his characteristic attention to detail, gave an overview of the South African Conference in a letter to WCW, July 2, 1900, and to WCW and E. R. Palmer, June 20, 1900, CAR. A description of the sanitarium financial woes in Denmark is found in AGD to Brother and Sister White, November 25, 1900, CAR.

[7] AGD to George Irwin, March 14, 1900, ASTR; Valentine, *Prophet and Presidents*, 176, 177.

[8] AGD to EGW, May 17, 1900, CAR. Valentine, *Prophet and Presidents*, 179, 180.

[9] AGD to WCW, May 4, 1900, CAR.

[10] AGD to EGW, May 17, 1900; AGD to WCW, May 17, 1900, CAR.

[11] AGD to Henry Wessels, June 3, 1900, CAR.

[12] EGW to Brother and Sister [John] Wessels, May 18, 1897, EGW Research Center, SWAU.

[13] AGD to EGW, May 17, 1900; AGD to WCW, May 17, 1900.

[14] EGW to W. S. Hyatt, November 9, 1899, EGW Research Center, SWAU.

[15] AGD to George Irwin, July 31, 1900, CAR.

[16] Ibid.; *RH*, September 4, 1900, 11.

[17] AGD to George Irwin, July 31, 1900.

[18] Ibid.; Valentine, *W. W. Prescott*, 145; AGD to WCW, August 23, 1900, CAR.

[19] AGD to WCW, August 23, 1900.

[20] *RH*, October 23, 1900, 13; AGD to EGW, October 4, 1900, CAR; GCCMin, fall session, October 25, 1900.

[21] AGD to EGW, October 4, 1900.

[22] Ibid.

[23] GCCMin, fall session, October 21, 25, 28, 1900; Calvin W. Edwards and Gary Land, *Seeker After Light: A. F. Ballenger, Adventism, and American Christianity* (Berrien Springs, MI: Andrews University Press, 2000), chap. 3.

[24] AGD to Brother and Sister White, November 25, 1900, CAR.

[25] AGD to EGW, January 8, 1901, CAR.

[26] AGD to WCW, January 24, 1901, CAR.

[27] On the rumors surrounding Daniells's installation as General Conference president in 1901, see the complete discussion in Valentine, *Prophet and Presidents*, 180–190.

[28] Ibid.; AGD to George Irwin, July 31, 1900.

[29] General Conference of Seventh-day Adventists, *Annual Statistical Report for 1901.*

[30] Barry Oliver's *SDA Organizational Structure: Past, Present, and Future* (Berrien Springs, MI: Andrews University Press, 1989) is the best general study of the topic. George Knight, *Organizing for Mission and Growth* (Hagerstown, MD: Review and Herald®, 2006) is an excellent short introduction. Malcolm Bull and Keith Lockhart, *Seeking a Sanctuary: Seventh-day Adventism and the American Dream*, 2nd ed. (Bloomington: Indiana University Press, 2007), 118.

[31] For a clear discussion of the problems leading up to the 1901 General Conference reorganization, see Schwarz and Greenleaf, *Light Bearers*, 246–250.

[32] EGW, *The Ellen G. White 1888 Materials* (Washington, DC: Ellen G. White Estate, 1987), 4:1498; EGW, *Testimonies to Ministers and Gospel Workers* (Mountain View, CA: Pacific Press®, 1923), 320; EGW to G. I. Butler, October 14, 1888. A convenient compendium of documents dealing with organizational reform in this age is found in Bert Haloviak, compiler, "Documents on Church Organization, 1883–1907," ASTR. Although George Butler's reputation as a hard-nosed General Conference power broker remains intact, he has found a sympathetic biographer in Emmet K. Vande Vere's *Rugged Heart: The Story of George I. Butler* (Nashville: Southern Publishing Association, 1979).

[33] Speed Mosby, "The New Nobility," *The Public*, September 8, 1900, 343. Loughborough's positions taken from 1891 *General Conference Daily Bulletin*.

[34] Oliver, *SDA Organizational Structure*, 160, 161; AGD to WCW, August 23, 1900.

[35] Oliver, *SDA Organizational Structure*, 104–106; A. L. White, *The Australian Years*, 120–122; Valentine, *Prophet and Presidents*, 214. It had been a year before the experimental union conference in Australia that Robinson innovated the new church structure in the young South African church. He realized that the limited Adventist personnel prevented the staffing of the usual array of independent auxiliary associations. Robinson's plan did not meet with approval from church leaders in Battle Creek (though being thousands of miles away from headquarters, he had already instituted it), but Robinson's description of it in an exchange with Willie White clearly influenced the latter in his new Australian plan. See Oliver, *SDA Organizational Structure*, 73–81.

[36] Valentine, "A. G. Daniells as Evangelist and Administrator," 36; EGW quote from "Talk by Ellen G. White in College Library," April 1, 1901, unpublished stenographic transcript, EGW Research Center, SWAU.

[37] Oliver, *SDA Organizational Structure*, 161, 162.

[38] GCCMin, March 29, 1901.

[39] GCCMin, March 24, 1901; *GCB*, Extra No. 20, April 25, 1901, 457; AGD to E. R. Palmer, May 3, 1901, ASTR.

[40] EGW, "Talk by Ellen G.White."

[41] *GCB*, Extra No. 3, April 5, 1901, 66.

[42] *GCB*, Extra No. 1, April 3, 1901, 17.

[43] Ibid., 19.

[44] Ibid., 23, 25, 26.

[45] Ibid., 27–29.

[46] Committee on Counsel Minutes, April 2, 1901; *GCB*, Extra No. 2, April 4, 1901, 34.

[47] Daniells's talk and subsequent discussion found in *GCB*, Extra No. 4, April 7, 1901, 89–92.

[48] GCCMin, April 8, 1901, 39; *GCB*, Extra No. 7, April 10, 1901, 169.

[49] *GCB*, Extra No. 8, April 11, 1901, 185, 186; Extra No. 9, April 12, 1901, 201, 202, 205, 206.

[50] *GCB*, Extra No. 8, April 11, 1901, 186, 187.

[51] Daniells provided a useful summary of the changes in the next-to-last *General Conference Bulletin*, no. 3, 1901, pp. 513–515. He reflected on the event two years later in "The President of the General Conference in the Light of the Constitution Adopted in 1901," statement by A. G. Daniells in a letter to Dr. C. C. Nicola, July 30, 1905, EGW Research Center, SWAU.

[52] George Knight provides insightful commentary on the reform in his *Organizing for Mission*, 108, 109. Jerry Moon's *W. C. White and Ellen G. White* and Barry Oliver's *SDA Organizational Structure* also have illuminating thoughts on 1901.

[53] Barry Oliver provides a complete discussion of the competing philosophies of General Conference reorganization in *SDA Organizational Structure*, 194–227; Jones's sermon in *GCB*, Extra No. 2, April 4, 1901, 37–46; Daniells quoted by Oliver, 224.

[54] AGD, "The Field," delivered April 3, 1901, *GCB*, Extra No. 2, April 4, 1901, 47–50.

[55] Robert Wiebe's *The Search for Order: 1877–1920* (New York: Hill and Wang, 1967) is the classic statement of these developments. *GCB*, Extra No. 11, April 15, 1901, 228.

[56] See Max Weber's two essays, "The Sociology of Charismatic Authority" and "Charismatic Authority and its Routinization," both in *Max Weber on Charisma and Institution Building*, ed. S. N. Eisenstadt (Chicago: University of Chicago Press, 1968).

[57] *GCB*, Extra No. 3, April 5, 1901, 68.

[58] Ibid.; Extra No. 10, April 14, 1901, 216–219; Extra No. 18, April 23, 1901, 410–414.

[59] GCCMin, April 18, 1901.

Chapter IV

THE OFFICE OF PRESIDENT

Arthur Grosvenor Daniells, Seventh-day Adventism's new world leader (president in all but title), entered office in the prime of life. At age forty-two, he brought energy, experience, a passion for missions, and a talent (one is tempted to say genius) for administration. He also, on occasion, conveyed an air of imperiousness. The most famous photograph of him suggests a man comfortable with command. In fact, he had to learn lessons in humility while still in Australia. But the Adventist Church needed his strength in the new century. O. A. Olsen and G. A. Irwin, fine Christians both, lacked the fire or self-confidence to direct an increasingly complex organization. Daniells would bring both. Just as important, he had the confidence of Ellen White and the close friendship of her son Willie. His wife, Mary, though sharp-tongued, was completely devoted to him. Given these ingredients for his success, it should not be so surprising that he would head the church for the next twenty-one years.

Daniells would soon face some of the most vexing problems any Adventist leader has known. Yet he was fortunate to come to power at a time of prosperity and great national confidence. The Spanish-American War was just past, and America was flexing newly found imperial muscles. It was a young nation, with a median age of under twenty-three years. And driven by the high level of trans-Atlantic male migration, there were more men than women in the population of some 76 million. Furthermore, a time of human movement—from nation to nation or from farm to city—when people are establishing new roots, is often a time when they are more receptive to new religious traditions. All in all, it was a propitious moment for the Adventist movement.[1]

What did A. G. Daniells make of his elevation to church leadership? We have little sense of his private reflections during the several weeks of the General Conference session. His days were too filled with meetings to allow for much correspondence; in any event, nearly every leader of note was present in Battle Creek. But in the following month he conveyed his personal response in letters to fellow Adventist workers. He exuded enthusiasm for the accomplishments of the session. "I doubt whether any such meeting has been held since apostolic times," he told E. R. Palmer in what one assumes was tongue-in-cheek hyperbole. One might also be suspicious of his testimony that during the session "not a word was uttered that needed to be retracted. Not a single measure submitted received unkind treatment. . . . It was all done by common consent." Whether or not such universal harmony prevailed, it is clear that Daniells felt privileged to have participated in what he recognized as a special moment in the Advent movement.[2]

PRIVILEGED AND PROUD

"I had quite a hand in the revolutionary measures that were brought forward," he confided to Palmer. But pride came less naturally to Daniells than a nagging feeling of his limitations. Early in the sessions he sensed the drift of things; his descriptions of Australian organizational achievements were clearly influencing delegates. His leadership there and the lack of any other obvious choice for leader scripted the handwriting clearly on the wall. "I felt unreconciled to that which I saw was coming," he wrote veteran worker in Australia E. W. Farnsworth. "But the Lord gave me the fullest assurance it was my duty to remain here [rather than return to Australia] and join the brethren." Thus, when his election came, he was at peace with the promotion, even telling "the brethren of my experience."[3]

Two further things helped Daniells assume leadership with a measure of confidence. He took as a good sign that he was invited by conference presidents to visit virtually all camp meetings that summer. They well knew his position on vigorous financial support for foreign missions, yet they still offered him their pulpits—an indication of "heart work" at the sessions. Second, Daniells was granted the experienced workers he requested to be at his side, notably Prescott, W. A. Spicer, and other "wide-awake yet consecrated men." Daniells, the preternaturally talented administrator, understood the vital importance of competent help. He also understood the delicate matter of dealing with an immediate past president. George Irwin, a respected though not always highly effective Adventist leader, had at age fifty-six some years of service left in him. (Unfortunately, Irwin carried a sense of failure about his time as head of the church.) It came as a relief to Daniells (who could better carry on without the old guard hovering about) that Irwin was posted as far away as could be imagined: Australia. Being made head of the Australasian Union gave him a graceful, honorable exit. Essentially, he and Daniells swapped jobs. The latter greatly appreciated Irwin's being a good soldier about the change. "He has taken the revolution that has come in the best spirit possible." It was even arranged for Irwin's son, a college professor, to accompany him and teach at Avondale. Adventist church leaders, at a moment of institutional stress, passed the test of graceful consideration for one of their own.[4]

TASKS FOR A NEW LEADER

What exactly did a General Conference president do? In the largest sense he had the task of coordinating and moving forward the worldwide effort of his church. In the case of Seventh-day Adventism this meant conveying a prophetic message of Christ's soon return. The urgency of the Advent message imposed a unique pressure on leadership. God's timetable depended on their success. Thus, an important part of Daniells's work was exhortative, and he used the pages of the *Review and Herald* to urge members on to faithfulness and action. But Daniells lacked charisma, both in the religious sense (as Ellen White had it) and in the vernacular sense of an aura of personal magnetism that drew people to him. Perhaps the closest thing to charisma Daniells possessed was a passion for the Adventist mission, which he effectively conveyed to all who would listen. But administrative giftedness, rather than charm, provided the underpinning of his long tenure of leadership.

At the heart of Daniells's task was communication. He lived in a state of continuous communication and conferral, primarily with other leaders. The communication took three forms: attending endless meetings; corresponding with far-flung leaders; and traveling thousands of miles to meet local leaders, observe the grass-roots church, and speak at camp meetings.

The Adventist Church has long been characterized by its penchant for frequent and protracted administrative gatherings, driven by a desire for denominational unity and consensual decision making. Daniells had scarcely finished the grueling three weeks of the General Conference session when he had to chair regular meetings of the General Conference Committee (the executive body of the world church) and the Foreign Mission Board. The former committee he first chaired on April 19, when it took up the laborious chore of filling an array of committees and leadership positions. The latter committee would sometimes meet daily when Daniells was in Battle Creek. The Mission Board convened three times on May 27, for example (the first at 5:30 A.M.), to consider mission efforts in the South Pacific's Society Islands. It established legal procedures for transferring an Adventist missionary's property to the church and further voted $2,500 for the purchase of a boat for use in the islands.[5]

There was more. Daniells also served as the first president of the Lake Union Conference, perhaps because its territory included the General Conference headquarters. This duty quickly proved onerous, but he nonetheless trudged ahead in the position until 1905. He also chaired the General Conference Association (the legal entity of the church that owned property).

When not in meetings, Daniells spent an extraordinary amount of time on correspondence. Before a national long-distance phone network existed, the Adventist Church depended heavily on the U.S. Postal Service. In his twenty-one years as General Conference president, Daniells produced a flood of letters. On July 17 (to choose a not uncommon day), while attending education meetings in Berrien Springs, he found time between sessions to compose at least six letters (there may have been more). These were often multipaged, typed epistles dealing with a variety of church concerns, sent as nearby as Battle Creek or as far away as Toronto, Cape Town, or Cooranbong, Australia. In Adventist centers he generally had a stenographer, but on the road he did his own typing on an early model portable machine. Daniells maintained a direct but cordial tone in his missives. They are business-like, relatively formal, and to the point; no chattiness and only occasionally a reference to his family. But they also convey an ease of communication with a wide range of people. No hint of imperiousness or *primus inter pares* marks his early letters.

Daniells recognized that a leader could not always manage an organization from afar. He traveled thousands of miles each year. Occasionally, he caught a steamer across one of the Great Lakes or along the coast, but mostly he moved by train. Daniells benefited from living at the height of railroad passenger service in America, ranging from elegant transcontinental sleeping car routes to electrified interurban short lines (extending even to Berrien Springs). Midwestern railroads like the Grand Trunk found it useful to place timetable advertisements in the *Review and Herald*. How to secure favorable passenger rates was a frequent conversation of church leaders around General Conference time.

What drove Daniells to such endless toil? One has to look no further than his passion for the Advent message. From the time of his decision to enter church work during his early twenties, his dedication appears unflagging. He might have had moments of uncertainty about his abilities or the state of his soul, but about the urgency of the Adventist truth he seemingly had no doubts. For those who seek more overtly psychological roots of behavior, Daniells offers a tempting case study. His compulsion to work might be seen as an effort to impose control on his life, a desire fed by the insecurities of his early youth (losing his father and placed for a time in an orphanage). In this reading, his youthful stammer and his lifelong work habits have the same etiology. But such an interpretation seems strained. With Daniells, one generally got what one saw.

A COMMITTEE MAN

There is no better way to understand the work of a General Conference president than by following Daniells through the first months of his tenure. The level of energy Daniells brought to his job may have been unusual, and the challenges facing the church in the early 1900s were unique, but in most respects the contours of his work resembled what other church executives have faced.

The landmark General Conference Session of 1901 concluded in mid-April. As already noted, the next several weeks brought follow-up meetings of the General Conference Committee in Battle Creek. For Daniells, who had been in America scarcely half a year, the endless sessions offered a chance to become more familiar with church leadership. He was a shrewd judge of men, and perhaps his most important early task was to size up the people surrounding him. Like the men who enter the White House, Daniells took for trusted counselors those individuals he had long known. Willie White was his chief confidant, along with Willie's mother. The bonds formed during the Australian years served Daniells well. Ellen White's advanced age, recurring ill health, and—most important—unique prophetic stature, meant that Daniells had to seek her counsel in careful ways (more on this in a later chapter). But to Willie he could write with what appears complete candor. "I hardly know where to begin nor what to say," he confessed in October of 1901. "I would give a great deal if I could have a full day's conference with you under some tree where no one would disturb us."[6]

The Whites, though, lived in California and only occasionally ventured east. So the individual Daniells consulted more frequently on a face-to-face basis was W. W. Prescott. His yearlong visit to Australia in the 1890s formed the basis of Daniells's high opinion of him. After some difficult experiences with attempted educational reform at Battle Creek College, and with unsuccessful efforts to put Adventism in England on a firmer institutional footing, Prescott had returned to Battle Creek in 1901 (at Daniells's insistence). Here, at Daniells's side as head of the Foreign Mission Board, Prescott found renewed influence. Prescott and Daniells traveled together extensively in the early summer, taking stock of the church. "It has been such a help to me to have him for a counselor," Daniells effused to Willie White. "He is better acquainted with the men in the field than I am. . . . He forms a quick, accurate judgment, and has a lot of courage. I am satisfied that we have done well to get him out of England, and to get his mind onto a broader range." "Broader range" in this case meant that Prescott was effectively second in command to Daniells.[7]

A younger and newer acquaintance who also became a trusted advisor to Daniells was William A. Spicer. As Mission Board Secretary (and influential General Conference president after Daniells), Spicer proved capable. When important matters came up, Daniells observed, Spicer had "an intelligent statement or proposition to make regarding the weighty matters." Further, "he communicates inspiration and instruction that is really helpful to the workers." It took a load off Daniells's mind to know that during his frequent travels matters at the home office were well attended to by Spicer.[8]

These lacks often had to do with money. The Seventh-day Adventist Church had never been flush with funds, but as mission activities expanded in the 1890s and when economic conditions in the nation were distressed during mid-decade, shortfalls were chronic. In May, the church owed its workers some $17,000 but had on hand only $1,500. It was not the first time church employees would wait months for their wages; this had been true frequently in the 1890s. But an organization that wished to consider itself modern and efficient could not countenance fiscal irresponsibility. The General Conference Committee voted to immediately borrow funds to meet church obligations. John Harvey Kellogg took matters a step further, proposing a double tithe. The cash-strapped leaders jumped on board, voting to ask local conferences to make an appeal. The double tithe initiative was pursued for some time, helped perhaps by new prosperity in America.[9]

Matters of church finance were more complicated than a simple shortfall of funds. Church leaders, too, often lacked sophistication—occasionally even common sense—in handling money. H. E. Osborne, secretary of the General Conference, deplored the "astonishing laxity" of workers regarding money. Their readiness to take on debt, and worse, their careless attitude toward such obligations, was "breaking down the confidence of our people generally." He regretted that Adventists did not share the "splendid reputation" of the Quakers in honesty of dealing. The new union conferences, moreover, displayed an independence in financial matters that left General Conference leaders strapped for funds. Instead of passing along tithe funds, for example, the Eastern Union Conference sent only credit memos. This was not mere contrariness on the conference's part. As union president H. W. Cottrell wrote Daniells, "We do not have nor neither will we have money enough." But if this practice continued, many church workers could not be paid and would have to look for work elsewhere. More happily, the question arose of what to do if a conference brought in tithes and offerings beyond its needs. This issue faced the Michigan Conference. Should it bank the surplus for future rainy days? Daniells thought not. Not when there were pressing needs elsewhere. One suspects that Daniells was thinking of General Conference needs. But that suspicion is contradicted by his comments to a Michigan elder regarding whether members might pay their tithe directly to a mission field. Church leader though he was, and presiding over a church entity then in grave need of funds, Daniells still refused to demand that tithe must go only through "proper channels." "That is a question between him and his God," Daniells opined. "I would not dare to advise any one in this."[10]

Another organizational problem that the General Conference Committee moved to address concerned the Foreign Mission Board and International Tract Society, which were headquartered in New York City. Having a strong church presence in the great metropolis had seemed a good idea, but Gotham's Adventism had been vexed by personality divisions. Further, an independent Mission Board proved challenging to coordinate with Battle Creek headquarters. The 1901 General Conference Session decided that the Mission Board's work would be taken on by the General Conference Committee (a change completed in 1903). The Tract Society had an even quicker demise. Its books would be audited, and its New York office closed by May 10. Daniells estimated the church could save $2,000 a year by consolidating its operations as a department of the General Conference with no loss of effectiveness. Likewise, the Chicago office of the *Sentinel of Liberty* (the church's religious liberty publication) was closed and operations moved to Battle Creek. The consolidation of independent church bodies, a major organizational goal of the General Conference session, proceeded rapidly.[11]

Another primary concern of the General Conference Committee was personnel issues—matching the right person to particular needs of a local field. Asking an individual to serve in a faraway mission could be a way of removing a troublesome person from the center of power in Battle Creek (as in tasking Prescott to England). More often, though, decisions were made on judgments of suitability to event or locale. Thus, one meeting in late April assigned church leaders to various summer camp meetings. Making decisions about regular postings clearly occupied a large share of the committee's energies, and Daniells's influence on such appointments provided regular opportunities to shape the face of the institutional church.[12]

Daniells presided over a General Conference Committee that often featured a collection of the most able—and strongest willed—individuals in the denomination. The session of April 29 is an example. Held in the Review and Herald chapel, the meeting was attended by seventeen men, including Daniells, Prescott, Willie White (still in Battle Creek after the General Conference Session), A. T. Jones, E. J. Waggoner, J. H. Kellogg, former General Conference presidents O. A. Olsen and G. A. Irwin, influential education reformer E. A. Sutherland, redoubtable church pioneer J. N. Loughborough, plus other leaders less well known to Adventist history but competent in their fields. Bringing singleness of mind to such a group must have presented unending challenge to Daniells. (Indeed, as will be seen in future chapters, it proved a challenge sometimes beyond his formidable powers of persuasion.)

A study of the General Conference Committee minutes reveals a body that necessarily exercised broad powers over the church. Even though a major goal of the 1901 General Conference Session was to empower the new union conferences with oversight of local conferences, at the beginning these new entities needed guidance. Establishing the new departments to replace the old Tract and Missionary societies, Sabbath School, and Religious Liberty Associations required ongoing superintendence. The reward for this effort, they hoped, was a more unified approach to church mission.

They sought not only greater unity but also helping General Conference leaders maintain steady focus on the big picture. The details of church administration were to be removed from Battle Creek to those leaders who were "on the ground." "Our hope," wrote Daniells in a memo to fellow General Conference Committee leaders, "is that we shall be left almost entirely free to study the large questions of policy affecting the entire field," especially foreign ones. Rationalizing organization, a central theme of government and business in the Progressive Era, was apparent in the Adventist Church as well.[13]

Never far from Daniells's mind during his first year in office was the church's chronic indebtedness. An inescapable fact bedeviled the church: the General Conference employed more people than it had funds to pay. By mid-1901 the church still owed nearly $25,000 to its laborers. This was a liability, as Daniells bluntly put it, "with no assets to offset it." Clearly, the church could not go forward without a plan.[14]

It was to address these nettlesome problems that Daniells had been voted leader. He was capable of institutional problem solving, forceful expression of his analysis, and the implementation of a solution. In this case, the answer lay in the just-formed union conferences. The point of these new organizations—intermediary between local conferences and the General Conference—was to provide administrative oversight to their regions. More to the point, the unions would oversee the employment of conference ministers. Most of the funds that previously went to Battle Creek would now stay at the union conference level, where the burden of determining how many workers could be supported would now lie. State conferences would pay two "tithes" of their members' contributions, one to the union conference and one to the General Conference. Daniells projected that the Eastern Union Conference (if local conferences faithfully paid both tithes) would have roughly $15,000 per year to cover its $10,000 obligations for workers' salaries. Daniells admitted that it was "impossible to speak with certainty as to how many of the State Conferences will pay the second tithe," but he moved forward with the confidence required of an organizational president. In any event, church headquarters had few other options. General Conference income was going to be decreased, and the union and local conferences would have to pick up the slack.[15]

Daniells and the large committee met almost daily until May 1. The scope and intensity of committee work during these weeks resembled the famous Hundred Days of legislative activity after Franklin Roosevelt took office in the spring of 1933. Issues ranged from the relocation of Battle Creek College (effectively marking the beginning of the exodus from Battle Creek) to transferring ownership of church property to wide-ranging discussions of church finance to planning for the "colored work." Church leaders acted with an assurance born of a belief that God had commissioned their efforts.[16]

ON THE ROAD

With weeks of General Conference Committee work finally ended, Daniells had one day to catch his breath before he was off to Indiana. He must have wondered when he would find time to attend to family details. Now that it was clear that his family would not be returning to Australia, new roots must be set down. In the autumn of 1901, construction began in Battle Creek on their first American house, of which just the second floor would be theirs. Since only one in five American families then owned their own home, the Daniells's situation was not unusual. Moreover, they would not need large quarters. The three-member Daniells household was smaller than the typical American family of five, and there seemed little prospect of their family's growing.[17]

The house came later. For the moment, on the third of May, Daniells began his visits to state conferences, what would be over the summer a procession across wide swaths of the eastern and central United States. Rather like George Washington's heroic efforts to visit every existing state during the early years of his presidency, A. G. Daniells needed to be visible to Adventist leaders and laymen alike. If the reorganization of the Seventh-day Adventist Church was less momentous than the founding of the American nation, the parallels were nonetheless real. A new administrative structure existed on paper—and most clearly, in the mind of Daniells himself. But the translation of that vision into a functioning organization required immense effort. The inchoate telephone network did not allow him ready contact with the far-flung church. An efficient post office was an invaluable aid. But the situation demanded Daniells's presence in the East, South, and Midwest.

He started with a trip to Indianapolis. The Indiana Conference, so troubled by the "Holy Flesh" movement the previous year, was settling back into a more traditional Adventism. Ellen White's testimony about the Indiana situation, delivered at the recent General Conference session, had good effect. "The brethren who had led in the wrong course," the *Review* reported, "confessed to this, and placed themselves in the attitude of perfect willingness to aid in every way possible in putting the affairs of the Conference on a better basis." This special constituency meeting of the Indiana Conference was attended by an all-star collection of leaders: Daniells, Willie and Ellen White (who were on their way back to California), A. T. Jones, P. T. Magan, and W. W. Prescott.[18]

The 120 delegates heard Daniells open the weekend meetings on a Friday evening with a sermon based on Joshua 3:5. "Sanctify yourselves: for to morrow the Lord will do wonders among you." Prescott and Jones followed the next day with traditional Adventist sermons on the sanctuary and the priesthood of Christ. But as the featured church speaker, Ellen White devoted herself to the dominant message of her later life: Christ's love and presence among His people. That night the business meeting of the conference was held, a gathering so spiritual that Jones enthused that it was "not distinguishable in spirit from [those] that had been held even on the Sabbath." The agreeable spirit carried over to the next morning, when Ellen gave frank counsel to the Indiana delegates about the proper (and improper) course. With new leadership installed, Indiana Adventism appeared to be again on a firm foundation. Daniells returned to the Hoosier State in the fall and expressed relief that there was nothing "to remind us of the trouble that existed here last year."[19]

From Indiana Daniells traveled east to Ohio, where he spoke at the Mount Vernon Academy graduation. He lingered for several days, acquainting himself with Ohioans and vice versa. His words "of earnest admonition and instruction," the *Review's* correspondent testified, "had a marked effect." The "good will" engendered by Daniells's visit was exactly what he intended.[20]

The end of May brought a trip to the plains of central Kansas. A local camp meeting of the Kansas Conference, held at McPherson, was actually two events—an English-speaking set of meetings and a larger German-language set of gatherings. Daniells and Prescott assisted members in matters of church organization. Daniells would return to Kansas in July for a full conference camp meeting.[21]

The next stop on the camp meeting trail was in Des Moines. Iowa had been an important early center of the Adventist Church (also a center of early heresy), and it remained one of the larger conferences. A. G. Daniells never shrank from sharing with his colleagues his opinion of various gatherings. About the Iowa meetings he was ecstatic for many reasons. The business meetings and elections went smoothly, and a progressive spirit was manifest. The vexing theological issues of the past appeared to be finally laid to rest. "When all had been done that could be done by the people, the Lord came graciously near and set the seal of disapproval upon it all," Daniells wrote Willie White in prophetic language reminiscent of his mother's. Daniells also loved the evangelistic preaching, as did many in the congregation. The eleven o'clock church service extended to mid-afternoon. In place of the usual altar call, particular groups were sent to other tents. Scandinavians went to one. To another were sent those "who were conscious of their unconverted and thoroughly-backslidden state." This was a large group, described by Daniells as "very earnest seekers for deliverance from the bondage of sin."[22]

An ordination service came later in the day, followed by an old-fashioned testimony service where two to three hundred spoke, Daniells estimated. "Thrill after thrill passed through the congregation, as they gave their short, ringing, pointed testimonies of joy in God and hope and courage for the future." Sunday morning (at 5:30!) Daniells made the obligatory appeal for the support of foreign missions. But he did not make an immediate call for funds; instead he wanted to give P. T. Magan an opportunity to appeal for the church's major fund-raising effort of the age, the "Relief of the Schools campaign."[23]

This campaign addressed one of the thorniest problems General Conference leadership had faced in the years preceding Daniells's arrival: overwhelming indebtedness by most of the recently started schools. The 1890s was the epic age of educational institution founding, with colleges (Walla Walla and Union colleges) or more modest training schools (Southern, Southwestern, and Oakwood) sprouting up in every part of the country. But the deep recession through much of the decade undermined the ability of members to support them. A collective debt of $350,000 threatened to sink the church. To shut the schools down would be to admit institutional failure of a high order. This was clearly not an option. At this fateful juncture, when the future of Adventism education was at risk, church leaders displayed a heartening ingenuity. In 1899, Ellen White (still in Australia) had volunteered to dedicate the royalties from her recently completed "The Parables of Jesus" (published as *Christ's Object Lessons*) to the redemption from debt. But her donation came on condition that church leaders and publishing houses unite to promote an unprecedented sales campaign. The resultant effort was probably General Conference president George Irwin's finest hour. In the spring of 1900, a special committee was set up to oversee the campaign. P. T. Magan did little else for months besides head the effort. Pacific Press and Review and Herald Publishing each produced a massive run of 150,000 copies. They did this reputedly at cost. The tract societies handled sales commission free. Everything was to go to the schools, and for this reason they were to mount an aggressive selling campaign. Indeed, an army of church members was called on to sell the book.[24]

The "Relief of the Schools" work (what the *Review* styled "a Herculean task") proceeded over the next few years. But it started slowly. P. T. Magan had to prod members with urgings to recover "a little of the old-time spirit that used to be in 1844." He publicly commended the "noble South Dakotans," who, though poor, followed in the way of the "churches of Macedonia" in their support (the names and donations of Dakotans were printed in the *Review*). The church paper kept the campaign before members with a drumbeat of exhortations seldom equaled in denominational history. Letters were published in the *Review* testifying to the increasing broad spirit of enthusiasm among members. In one small church, a revival of commitment to the project resulted in members ordering 378 books for public sales. The canvassing project, indeed, became a means of church revival. One leader estimated that given the 50,000 members in America, each would only have to be responsible for selling six copies (at $1.25 each). It seemed simple on paper. But a church body of modest means found it challenging to raise the $50,000 to cover the cost of materials that went into the 300,000 copies. The *Review* weekly published the list of the faithful donors, with usual amounts ranging from $1.00 to $25.00.[25]

The plan might have appeared simple in concept. But the complexities of printing and distribution made the effort more than General Conference leaders had bargained for. A. G. Daniells inherited the project and devoted considerable energy during his first eighteen months in office to it. The plan required tweaking so that the two publishing houses would not, on the one hand, be beggared by the endeavor, but on the other, produce the books in a timely fashion. The expensive and protracted effort occasionally strained administrative patience. "It makes my heart sad when I think of the awful indifference our people have manifested toward this heaven-born plan," Daniells lamented at one point. Campaign leader Magan was reduced to hard negotiations with one union conference leader to persuade him to purchase the book at agreed-on prices from Pacific Press. Magan was frustrated that even the shrewd Daniells failed to understand how the West Coast press's higher shipping costs added pennies to the per-copy cost. By the fall of 1900, proceeds from sales reached $35,000, which represented only a tenth of the indebtedness.[26]

From his leadership perch at the newly established college in Berrien Springs, E. A. Sutherland shared with Daniells his own attempts at getting the crusade in high gear. Sutherland, never shy about letting church comrades know how things should be done, laid out for one conference president a plan for getting all his workers on the task. But the leader bridled at the intrusion on his prerogatives. Slow and steady, was his approach.

Sutherland fretted to Daniells that what could be accomplished in weeks would drag on for months.[27]

The campaign also weighed heavily on Daniells. Not until the spring of 1902 did he find cause for real optimism about the program's success. The turning point, he felt, came in Michigan, the largest conference and something of a bellwether for the church. Conference leadership finally exhibited enthusiasm for the effort. It came following a troubled night for the Michigan Conference president, J. D. Cowell. He awoke with what he was convinced was a plan from the Lord. The state was divided into districts, with a local minister assigned to each. A quota of books was given each district (minister) to sell. The genius of the plan, however, lay in a pointed incentive for the ministers. Instead of receiving their regular salaries, they would get paid only out of the commission of their book sales. The pastors "cheerfully agreed to this plan," Daniells reported with uncharacteristic naiveté. "They did not feel they were whipped into the work," Daniells assured Willie White. Whatever level of true volunteerism existed, book sales did pick up mightily. Daniells also planned during his first visit to Europe in spring 1902 to urge leaders to adopt the sales plan. The transatlantic economy was strong. There was no excuse for not walking through the door God had opened. It just took work. No one could contradict Daniells's observation that the *Christ's Object Lessons* campaign was "designed to make God's people a working people."[28]

For all its problems, by the fall of 1902 the campaign enabled some of the schools to reduce their debt by over half, others less than that but still by substantial amounts. The campaign continued into the fall of 1903, by which point, most admitted, it had begun to flag. Church leaders considered utilizing Ellen White's more recent book, *Education,* in a fund-raising fashion similar to *Christ's Object Lessons*. But despite the appropriateness of its subject for such an effort, momentum was never achieved. The financial ball was passed back to the various union conferences, who were the legal owners of their local college or training school and upon whose shoulders the burden of support would thereafter be laid. Ellen White may have benefited in another way, though. Her gift of *Christ's Object Lessons,* according to son Willie, may have counteracted an undercurrent of criticism about the book royalties she earned.[29]

The campaign's ultimate success led Daniells and Spicer to envision a similar effort to defray other General Conference indebtedness. Salaries for ministers were running some $40,000 above what tithes were providing, and there was no ready means of closing the gap. But a recent work of E. J. Waggoner, *The Everlasting Gospel*, suggested an answer. By early 1902 it had been published only in England (where Waggoner had been working for several years). Daniells considered it a great work: "One of the best books published by our people." "It strikes the great key-note of the Reformation, namely, justification by faith." If thirty thousand to fifty thousand copies were published in America, put in all Adventist homes and then sold to their friends, it could be both a spiritual and financial blessing. The plan, however, sound though it seemed, never came to fruition.[30]

Magan, on an early Sunday morning at the Iowa camp meeting, touched a generous nerve in his hearers. Some $1,500 in cash, pledges, and objects (a gold watch and pottery with an estimated worth of $150) poured in. Even more came in verbal pledges for the campaign and missions, including a promise by a woman in Minnesota to donate her farm. But members were asked to do even more. "The ground was canvassed for the 'Signs,' and the 'Missionary Magazine.' " Overstocks of the Tract Society's *Good Health* and A. T. Jones's massive anti-Catholic screed, *The Two Republics*, were successfully hawked. "Poor old Iowa has not experienced so much life and enthusiasm for a long time," Daniells reflected happily.[31]

With all this salesmanship on display, one might be tempted to wonder if Daniells and his compatriots were the inspiration for Professor Harold Hill, the fictional "Music Man," who plied Iowa towns in this era looking for a scam. But such cynicism would be misplaced. Daniells and his fellow Iowans shared a commitment to a message, the proclamation of which was worth their worldly wealth.

Not that Daniells shied away from thinking about financial needs or asking for funds. "There is a great wave of prosperity in this country at the present time," he noted. "Our people are making money. They have lots of it." Indeed, the prosperity of the new century was turning people's hearts to mammon, even within the church—and even within the ministry. Daniells told of one minister in the Iowa Conference so well-to-do that he had recently purchased a farm. But when a fellow minister sought a loan to make a contribution to the struggling work in Scandinavia, the prosperous Pharisee would do so only at 7 percent interest. "I need not tell you that this minister has but little influence among the people, especially when he preaches on the nearness of the Lord's coming."[32]

Daniells became an outstanding administrator in part because he was capable of realistic self-reflection about his work. He found the Iowa meetings instructive. "I think that I learned a number of lessons that will help me very much in my work," he told Willie. "I see that the General Conference Committee must come into closer touch with the masses of our people. We must make them acquainted with what we are endeavoring to accomplish." Daniells had confidence that once his Adventist family saw a need they would step forward, as he saw happen in Des Moines.[33]

The ensuing Minnesota camp meeting proved as disappointing as Iowa's had been exhilarating. Held at Anoka, the gathering was brief, attendance was small, and enthusiasm was lacking. Daniells and Prescott arrived just as things were wrapping up and had time for only short sessions with conference workers. "I accomplished nothing, so far as I can see," he despaired. He experienced a larger sadness in the missed opportunities the camp meeting represented in terms of funds expended for the event, wearisome travel by members, modest funds raised for missions, and lack of clear direction for the conference's future. But even in frustration, as Daniells admitted, useful knowledge could be gleaned. He gained a sense of the field and of conference leadership. He must not avert his eyes from the challenges he faced in the field.[34]

DEFICIENCIES OF LEADERSHIP

Church leaders no doubt undertook the reorganization of 1901 with eyes open to the many and necessarily unanticipated difficulties they would encounter. But even an administrator as experienced as A. G. Daniells met hurdles that challenged his optimism. His next stop, the Wisconsin camp meeting, forced him to confront a truth that had been stealing upon him for some time: ineffective leadership stalked the denomination. Indeed, not only here but during visits to Ohio, Minnesota, and Michigan camp meetings, where he had a chance to observe state conference leadership firsthand, Daniells came face to face with the human limitations with which the church struggled.

In Wisconsin, poor leadership compromised the camp meetings (which were the most important conference events of the year). "I never saw anything more lamentable than the situation in Wisconsin," Daniells complained. "They were not only without leadership, but without knowledge as to what to do." The conference president was well meaning but clueless about his task. Rank-and-file pastors were likewise deficient. "It makes me sad to see how a great many of our preachers spend their time, and how little they improve." A few worked hard "along progressive lines," but the "great majority of our ministers are taking it easy, and not only failing to grow, but are really retrograding." Pastors must be encouraged and helped to grow, but those who make no improvement should be encouraged to give way to "men of energy and push and consecration." The 1888 righteousness by faith message also seemed to have made little headway among the ministry. "I believe we are doing our people a positive disservice by keeping this light away from them," Daniells complained to Willie White. "Ministers in whom they suppose they should have confidence are giving them error and darkness for truth and light." Some younger pastors interested in the Minneapolis message felt constrained by their leaders from promulgating it. At the same time, he recognized that many Adventist clergy were woefully underpaid. "It is impossible for our laborers to live as they ought to on the wages they are receiving."[35]

During a return visit to Ohio later that summer, Daniells enjoyed a "splendid meeting" and fellowship with a "fine lot of Sabbath-keepers." But the leadership, he confided to Willie White, was "dreadfully weak." Daniells was dismayed by how "leadership in this country has degenerated. . . . It has to be seen." The situation was most acute in Michigan, largest of the conferences. The first signs of trouble came with the indifferent attendance at camp meeting, reduced by half from previous years. "The conference has been running down for some years, and I fear it will go several notches lower before the thing turns on the upgrade." Why? The problem started with the conference president. "Brother Cowell is a good old, honest farmer; but he has no more business to be at the head of this great Conference of 8,000 people than anything in the world. He has no plans," Daniells fretted, "no decision, no force, no progressiveness; so far as I can see, he is simply a figure-head." Which was a second problem: a group of strong pastors benefited from having a weak president. "They can work when and where and as much or little as they please, and they can draw their money just the same. There is plenty of it, and there is no trouble to get it."[36]

Daniells had an abrupt lesson in the limitations of even the highest-ranking General Conference leadership when facing determined local opposition. With a constituency meeting underway to choose conference leaders, Daniells spent an extended amount of time with Cowell and the nominating committee. He thought he had the outcome stage-managed: Cowell would become a committeeman and a more suitable president would be elected. But at the key moment during the meeting, "Brother Cowell showed the white feather, and gave away the whole thing by his milk-and-water attitude." Something of a backlash occurred among committee rank and file, who "got it into their heads that we were trying to crush Brother Cowell." Heels dug in firmly, and Daniells finally had to admit defeat. The same leadership group would return for another year. Complicating this tragi-comedy, Cowell had "heard that Sister White had said he was not the right man for the place." If he were certain she had said this then he would step down, but lacking this direct command he feared refusing the mantle that the Lord had seemed to bestow. This sense of calling, of appointment, genuinely felt if not always genuinely conferred, complicated selection of leadership. Willie White, empathizing with Daniells's frustration, confided to him that these shortcomings of democratic leadership might need to give way to plain speaking by the small group of leaders (especially himself and Daniells) "who have had clear light" about managing church work.[37]

The emotional toll of these frustrations on Daniells was huge. "Sometimes I almost despair of a full and complete reformation. . . . I almost wish that I had never left Australia, or that I had stopped in England and Europe." But with the resiliency that marked his remarkable tenure as president, after a good night's sleep he would awake "with renewed courage to battle on." This required unceasing effort to hold before the state conferences "right principles" of organization in the confidence that sanctified common sense would ultimately prevail. Addressing the general quality of the Adventist pastorate took longer. Not until after his presidency would he be able to undertake systematic efforts at improving the training of ministers.[38]

NORTH, SOUTH, AND NORTH AGAIN

Arthur G. Daniells enjoyed a brief respite at home in Battle Creek following the Wisconsin camp meeting. But on June 21 he rode the rails again to Toronto for the Ontario camp meeting. Then he made his way south to Graysville, Tennessee, where one center of educational work in the Southern Union was located. His stay was abbreviated by a sudden call to visit New York City. Rail travel could be slow, and Daniells earned no frequent-flier miles. Still, he never stood in line at security checks nor dealt with the frantic pace of airline travel. Given his predisposition to push himself mercilessly, the enforced calm of train travel may have been therapeutic. And it certainly was not wasted time, not with his trusty typewriter ever ready to assist his stream of letters.

As Daniells headed to Tennessee, he must have reflected on the unique problems Adventism faced in seeking to extend its presence in the South. Adventism was a "Yankee" faith, born in New England. The original Millerite message did not find much resonance below the Ohio River, and the consequent Advent movement spread west rather than south. The church's solid identification with the Union during the Civil War and its Republican Party leanings thereafter threatened to drive a wedge between it and the subjugated former Confederate states. The region was poor, religiously conservative, and rent by racial antagonisms. Evangelistic work among whites had proceeded fitfully, and efforts with the impoverished black population had started just a few years earlier when Edson White bravely pioneered work in Mississippi.[39]

Despite the difficulties, Adventist leadership made the Southern work a priority, partly because Ellen White continually prompted them to do so. She was delighted her wayward son Edson was back in the church and attempting constructive work. The General Conference showed its good faith in this effort at the spring meetings, where financial support for the nascent Southern conferences was promised. Schools at Graysville (for whites) and Oakwood (for blacks) were well underway. Encouragement for colporteurs and other church workers to head south appeared frequently in church papers. In late fall 1901, the *Review* prompted members to "Spend Your Winter in the Sunny South." Colporteurs, in particular, who anticipated slow sales during the winter, were urged to enter those states thus far scarcely exposed to Adventist literature. Church leaders wanted so much to make this happen that they promised three months' room and board to people willing to work in what was styled "a world of its own." In May, the Tennessee Conference sent workers laden with reams of literature to the Confederate Veterans Reunion at Memphis. Here, on the fiftieth anniversary of the Civil War's beginning, former rebels were exposed to the teachings of a church that itself had earlier rebelled against denominational orthodoxy.[40]

Daniells understood that his visit to Graysville carried potential awkwardness. He would be meeting with Edson, whose erratic ways and financial irresponsibility were frequently the bane of Battle Creek leadership. But he was also Ellen White's son, a fact Daniells could not overlook. For her part, Ellen White struggled to strike a balance between endorsing Edson's work in the South and acknowledging his limitations. Earlier in 1901, Edson had moved the operations of the Southern Missionary Society to Nashville. Shortly thereafter the Southern Union Conference was organized (likewise headquartered in Nashville), followed by schools and the Southern Publishing Association. The southern field gave every indication of a bright future. But church leaders had little confidence in Edson. Thus, it was vital for Daniells to make a personal visit.[41]

Graysville, pleasantly situated in a valley just east of the Cumberland Plateau and a few miles north of Chattanooga, was the original sight of the Southern Training School. It was also conveniently sited on the Southern Railway, which gave Daniells and others easy access. The entire conference committee attended. The delicacy of Daniells's mission was highlighted in contrasting letters he had received only days earlier from the Whites. Ellen White had written him twice in June arguing for the special nature of the Southern field and that the "kingly minds" of Battle Creek ought not to control all the funds going there. "All that Edson has presented to you regarding the necessity of special plans for the book work in the South is worthy of consideration." But Willie was more circumspect about the situation. He had been hurt by his brother's charges that he unduly influenced their mother's opinions. "I am trying to look beyond the man to the work," he wrote Daniells, "and I am sure that you will do the same, and with much better grace than I do." Willie, with his usual voice of caution and moderation, urged his friend to give the imperfect efforts in the South a fair hearing.[42]

Neither Mrs. White nor either of her sons could have wished a better outcome. "Matters that had been causing controversy were fully discussed and satisfactorily settled," Daniells later reported to Olsen and Prescott. Southern Publishing Association in Nashville gained recognition as the church's book distributor in the South, and colporteur work in the region would be actively fostered. Edson must have been delighted. A bit more discussion at previous sessions, Daniells concluded, would have prevented needless friction. Furthermore, "my confidence in Edson's work has increased." Daniells wrote repeatedly over the next month that his general interest in Adventism's progress in the South—especially among blacks—had increased tremendously.[43]

Daniells had planned to accompany Edson White to view the new church facilities in Nashville, but the call from leaders in New York changed his itinerary. He did, however, take a day off to visit Chattanooga's Civil War sites. Edson and others escorted him about Orchard Knob, Missionary Ridge, and the spectacular vista from atop Lookout Mountain. Other than his early experience in Texas (whose culture was more Southwest than Southern), this was Daniells's first exposure to the South. He may have drawn some stares, in this Jim Crow era, when he traveled north toward Washington accompanied by "Brother Armstrong," an African American church worker. Armstrong tutored Daniells regarding the work among that segment of the population.[44]

The twenty-four-hour trip from Chattanooga to the nation's capital allowed Daniells to arrive just in time to enjoy a Sabbath with believers there. He here encountered a more direct and potentially explosive racial divide than he had ever—or would ever—experience. The District's Adventist church was holding evangelistic tent meetings that appealed to both whites and blacks. However, in what was still an essentially southern city, integrated meetings were a problem. Further, a dynamic young pastor, Lewis Sheafe, was prepared to push an agenda that caused Adventist leaders discomfort. (This story, a troubled one for Daniells's presidency, is the subject of chapter 7.)[45]

From Washington, Daniells proceeded directly to New York City. The urgency of the visit resulted from the need to see Elder G. W. Reaser before he sailed to a mission posting in Natal, South Africa. The trip, at Reaser's urging, was a measure of how quickly church men were coming to value

Daniells's counsel. O. A. Olsen had decided not to join Reaser in Africa, and the latter needed reassurance about the daunting challenge he would face on his own. Having made the long detour to New York, Daniells used the visit to investigate the troubled New York Conference and the nascent organization of the Atlantic Union Conference.[46]

Daniells returned to Berrien Springs, Michigan, in mid-July. Two important gatherings occurred simultaneously on the banks of the St. Joseph River: Lake Union Conference meetings and a church-wide educational conference. Conveniently for Daniells (who needed to attend both), union meetings were held in the morning and education meetings in the afternoon.

High on Daniells's agenda for the Lake Union meetings was finding a vice president who could relieve him of its administrative details. That Daniells had to assume union presidency reveals just how little administrative experience the church then had. Fortunately, W. H. Thurston, having returned stateside after pioneering the Adventist work in Brazil, fit the bill nicely. Thurston was in the "front ranks of our reform work," Daniells enthused. "He has clearer views of the work than most of the men who have remained in this country." Daniells was also cheered by Lake Union delegates' quick acceptance of reform measures, including a democratization of local conference constituency meetings (every church member present would be a delegate) and the furthering of a second tithe to the General Conference to support foreign missions.[47]

But greater excitement attended the education meetings. Adventism was in the midst of its great age of school founding. Although the denomination's ambitions were greater than its pocketbook, it nonetheless displayed a commitment to education that would be unwavering; indeed, this investment would uniquely stamp it among Protestant denominations. Colleges, secondary schools, and now especially, primary schools began sprouting where pockets of Adventism existed. This efflorescence resulted from a combination of things. The generally strong American economy enabled growth. More important, a self-generated reform movement within Adventism undergirded rapid expansion. It came in part from Australia and in part from Battle Creek. Australia's Avondale School, founded under Ellen White's watchful eye, provided a new "blueprint" for American schools. A series of articles in the *Review* in the late 1890s inspired an educational awakening among Adventist readers stateside. In Battle Creek, Sutherland took charge of the college and instituted far-reaching reforms. With a fervor that can only be described as evangelical, he exhorted college students to go out from Battle Creek—even before they had graduated—to populate Adventist grammar schools with teachers. Many youth accepted the challenge. Between 1895 and 1900 the number of schools increased from 18 to 220. Adventist education would never look back.[48]

The July education meeting in Berrien Springs was the second one sponsored by the General Conference. The first, a decade earlier (setting a precedent for the ongoing decennial education conferences in the North American Division) in Harbor Springs, Michigan, began to wean Adventist education off the prevailing classical curriculum toward one based on biblical studies. The 1901 conference pondered what Christian grammar education ought to be. The roughly one hundred teachers, from all about the country, and many of them still teenagers, camped in tents pitched in oak groves along the St. Joseph River. The tents were provided free of charge, as was the tuition for the six-week school session. Daniells, who arrived after the conference had begun and left after a week, liked what he saw. "They are a bright, consecrated lot of young people," he noted, "and are having a good experience in their work."[49]

But Daniells, the eagle-eyed administrator, was also alert to larger problems in the still-immature educational system. In truth, there was no system. Adventist education was in "a formative state," as Daniells kindly phrased it. The relationship of local churches to their church schools was uncertain. "The brethren and sisters in the churches do not know just how they should act toward the teachers, nor what demands they should make of them." The teachers, for their part, young and inexperienced, had good intentions toward their students but little beyond that. "We have not the qualified teachers to send to the churches." These were not disabling problems. "It is very plain to me that the church school work is becoming a great work," Daniells confidently predicted, one worthy of denominational leaders' attention. The situation called for "some splendid organizer to take charge of the whole school business and develop it." No "czar" of Adventist church school organization appeared. But Daniells, whose heart was always with evangelism and foreign missions, must be credited with an early understanding that education would soon become "one of the largest and most important" aspects of the church.[50]

Why did these two important church meetings occur in the rural groves of Berrien County rather than in or near Battle Creek? Because the grounds were under strong consideration as the new site for Battle Creek College's successor. Under Ellen White's prodding, the decision to move had been made during the General Conference session in March. (Kellogg had agreed to purchase the Battle Creek campus for his own institution of medical education.) But where to go? Sutherland and P. T. Magan had located a prime site, a hundred-acre farm, convenient to Benton Harbor and Lake Michigan but suitably rural, as Ellen White recommended, and perfect for the work-study training the two reformers envisioned for Adventist education. When he at last saw it, Daniells considered the Garland farm to be in "the finest state of cultivation" he had ever seen, and the $10,000 price tag seemed within reach. Daniells's mental wheels were spinning. The college would not need the entire acreage, he calculated, so plots could be sold to teachers and others affiliated with the school (at a higher rate than the total per-acre purchase), which would defray about half the cost. This, combined with funds from the sale of Battle Creek College, would allow the new institution—Emmanuel Missionary College—to get its start debt free. In October, sixteen railroad cars laden with college gear snaked their way to the new college site on the St. Joe. The exodus from Battle Creek, which would pick up momentum over the next two years, had begun.[51]

CAMP MEETINGS AND MORE CAMP MEETINGS

Adventist culture revolved around camp meetings. The historic Christian calendar held little allure for most Adventists (shades of papism), but rusticated revivalism, so much a part of nineteenth-century evangelical culture, bit deep into Adventism. Camp meetings were then still considered a means of evangelism. Daniells mildly complained when certain conferences placed their meeting sites so far away from general populations that proselytizing was difficult. But camp meetings increasingly were becoming what we know today: occasions for members flung across the conference to renew friendships and experience spiritual growth through sermons by the church's leading figures (Ellen White, quite naturally, was the leading attraction). Additionally, camp meetings were convenient times for conference constituency meetings.

The latter was one reason A. G. Daniells sought to attend as many camp meetings as he could in that first, crucial year of reorganization. He did not carry the star power of White, but he was nonetheless in heavy demand on the camp meeting circuit. Indiana leaders postponed their event so that he could attend. Daniells regretted that he could not always supply the prominent figures, such as himself, Prescott, or Jones, as headliners.[52]

Through June, July, August, and September 1901, Daniells circumnavigated by rail America's East and great hinterland: to Kansas in late July; early August, on to Cleburne, Texas; return east to Lansing, Michigan, and Canton, Ohio; then zigzag to Kankakee, Illinois, and Greenfield, Indiana. In early September it was back to New York State for the camp meeting at Oswego before decamping for Trenton, New Jersey, and the Atlantic Conference meeting. On the train from Indianapolis to New York the normally hearty Daniells became ill and convalesced in Buffalo for several days. Here he experienced a brush with history at the Pan-American Exposition then underway. His illness impeded the usual fair sightseeing, but he did attend President McKinley's address. He found a spot directly in front of the stage and took his measure of the nation's leader. "His manly bearing and manifestation of intelligence greatly impressed me," he wrote Willie. But the next day, when McKinley returned to the fairgrounds he was shot by anarchist Leon Czolgosz. "This was a terribly cruel assassination," Daniells continued. "I can hardly feel reconciled to it."[53]

He had traveled more than ten thousand miles since June, to twelve meetings. But there was more. Later in September he made a westward swing to Denver, Colorado, returning through Lincoln, Nebraska. He had a break from the circuit for just over a month before going to the deep Southeast to Florida camp meeting in November. "I will not spend another summer just as I have this one," Daniells vowed.[54]

The Florida visit had particular poignancy. Daniells was reunited with G. I. Butler, the old church warhorse, who had baptized him in Iowa, later hired him to his first pastorate, and then suggested he take a mission posting in New Zealand. They had not seen each other since Daniells had gone to the southern hemisphere fifteen years earlier. Butler had "retired" in Florida but found himself inextricably pulled into conference work. "I looked upon you as a father," Daniells confided to Butler in an earlier letter. But the reunion was somber. Lentha, Butler's wife of many years (who in her youth had, along with her parents, responded to William Miller's preaching in Vermont), passed away in Bowling Green, Florida, shortly before Daniells arrived. The man who as a youth was nurtured by the Butlers now became the patriarch's support.[55]

The summer's perambulations meant that Daniells spent much time in tents and eating camp food. He made a discovery—and it was not a pleasant one. The camp facilities were frequently awful. "In some places we have had damp, musty tents, and sometimes damp beds." But the food was worse. "I have been astonished at the ignorance or the carelessness of the Conferences in their food preparations," he confided to Willie. Only a couple of the meetings provided anything suitable. More often "the food has been cheap, sloppy, and unpalatable." He was even more aggravated by having endured protracted committee meetings only to then wait in the back of long lines for a lunch gone cold. Daniells, who had a highly developed sense of personal dignity, at one meeting refused to be part of the hungry, jostling crowd and simply went without. How could it be, he wondered, that after decades of experience with camp meetings the conferences still managed them so poorly? Always the administrator, Daniells determined that not another season would go by without clear instruction on how to run a session.[56]

Daniells found one exemplary effort in the Texas camp meeting held at Cleburne, Texas. It was well situated in a major rail center, making for convenient access. Likewise, the campground tent was centrally located near the county courthouse in the middle of town. The tent overflowed with attendees—Adventists, of course, but also Cleburne residents, who during the days leading up to the effort had been deluged with papers and personal invitations. The camp grounds were clean, well lit by electricity (not always the case at campgrounds), boasted plenty of clean water, and served meals overseen by a "sanitarium-trained cook." Daniells could not have been happier. He was sure that a fine church in town would result.[57]

In later years, as Daniells felt confident in leadership, he welcomed open forums at camp meetings. At the Colorado camp meeting in 1906, for example, he held a set of "Q & A" sessions, where he fielded candid inquiries about Ellen White's ministry. Daniells learned that members had concerns about rumors of improper influences on "the Spirit of Prophecy" (this coming during the culmination of the struggles with Kellogg and A. T. Jones and the charges they were making). Daniells also got an earful of complaints about the meat, tea, and other proscribed foods that had made their way into the camp meeting kitchens. Perhaps nowhere else was the political adroitness of Daniells better on display than in his fielding difficult questions before church laity.[58]

THE MANTLE OF LEADERSHIP

A. G. Daniells quickly became (after Ellen White) the face of the official Seventh-day Adventist Church. He achieved this through tireless travel and endless public speaking. But he also won the loyalty of his administrative and ministerial colleagues by his manifest love for the church and an uncommon good sense about how things should be managed. These qualities help explain his two decades of leadership.

Leadership, by its nature, deals with problems. Many problems concerned human conflict (some famous examples comprise the next two chapters). Others involved the never-ending search for funds sufficient to support outreach. The corollary of that challenge was setting priorities for scarce financial resources. Daniells also faced, in his early months, the biblical problem of laborers being too few for the gospel task. At the occasion of Emmanuel Missionary College's opening in October he issued a call for workers in the *Review*. "Never in the history of Seventh-day Adventists," he announced portentously, "has there been such a call for earnest, consecrated workers." Preachers, physicians, nurses, teachers, canvassers—even business men and women (whose financial support was much needed)—had to be found. But these professions required training, and existing schools had "sadly missed the mark." "Brethren, we must get our bearings," Daniells candidly continued. Fortunately, the newly opened school in Berrien Springs intended to be a "training school for missionaries," and he urged all who could to attend.[59]

Successful leadership must also cast a vision, or at least reiterate in fresh, persuasive ways the accepted vision of a group's past. Daniells was not a man to point the church in new directions (that was the task for the church's prophet). But he could forcefully—and at times even eloquently—call members to renewed commitment. In an October sermon at the Battle Creek Tabernacle, Daniells exposited Isaiah 62. The Adventist people, like the Old Testament prophet, must not keep silent in a time of great darkness in America. Individuals must consecrate themselves anew to the evangelistic task. Then they will be called the "Holy People, the Redeemed of the Lord" (verse 12, NIV). At year's end Daniells reported on a Week of Prayer in Battle Creek (which he may have helped organize). Meetings were held every afternoon and evening in the Tabernacle, the Sanitarium, and the Review and Herald press building. Prayer, doctrinal study, "inquiry" (gatherings for those seeking release from particular sins), and, above all, a "revival of faith and hope in the sure and speedy triumph of the Third Angel's Message," said Daniells, marked the meetings. His sharing in the occasions of renewal increased church members' respect for him, not only as a brilliant administrator but also for his passionate commitment to the Advent message.[60]

Thus concluded Arthur Daniells's first nine months in office. These were important months. Not only a new century but a new organizational form had been birthed the previous spring, one that needed Daniells's attentive care if it was to step forward on spindly young legs. Daniells's patience was repeatedly tested. But his genius for leadership and organization was widely appreciated. Despite immense pressures and unrelenting work, Daniells thrived personally (in tip-top health, he testified, gaining eight pounds) and his church flourished. He had determined that as president he would have no controversy with anyone. An admirable goal, without question. But he would shortly face challenges from influential and strong-willed individuals who would force Daniells to abandon his vow.[61]

---

[1] United States Census Bureau, "A Century of Change: America, 1900–1999," accessed April 25, 2011, https://www.msu.edu/~bsilver/pls440century.html.

[2] AGD to E. R. Palmer, May 3, 1901, ASTR.

[3] AGD to E. W. Farnsworth, [May] 3, 1901, ASTR.

[4] Ibid.

[5] GCCMin, April 19, 1901; Mission Board Minutes, May 27, 1901.

[6] AGD to WCW, October 9, 1901, CAR.

[7] Gilbert Valentine gives extensive detail to these years of Prescott's career in his *W. W. Prescott*, 124–150; AGD to WCW, July 1, 1901, CAR.

[8] AGD to WCW, July 1, 1901, CAR; H. E. Osborne to AGD, September 8, 1901, ASTR.

[9] GCCMin, April 22, 1901.

[10] H. E. Osborne to AGD, May 31, 1901, ASTR; H. W. Cottrell to AGD, July 5, 1901, ASTR; AGD to H. R. Johnson, July 16, 1901, GCPL.

[11] GCCMin, April 24, 1901; April 26, 1901; Valentine, *Prescott*, 148, 149; AGD to WCW, October 9, 1901.

[12] GCCMin, April 29, 1901.

[13] AGD to Members of the General Conference Committee, August 2, 1901, ASTR.

[14] Ibid.

[15] Ibid.; for his memo to General Conference Committee members, Daniells had laboriously studied rosters of General Conference workers and their wages to propose a scenario for their transfer to the Eastern Union Conference.

[16] The index to the General Conference Committee Minutes for spring 1901 provides a convenient overview of topics.

[17] S. H. Lane to AGD, December 6, 1901, ASTR; United States Department of Labor, "100 Years of U.S. Consumer Spending," 3, accessed April 24, 2011, http://www.bls.gov/opub/uscs/report991.pdf.

[18] *RH*, May 14, 1901, 12, 13.

[19] Ibid.; AGD to WCW, September 2, 1901, ASTR.

[20] *RH*, June 4, 1901, 11.

[21] Ibid., June 25, 1901, 11.

[22] AGD to WCW, June 12, 1901, ASTR.

[23] Ibid.

[24] GCCMin, December 25, 1899; April 1, 1900; October 16, 1900; *RH*, May 1, 1900, 11.

[25] *RH*, August 7, 1900, 12; January 8, 1901, 12.

[26] AGD to G. A. Irwin, March 25, 1902, GCPL; P. T. Magan to H. W. Cottrell, August 13, 1902, and August 24, 1902, ASTR.

[27] E. A. Sutherland to AGD, March 10, 1902, ASTR.

[28] AGD to W. B. White, April 17, 1902; AGD to WCW, April 8, 1902; AGD to M. R. Brown, April 9, 1902. AGD to G. A. Irwin, March 25, 1902, GCPL.

[29] GCCMin, October 16, 1900; October 21, 1900; November 24, 1902; October 19, 1903; WCW to AGD, May 22, 1903, ASTR.

[30] AGD to WCW, May 12, 1902; AGD to C. McReynolds, May 15, 1902, GCPL.

[31] AGD to WCW, June 12, 1901, ASTR.

[32] Ibid.

[33] Ibid.

[34] Ibid.

[35] AGD to WCW, June 19, 1901; May 12, 1902; AGD to W. C. McQuaig, May 9, 1902, ASTR.

[36] AGD to WCW, August 23, 1901, ASTR.

[37] Ibid., WCW to AGD, September 2, 1901, ASTR.

[38] AGD to WCW, August 23, 1901, ASTR.

[39] Ronald D. Graybill's *Mission to Black America: The True Story of Edson White and the Riverboat Morning Star* (Mountain View, CA: Pacific Press®, 1971) tells the story of Edson White's work.

[40] EGW to AGD, June 28, 1901, CAR; *RH*, December 3, 1901, 14; June 18, 1901, 13.

[41] Arthur L. White, *Ellen G. White: The Early Elmshaven Years 1900–1905* (Washington, DC: Review and Herald®, 1981), 168, 169, 189, 190; Schwarz and Greenleaf, *Light Bearers*, 232–234.

[42] EGW to AGD, June 5, 1901; June 28, 1901, CAR; WCW to AGD, June 19, 1901; *RH*, June 4, 1901, 13.

[43] AGD to WCW, July 4, 1901, ASTR; AGD to W. W. Prescott and O. A. Olsen, July 11, 1901, GCPL.

[44] AGD to WCW, July 21, 1901, ASTR.

[45] AGD to WCW, July 21, 1901, ASTR.

[46] AGD to G. W. Reaser, July 4, 1901; AGD to H. E. Osborne, July 4, 1901, ASTR; Mission Board Minutes, April 28, 1901.

[47] AGD to W. W. Prescott, July 21, 1901, GCPL.

[48] Schwarz and Greenleaf, *Light Bearers*, 197, 198. An example of the exhortations to churches to start a school is found in *RH*, June 11, 1901, 14.

[49] Schwarz and Greenleaf, *Light Bearers*, 197, 198; *RH*, July 23, 1901, 10, 16; AGD to W. W. Prescott, July 21, 1901, ASTR.

[50] AGD to Prescott, July 21, 1901.

[51] Schwarz and Greenleaf, *Light Bearers*, 259–262; AGD to W. W. Prescott, July 21, 1901; Meredith Jones-Gray, *As We Set Forth*, 88–91.

[52] AGD to G. E. Thompson, July 12, 1901, ASTR.

[53] "Camp-Meeting Arrangements," GCPL; AGD to WCW, September 20, 1901, ASTR.

[54] AGD to WCW, September 2, 1901, ASTR.

[55] AGD to George I. Butler, July 25, 1901; *RH*, November 26, 1901, 16; December 3, 1901, 14.

[56] AGD to WCW, September 2, 1901.

[57] *RH*, August 20, 1901, 7.

[58] "Questions-Box Service on the Spirit of Prophecy," August 28, 29, 30, 1906, EGWE.

[59] *RH*, October 22, 1901, 16.

[60] *RH*, October 8, 1901, 16; December 31, 1901, 9.

[61] WCW to AGD, June 19, 1901, ASTR; AGD to Brother Llewellyn, December 17, 1901, GCPL.

CHAPTER V

TAKING ON BATTLE CREEK

An axiom of executive leadership is that if collective pain must be endured by an organization or nation, it should be dealt with early in a leader's tenure. Navigate the storms of economic recession, conflict, or controversy, then right the ship and sail into more peaceful waters. A. G. Daniells did not intentionally choose this course. Few leaders seek out conflict. But as events transpired, he would face his most difficult challenges in his first years as General Conference president: the decision to move both General Conference headquarters and the Review and Herald publishing company from Battle Creek to Washington; the contention (especially with A. T. Jones) over Daniells assuming the title of "president"; the knock-down struggle with John Harvey Kellogg and the Battle Creek medical establishment; and the racially explosive controversy with Lewis Sheafe, pastor of a large congregation in the nation's capital. Although problems would remain his stock-in-trade, after contending with these big issues Daniells's presidency progressed more smoothly, at least until World War I rudely imposed itself on the international church.

TRAVAILS WITH PUBLISHING

Daniells also faced in his early years struggles with Adventist publishing. The church's publishing houses were then (until the medical work surged to the foreground) the bellwether institutions of the movement. Before the denomination had a governing structure it had a printing press, and the Adventist message had spread largely through the printed word. The Review and Herald press was established in 1861, followed by the Pacific Press in 1874. Presses in Europe and Australia carried Adventist doctrine to those regions. Books, periodicals, and tracts were distributed by an army of members, organized by Tract and Missionary societies in each conference. Soon, full-time colporteurs working for conferences or directly for the publishing houses were hawking publications. James White was the great promoter of the publishing work. His wife's writings constituted the core of church publications during and after her lifetime. But other best-selling works also appeared in the 1880s, such as Dr. Kellogg's *The Home Hand Book of Domestic Hygiene and Rational Medicine* (which introduced subscription sales to Adventist publishing) and Uriah Smith's *Thoughts on Daniel and the Revelation,* long a staple of Adventist publishing.[1]

Review and Herald and Pacific Press were impressive operations. The Review's Battle Creek facility, among the largest printing facilities in Michigan, employed some 275 workers and boasted more than a half million dollars in annual sales. By church standards they had become big business. Competition and accompanying hard feelings between the two houses inevitably followed, resolved through the typical corporate expedient of that age: cartel agreements to divide up the American territory so as to reduce competition (an agreement that lasted well into the twentieth century). Unlike secular American business, where competition was embraced (at least in theory) as a virtue, Adventist culture assiduously sought to avoid anything resembling competition within its ranks.[2]

In truth, publishing, rather than medical work, was the "right arm of the gospel" during the late nineteenth century. But like the medical field, publishing was populated by strong—even contentious—personalities, could be operated well or poorly, and even more than health care, was subject to the vagaries of the economy. The national depression beginning in 1893 cut deeply into colporteurs' profits. Sales of more than $800,000 in 1891 fell to $250,000 four years later. Even after the economy recovered in the later 1890s, Adventist publication sales remained flat, in part because morale was low among colporteurs and conferences leaders. In the Lake Union Conference (largest of the conferences), for example, 1891 sales of $84,000 had fallen 90 percent a decade later. It was worse in some areas of the country, such as Missouri, where drought destroyed crops and demoralized the subscription book business.[3]

For most of the country, the new century brought renewed prosperity. In Michigan "crops have been excellent," Daniells wrote church administrator Allen Moon. "Prices are good. Factories are humming. . . . Money is plentiful and circulating freely. This part of the country is enjoying unparalleled prosperity. . . Now is our time to do something."[4]

Daniells had two things in mind. First, he called back from Australia Edwin R. Palmer to head up the Lake Union's colporteur effort. They had been colleagues in the Australian field, and Daniells had high regard for him. Palmer restructured the bookselling business to make the local conference tract societies (rather than the publishing houses) directly responsible for sales. As with the union conference model and the educational blueprint of Avondale, the publishing reorganization was yet another Australian contribution to North American Adventism. With Daniells's unwavering support, Palmer took up his new task in October 1901, reviving first the colporteur and then the publishing work. A great bookselling campaign was planned for the months following the abundant fall harvest. "The farmers will have more leisure, and all classes will have more time for reading during the long wintry evenings," Daniells reasoned. An ambitious call went out for a thousand men and women to travel frozen Wisconsin, Illinois, Indiana, and—particularly—Michigan roads in a massive colporteur effort. Conference and local church leaders were tasked with inspiring the laity. Ten ministers, exhorters of a sort, were sent from church to church, setting before the brethren and sisters the importance of the sale of our literature, seeking to "arouse the whole state to energetic action." Few things excited Daniells more than the prospect of fielding a volunteer army of literature evangelists.[5]

Daniells and Palmer understood something quite important: that for Adventist bookselling to thrive, the conferences and churches, through the agency of the tract societies, must take ownership. If the publishing houses headed the effort, as was becoming truer in the 1890s and early 1900s, apathy and indifference among church members were sure to follow. The state tract societies must be revived, and to Palmer's great credit, he did just that.[6]

The problems at the publishing houses went beyond their attempt to control book distribution. Thus, Daniells's second task involved matters of personnel changes and changes of heart in Battle Creek.

Some of the personnel changes happened inadvertently—and not for the better. Printing was a blue-collar occupation peopled by skilled workers who shared a culture unfamiliar to most Adventists. Pressmen could be demanding and adversarial. Their belief that Review and Herald press management was enjoying raises without sharing the wealth with the floor led to many resignations of experienced printers. The Review had no recourse but to employ relatively unskilled "tramp printers," many of whom were not church members. A despondent Daniells reported to Willie White that twelve workers had recently spent time behind bars for drunkenness. "You can imagine the influence of this, and the effect it has upon the business of the office."[7]

The most vexing and chronic dilemma Adventist publishing faced was whether to accept nonchurch printing work. The economics of printing seemed to demand that presses be kept running. Church journals and books seldom filled that demand, so large printing jobs were bid on. The press, after all, was a business. Despite Ellen White's warnings against creeping commercialism, the tendency was hard to avoid. Merchandising catalogs, dime novels, and religious literature of various persuasions came off its presses. The loss of original spiritual focus contributed to a nettlesome spirit within the press and between press and church leadership. A. R. Henry, the press manager until 1895, had been largely responsible for bringing growth to the Review but also a contentious spirit. His legacy (and ongoing influence on the Review board) was largely an acrimonious one.[8]

But it was not just management or the "mixed multitude" labor force at the Review press that caused problems. There seemed to be a general religious apathy even among Adventist workers (and in the Battle Creek Church more generally). Daniells addressed this problem in the time-honored fashion of revival meetings. The year-end evangelistic meetings in Battle Creek included, at the request of its managers, special prayer sessions at the publishing house in order to "work a reformation among the employees." Morning and noon meetings were supplemented by the offer of private sessions for discussion, study, and prayer for any who so desired. Daniells himself made special efforts to be available to the workers "to see if they could not be reached." In one of the evening meetings he made an "appeal to them to cleanse the Review and Herald office from the evil that has been injuring the institution for years." He continued at the next day's meeting, which "started a reform current that has been deepening, I think, ever since."[9]

A century later it is difficult to evaluate the impact of Daniells's work in prompting revival at the Review office. Problems at the press clearly did not cease. But his effort reveals a leader not content with sitting in his office fretting over how he wished things would be or even planning and then issuing orders to others. He walked out his office door to participate in effecting change. Later experts on leadership would commend this approach.

But Daniells also displayed leadership in a willingness to make far-reaching changes, in this case, changes at the Review office. He met with the Review's board of directors, who proposed that they must "sweep the place clean." This included changes at the top if the publishing house were to "stand as a beacon light in Battle Creek." Daniells sought to entice C. H. Jones, the highly successful manager of Pacific Press, to take over the Review and Herald. "Every member of the Board wants you to come," he wrote him. Even current manager I. H. Evans (an experienced denominational treasurer, but perhaps out of his depth here) admitted that the change would be beneficial. The plant needed someone who really knew the business. But for all of Daniells's considerable persuasive powers, he could not lure Jones east. In the end, he stayed with Evans, but buoyed up leadership by including his trusted deputy, W. W. Prescott, along with himself on a steering committee of the Review board.[10]

Jones's loyalty to Pacific Press (and to Ellen and Willie White) hinted at the rivalries among the two major publishing houses and upstart Southern Publishing. The complicated division of the Adventist book and periodical market among the three had been imperfectly implemented. Further, Pacific Press and Southern Publishing suspected (rightly) that the senior press in Battle Creek sought to make the other two into branches of itself. The houses always scrambled to get the rights to the best-selling works, even if they had not originally published them. Willie White, who inherited his father's interest in publishing matters, used his insights to advise others unschooled in the perplexities of the publishing world. Southern Publishing, for example, wanted rights to the popular *Bible Readings for the Home* and *Daniel and the Revelation*. Accomplishing this was not a matter of church coercion but of "negotiation," White advised G. I. Butler (president of the Southern Union and advocate for Southern Publishing). Persuading the author to approach the original publisher and ask for the plates that could then be shared with another house, he felt, was the best approach.[11]

Discussions of Adventist publishing were complicated by one unavoidable fact: Adventism's most prolific and influential author was also a prophet. Her opinions carried unusual authority. If White lacked extensive formal education, she nonetheless possessed a shrewd sense of the publishing business. She and Willie had well-informed opinions, which they freely shared with Daniells and publishing house managers. Their complaints were aimed most often at the Review and Herald. The quality of paper, binding, and other press work were criticized. More personally, Mrs. White complained about how she had been persuaded to accept a lower rate of royalty with the promise that the publishers would then "push *Great Controversy* and *Patriarchs and Prophets* with all their might," a promise she felt went unfulfilled. She had no compunction about requesting the printing plates to one of the books be returned so that she might shop them elsewhere. Furthermore, after the Review fire, when talk of relocating the press got serious, she quickly talked of purchasing the rights to her major works so that they might be reassigned to a newly formed Review and Herald publishing company. Bickering over business details might seem unbecoming the station of a prophet; in fact, White depended on her royalties not just for her own sustenance but also to maintain her ongoing support of various church mission projects.[12]

Ellen White's repeated and very pointed comments on Adventist publishing concerned much more than her own pocketbook. The historical centrality of publishing and literature evangelism to the church's mission helps explain why everyone felt so much was at stake. She delivered testimonies regarding publishing over many years, culminating in a large portion of Testimony No. 35 (published in 1902 as *Testimonies for the Church* volume 7) being devoted to the topic. She understood publishing houses to be missionary agencies. "When the workers in the publishing house are educated to think of this great center as related to God and under His supervision," she instructed, "they will regard it with great respect and reverence."[13]

But Ellen White's prophetic status meant that church leaders sought to influence policy by employing the oracle's words to bolster their position. Daniells was as guilty of this as anyone. When he sought to persuade C. H. Jones to head the Review and Herald, he asked Willie to broach the matter with his mother. But Mrs. White refused to be led down his path.

"She talks freely about the general situation," Willie reported, "but when it comes to pressing her to say just what we shall do, she says that that is not her part of the work, but that you must study and pray." Ultimately, she advised Daniells and Prescott to take the lead in reforming the press (which is what happened). The battle for prophetic sanction can be seen more dramatically in the jockeying for market share among the publishing houses. In theory, the nation's territory was carefully divided among the three. But branch sites, such as Pacific Press's New York office, or efforts to gain rights to marketable books, eroded simple boundaries. Battle Creek and Oakland managers continued to quibble over turf.[14]

The great lurking fear was that the elder statesman of Adventist publishing, the Review and Herald, would seek to bring all work under its purview. Mrs. White had cautioned against such a development (Pacific Press took her statement as a sort of Magna Carta of its independence). But in 1902 the issue turned on Pacific Press. Its New York City branch was an attempt to gain entree to the large markets of the East. Part of the decentralizing thrust of the 1901 reorganization (and the heart of Daniells's reform of colporteuring) was to put the bookselling business squarely on the shoulders of the conferences. This implied, in General Conference leadership eyes, transferring the New York press to the Atlantic Union Conference. But Pacific Press managers saw things differently. At a board meeting in Oakland to consider the request, C. H. Jones reviewed past testimonies in which White counseled the press's independence. At Willie White's request, Jones sat down with the aging church mother to seek her counsel. After summarizing the issue for her, Jones wrote Daniells, White responded simply, "I have no further light." Jones added White's summary comment (no doubt with great satisfaction): "Is not that which I have written plain enough?" He then proceeded to quote White's comments about the Pacific Press's need to maintain its branches.[15]

As if that were not enough, Daniells had to endure an epistolary lecture from S. N. Curtiss, who ran the New York branch for Pacific Press. He reminded Daniells that God's messenger had instructed church leaders that "business men [should be] for business and preachers for the ministry." In other words, Battle Creek leaders ought not to interfere in complex matters of publishing. Curtiss went on to quote Ellen White at length on the independence of Pacific Press (which he understood to include its branches). Daniells and Prescott were checkmated by testimonies counter to their plans. Daniells's usual ally, Willie White (who had close ties to Pacific Press), advised that change occur slowly. Pacific Press would keep its branch office in the East for some time longer.[16]

Ellen White's involvement was even more direct in the matter of Southern Publishing's uncertain early existence, a high-stakes dilemma for Daniells and the General Conference. The incident was so significant to Daniells that nearly thirty-five years later he devoted a chapter to it in his book *The Abiding Gift of Prophecy*.

The small publishing house had been privately started in 1900 to provide inexpensive literature for the southern United States. But Edson and his mother called for a larger, denominationally sponsored press, essentially a third American facility—this at a time when the two established houses were scarcely running half time and forced to accept commercial work to survive. Daniells lacked enthusiasm from the start. Further, as mentioned earlier, few church leaders had confidence in Edson White's financial or managerial abilities. But he remained the son of the church's prophet, and in the early twentieth century she championed the advancement of the work in the South. Thus, Daniells had to approach Edson's publishing brainstorms with a modicum of respect.[17]

This was not easy, for when Daniells made an inspection of the Nashville plant in 1902 he saw red ink everywhere. "The situation looks appalling to me," he told Southern Union president R. M. Kilgore. Monthly losses of $1,200 to $1,500 were a huge strain on the church. Daniells cryptically alluded to matters even thornier than financial loss. Edson White did not improve matters when he dunned Daniells for a larger General Conference appropriation and higher pay for himself. "It is hard for me to understand your letter and your attitude toward the General Conference," wrote an exasperated Daniells to White. "We are sending more money to the South than to any other one mission field in the world," he reminded the profligate Edson. Furthermore, in harmony with new church organization, the Southern Missionary Society ought to look to the Southern Union Conference for support and direction.[18]

Daniells understood that the financially modest Southern Union was in no position to salvage the press. Thus, the General Conference Committee felt it had no choice but to pull the plug. The equipment would be sold to a junk dealer and the building converted into a book depository. North America needed only two printing presses.[19]

The decision rested uneasily upon the committee's collective conscience, however. How could they reconcile their action with what seemed clear earlier counsel to establish the plant? A rationalizing answer came in the suggestion that Ellen White's instructions only meant that a means of circulating literature in the South required an assist, not necessarily a need for a printing press. "We made ourselves believe," Daniells later reflected, "that it was our *misinterpretation* of the counsel that was at fault, not the instruction itself." After all, Daniells rationalized, she had also instructed that the church was not to incur heavy debt that would burden members.[20]

Yet the situation was unsettled enough that in mid-October 1902 a delegation traveled to California. Daniells, Willie White, A. T. Jones, W. T. Knox, J. O. Corliss, and E. R. Palmer traversed up the hill to Elmshaven for an audience with Ellen White. News of Southern Publishing's debt and the recommended closing distressed her deeply. But she finally concurred with the group's judgment. A relieved group of administrators returned to Battle Creek. But a few days later Daniells and others received a letter from White. She admitted a mistake. "The Lord instructed me that I had taken a wrong position." A way must be found to save the publishing house. Light was to "shine forth" from Nashville to the entire South.[21]

"Disconcerting" was the term Daniells used to describe this turn of events. Some could not understand how such a quick prophetic reversal could occur. The biblical story of Nathan's change of heart about David's building the temple provided a reassuring precedent. And just as David accepted the prophet's instruction, so did the General Conference Committee. Southern Publishing would live to see many more days. Its turnaround was not immediate, but with attention given to details of economy, the press became profitable within a few years. Not only that, but the other two presses, Daniells later recalled, were able to forgo outside work and keep busy with church publications. The moral seemed clear to Daniells: Although God's messages might at first seem difficult to understand, this experience "confirmed my confidence in the divine leadership of God's people through the prophetic gift."[22]

His confidence withstood even a quite severe personal rebuke from Ellen White. Her initial agreement to the closure of Southern Publishing rested on the visiting committee's grim assessment of the "terrible financial embarrassment resting on the work there." But the Lord had given her another perspective. "My brother, the Lord never placed on you the burden of reorganizing the work in Nashville." "You did not speak intelligently nor by the inspiration of the Holy Spirit." Daniells needed to spend time working in the South to see the particular difficulties there firsthand, she concluded, "before you feel at liberty to come to the conclusions to which you have come." Furthermore, the testimonies "have not been heeded." "Backbiting" and quick criticism of others must cease (an allusion, clearly, to the Battle Creek posture toward Edson and his Nashville associates). "I know that it is time for you to criticize yourself closely," she added. "My brother, I want you to make an unreserved consecration to God, that the whole tenor of your experience may be changed." At the time he received this testimony, the future success of Southern Publishing appeared unlikely. Thus, for a man of Daniells's decisive will to graciously accept such reproof speaks to both the regard in which White was held by leadership and a streak of humility that was a saving grace of Daniells.[23]

CHANGE AT THE REVIEW

Not only did the Review and Herald press come under scrutiny but the *Review and Herald* publication as well. The *Review*'s redoubtable editor, Uriah Smith, proved antagonistic to Daniells's reforms. Smith had edited the church paper (save for a short stint by A. T. Jones) since before Daniells was born. Now, the new General Conference leader's call for spiritual reform in the publishing house—and worse, wondering aloud if the publishing association in Battle Creek ought to be abolished in favor of direct control of the press by the General Conference—set Smith on the warpath. He opened 1902 with an editorial recounting his own denominational pedigree and the distinguished service the publishing association had given the church. "There are rumors afloat now that the cause is suffering under a heavy load of odium," Smith reported to the Adventist public, and that such odium could only be relieved by a drastic change of control at the Review.[24]

Thus, at a key moment in the effort to consolidate church reform, Daniells faced a challenge. Smith's influence within the church could not be ignored. And he was not alone. Two other venerable church figures, G. I. Butler and Stephen Haskell, also resisted the reorganization (if less directly than Smith). It was probably no coincidence that individuals who lacked enthusiasm for the 1888 righteousness by faith movement similarly resisted a fundamental rethinking of church governance. The old ways, to the thinking of some, are always the best ways.[25]

But Daniells could not permit overt opposition in such an influential venue as the *Review*. Too much was at stake. Thus, he maneuvered to get himself, his right-hand man, Prescott, and I. H. Evans on the key General Conference subcommittee overseeing the paper. The troika quickly moved to replace Uriah Smith as editor. Smith had become vulnerable for a number of reasons, including racially insensitive remarks in the *Review* and ongoing cavils against the 1888 message. Further, it was apparent that his energies were flagging. He left much of the day-to-day work to his assistants (including his son Leon). In the all-too-frequent manner of founders, Smith had overstayed his effectiveness. The General Conference Committee, with "remarkable unanimity of opinion," voted to replace Smith with Prescott. Prescott, out of deference to Smith's feelings, refused to be designated as editor in chief; instead he was listed more modestly as managing editor. Thus, Smith was kept on the masthead as associate editor (along with W. A. Spicer), but the blow to him was considerable. He lived only another thirteen months.[26]

In certain quarters, Daniells's reputation took a hit for what some perceived as peremptory, even unchristian, treatment of Smith. Daniells had to mend bridges with people such as Butler. He regretted that Butler's "son" (as Daniells styled himself) "had not proved very pleasing" in his actions. Nor did he intend to offend the thin-skinned Butler when he advised him against traveling to Battle Creek for meetings. Daniells's efforts to reassure the old warhorse that he was indeed a valued leader (he was still a member of the General Conference Committee) led to an unusual moment of confession. He told of an experience during childhood when his mother punished him for an act he did not commit, without giving him an opportunity to defend himself. The incident left an impression. Daniells now valued "very much the right of every human being to speak for himself before he is judged and condemned." He wanted his former mentor to grant him that right of explanation before drawing hasty conclusions.[27]

With the *Review and Herald* safely in the hands of Prescott, Daniells could now count on editorial support for the reorganization effort. "I know that we could never hope to carry through the reforms we are called to effect," Daniells assured Prescott, "with the paper standing as it did." Prescott wasted no time redesigning and updating the venerable journal. An illustration now adorned the front page, and a more modern typeface was adopted. More important for Daniells, Prescott ensured that the paper would be an instrument of education and revival in the church. Prescott made it, in biographer Gilbert Valentine's description, "both visionary and informative, reviewing and heralding."[28]

Daniells's newfound influence on the church paper and at the publishing house represented another large step toward securing church reorganization. Pockets of resistence remained, to be sure, particularly in Battle Creek. But two events, one toward the beginning and the other at the very end of 1902, served to open a door for even more sweeping changes in church governance.

OUT OF BATTLE CREEK

In the cold early-morning hours of February 18, a fire broke out in the Battle Creek Sanitarium. Its origins would never be precisely determined, but with the wooden construction and gas lighting of the age, little encouragement was needed. Overwhelmed city firefighters were reduced to a spectator's role. "It seemed to be absolutely under the control of other than human power," observed I. H. Evans. Two main structures became rubble and ashes within two hours. Miraculously, given the four hundred patients in residence (including eminent chorister Ira D. Sankey, who escaped down a fire escape), only one fatality occurred. Dr. John Harvey Kellogg never thought twice about rebuilding on the same location.[29]

On the next-to-the-last day of that same year, with church members gathered for prayer meeting in the Battle Creek Tabernacle, a cry went up that the Review and Herald publishing building was on fire. In short order the three-story structure burned to the ground, though without casualties. In an odd bit of role reversal, Daniells had written to Ellen White a year and a half earlier that he worried that the complex of wooden buildings at the press were a firetrap. "The whole arrangement is a nuisance and a danger." His baleful prophecy came true, and with it a nudge toward relocation that quickly took on irresistible momentum.[30]

For several years there had been loose talk about the desirability of moving General Conference headquarters out of Battle Creek. Why would church leaders consider leaving their historic home, the city where the church first organized? For several reasons, some openly discussed and others quietly shared.

The most common reason given for a move was to end the clustering of believers in Battle Creek. If Battle Creek was a "city on a hill," there were nonetheless other hills that needed to be evangelized. "Too many are there now [Battle Creek], and too many interests are being piled up in Battle Creek," said Ellen White. Those interests ought to be "divided and located in other cities."[31]

Part of the discontent with Battle Creek was Adventism's growing status as a world church. The church now seemed to require a home more distinguished than a parochial Michigan town. *Signs of the Times* editor M. C. Wilcox dared to verbalize this conviction to Daniells. "I feel profoundly convicted myself that the [publishing] work would be very much better if the headquarters were located in some coast city, like New York than in an interior city like Battle Creek, against which there has gone out a great deal of prejudice." Christ might have come from Nazareth, Wilcox noted, but he went from there to Capernaum. Indeed, one of the reasons later put forward for choosing Washington, D.C., was the desire for the American capital's postmark on church correspondence. Also hinted at but not directly admitted was a need to escape the influence of the Adventist medical establishment's influence. Kellogg and his Battle Creek Sanitarium had more employees than the General Conference; its national renown exceeded that of the formal church. And rivalry—even bitterness—increasingly characterized the ministerial-medical worker relationship (a subject of the next chapter). Better to draw some space between the arms of the gospel.[32]

This contentious spirit, not only with the medical establishment but also within the publishing house, comprised a common rationale for a move. Adventist workers seemed unable to work in harmony in Battle Creek. Perhaps the four decades there had engendered too much institutional inbreeding. Perhaps the problems were the inevitable by-product of growth. In any event, the atmosphere had turned rancid. And although Ellen White no longer lived there, her voice sounded the loudest call for change. Additionally, although the church had been enjoying growth throughout the Midwest, California, and even, tentatively, in the South, the urban centers of the East lagged. Church leadership felt strongly that in order to advance the gospel there, a robust institutional presence was required.

Finally, leaders and members agreed, the two devastating fires of 1902 could not be coincidental. Shortly after the fire, Ellen White wrote Daniells that she had previously recorded in her diary a vision of "an angel standing with a sword as of fire stretched over Battle Creek." Although fire was an ever-present reality in American life of that age, to have two landmarks taken in quick succession suggested—no, proclaimed—God's intention for dispersal. The denomination had mistakenly clustered too tightly in Battle Creek. "The Lord desires the truth to be represented in other places besides Battle Creek," she instructed Daniells. Never again should this be allowed to happen. Like the Jews being dispersed from Israel, the Adventist diaspora from Michigan was intended to be a great missionary movement throughout America.[33]

Notwithstanding these calls for change, the final decision came with difficulty—and some would not move at all. After the sanitarium fire in February, immediate discussion centered not on a move but on what scale the sanitarium should be rebuilt. Daniells, who was in Kansas when the tragedy occurred, immediately counseled Prescott (who was in Battle Creek) to restrain any impetuous move by Kellogg. Prescott did his bidding, and the latter pledged prudence. Kellogg, after all, already had significant debt on the structure, and insurance was not nearly going to cover the estimated rebuilding costs. Just four days after the fire, Kellogg wrote Daniells a long letter that appeared the model of candor. In his typically irrepressible manner, Kellogg purported to see the fire as providential and laid out a seemingly clear path to financing rebuilding. He also attempted to deflect the calls already heard to relocate the sanitarium. "There is a certain class of patients," Kellogg argued, "which cannot be turned over to our branches: senators, lawyers, governors, etc., will insist on going to headquarters." Kellogg could not wait to see Daniells when he returned to Battle Creek. "He wants your help," Sutherland confided to Daniells. "I think that now is the time for you to do some good work with him."[34]

Whatever that "good work" might have been, Kellogg proceeded full speed ahead. The ashes had not cooled before Kellogg made brave public pronouncements about building on a scale grander than ever, aided by wealthy local patrons appreciative of his institution's work. But Ellen White had advised a smaller scale and perhaps a rural environ. For over a month the board of trustees reflected on the "lessons" the fire held for them before giving a green light to rebuilding. In a long report to *Review* readers, Kellogg described the process whereby the decision was made to rebuild on the same spot. The Battle Creek Sanitarium's "brand name" was invaluable, the board felt, holding for the public a distinctive approach to good health. To take the institution elsewhere would be like attempting to move a deeply rooted giant oak. Further, Kellogg wrung generous pledges (never fully realized) from local residents to support rebuilding. But on what scale should the complex be built? Kellogg regaled *Review* readers with a confusing barrage of details of the new building, but the bottom line seemed clear: reconstruction would be only slightly less grand than before.[35]

Daniells found himself cast in the unusual role of defending the rebuilding decision. When a letter highly critical of the plans reached him, he responded defensively. He acknowledged White's warnings but no prohibition. "Sister White has had plenty of time and full opportunity to express herself with reference to rebuilding the Sanitarium in Battle Creek, but no word has come from her forbidding this." As was often the case, Daniells's decision-making became an awkward mix of inspired counsel and pragmatic considerations. He would seek her counsel; but if no specific advice was forthcoming he had no trouble making decisions based on the pertinent factors as he understood them.[36]

So Kellogg fatefully cast his lot with Battle Creek while denominational leaders would move on. To some outside observers the debate portended division. The *Detroit News* predicted a break coming to the denomination. The decision to move the printing press, though sealed only in the spring of 1903, seemed foreordained by the Review and Herald fire of the previous December. The cover of the first issue of the *Review* after the fire dramatically juxtaposed an engraving of a thriving printing house with a photograph of the charred remains resembling Atlanta after Sherman. What was interpreted as Old Testament–style judgment on the church grabbed the attention of the entire North American church. "I am afflicted with all who are afflicted," Ellen White wrote Daniells when she got the news. But she was not surprised. "In my diary I had written out the description of a scene that had been presented to me, in which I saw an angel standing with a sword as of fire stretched over Battle Creek."[37]

The *Review* staff gamely soldiered on to produce a paper each week (published elsewhere). "In the shadow of a great calamity we are of good courage," Uriah Smith (who was still allowed some editorial privileges) reassured readers. But the main building of the printing house was gone, along with its huge capacity for production of the printed word. Administrative agendas suddenly altered. Daniells and his cohorts had to drop everything to help out the three hundred people thrown out of work. It might have been worse. The warehouse with most of the Review's inventory was unscathed.[38]

Although Daniells asked for her advice on the meaning of the catastrophe, White would not give an immediate reply. "I dare not give advice," she responded, noting that she had been unable to effect Battle Creek reforms that might have prevented "the falling of the fiery sword that was hanging over Battle Creek." But if she would not, many others would. Beginning in early January, Daniells received letters from across the country pointing out what seemed to them obvious: it was time to disperse. "From every quarter we are receiving words of sympathy from our brethren," Daniells reported, "but every one warns us against building up another large printing house in Battle Creek." But General Conference leaders were not to be stampeded into any course of action. The Review and Herald directors would not "move hastily" into a decision. Yet once an early April vote was taken at the Oakland General Conference session to move church headquarters, it was inevitable that the Review and Herald would soon follow. Debate over a move lacked acrimony. Certainly not after word came from Ellen White about the need for a move. One delegate asked why it was assumed that a move would be to the East. Another questioned the expense, despite assurances being given that no debt would be incurred by the move. The action to move was only one vote short of unanimous.[39]

Initial indications pointed to New York City as the new home. The General Conference Committee voted on May 1 to "favor" a New York location, influenced in part by a memorial from Atlantic Union Conference delegates that a site near New York would be ideal. Moreover, there was strong interest among Ellen White and other denominational leaders for Adventism to have a pronounced presence there; further, the city that had emerged as America's great metropolis would add luster as headquarters for the world church. A locating committee of eight men scoured locations from Long Island to Rhode Island. The location Daniells found most appealing was actually rural (in harmony with White's wishes), north of the city and east of the Hudson River near a village inelegantly styled Fishkill. Situated along a colonial military road between New York and Boston, Fishkill village enjoyed convenient train connections in several directions. It had been the estate of a wealthy gentleman who later decided to construct a resort hotel on the estate's nearly one hundred acres. Daniells waxed eloquent to Willie White about the hotel's modern features (including gas lines and its own ice house) that would make it suitable for church use. "I do not remember seeing anything better anywhere." It might be used for a sanitarium, training school, or—most to the point—General Conference headquarters.[40]

But Washington, D.C., also had its supporters. None was more enthusiastic in advocating for the nation's capital than J. S. Washburn, then living in the District area as pastor and functionary of the church's Religious Liberty Department. Throughout the spring and early summer, Washburn conducted a nonstop campaign to persuade Daniells, Ellen White, and whoever else would listen that the denomination would be best served by heading to the Potomac. He told of seeing senators on streetcars, of meeting a presidential bodyguard who promised the gullible Washburn "an interview with the President any time." Yet he made some compelling arguments. Seventh-day Adventism needed to have a lively presence at the seat of national power, he wrote Ellen White, particularly as we entered the age when Sunday laws were becoming mooted about by Congress. Further, as church missionary work focused on Europe, Africa, and Asia, headquarters near the seat of American government could be beneficial. Not only in the East, but also on the sectional border between North and South, Washington's geography recommended itself in that troubled age of race relations. Unlike New York, clearly a northern city and thus a source of cultural suspicion to southerners, Washington was a traditionally southern town. "Our publications bearing the imprint of Washington, D.C.," Washburn argued, "would circulate freely through the South."[41]

Strong arguments, but Daniells remained smitten with the Fishkill estate well into June. Washburn was reduced to begging that before a final decision was made the General Conference locating committee (including Daniells) should visit Washington. Washburn had done his due diligence. Knowing that a rural (or at least suburban) location for a sanitarium was desired, he scouted out a community on the Northeast side of the District that fit the bill. Takoma Park, partially in and partially outside the District, seemed to meet all requirements, including a trunk rail line running through it and convenient municipal transportation to the capital. Further, its mayor cooperated in the bid to attract the headquarters of a small but growing denomination. The enterprising Washburn even found a suitable building for the Review and Herald to rent in the center of the Federal District while its own new headquarters were constructed. "I feel that it would be only fair that I have a chance to talk with you about the situation before the location is definitely fixed," he pleaded.[42]

Washburn's persistence—and his logic—paid off. The visiting committee toured Takoma Park's environs in late May (normally a pleasant time of year in the region). They were impressed. Further, although Mrs. White refused to offer definitive counsel on the move, Willie made it clear to Daniells that Washburn's appeals on behalf of Washington had their effect. She leaned toward the site on the Potomac. "We are many years behind in giving the message of warning in the city that is the capital of our nation," she wrote Daniells in June. Through most of June no final decision on location was made. However, the General Conference Committee determined in mid-month that despite legal complexities that impaired a quick relocation of the publishing house and despite not knowing where they were to go, the headquarters must find a new home.[43]

Church leadership's interest in improving its outreach in Washington had manifested itself the previous fall when the General Conference Committee authorized the unusual step of a national appeal to fund construction of a local church. (This was not unprecedented. In 1879, the Dime Tabernacle in Battle Creek had also been erected after a national fund-raising effort.) This would not be the first Adventist church in the capital. But the previous congregation was predominately African American, and in an age of ferocious racism it was thought that a white congregation was needed (more on this in a succeeding chapter). Leaders had their eyes on (and later purchased) a handsome stone structure from the Methodists at the prime location of Twelfth and M streets. It was believed the site would help to attract leaders of business and government to the message. The congregation's pastor, J. S. Washburn, prophesied that the new church would "be as a city set on a hill—a light shining brilliantly." This was particularly important, Washburn insisted, when Sunday laws threatened the District itself. The *Review* certainly did its part to promote the church fund, making space in one issue to two extended calls for help by Washburn and A. G. Daniells.[44]

But where exactly would the sanitarium and headquarters go? Aided by Washburn's early legwork, Daniells and his associates on the locating committee spent four days exploring the D.C. area. The Washington of the early 1900s was still a relatively sleepy town with a distinctly southern flavor to its culture. Unlike virtually every other major city in America, Washington had no industrial base—and consequently none of the influx of European immigrants. But it hosted many European visitors. One such traveler noted that the nation's capital carried an air "of comfort, of leisure, of space to spare, of stateliness you hardly expected in America." The Federal District was not yet the elegant, manicured space today's citizens know. But the city's transformation was imminent. Just the year previous the Park District had adopted an ambitious program of renovation. "The City Beautiful Movement," building on the original plans of Pierre L'Enfant, provided a blueprint that in succeeding years refashioned the capital's center into a showpiece.[45]

The expense of land and the desire for a more rural setting led Daniells and his helpers to look outside the District. Attention returned to Takoma Park. Boasting both a stop on the Baltimore & Ohio main line to Baltimore and a trolley line right into the heart of the city, it was the sort of idyllic suburban environment that Americans would value throughout the twentieth century. But would affordable land be available? In a manner church leaders could only describe as providential, fifty prime acres at a bargain price came on the market. "It is a magnificent place," Daniells enthused. "We could purchase all the land we required at a very reasonable rate." He wished Ellen White could come and inspect it before a decision was made. Daniells, a global denomination's leader, was still anxious to get the imprimatur of his church's prophet.[46]

By late June the decision for suburban Washington was sealed. The lovely fifty-acre parcel, bisected by Sligo Creek, would be the site of a sanitarium and training school (later Washington Adventist Hospital and Washington Adventist University). Another smaller acreage was found right on the Maryland-District of Columbia boundary, where the world headquarters and the Review and Herald press would be located, the latter just over the border in Washington so that the valued publication imprint could be claimed. In the interim, a building was rented only blocks from the nation's Capitol for both headquarters and press.

Daniells's pleasure at having found the just-right home for his beloved church was tempered by two nagging worries. First, the closing of the old Review corporation was proving more difficult than hoped, which threatened an easy transition to the new. The Review fire, of course, had interrupted production of new books (though the fortunate sparing of the main warehouse allowed the ongoing sale of books). Local commercial printers took up production of the *Review and Herald*, so it suffered no lapse. Its control board in the spring of 1903 debated how to pick up the pieces—and where to set them down. Like most early Adventist organizations, the Seventh-day Adventist Publishing Association had been organized on an independent basis, formally owned by stockholders who had invested not for profit but for support of evangelism. In theory, these stockholders would acquiesce in the planned move and dissolution of the corporation, considering their investment as a form of contribution to the church. But certain individuals, unhappy with the course of events and perhaps having tenuous ties to the church, challenged the closure and move. The business meeting to consider surrendering control to the General Conference was long and contentious. The change carried by a narrow margin. But die-hard individuals took the matter to the courts, insisting on a generous cash settlement for themselves.[47]

As if Daniells and Prescott did not have enough on their minds with a momentous decision to make about the move, they now faced an injunction against the removal of the press. A. R. Henry, quarrelsome and formidable former manager of the press, headed the effort. This challenge to what seemed a divinely ordered change upset Daniells. He did not use the word "blackmail" to describe the blocking move by the relatively few stockholders, but he may have entertained the thought. At a time when the still-functioning publishing association had large outstanding bills and little income, major stockholders began drawing their money out in large chunks, threatening bankruptcy for the association. I. H. Evans, who as treasurer was intimately involved in the negotiations, told Daniells that he considered these actions an attempt "to crush the Review and Herald completely." Ultimately, Daniells had no choice but to give in. The General Conference Committee voted a settlement with the intransigent stockholders for the sake of moving forward with the new Review and Herald. This meant depleting the church of much of its precious cash reserves (and required pleading with conferences for appropriations). Daniells was reminded yet again that successful administration sometimes required distasteful compromises.[48]

The other worry concerned the reaction of Battle Creek members to the move. Ellen White had warned him that "the enemy [Satan] will work to defeat the plan of entering Washington." Daniells knew of discontent, partially related to but going beyond issues at the press. The ticklish matter of relocation came at a time when Battle Creek's developing reputation as breakfast cereal capital brought a booming local economy. Many Adventists found venturing into real estate a lucrative endeavor. Kellogg's Battle Creek Sanitarium, though in the midst of rebuilding, was a linchpin of the local Adventist economy. Why threaten all this with a move?[49]

Possessing the courage to lead an organization that now faced a fractious moment, Daniells determined that he must go before the Battle Creek Church family and explain the decision for a move. He, Prescott, and Willie White planned strategy in New York City. He expected an "unfriendly attitude" that late July Sabbath as he stood before the congregation, having received word of "mutterings" among members. During the morning service Daniells summarized the reasons for the move and reviewed Ellen White's many statements about the unsatisfactory situation in Battle Creek and suggestions of where to move. In the afternoon, another meeting brought more testimonies, some which pointed out the dangerous course of those who stubbornly opposed the move (Daniells clearly found White's advice to be useful cover for the locally unpopular decision). The results were as satisfactory as he could have hoped. Although he recognized that those most adamantly opposed probably did not attend, he took comfort in the lack of criticism from those present.[50]

Daniells was in fact so pleased with his Battle Creek encounter that he decided to write up a report for the entire church. As head of the church, it fell his lot to explain a decision of this consequence. Daniells's retelling of the relocation story, which he did in a two-part set of *Review* articles, said something about how he wanted the incident remembered. Notably, he failed to reveal the enthusiasm he originally had for the Fishkill estate. Nothing should interrupt the narrative of God's providence in leading them to the D.C. area. He assured Adventist readers that Ellen White's counsel had been sought and diligently followed. There was a clear progression in her counsel, from admissions that she had no definite word on where to relocate to later counsels that were couched in clear language of inspiration. Nothing was said of her advice in late June that a sanitarium be established without delay on the New York property (direction never followed). Daniells also gave credit to the work of the locating committee, which was more than the *Review's* associate editor Leon Smith did in another summary article about the move. In Smith's haste to assure members that White's advice was decisive, he went so far as to claim that her letters of counsel were "entirely independent of any statements or representations made to [her] by members of the committee. Nothing whatever from any member expressing any opinion or preference in the matter had been written her." Technically this was true, but it masked the great influence of Washburn (who was not a committee member) on White's thinking about the matter. This slanted version of prophetic advice may well have been intended to dampen the expected resistance in Battle Creek. In any event, propagating White's prophetic messages as a pure distillation of divine counsel—free of human influence—would ultimately return to haunt the church. Daniells, who knew of Washburn's part in the selection process, must have winced when he read Smith's claim. The incident may have contributed to Daniells's later attempts to mold a balanced view of inspiration within his church.[51]

The physical move itself culminated on August 10, 1903, when four boxcar loads of furniture, files, and other essentials from Battle Creek reached Washington. Everything went to the temporary headquarters and printing facility on Capitol Street. The General Conference staff trickled in throughout the day. Daniells arrived around noon, coming straight from the Ohio camp meeting. He unintentionally contributed his own bit of historical fabrication, telling *Review* readers that the six-story interim building they were renting had been a frequent place of entertainment for George Washington on his visits to the city (a story no doubt recounted to him by a local booster, which Daniells naïvely believed).[52]

On the evening of August 24, just two weeks after arriving, a dedication service was held at the temporary headquarters. Small though it was, and incomplete as the move to Washington remained, the moment nonetheless carried significance for the self-understanding of the church. Indeed, so important was the service for the North American church that the *Review* devoted three pages of verbatim reportage to the event. The service included a dedicatory prayer by W. W. Prescott, testimonies by various workers, and an address by Daniells. If not eloquent, it was heartfelt and hopeful. In ways, Daniells took on the mantle of John Winthrop, the great leader of the Puritan migration to America (comparisons between the two men are fruitful). Upon the landing of the three ships in Boston Harbor in 1630, Winthrop delivered a sermon to the few hundred who left a familiar land for nearly uncharted terrain. He told his fellow believers of their great calling, of what they might accomplish if they remained faithful, of what God expected of them. Daniells did the same. He reminded his hearers (and readers) of God's past leading, of the portents suggesting a move, of divine guidance to Washington. In words that except for details of place and time might easily have been Winthrop's, Daniells said, "The Lord led us out of Battle Creek that we might have different conditions, and that we might place a different mold upon the work. . . . We must be converted anew, that we may keenly sense the solemn responsibility we accept in coming here. Only thus can we start and conduct the work aright."[53]

Daniells was not prophetic in every case. One way he suggested that the new community might avoid falling into the "easy-going way" of Battle Creek was to avoid establishing a large congregation in one place. Likewise, E. R. Palmer predicted at the dedication that Adventism had learned the folly of putting its confidence in large institutions. God's judgments have taught the church not to "secure a standing among denominations from that point of view." Of course, Daniells and Palmer were as wrong as could be. Adventism is a movement of institutions. Although leaders were determined to avoid the spirit of Battle Creek, the mother city's institutional landscape of large church, sanitarium, college, and headquarters was replicated. Two future large centers of Adventist institutional life were also founded about this time. The future center of theological training (later known as Andrews University) had been established the year before in Berrien Springs. And Adventism's signature medical institution (later Loma Linda University) would be founded two years later.[54]

The 1903 move to Takoma Park, linked with Ellen White's permanent residence in northern California, created a bi-coastal church. True, the heart of church membership remained in the Midwest and Great Plains. But the church's direction now came from the East and West coasts. In retrospect, there is an air of inevitability about the move, even if conditions in Battle Creek had been more salutary. A worldwide church had simply outgrown a provincial Midwestern city (even if that city was becoming breakfast food capital of the world). The church was developing a reach and a sophistication that required a higher-profile location. Finally, the departure from the place where the church had its firmest roots marked an unspoken step away from dependence on its founding family. Ellen White survived another twelve years, and her correspondence with Daniells continued apace (though often, now, through her son Willie). But church headquarters were a continent away from Saint Helena. For all of Daniells's belief in the prophetic office of Ellen White and his solicitation of her advice, his career represented the bureaucratization of church leadership. Increasingly, he would depend upon the decision making of himself and church officers.

Fortunately, he still had Ellen White as an ally in the most difficult administrative struggle of his career: that with the medical establishment personified in the figure of John Harvey Kellogg.

---

[1] On the history of early Adventist publishing, see Donald R. McAdams, "Pacific Press Versus Review and Herald: The Rise of the Territorial Monopolies," *Spectrum* 8 (August 1977): 11–21.

[2] Ibid.; Valentine, *Prescott*, 192.

[3] Donald R. McAdams, "Edwin R. Palmer: Publishing Secretary Extraordinary," *Adventist Heritage* 2, no. 1 (Summer 1975): 51–62; AGD to E. R. Palmer, August 25, 1901;

AGD to E. R. Palmer, July 26, 1901, ASTR.

[4] AGD to Allen Moon, September 27, 1901, ASTR.

[5] McAdams, "Edwin R. Palmer," 52–54; AGD to WCW, September 27, 1901, ASTR; AGD to S. N. Curtiss, March 27, 1902, GCPL.

[6] McAdams, "Edwin R. Palmer," 54, 55.

[7] AGD to WCW, September 2, 1901, ASTR.

[8] Schwarz and Greenleaf, *Light Bearers*, pp. 248–250; A. L. White, *The Early Elmshaven Years*, 229, 230.

[9] AGD to C. H. Jones, December 27, 1901, ASTR.

[10] Ibid.; Valentine, *Prescott*, 194.

[11] A. L. White, *The Lonely Years*, 228; WCW to AGD, March 1, 1907, ASTR; Gilbert Valentine's *The Prophet and the Presidents*, pp. 147–156, provides thorough background discussion to the issue during the 1890s.

[12] EGW to AGD, June 5, 1901; EGW to AGD and I. H. Evans, January 22, 1902; WCW to AGD, September 2, 1902; WCW to AGD, June 19, 1903, ASTR. In a notable instance, Ellen White took a new manuscript, *Steps to Christ,* to a non-Adventist religious publisher, Fleming H. Revell. This was not out of pique but rather from a belief that this, her crowning work of devotional literature, would find a wider Christian reading audience. It was later republished by Adventist houses.

[13] EGW, *Testimonies*, 7:193.

[14] WCW to AGD, February 8, 1903; I. H. Evans to AGD, May 18, 1902, ASTR.

[15] C. H. Jones to AGD, May 11, 1902.

[16] S. H. Curtiss to AGD, March 19, 1902; WCW to AGD, May 28, 1902; July 11, 1902, ASTR.

[17] AGD, *The Abiding Gift of Prophecy* (Mountain View, CA: Pacific Press®, 1936), 325. EGW to AGD, June 28, 1901, ASTR.

[18] AGD to R. M. Kilgore, September 22, 1902; Edson White to AGD, April 16, 1903; September 24, 1903; AGD to Edson White, April 10, 1902, GCPL; O. M. Hayward to AGD, March 8, 1903, ASTR.

[19] AGD, *Abiding Gift of Prophecy*, 324, 325.

[20] Ibid., 325; emphasis added.

[21] Ibid., 325–327.

[22] Ibid., 328, 329.

[23] EGW to AGD, December 7, 1902; November 16, 1902, EGWE.

[24] Valentine, *Prescott*, chap. 12; *RH*, January 7, 1902, 8. My account of Smith and the *Review* draws heavily on Valentine's work.

[25] AGD to G. I. Butler, April 11, 1902, Valentine, *Prescott*, 195; AGD to WCW, April 15, 1902, GCPL. Even after Smith was removed as editor, he continued, in Daniells's view, to oppose the theological positions of Jones and Waggoner, which were supported by the Spirit of Prophecy.

[26] Valentine, *Prescott*, 194–196; AGD to R. H. Kilgore, April 13, 1902; GCCMin, February 15, 1902.

[27] AGD to G. I. Butler, April 13, 1902, GCPL.

[28] AGD to G. I. Butler, April 11, 1902; AGD to W. W. Prescott, April 13, 1902; *RH*, April 8, 1902, 24; Valentine, *Prescott*, 198.

[29] I. H. Evans to AGD, February 19, 1902; *RH*, February 25, 1902, 13, 14.

[30] AGD to EGW, June 25, 1902, ASTR.

[31] EGW quoted in *RH*, August 11, 1903, 5.

[32] M. C. Wilcox to AGD, May 24, 1901, ASTR.

[33] EGW to AGD, January 5, 1903; EGW to AGD and W. W. Prescott, July 1, 1903, ASTR.

[34] Valentine, *Prescott*, 170; J. H. Kellogg to AGD, February 24, 1902, E. A. Sutherland to AGD, March 10, 1902, ASTR.

[35] *RH*, February 25, 1902, 14; April 8, 1902, 21–23; Richard William Schwarz, "John Harvey Kellogg: American Health Reformer," PhD dissertation (Ann Arbor, MI: University of Michigan, 1969), 186–188; Valentine, *Prescott*, 171. Kellogg's dissembling to Battle Creek residents about rebuilding plans (he later admitted to Daniells that he never considered a move from their city, but only sought to worry them into support) contributed to the latter's loss of confidence in him.

[36] AGD to Clifford G. Howell, March 27, 1902, GCPL.

[37] *RH*, January 6, 1903, cover; EGW to AGD, January 5, 1903, EGWE; I. H. Evans reported the *Detroit News* article to Daniells in a letter, January 12, 1903, ASTR.

[38] *RH*, January 6, 1903, 2, 4; AGD to J. S. Washburn, January 6, 1903, GCPL.

[39] *GCB*, no. 6, 1903, 84–88; no. 7, 102, 103; AGD to J. S. Washburn, January 6, 1903; AGD to M. A. Underwood, January 6, 1903; AGD to W. A. Colcord, January 7, 1903, GCPL.

[40] GCCMin, May 1, 1903; A. L. White, *The Early Elmshaven Years*, 248; AGD to WCW, June 21, 1903; *RH*, August 11, 1903, 5, 6.

[41] J. S. Washburn to EGW, March 2, 1903; J. S. Washburn to AGD, March 6, 1903, ASTR.

[42] J. S. Washburn to AGD, June 4, 1903; May 5, 1903; J. S. Washburn to EGW, June 5, 1903, ASTR.

[43] J. S. Washburn, Memo on Washington, DC [June 1903]; WCW to AGD, June 19, 1903; EGW to AGD, June 26, 1903, ASTR.

[44] *RH*, January 13, 1903, 6, 12–14.

[45] Constance McLaughlin Green, *Washington: Capital City, 1897–1950* (Princeton, NJ: Princeton University Press, 1962), 77, 132–135.

[46] J. S. Washburn to AGD, May 5, 1903; June 4, 1903; June 11, 1903, ASTR; A. L. White, *The Early Elmshaven Years*, 273, 274.

[47] Valentine, *Prescott*, 201–203.

[48] I. H. Evans to AGD, June 3, 1903; June 12, 1903, ASTR; GCCmin, June 18, 1903; July 7, 1903; Schwarz and Greenleaf, *Light Bearers*, 262, 263.

[49] EGW to AGD and W. W. Prescott, July 1, 1903, EGWE.

[50] AGD to EGW, July 27, 1903, ASTR. *RH*, July 28, 1903, 24. The curmudgeon Henry

could not be pacified. Even after the settlement, he continued to vex leadership. "I am absolutely disgusted," Evans confessed to Daniells, "with a man who will go around, year after year, with chips on his back, making war against this cause." For all his troublemaking, however, Henry never left the church. I. H. Evans to AGD, November 10, 1903, ASTR.

[51] *RH*, August 11, 1903, 5, 6; August 20, 1903, 4, 5; EGW to AGD, June 26, 1903; WCW to AGD, June 19, 1903, ASTR; *RH*, July 28, 1903, 24.

[52] *RH*, August 20, 1903, 6.

[53] *RH*, September 20, 1903, 10.

[54] Ibid., 10–12.

CHAPTER VI

THE CRISIS OF 1903

Arthur Daniells approached his leadership role in the Seventh-day Adventist Church with a clear sense of mission. He sought to inspire and enable fellow believers—both church workers and laypeople—in their task of spreading the gospel. Time was short; the world's end was near. Of this he had no doubt, a certainty permeating his letters and public addresses.

But the clarity ended there. As head of a worldwide religious movement, he faced challenges unknown to James White. The complexity of church structure increased rather than diminished with the reorganization of 1901. Laudable goals of mitigating "kingly power" at the General Conference level and empowering local regions had by the law of unintended consequences created new centers of power in union conferences. Further, church finances showed little sign of immediate improvement. Nagging worries about debt followed Daniells everywhere. Even so simple a matter as what the head of the church should be called vexed him, with the unrelenting Alonzo Trévier Jones leading the charge. And then there was the "right arm of the gospel." The International Medical Missionary and Benevolent Association (IMMBA), under the leadership of the irrepressible Dr. John Harvey Kellogg, seemed poised to usurp the church's apocalyptic message with its gospel of health. From Australia days, dilemmas of organization and finance were old hat to Daniells. But how would he handle the new challenges of forceful, determined personalities?

COMPLETING REORGANIZATION

These conflicts, probably the most famous and consequential in the history of early twentieth-century Adventism, occurred against a backdrop of completing the organizational reforms of 1901. Daniells was preoccupied throughout 1902 with evaluating the changes already made and carrying through what had begun. Three new union conferences were birthed in 1902, the Northern, the Central, and the Pacific, making eight in all. The unions now held responsibility for administering the churches and denominational institutions therein (publishing houses and sanitariums excepted). Ownership of Union College went to the Central Union Conference, Keene Industrial Academy to the Southwestern Union, Walla Walla to the Pacific Union, and the Graysville and Huntsville schools to the Southern Union (though Oakwood would later revert to the General Conference). The General Conference was becoming, as Daniells observed, an advisory body "to the great field over which it presides." The General Conference Committee took on the function of the Mission Board, "looking after the welfare of the Union Conferences throughout the world" (indeed, logic of this development led to the Mission Board's abolishment at the 1903 General Conference).[1]

But old patterns of behavior persisted. Daniells, an admirably patient administrator, recognized part of his task to be educating local leaders about new realities. For months he received requests (especially from Edson White) for reimbursement from General Conference funds. This procedure, Daniells sought to make others understand, must now be redirected toward the local or union conferences. Some workers also objected to having their ministerial credentials issued by the local conference rather than the General Conference. Perhaps they thought there was something second rate about local credentialing, or they may have worried that their salary would be less sure. In some cases their fears were realized. Old warhorse Stephen Haskell found his pay reduced by his new employer, the Atlantic Union Conference, when hard times came.[2]

But church employees should have been concerned about the downside of staying on the General Conference payroll. The fact of the matter was that Battle Creek (later Takoma Park) headquarters was no longer the mother lode of funds. Tithe money now stayed in the unions, which paid only a "tithe" of their tithe collections to the General Conference. "The regular tithe that used to come to the General Conference treasury now went to the treasuries of the Union Conferences," Daniells confessed to A. M. Neff. To a degree that church leaders may not have anticipated, headquarters faced an acute cash flow problem, this at a time when long-standing debt plagued the church. Money problems contributed directly to the Daniells-Kellogg rift, as will be discussed later.[3]

Early plans called for the General Conference session to be held in the fall of 1902 (there were as yet no firm rules on their frequency). Certainly much business awaited attention. But Daniells and other members of the executive committee decided to defer until the following spring. So many state and union conference meetings had occupied their time during the previous months that leaders needed time to catch their breath. Daniells was also preoccupied with overseas matters following his long journey to Europe that summer. Additionally—and to Daniells surprise—there was little enthusiasm among the California brethren (and Ellen White) for hosting the session in their territory.[4]

Daniells may have been relieved for the delay; he dreaded the showdown that he knew was coming. Tensions had been building since the previous fall. The church would either move forward with its reorganization or step back. In Daniells's mind there was no question about the direction they must go.[5]

The General Conference Session, which lasted more than two weeks from March 27 to April 13, required extensive planning. Daniells had help from the other officers, but much of the burden fell on him. Despite earlier reluctance by California leadership, meetings were held at the church in Oakland, California, the center of West Coast Adventism. Ellen White, quite late in the planning, encouraged leaders to consider moving the site to Healdsburg, where she resided, offering the homes of local members to accommodate delegates. The General Conference Committee pondered her suggestion respectfully but finally deemed the notion impractical. Indeed, the expense of travel to a far-west location had already led to the decision that this be a smaller conference. Only 130 delegates were expected (fewer actually came, plus the usual clutch of visitors). Sleeper accommodations on the Santa Fe Railroad out of Chicago were arranged. But lest any member think leaders cosseted themselves, committee minutes stipulated that travel would provide "opportunity for counsel while en route." A narrow escape by George Butler offered a reminder that train travel, even in the twentieth century, could not be taken for granted. His train, wending its way through the mountains of Colorado, fell victim to a landslide, which wiped out a section of track along with the engine and some coaches.[6]

Adventists were an economically modest people. Public accommodations would stretch budgets. Thus, most delegates resided with local Adventist families. Lunches and dinners were catered by the San Francisco Vegetarian Café in a spacious tent across from the church. "The menu is liberal," the *Review* reported with appreciation, "the food thoroughly hygienic, and the service excellent."[7]

Per the usual format, the Oakland General Conference combined church business with devotional messages (the latter at 8:00 A.M. and then again in the evening). As in all later General Conference sessions, the church showcased its preeminent figures, including W. W. Prescott, A. T. Jones, L. R. Conradi, A. G. Daniells, G. A. Irwin, and of course, Ellen White. Sermons, though powerful in their own way, were generally shorn of the anecdotes and illustrations to which modern listeners are accustomed. Instead, addresses were exhortative and heavily doctrinal, stressing the particular prophetic work to which Adventists were called, in particular the nearness of the Second Advent. Speakers were hard on themselves and on their listeners; there could be no excuse for shirking the duty God had given. The handful of surviving pioneers, such as White and John Loughborough, stood as paragons of faithfulness to the original message.

The 1903 General Conference was the first for Daniells as leader of the church. Appropriately, he took center stage, delivering the devotional talk on the first Saturday night, then presenting his agenda at the Monday morning business meeting. His sermon displayed a homiletic power often undervalued in assessments of his career. "The time, the movement, the providence," comprised Daniells's theme. He led his hearers through a review of Bible prophecy and end-time events. It was familiar territory but well paced and effective in presentation, a message crafted to instill confidence in the Advent movement—and more—to inspire redoubled dedication to the task given a remnant people. "Let us lay aside every weight; let us lay aside every hindrance," Daniells concluded. "Let us bury everything that operates against the consummation of this work."[8]

Daniells sincerely hoped that all differences among delegates might be buried when he stood to speak on Monday morning, when the work of the session really began. He delivered, essentially, a state of the denomination address. In the manner of all astute politicians, he accentuated the positive, celebrating collective achievements. Reorganization, of course, was chief among these. Twelve union conferences and three mission conferences now existed to coordinate outreach. Why was this better? Because God's work was "placed in the hands of those to whom it belongs," giving responsibility to those closest to the field. Decentralization was accompanied by simplification, as superfluous bodies were eliminated. Further, the crushing debt that burdened the denomination when he took office, while still considerable, was becoming manageable. Christiana Publishing House in Norway had single-handedly crippled the European work. And stateside, the many new schools likewise imposed a collective debt of some $350,000. But Daniells and his compatriots determined that the only honorable course was to repay every penny. Through sacrificial giving by church members and helped by the difficult but ultimately successful *Christ's Object Lessons* campaign, great strides had been made in this direction. Daniells was perhaps most proud of what members in the pews had done for foreign missions. The preceding two-year period witnessed the greatest outpouring of mission offerings in the church's history (helped certainly by a recovering economy). Individual conferences had on their own sent out missionaries. Moreover, all new initiatives of the past biennial were accomplished with no new debt.[9]

Daniells also spoke with admirable candor about ongoing challenges. The rapid reorganization, for example, could not be done "without causing some confusion and apparent loss." He would not "presume to claim that the work done has been perfect." There was, in modern parlance, a steep learning curve for church administrators. The other continuing challenge was the Southern work. Ellen White's unrelenting call for greater attention to the South bore fruit. "I am satisfied," Daniells confessed, "that we have not done all for the Southern field that should have been done." Somewhat defensively, Daniells pointed out that more than $300,000 had been allocated there in the past decade. It was less increased funds the region needed, he postulated, than "intelligent, thoughtful, and studious cooperation of our people in the North."[10]

Effective leaders understand the importance of drawing on tradition and the contributions of others. Daniells's address included poignant remembrances of the workers who had fallen since the past session (fifteen ordained ministers and six missionaries). In particular, he eulogized Uriah

Smith (whose death, a few thought, was hastened by his unceremonious removal from the *Review and Herald* editorship).[11]

Interspersed in Daniells's state-of-the-church message were formal recommendations of the General Conference Committee to the full session for approval. These included exhortations for even more active mission work by union and state conferences and, most significantly, that all future denominational work be carried forth "on a strictly cash basis." Further, the General Conference should not be held responsible for debts it did not assume by formal action. Though stated indirectly, it could only be read as a thinly veiled statement by church leadership that they were prepared for a showdown with Kellogg's medical establishment. This was made abundantly clear when, after Daniells sat down, trusted party man C. H. Parsons immediately got the floor and moved that a committee be formed to "examine into the financial standing of all our various institutions, and to investigate their relationship to the Seventh-day Adventist denomination." If that was not meddling enough, Parsons (in what was clearly a well-rehearsed motion) went on to charge this committee with devising a plan to bring all institutions "under the direct ownership, control, and management of our people [the General Conference]." The gauntlet had been cast down.[12]

Notably missing in this agenda-setting session was an item that proved almost equally explosive. The committee on the constitution just a few days before the session's close brought in a recommendation that in some eyes evoked the specter of Babylon. The Seventh-day Adventist Church was again to have a president.

"WHAT'S IN A TITLE?"

Almost overlooked in the bundle of administrative changes made two years earlier was a redefinition of the executive power of the Seventh-day Adventist Church. Technically, A. G. Daniells was not elected president; he was chosen by the General Conference Committee as chairman of that body for an undefined term (though presumably until the next General Conference session two years later). The putative General Conference president was technically just the chair of its executive committee.

Why? Because there was a collection of church leaders, notably, A. T. Jones, E. J. Waggoner—and even for a time, W. W. Prescott—who took quite literally Ellen White's admonition that no "kingly power" should dominate the church. Their opposition to the office of president had deeper roots. It partook of a highly spiritual, almost mystical view of church leadership. Christ was the true head of the church; thus no strong authority figure was needed—or desired. The implication of this view of ecclesiology was radical decentralization of authority. Although Jones and Waggoner had been promoting their views since General Conference sessions of the late 1890s, it is unlikely that most leaders really understood what they were voting in the final days of the 1901 Battle Creek meetings.[13]

Certainly Daniells did not feel inhibited by his title of "chairman." Within weeks of the General Conference session he was publically signing correspondence "president," and the title remained on the letterhead stationery. Legal documents, in particular, required signature by an official head. Prescott, who possessed a sense of pragmatic realism, ended his opposition to the title. He and Daniells deconstructed Ellen White's testimony against vesting too much authority in one person and concluded (quite reasonably) that her counsel "was to the effect that the one man acting as president . . . was not to be cumbered with the details of the entire conference." Daniells was persuaded that the new union conference system sufficiently distributed authority.[14]

The issue hardly rose above an annoyance to Daniells, but in California Willie White saw more directly the depth of feeling it aroused in A. T. Jones. "He tells our people that the General Conference has no president any more," he complained to Daniells, "that our state conferences are not to have presidents, and that the office of president of the Union Conferences will soon be done away." Indeed, some conferences began trimming their leader's title under member pressure that to continue using the title after the prophet had spoken so plainly constituted apostasy. White did not put much stock in the need to discard a title. "It has seemed to me that if the president understood that his work was to preside, if our people understood that it was his duty to preside rather than to act as a dictator, there is no great harm to come from the continuance of a title which seems business-like and is generally understood."[15]

Over the subsequent two years before the Oakland General Conference, Daniells continued unapologetic in his use of the title.

The matter appeared on its way to becoming a nonissue. But Jones was not a person to let anything go that he believed a matter of principle. (It should be noted, though, that Jones's principled opposition did not prevent his accepting the presidency of the California Conference in the summer of 1901.) At the Fall Council in 1902 Daniells got his first hint of the discontent over the presidency title. Not much was to be done, however, until the issue came to a head at the next General Conference session. Near the end of the Oakland meetings a revised church constitution was recommended by the committee on constitution. It called for the formal return of the office of president.[16]

Why the committee felt it necessary to introduce the few changes as a new constitution rather than simply a series of alterations to the old is unclear. For one thing, there were other matters of importance that the new constitution embodied. Perhaps there was also the thought that embedding the controversial title change within an entire document would render it less obvious. But there was no way of hiding a change some deemed subversive of the proper course of church administration—particularly so when some of the objectors served on the subcommittee. Thus, when the group brought back its report to the full conference on April 9, there were actually two reports, a majority and a minority.[17]

The majority report, bringing the recommendation for a revised constitution, was signed by ten members, including Willie White (but not Daniells, who was not a member). The minority report, signed by E. J. Waggoner, David Paulson, and Percy T. Magan (Jones was not a member), asked that the constitution of 1901 "be given a fair trial before it be annihilated." After the minority lost its motion to substitute its report for the majority's, the losing group immediately grabbed the initiative in the debate. Daniells did not chair these sessions (H. W. Cottrell did) and until near the end largely remained on the sidelines, as he realized the discussion to some degree constituted a referendum on his leadership.[18]

Waggoner took the floor and did not surrender it for at least thirty minutes. Approaching the end of his long posting in Great Britain, and (in retrospect) moving increasingly toward the theological margins of Adventism, Waggoner's objections to a General Conference presidency seem not to have resulted from personal animosity toward Daniells. The two had been long planning for Waggoner's return to America.

Rather, Waggoner interpreted these matters of administrative structure in overtly theological terms.

How so? Because the proposed constitution violated the biblical principles of local congregational control and equality of believers in Christ. The exaltation of any man in leadership contradicted clear New Testament teachings. Waggoner's theological cautions about central power were to the point. But he could not leave it at that. He felt compelled to invoke the specter of a church creed and the papal structure as just around the corner. He did not particularly care for the present church constitution, but it was preferable to the proposed "worst constitution ever devised among Seventh-day Adventists." An ideal church organization (which Waggoner knew was not in the works), though recognizing the need for leaders, would also understand that authority "rests in the individual and his relation to God, and not in the position to which he is elected." Energy devoted to constitution writing, in Waggoner's naïve understanding of organizations, was mere child's play.[19]

Waggoner's peroration foretold a long debate. Indeed, at the start of the subsequent session a motion was proposed to restrict individual comments to five minutes. Jones, who was gearing up for an even longer speech, quickly objected. Daniells, seeking to maintain a perception of fairness to dissidents, spoke against the motion, and it died. But before Jones got the floor, P. T. Magan got in licks of his own. Both he and Paulsen represented the church's medical interests, and they saw the matter of a strong presidency tied to another mischievous provision of the new constitution: denominational ownership of all institutions. Magan, more measured than Waggoner, focused on practical matters of organization (though he was not above playing the "papacy card"). Like Jones, Magan deeply regretted that the 1903 constitution represented a "step back" from those of 1897 and 1901. The issue of authority had dogged General Conference sessions since the late 1880s (James White's and George Butler's names were not mentioned, but their strong-willed ways had prompted calls for change). But just when the 1901 decentralizing reforms seemed ready to put the church on the right track, a constitutional reversal was attempted. The earlier reforms needed to be given a chance.[20]

If Magan sought a tone of judicious persuasion, Jones brought his typical debater's tenacity. He likewise deplored the retreat from earlier progress, but more than any other speaker, he invoked Ellen White. "It is not wise to choose one man as president of the General Conference," critics loved to quote (from a letter dated August 1896). Jones did not stop there, trotting out long passages of White's criticism of church leadership. He likely took particular enjoyment in reading to the brethren her admonition that "no one is to claim kingly power over God's heritage in the medical missionary work" (Jones and Kellogg had discovered their mutual interests, which would strengthen their bond all the way to their respective departures from the church). Jones may not have shared Waggoner's mystical theology, but he did share his belief in authority at the local church level. And why should the local church be restricted to one elder, he reasonably asked, instead of the biblical model of multiple elders?[21]

Jones had to respond to the awkward question of why, given his adamant stance, he had accepted the presidency of the California Conference. For the simple reason, he explained, of using that position to illustrate how a conference run on proper principles would operate. His conference model eschewed hierarchical direction for consultation and individual empowerment. But, asked one delegate, what would be done with a pastor who did not preach as the conference thought proper? "Let him preach the gospel," Jones responded confidently. "He belongs to Jesus Christ, and the committee must belong to Jesus Christ." One imagines Daniells shaking his head at this bit of glibness. No religious organization could long proceed on such a basis.[22]

Waggoner and Jones may have been seeking to reprise—with a different issue—the impact they exerted on the 1888 General Conference. But where they brought a fresh, much-needed (if controversial) message to the church in 1888, their agenda in 1903 seemed carping rather than substantive. Not that organizational structure and oversight of leadership are insignificant, but the two men's rationales, rooted in mystical theology or labored readings of Ellen White, lacked persuasiveness (except to those whose personal agendas made them appealing).

If parallels to early American history were to be invoked, Jones and Waggoner would be modern-day Patrick Henrys. Henry, the great spokesman for American liberty before and during the American Revolution, uncompromising and rhetorically powerful, was a figure whom Jones especially might admire. Serving a prophetic role in thundering against real or imagined abuses and calling a people to action were both men's forte. But intrepidity frequently devalues patience and grasp of the complexities of life. The very qualities that made Daniells an effective administrator were those Jones would be temperamentally unable to appreciate.

The Patrick Henry comparison is particularly apt, because the 1903 General Conference bore one striking resemblance to the 1787 Constitutional Convention. An essential issue in both events was the same: Would there be one leader (designated as "president" and elected by delegates representing the church constituency) who could exercise executive authority? Under the Articles of Confederation (America's first governing system) there was no single executive but rather an executive committee. And the 1901 General Conference Constitution provided for a similar executive committee structure presided over by a chairman (though Daniells continued to behave as a president). A similar dynamic persuaded both groups to eschew a strong executive. During the Revolutionary Era, American leaders—Henry notable among them—feared tyranny and determined not to endow a single person with potency. They had seen literal kingly power and felt safer in distributing power throughout the nation at the state level. The 1901 Battle Creek sessions were likewise concerned with kingly power and fashioned a document intended to distribute authority across the country (the world, really) through various union conferences.

But America struggled under the Articles of Confederation. Thus, our Founding Fathers concluded that power was too decentralized; we needed a stronger national authority headed by a president. Patrick Henry was so incensed by this movement that he refused even to attend the Philadelphia Convention (he "smelt a rat"). Like Henry, Jones and Waggoner were appalled that the "spirit of '01" could so quickly be dismissed in a rush to crown a president. The earlier church constitution had not been given a fair chance, they repeated. Just as the proposed United States Constitution appeared to compromise the principles of liberty embedded in the Declaration of Independence, so the reformed 1903 constitution implied a "rejection of the principles of organization given us by the Spirit of God two years ago."[23]

History has proven Henry and his fellow Antifederalists wrong. National progress required a stronger central government headed by a strong executive. Likewise, Adventist Church history bears out the wisdom of the 1903 administrative change (a tweaking, really, of the 1901 constitution). Patrick Henry, essential though he was in the halcyon days of the Revolution, proved an unhelpful contrarian during the nation-building period. Jones and Waggoner, forever remembered as champions of the 1888 righteousness by faith message, were unable to grasp the administrative imperatives of the twentieth century.

It is hard to know what the impact of Waggoner's, Magan's, and Jones's speeches on the delegates at Oakland would have been if no effective response had been made. We do not know because Willie White next got the floor and delivered a *tour de force* of argument. Other delegates might quote Ellen White, but no one could claim to interpret her words with the authority that her son could. He proceeded to put her words about "kingly power" in a useful context. He then gave a pellucid narrative of recent Adventist Church organization and the streamlining effects of the 1901 reforms. In a masterly stroke, he demonstrated that Jones's concern for consultation among individuals and departments was achieved in 1901 and now further advanced with the 1903 emendations. His words were brilliantly disarming. "I do not think that there is very much in a name," he reassured about the disputed title. "He is not a king, but a servant."[24]

White prepared the ground for Daniells, who had with the exception of two interjections intended to ensure utter fairness for his critics, held his counsel until now. He probably sensed that his alter ego had changed the momentum of the debate. Daniells's tone was conciliatory; he recounted how he and Jones had worked together "quite pleasantly in the matter of reorganization." He added (wishfully), "I am sure that there is some misunderstanding, not a difference of view in the real principle." This was the rhetoric of an administrator who may know better but who must speak the language of organizational unity.

After a bow to group harmony, Daniells proceeded to realities. "We face conditions, and not theories," he bluntly stated. The consummate administrator had little patience with Waggoner's mysticism or Jones's idealized congregationalism. One contested feature of the new governing document, for example, was a provision that five members of the General Conference Committee (including either the president or vice president) could constitute a quorum and conduct business. The proposed quorum of five was notorious in Jones's eyes, a recipe for encroachment on other entities of the church. But Daniells pointed out the difficult realities leaders faced. "Letters come from India, from Africa, and they have to be dealt with. Calls come; demands come; every day we are living there are living problems cropping up. Somebody has to meet those problems, and meet them right on the spot. We (the twenty-five member General Conference Committee) can not take our seats, and keep still the whole year. Now, who is going to do it?" Daniells's logic was impeccable. If the president was on, say, the Pacific Coast, "let him with four or five men [Executive Committee members] get together, and help each other out." This would be true all around the country.[25]

Daniells brought his own array of Ellen White's comments. He made a telling point when he quoted her reference to the General Conference president *after* her famous counsel about not choosing one man as president. He argued that her intent was not to eliminate the office of president but to have sufficient decentralization throughout the union conferences so that decision making does not fall chiefly on him. Daniells's interpretation of White's words, in retrospect, seems proper.[26]

The back-to-back speeches of White and Daniells probably sealed passage of the constitution, but veteran Adventist leader George Butler was called to the front for some historical perspective. Butler proceeded to deliver a rambling series of Adventist history recollections. After the civil but wearying debate and unending string of Ellen White references, Butler's folksy tone must have been a welcome relief. A casual listener might think he had no point. But in fact, Butler was cleverly driving toward a middle position, arguing that under any system of governance the essential matter was for a leader to have the right heart. In the end, the old warhorse could not resist supporting current leadership's position. The return to having a president who was elected by delegates for a specific term (rather than selected as chair by the General Conference Committee for an indeterminate period) would appeal to a former president who was never shy about the exercise of authority.[27]

With the repeated invocation of Ellen White's words on the subject of leadership one might wonder where her voice was during the debate. She had retreated into oracular silence, offering comfort to neither side. White delivered a devotional talk, as was her custom, and in the final days she delivered a long exhortation on the importance of supporting the Southern work—a topic dear to her heart. But White chose not to intrude into controversy, even when clarifying words might have hastened resolution. With a legion of men parsing her words in support of their positions, she refused to become the designated authority of last resort.[28]

Though acceptance of the new constitution seemed likely, there were nonetheless, details to be worked out. And since the floor had earlier been dominated first by the Jones/Waggoner contingent and then White/Daniells, a number of other delegates wanted to have their say. There was concern that the General Conference Committee have a well-rounded representation; that folding the Mission Board into the General Conference might mean the president's attention would be unduly concentrated on the world field; and that a quorum of five leaders, even if necessary at times, seemed dangerous. To the latter point, A. T. Jones regained the floor to object to the five-person quorum provision, which other delegates also disliked. Daniells thought he had answered this point, but he proved flexible. His larger objectives were straightforward: church leaders had to be able to transact business as they traveled about the country. The constitution should reflect this administrative reality.[29]

Fine tuning of the document continued till all who desired had had their say. Jones won the skirmish over the use of "quorum"; it was dropped in favor of the more modest empowerment to "transact executive business." When chair H. W. Cottrell finally called for a vote on April 9, 120 stood in favor of the new document; 20 voted no. Delegates went on to elect Arthur Daniells as General Conference president, Conradi as first vice president (based in Europe), and W. W. Prescott as second vice president (in America). The reorganization begun in 1901 had been completed.[30]

The 1903 revision did not represent a sharp turn toward centralized power, in the sense that the 1787 United States Constitutional Convention did. It was a moment of Adventist pragmatism. The matter of having a president was never seriously questioned again, except by hard-core opponents such as Jones, who continued to grouse. During the summer of 1903 Jones wrote, and Pacific Press published, a short pamphlet entitled *One-Man Power*. The work was purportedly about the overweening power of the business trusts (then a major concern of American reformers) and the continued danger of the papacy (aided by American policy in its occupation of the Philippines), highlighted by a quick review of despotic rule throughout Western history. But clearly, Jones meant this as allegory that spoke to current church matters. "The logic of a one-man rule is always a despotism." Jones's work in religious liberty provided a plausible pretext for his writing. But its timing and his bulldog refusal to give up on an issue he deemed "principle" suggests the work was a yet another snap at Daniells's leg.[31]

Despite Jones's and Waggoner's protestations, the Seventh-day Adventist Church would not return to the pre-organization days of the early 1860s. The organization man, A. G. Daniells, represented the future, signaled by the ease of his election near the close of the 1903 sessions. But if he readily carried the day over a call to "holy anarchy," he would face a much tougher battle with a man who also believed in strong organization. For Daniells, the major crisis of 1903 was not with Jones but with Dr. John Harvey Kellogg.

CONFLICT WITH THE RIGHT ARM OF THE GOSPEL

Prompted by Ellen White's vision about health reform in 1863, Adventists rather quickly added a doctrine of healthful living (if more slowly to adopt the practice) to their otherwise biblically based doctrinal teachings. The array of illnesses Adventist pioneers endured encouraged an appreciation of healthful living, and in the last half of her life White wrote extensively about matters of diet, exercise, and temperance. Merritt Kellogg took the half-year training course at Russell Trall's Hygiea-Therapeutic College and became Adventism's first physician. Half-brother John Harvey was among four bright young men (the two White sons included) sponsored at Trall's in 1872, James White needing trained workers to staff the church's Western Health Reform Institute in Battle Creek (forerunner of the Battle Creek Sanitarium). But John Harvey quickly became dissatisfied with Trall's water cure regimen, which disparaged a scientific basis of medical study. Kellogg's strong interest in organic chemistry was in line with evolving practice in medical education. He left, and with the encouragement of James White entered first the University of Michigan's medical school and subsequently Bellevue Hospital Medical College in New York City, both highly regarded institutions. Kellogg's education set the Adventist Church on a path away from increasingly marginalized medical traditions and toward orthodox medical training and practice.[32]

Kellogg quickly became the golden boy of Adventism, invited to be the physician-in-chief of the Health Reform Institute even before he had finished his training. As the protégé of James White (head of the board), he was assured of quick advancement. In 1876, he agreed to a one-year appointment as medical superintendent—a term that stretched to nearly seven decades. His forceful ways and political legerdemain were such that when the equally forceful but increasingly enfeebled White proved an obstacle, Kellogg angled to get him off the board. He also engineered a renaming of the institution—Battle Creek Sanitarium. A stroke of marketing genius, the name endowed the establishment with a memorable geographic locale and a new word in the English lexicon, "sanitarium," bespeaking Kellogg's determination that the institution was more about teaching health than curing disease. By the mid-1880s he was director and within a few years became by far the single largest stockholder (it was a nonprofit organization wholly subscribed by Adventists). The Battle Creek Sanitarium was closely identified with the Seventh-day Adventist Church, but it was essentially his.[33]

Kellogg's prominence within Adventism increased proportionate to the growth of the Sanitarium and the prominence of health reform within the church. Well into the early twentieth century he maintained a confiding relationship with Ellen White, who served as his personal spiritual counselor. Kellogg had great ambitions both for his institution and for the possibilities of Adventism as a movement that might revolutionize American health habits. Adopting healthful living was one aspect of sanctification—and perhaps the most important part. But he saw a major impediment to his dream's fulfillment: the Adventist clergy, and particularly those in leadership positions. Despite Ellen White's thickening stack of articles on diet and health, some ministers embraced reform reluctantly or not at all. A. G. Daniells apparently never gained the victory over red meat and, indeed, may not have put up much of a fight. As late as 1919 on a visit to Japan, he advised the missionary family with whom he stayed to supplement their Asian diet with meat. This unconcern about something so important to Kellogg continually irritated him and fed his undercurrent of distrust toward the ministry.[34]

The distrust could occasionally pass over to genuine animosity. Adventist clergy sensed (accurately) that Kellogg condescended to them. He viewed them as intellectually second rate, parochial, and often self-serving. As noted earlier, Daniells would have grudgingly agreed with portions of this indictment. But they were, finally, his ministers, and he quietly resented Kellogg's hauteur. Brilliant, quick-witted, and possessing the fanatic's utter confidence, Kellogg was temperamentally as different from the plodding Arthur Grosvenor Daniells as could be. And yet, in Daniells, Kellogg eventually found his match.[35]

CONTENTION OVER DEBT AND THEOLOGY

The conflict between Dr. Kellogg and the Adventist Church had three sources. Initially, it arose from his frustration with Daniells's "no-debt" policy, especially as it interfered with his hopes to establish a sanitarium in England. This was aggravated by his ongoing resistance to the General Conference leadership's desire to exercise clearer ownership of medical institutions. And finally, he resented leadership's failure to support rebuilding plans in Battle Creek, particularly as Daniells withdrew support for an aggressive campaign to sell Kellogg's *Living Temple* as a rebuilding fund-raiser. This latter issue quickly devolved into open questions about Kellogg's theological orthodoxy.

But underlying all these conflicts was a social cleavage that stole unawares over the church. Adventism had from its beginnings been a movement of modest farmers and tradesmen. Literate, certainly, even given to deep study of Scripture; but not learned (with the occasional exception of a J. N. Andrews or the Dartmouth-educated Prescott). Even though physicians of the nineteenth century did not hold quite the social cachet that they would in the twentieth, Kellogg and his Adventist medical brethren represented a new professional class in the church. Adventism's embrace of mainstream medicine, including top-flight medical training at the College of Medical Evangelists (founded in 1909 and later known as Loma Linda University), brought into its bosom a new sort of leader, whose professional ethic and loyalties would not long be subservient to the traditional clerical elite, who still lacked the professional training and credentials increasingly held by physicians. Other than the prophet herself, Kellogg was easily the most renowned Adventist in America. His reputation within the national medical community as author, surgeon, inventor of fitness equipment, and, of course, corn flakes, was formidable (though controversial). He bestrode Adventism like a colossus. The antagonism of Kellogg and Daniells highlighted a fundamental division that in retrospect could hardly have been avoided.[36]

The IMMBA, dominated by Kellogg, was the linchpin of the church's young medical work. It survived the 1901 purge (when most other church associations turned into departments) because Daniells and other church leaders did not want to tangle with the medical establishment. Thus, even after the move of Battle Creek College to Berrien Springs, Kellogg had a formidable institutional base from which to influence the church's medical efforts. And a far-flung work it was, with the church operating sanitariums across the nation and in Europe, Australia, and Mexico. But trouble began when the denomination began to consider founding a sanitarium in England.

Kellogg's ambitions for a medical presence in England was generally shared by church leaders. When Daniells visited England and Europe in late spring and summer of 1902, one task was to spy out possible sites. He assumed operations would start modestly by renting a location in London. But Kellogg also crossed the Atlantic, and he had grander plans. He wasted little time in locating what he considered an ideal location. It was on the Isle of Wight, off the southern England coast, in an available building near the queen's palace. He sent a call to members of the General Conference Committee, then in Denmark, to come over to examine it, noting Ellen White's advocacy of locating institutions near the wealthy. These events transpired when Kellogg and Daniells were still in the extended honeymoon after the latter's initial election as leader. But Kellogg's unrelenting ambitions were making Daniells uneasy. He smelled more debt. His inclination was not to make the trip across the Channel. But he made a tactical error that he later regretted. Daniells agreed to travel to England with Kellogg—but only if others requested it. Daniells's confidence that the frugal leaders would wave off the idea was misplaced, as they agreed to the suggestion. "I should have then and there told the doctor plainly such a location would not do."[37]

With a decision to visit England settled, Daniells at least sought to persuade the committee members that a London location must be the answer. A vigorous discussion ensued before Daniells persuaded the entire delegation to defer their trip to Switzerland and accompany him to

England and seek an alternate site. With support behind him in what he feared was a looming confrontation, Daniells felt relief. They set off on the train/boat journey.

But premonitions of trouble returned. He fell into a troubled sleep—and then had something akin to a visitation. "Late at night a voice seemed to be speaking to my conscience telling me that I must not surrender to wrong principles, and thus bring serious troubles upon the cause of God." Not knowing what it meant, Daniells reports that he, like his biblical namesake, "cried for understanding." When he awoke in the morning, the warning voice still sounded. "But before reaching London, I received light." He felt firmly impressed that he must not give approval to any plan that "would plunge God's people further into debt." And he knew that he would have to stand up to Kellogg.[38]

This quasi-revelation to which Daniells testified may strike some as presumptuous—or at least odd in an age when Adventism had a designated prophet. But it was not so unusual. Various church figures spoke of dreams, apprehensions, or impressions. Adventists (and doubtless many Christians generally) would consider such things unexceptional. J. L. Loughborough claimed many such dreams. The difference was that Ellen White delivered general testimonies for others in the church or for church leaders themselves. The impressions such as Daniells and others received were for themselves alone, a kind of divine private counsel.[39]

Daniells, now steeled for the conflict, received immediate good news: the Isle of Wight property could not be used for a sanitarium because of its proximity to a royal residence. Undeterred, the doctor suggested forming a committee to find another site that could be immediately purchased. As he addressed the group he became more insistent that when the leaders return to America they immediately raise twenty thousand dollars. Kellogg had long been used to getting his way with church leadership. New medical facilities had been acquired over the past decade like so many party favors—but expensive party favors. The American delegation stood firm behind Daniells in not being railroaded into a decision. Then Kellogg called Daniells into a washroom for a private conversation. What followed was, in Daniells's later description, the "greatest crisis of my life since first surrendering my heart to God." While blocking Daniells's exit through the door, Kellogg harangued him for two hours with every imaginable argument, including a threat that Ellen White would "roll" him "over in the dust" if he remained obdurate. One visualizes the short, excitable doctor, dressed in white, poking his finger in Daniells's chest while looking up into the owlish face of the taller man. But throughout the unrelenting lecture, Daniells testified, he heard another voice "that even the doctor's arguments could neither silence nor drown." Daniells would not budge: There would be no purchase until funds were donated. Kellogg finally stalked away, muttering that he could not work with Daniells's cash policies.[40]

The issue of rebuilding the fire-destroyed Battle Creek Sanitarium also vexed Kellogg and church leadership. Kellogg's plans were ambitious (despite his assurance to the contrary), and pledged funds from Battle Creek residents did not live up to promise. But taking a page from the church's great success in reducing school debt with the *Christ's Object Lessons* campaign, Kellogg proposed a similar effort with a new book he had penned, *The Living Temple*. He would pay for the printing of 400,000 copies, which would then be promoted and sold through denominational channels. The project appeared innocent enough; church leaders, including Ellen White, initially got behind it. But then closer looks at the text raised concerns.[41]

Daniells seemed almost apologetic to Kellogg about raising the issue of pantheism. He gushed that the project could potentially become "the greatest feature we have yet performed in our book work." Yet he wanted to ensure that the denominationally sanctioned book be "free from any just criticism." In a book intended to be about health and the human body there is no need to introduce controversial theological notions. Better to "modify your language" and—in the spirit of ignorance being bliss—"present only a part of your thoughts." That same day Daniells wrote Willie White regarding the delicate issue of Kellogg's cryptic statements about "God in man." Daniells thought the matter handled best by having the manuscript "carefully and critically edited." Wearing an administrator's rather than a theologian's hat, Daniells's concern was for maximizing sales and minimizing controversy rather than seeking to discern what Kellogg's true views might be.[42]

Daniells possessed, indeed, an interesting mixture of human insight and theological naïveté. After examining *The Living Temple*'s proof sheets, he wrote W. A. Spicer: "There is nothing in it I do not fully indorse." Given that Daniells entitled a chapter "Denomination Saved From Pantheistic Teaching," in his much later book, *The Abiding Gift of Prophecy*, his earlier comment that Kellogg's book was "straight as string" comes as a surprise. It partly reflected his lack of philosophical sophistication and need to look to others for cues. He also understood that resistance to the book from some church leaders bespoke their opposition to what Kellogg stood for more generally. Many of the "brethren have fought health principles for a quarter of a century. . . . This element are going to fight advanced truth no matter how it comes," but especially if it came through the doctor. Daniells understood, too, that Kellogg was unlikely to bow to ministerial pressure and remove sections he considered important. The generosity Daniells displayed toward Kellogg in these early discussions of *The Living Temple* is the more remarkable considering it was but weeks earlier that the doctor had blistered his ear over the British sanitarium issue. No doubt Daniells resisted fighting a war with Kellogg on two fronts and desired conciliation with the doctor on the book matter. But disquiet with *The Living Temple* remained. When Dr. David Paulson, one of Kellogg's staunchest allies, testified to the book's orthodoxy, Daniells assented to his judgment, but then outlined the larger issue at hand. Why the need for inclusion of speculative philosophy in the book? If even the educated Paulson puzzled over parts, "what hope is there for the average man?"[43]

These troubling matters of debt and theology formed the backdrop of the church's Fall Council held in Battle Creek in mid-November 1902. The two-a-day sessions in the Battle Creek Tabernacle's north vestry attracted not only members of the General Conference Committee but a large number of doctors and other observers. As Daniells confided to others, minutes from the committee sessions euphemistically reporting an "extended interchange of thought" scarcely hint at the heat generated within the vestry room and outside of the meetings. The tone was set a few days before the opening, when Kellogg marched a cadre of his medical associates to Daniells's office to straighten out a small group of local members of the General Conference Committee. In what became a five-hour "tirade," Kellogg bitterly complained of the opposition of Ellen and Willie White. "He has apparently taken his stand positively, absolutely, and unswervingly against Sister White and her communications."[44]

Perhaps Kellogg had heard of a meeting Daniells and six others had with Ellen White at Elmshaven in mid-October, several weeks before the Battle Creek session. They engaged her in frank conversations about the acute problem of church debt. Inevitably, the talk turned to Kellogg, the current source of most debt. White had been increasingly distressed with James and her cherished protégé. She gave unqualified support to Daniells's no-debt policy (and she added, with even more personal pain, permission for leadership to take over from Edson affairs at the chronically mismanaged Southern Publishing in Nashville). A verbatim transcript was made of the interview, which Daniells tucked away as ammunition for future confrontations.[45]

Daniells and Kellogg engaged in verbal sparring even before the sessions. Daniells, steadfastly set against incurring more debt, told Kellogg that he would rather "pack my satchel" and "go to the heart of Africa" to "labor in peace." Kellogg, whose outbursts alternated with attempts at conciliation, wrote Daniells that he wrongly suspected Kellogg of "a personal dislike." But he also chided Daniells for lacking sympathy toward the medical work. "You do not wish to be a slave to any man nor any board; we [IMMBA] feel the same." The medical establishment did not want "war"; nor were they determined "to oppose you, or anybody."[46]

Daniells, heartsick from the rancor, but confident in the support of most churchmen and Ellen White, opened the session by laying out the grim financial picture of the denomination. Indebtedness stood, roughly, at two million dollars. Leadership had been working hard to clean up this "wreckage" (as Daniells later characterized it). To take on more debt to purchase medical institutions would be to betray church members who had been working so hard to redeem finances.[47]

Would leadership endorse plans to promote *The Living Temple*? Initial discussions were congenial yet direct. A motion to move forward with the project was slowed by Prescott, who argued that the prudent approach required a consideration of the "character of the book." In the debate that followed, Prescott opined that man—in his sinful state—could not be considered to be God's temple. Kellogg, as was his wont, did not dispute this theological distinction, but averred that he was not making a theological point but a physiological one. Discussion became sharper in a later session, as Prescott and others quoted what they considered incriminating passages. Daniells, sensing that no consensus was being reached, moved that a small committee be appointed to study the manuscript. But the four-member committee charged with evaluating the manuscript included Kellogg and two supporters (Jones and David Paulson), leaving Prescott as the only independent voice. Predictably (nonetheless to Prescott's chagrin), it reported to the larger Committee that no serious problems existed. Another committee had been formed to consider plans for a sales campaign for the book. Further, there had been much positive talk of assisting the rebuilding effort through the issuance of construction bonds, which the General Conference would encourage members to purchase. It appeared that Kellogg was on his way to victory.[48]

Yet Prescott's concerns about the book—and his influence—checkmated Kellogg. Prescott asked and received permission to give his minority report to the assembled session. In candid language he stated his reasons why the book should never be published. Kellogg, for the moment confounded, asked that *The Living Temple* be withdrawn from consideration. In a gesture of amity, a group was formed to study the possibility of championing another Kellogg manuscript, "How to Live a Century."[49]

The November meetings considered a variety of church matters: consideration of proper tithe use; assignment of missionaries to fields afar; more support for teachers and textbooks in Adventist schools (including consideration of free tuition). But most important, from the perspective of Kellogg and Daniells, a resolution was adopted that the denomination be conducted "on a strictly cash basis." A corollary action stated that from this time forward the General Conference "would not be held financially responsible for any obligations which they have not assumed by their own action." In other words, the church was not going to financially guarantee Kellogg's independent actions.[50]

Kellogg's frustration is understandable, but his larger sense of betrayal by Daniells (and Prescott) is hard to explain, especially in light of the latter's motion at the same Fall Council meetings that $20,000 be appropriated for a British sanitarium. Clearly, Kellogg, for all of his strategic retreats and overwrought declarations of contrition, brooked no real opposition. He dreamed large dreams; dreams too large for a cash-only approach. Minnesota Conference president C. W. Flaiz, having seen Kellogg in action at the meetings, had a measure of sympathy for the doctor. "He has had his own way so long and has domineered and berated every body that it is hard on him to be checked in his career." Through most of the 1890s Kellogg had dominated presidents Olsen and Irwin. He sensed in Daniells a formidable opponent, one who could not be left standing.[51]

Daniells was not above mounting his own campaign against the doctor. He constructed a network of support among conference and union leaders. Through his unceasing correspondence he reiterated the acute debt problem and difficulties with Kellogg. "The time has come for members of the General Conference Committee to take a definite stand," he wrote H. W. Cottrell. And to N. W. Allee he complained of the "heavy pressure" brought on the General Conference Committee "to be party to the debt making policy in carrying on the medical work." Daniells laid blame on the medical party for widening "the breach between the General Conference and the medical department." Daniells did not survive as church leader for twenty-one years without a sure sense of how to build political alliances.[52]

In Ellen White, Daniells had an ally of somewhat uncertain support. "Do not let him [Kellogg] beguile you by his statements," she warned him in September. But Kellogg, despite his semipublic rants against her, would not give up seeking endorsements of his own from the prophet. He telegraphed her in early 1903 pleading for her to support an immediate acquisition of a British sanitarium. Kellogg's entreaties had their effect. While she had originally counseled Daniells to stand fast, by early 1903 she reiterated to him the need for a British medical facility. Daniells did not dispute its desirability, only the timing. But her change of tone both emboldened Kellogg to pursue his agenda and cast a cloud of doubt over her support for Daniells's leadership. Decades later, in *The Abiding Gift of Prophecy,* Daniells would recall an unwavering support in the Kellogg wars. But at the time, it did not always appear so.[53]

Kellogg quickly reverted to his own wishes about *The Living Temple.* He commissioned the Review and Herald press to print five thousand copies. Once printed, these were soon consumed in the great fire of December 1902, a development some observers considered divine interposition. Not easily dissuaded by the arm of Providence, he sent the manuscript to another publisher. It appeared in early 1903 and was soon hawked about the country by a cadre of Adventist youth Kellogg recruited.[54]

Tensions mounted as the Oakland General Conference approached in the spring of 1903. The medical "party," planted firmly behind Kellogg, planned Daniells's removal from leadership (a not impossible accomplishment given that the chair could be removed at any time by a majority vote of the fifteen-member Executive Committee). Kellogg cultivated such veteran and influential figures as George Butler and Stephen Haskell to his side (with only partial success). But Daniells was not the only problem. Kellogg considered Prescott and Willie White to be his liegemen, among the "heartless men in prominent places" (and the latter poisoning his mother's mind). Treasurer I. H. Evans, influential in money matters, was close behind. Battle lines were firmly drawn.[55]

CONTENTION OVER CONTROL

Matters of pantheism and debt remained unresolved. But the 1903 General Conference was even more threatening to John Harvey Kellogg by jeopardizing his control of medical institutions, particularly the flagship Battle Creek Sanitarium. For him, loss of control was unthinkable.

The Adventist Church then operated thirty-one sanitariums across America and fourteen around the world. In addition there was a phalanx of treatment rooms, food companies, and vegetarian restaurants. Their existence was a testimony to how far the institutional church had grown since its formal inception forty years earlier. And to a considerable degree, they were a testament to the energy and vision of Dr. Kellogg.

When the 1901 General Conference refashioned the collection of independent associations into departments, the IMMBA was allowed to retain its autonomy. Many leaders accepted Kellogg's argument that the peculiar features of medical work required independence. And in terms of institutional politics, it was probably a necessary compromise. But some now called for a consistent church polity: church members, who contributed to their support rather than association stockholders, should own all Adventist properties. The Committee on Institutions consequently recommended that all institutions should be held either through the General Conference or subordinate conference or mission organizations. Understanding that state laws of incorporation differed, the committee showed sophistication in the details of its proposal.[56]

Predictably, though, Kellogg saw dangers lurking. Were conference committees actually going to manage institutions? Proponents of change sought to assure medical attendees that their boards would handle day-to-day administration, while being ultimately accountable to constituents. Would the policy apply only to future institutions or would existing ones be gathered in? C. H. Parsons, who as chair of the Committee on Institutions introduced the proposal and was major spokesman for it, carefully responded that the intention was for future institutions—but if feasible and agreeable to stockholders, existing ones would be also be reorganized as conference entities.[57]

With Daniells occupying the chair and saying little, Kellogg launched into a spirited, penetrating, and occasionally sarcastic defense of keeping the status quo. The sarcasm came at the beginning of his long domination of the floor. The resolution did not go far enough, he complained in mock seriousness. All property owned by any Seventh-day Adventist should come under denominational control. He detected a "communist" principle at work (this in the days before any nation had come under communist rule). "The people must rule, the people must control, the people must have ownership." His rhetoric was hyperbolic, but Kellogg was making a serious point. Must every institution started by a group of evangelical- or health-minded individuals finally be brought under direct church control? If so, the church was creating a major disincentive for members to step out in faith.[58]

The doctor continued to hector the delegates. He alluded to long-standing criticisms that his sanitarium's policies demanded unswerving loyalty from its workers. But was not binding workers to God's cause (the sanitarium) a laudable goal? he protested. And if, as some argued, all Adventists (rather than just the stockholders) who contributed to an institution through their church offerings should have a voice in its operation, then he was doing that. Faithful workers at the Battle Creek Sanitarium, unlike at other Adventist institutions, were rewarded by membership in the Association. But here, Kellogg ominously continued, is a "great monarch, a tyranny," which says "you shall not do it" to men who want to organize and run an institution along lines they see fit. Changing his political metaphor, Kellogg took aim at a value close to American hearts. People talk of "the blessed principle of republicanism." But "there is not a greater tyranny on earth than republicanism. What is it?—It is simply the tyranny of the majority over a minority." It was as if Kellogg had sat at the feet of John Calhoun, thundering now against General Conference oppression rather than that of Northern states over the South.[59]

As Kellogg thundered and Daniells sat quietly in his chair, the doctor built momentum. Suspicioned though he was by many, he still carried the prestige as Adventism's greatest institution builder. But Willie White, who in his youth had been like a brother to Kellogg, took the floor and showed again why he deserves to be remembered as more than Ellen White's dutiful son. He sought to defuse the tension by getting the discussion back to first principles—and to reassure Kellogg—through a quick historical review of Adventist organization founding.

The stock company organizational model had been promoted by his father, James White, at a time when the church had few funds. Individuals would contribute to a school or printing house through the purchase of stock (in most cases not expecting a return on their investment, other than the satisfaction of furthering God's work). But as the work grew, White continued, it became apparent that another basis of organization was needed. The people who dedicated their lives to the work, rather than the stockholders, were really the principle investors; as Kellogg insisted, those building up the institution should have influence. White agreed that ownership by membership rather than stock made sense. But ascertaining the balance of influence based on how much stock one owned versus being vested through work at an institution was difficult. Thus, the principle of "one man, one vote" seemed advisable. This could offset the ongoing problem of proxy voting at stockholders meetings. No plan that man devises could be "free from perplexities," White admitted. But "where the burden of labor is, there rests the burden of control," a sentiment fashioned to calm the agitated doctor.[60]

Alas, it could not be accomplished so easily. Kellogg professed agreement with most of White's speech—he made no brief for stock companies nor did he allow proxy voting at Battle Creek Sanitarium. But to say the institution should be "owned and controlled" by everyone in the denomination made no sense. Who comprises the denomination? There is no legal test of membership; thus, Kellogg argued, "you have no means of finding out who the denomination is." Further, he added in his cleverest bit of sophistry, if the coming persecution is soon, the property of the church will be confiscated. Better by far that its property remain in the hands of independent associations.[61]

Kellogg probably did not worry about apocalyptic events. But he did worry that an organized cabal of incompetent ministers were attempting to wrest control of his beloved sanitarium. In a final shot across the bow, he sarcastically observed how satisfying it was to be "posing before the world as the owners of all these institutions in all parts of the earth," and for leaders to think "that we can touch a button, and every man in all these institutions would respond and obey." It would be a puppet show, directed from General Conference headquarters. But it cannot work, Kellogg insisted, because no central control can ever know local needs sufficiently. How could decisions about the Adventist health message be made by men, who, like a dog, find it no problem to sit down to dinner and "gnaw a bone" (one wonders how Daniells, famously a carnivore, took that remark)? If these pointed rebukes were not enough, Kellogg left no equivocation: If the delegates made the resolution applicable to all institutions, he would "not expect to be bound by it in anything I have anything to do with."[62]

Daniells, like White and Parsons, sought a less threatening interpretation of the proposal. Denominational ownership did not necessarily mean denominational control. A managing board of directors would do that. But Kellogg would have none of that. "Don't be deceived," he commanded delegates. "Ownership always means control." Kellogg cast the gauntlet down at Daniells's feet. "Dishonesty, bad faith, and dishonor are in this thing." Wealthy donors had entrusted the IMMBA with funds for medical and other beneficent work with the stipulations that it was not for church work. Was that trust now to be broken through denominational control? (Kellogg's public statements about the Battle Creek Sanitarium being non-denominational—a necessary disclaimer in his mind—greatly troubled loyal church members.)[63]

John Harvey Kellogg's strenuous objections succeeded in having the constitution amended to state that only institutions that had been created through conference or mission field organization would be owned by the "people" through conferences. It was a form of victory for Kellogg. The Battle Creek Sanitarium would never be controlled by the Adventist Church (nor did he give up an affiliated sanitarium in Mexico). The cost was high, as it was becoming apparent that his alienation from Adventist leadership was virtually complete—and his alienation from the church in general would not be far behind.[64]

A. G. Daniells, just two years into his presidency, could not know for sure how events would play out. He must have sensed that most church leaders supported him. Kellogg's schemes to replace Daniells at the General Conference session had failed, but the Kellogg faction remained formidable. On both sides there was an almost desperate desire to harmonize the two factions. The Sunday following the contentious Friday session described above, private and very protracted informal session ensued. In the evening, a small group sought to prevail on Daniells to seek reconciliation with Kellogg. E. A. Sutherland, then principal of Emmanuel Missionary College, "talked to Daniells plainer than I ever heard any man talked to in my life," testified Percy Magan. The session went on till 3:30 in the morning, when Daniells finally gave halfhearted assent to meeting with the doctor. Magan then proceeded to Kellogg's room in the local hotel, where until 5:30 that morning he sought to seek similar concession from him.[65]

Ellen White remained unpredictable. During the Oakland session she delivered a devotional just an hour before Kellogg began his rant. Even as she reiterated the need for the Adventist diaspora from Battle Creek, she also commended the medical work, encouraged Kellogg in particular, and noted that Heaven did "not endorse the efforts put forth by different ones to make the work of Dr. Kellogg as hard as possible, in order to build themselves up." Such words must have emboldened Kellogg. Further, during the conference she wrote Daniells and his fellow leaders that they should say "nothing that will drive Dr. Kellogg to desperation." "Do not use the words that I have spoken under great perplexity and distress to hasten a crisis." And then, her classic warning to Daniells: "God would not have you suppose that you can exercise a kingly power over your brethren." White's admonition nudged Daniells and others to seek common ground with Kellogg. In retrospect, we detect in Ellen White less vacillation than efforts to seek by different means her central goal, which was to promote church unity for an effective advance of the gospel. This led her to alternately support or rebuke individuals on both sides. It is also clear that although church leaders always coveted her support, she frequently was unable to direct events along the path she wanted.[66]

The political context of these ecclesiastical discussions may not have been apparent to participants, but from a century later one is struck by their debt to the broader American political debate (discussed in chapter 3). The call for control by "the people" reflected a central theme of the Populist Movement in the 1890s. Likewise, Kellogg's invocation of "communism" was a typical smear against any perceived radicalism. Oddly, in this situation Daniells and the "establishment" became purported agents of radicalism, while Kellogg could take the conservative high ground of economic liberty. But Kellogg's defense of independent church organizations also anticipated chronic tensions in the later twentieth-century church: What should be the relationship of independent ministries to the North American Division? Percy Magan's and E. A. Sutherland's founding of Madison Institute is properly seen as the beginning of the self-supporting tradition in Adventism. But Kellogg should also be acknowledged as a champion of the movement through his incisive critique of efforts at institutional consolidation.

THE SEARCH FOR RESOLUTION

Arthur Daniells was dealing with one of those issues that awaken administrators in the early morning hours: an intractable policy dispute that is also a bitter personality conflict. The Kellogg-church leadership struggle remained chronic for another full year, with acute phases occurring during the subsequent fall and spring church sessions. The frustration must have been all the greater since both sides appeared ready to bury the hatchet in the weeks following the Oakland General Conference session.

In late April 1903, the IMMBA (dominated by Kellogg) held its legal meeting in Battle Creek. The meeting became a focused occasion for reconciliation. A. T. Jones read to Kellogg a testimony from Ellen White, which he tearfully accepted. Daniells and Prescott followed his lead. More dramatically, both Kellogg and Daniells appeared together at the Tabernacle the next day to publicly pronounce that "all our difficulties have been settled without being discussed," Kellogg melodramatically announced. He would surrender plans to control Adventist medical work and revise his theology in *The Living Temple* to boot.[67]

Things were not settled, of course, and no amount of lachrymose speech making would alter that fact. Adventist leadership suffered from a naïve view of conflict resolution. Bring the contending parties together; read a testimony; pray; profess a changed heart: the formula was standard.

But the underlying differences persisted, and the truces would be short-lived. In this case, the April *rapprochement* lasted but a few months before the animosities resumed.[68]

Troubles returned in part because Kellogg persisted in marketing *The Living Temple*, brazenly soliciting help from various conferences and sanitariums. He also was soliciting from churches the names of the brightest young people to make a part of the medical work in Battle Creek. Both conference presidents and laymen contacted General Conference headquarters wondering how they were to respond. Daniells was "greatly troubled over the efforts to draw our young people in large numbers to Battle Creek." He had a simple response: he was following the Lord's advice to take his family and leave the city. This may seem a clear answer, but Daniells fretted that he ought to do more. He confessed to Willie White that he was haunted "day and night" about whether he should in fact take a stronger stand and positively warn parents about the "perils to which [their children] would be exposed." Daniells hesitated to speak out, though, because "everything I say and do against this will be communicated to Dr. Kellogg, and will perpetuate the conflict." "I do not want to fight," Daniells wrote with unfeigned weariness. "I want peace."[69]

In the month and a half before the Autumn Council convened on October 7 (the first to be held in Washington), Daniells received a steady flow of reports from the field about Kellogg and his book. His most faithful correspondent was J. H. Washburn, who, while on the camp meeting circuit, kept Daniells current about the appeal for young people to come to Battle Creek. Washburn and others also gave reactions to *The Living Temple*, which, now published, had gained a wide reading among pastors, some of whom volunteered to Daniells their concerned reaction.[70]

More significantly, he received an unusually direct message from Ellen White (neither she nor Willie attended the upcoming meetings). She was drawing near the end of her patience with Kellogg, and from this point forward would advise Daniells to stand firm against his actions. Her new resolve came in part from her opening the pages of *The Living Temple*. She had resisted reading it until Willie finally persuaded her that she needed firsthand knowledge about the disputed text. She now understood the need for a public statement. Kellogg's claims that his words were her words were only slight exaggeration. "There is a similarity of expressions, it is true," White admitted, "and many of the words are the same as the words used by me." Such phrases as "God in nature" were used by both. But similarities were more apparent than real, she insisted. A mind "under the deception of Satan" might interpret Kellogg's meaning as hers. "But this is not so." She could no longer communicate directly with Kellogg, at God's command. So she depended on Daniells to champion truth. She counseled him to be cautious: "Do not precipitate a crisis, work silently." Like a five-star general exhorting his army, she commanded, "Quit you like men; be strong. Make no raid against any one, for you are warring not against men, but against principalities and powers."[71]

Daniells no doubt appreciated her support. But he hoped the fall church gathering would be the first general meetings in a year unvexed by Kellogg's affairs. Missions, budget, education: normal church business cried for undivided attention. But "the issue" could not be suppressed. A group of some ten Kellogg supporters (Jones, Waggoner, and Paulson notably—the doctor had not yet arrived in Washington) forced the matter into debate. The same tired discussion of *The Living Temple* ensued: Did it promote pantheism or did it not? Should the denomination promote it or not? Ellen White was far away, and apparently in the minds of many leaders, out of mind. When Daniells had a particularly painful encounter with David Paulson at the end of the day, he was discouraged.[72]

The despair was short-lived, though, because upon returning to quarters he found a reception party awaiting him. "Deliverance has come!" one told him. Their elation concerned testimonies from Ellen White that spoke to the issue of the moment. The next morning, Daniells, no doubt with unusual satisfaction, read her missive that, as the minutes recorded, gave "solemn warnings regarding the teachings of the book 'Living Temple.' " (As if this was not enough, Prescott reprinted the testimony in its entirety in the *Review and Herald* the following week—the entire church would see Kellogg's indictment.) In her very first paragraph, White wrote she felt "compelled to speak in denial of this claim" [that the book's teachings were sustained by her writings]. As Daniells read, he heard many "amens" from the assembled men. The moment, in Daniells retelling to White, was saved. A minister arose at the end of the reading and invited all who wished to "stand firm with Sister White in this great struggle" to stand. Nearly all did so. Kellogg, when he arrived, professed a similar spirit of unity, even meeting privately for theological discussions with Daniells and Prescott. The *Review* happily reported to the church that "our hope is renewed that this people will go forward with a united front, to accomplish the work committed to them in this generation."[73]

But rumors of reconciliation were always premature. Even Ellen White's ongoing flow of letters condemning the "sophistries" in the book turned the tide only slowly. Indeed, within a couple of months Daniells had cause to worry again that Kellogg's forces had gained her ear. Technically, Prescott was still charged with vetting *The Living Temple* to bring it into theological line. He had in fact given up the task. But word spread that the General Conference Committee would release an acceptable text of the book shortly; further, that Willie White had agreed to the minor changes. Most troubling, of course, were rumors that Ellen White herself was yielding to the doctor's blandishments. Percy Magan, an ally of Kellogg's who also found favor with both the Whites, circulated the disturbing report that she had commented that Daniells and Prescott were "trying to knife Kellogg." Could Daniells count on her support?[74]

Thus, in early 1904, with his spirits again low, Daniells appealed to the church's prophet in two ways. First, he pleaded with her and Willie to move to Washington for six months or a year. He needed her immediate advice on the pressing details of establishing new headquarters. And his desire to keep her close no doubt came partly from his desperate desire to have some control on who got her ear.[75]

Second, Daniells addressed to Ellen White perhaps the most remarkable letter of his career. As in all his correspondence, his tone is calm and measured. But his ten-page missive also conveys his depth of feeling about the Kellogg issue and its threat to the church's mission.

Daniells sought to impress on White the seriousness of the moment. How so? Because reconciliation between the medical and church leadership factions appeared unlikely. Daniells had lost confidence in Kellogg's sincerity, finding him "devious, misleading, and confusing." Although Daniells continued to protest that there was nothing personal "between the Doctor and me," that posture was now hard to credit. Too much roiling water had gone under the bridge. He recounted that water in some detail, beginning with the debate over rebuilding the Battle Creek Sanitarium and going on to the bitter dispute over purchasing land in

England. Daniells found appalling how Kellogg would mislead one group about his plans, then boast to Daniells about his dissembling. "He gloried in the success of his game of bluff." Even worse, Kellogg "worked to undermine my confidence in the Spirit of Prophecy." He recited example after example of times when the testimonies were untrustworthy. Daniells, who gave the appearance of possessing an administrator's proverbial tough hide, nonetheless was wounded. Kellogg's remarks "pierced my heart, and left a poisoned arrow there to destroy me."[76]

More recently, the unending dispute over *The Living Temple* was wearing him down. Kellogg would not give up on its publication and distribution through church channels. Daniells sought to discourage the book's promotion, both in America and abroad. Its teaching, he implied quite directly to G. B. Starr in Australia, were part of a devil's brew of false teachings that included theosophy, Christian Science, New Thought, Higher Criticism—all part of the "deadly science of evil."[77]

These "deadly germs," of which Kellogg's reputed pantheism was an example, could not be allowed to infect Adventism. But the possibility of this was real, most dangerously because Ellen White's supposed endorsement of *The Living Temple* (and criticism of church leaders) was being widely bandied about Adventist circles. "How many such letters [about *The Living Temple*] are being sent through the denomination no one knows." Daniells was perhaps feeling intimidated by the potent group Kellogg had gathered who were "squarely opposed to the policy of the General Conference Committee." And the fear that they had captured the church's prophet for their own purposes was foremost in Daniells's mind as he wrote to White. He chided her gently (and certainly unconsciously, since his respect for God's anointed was great) for not using her testimonies to give clear support to the church administration's position on the book. "It is this evil, deceptive trading on your influence that gives these men influence, causes great confusion, and makes our work terribly hard." Daniells insisted that he and his compatriots did not expect to be commended by name in her testimony. But the public must not think that "they [Kellogg's faction] have a private walk to your residence, and that they are in close personal touch with you."[78]

Looking back from more than a century later, one might be tempted to view Daniells as an alarmist. Could matters within the church have been that bad? Yet a union conference official had reported to him that David Paulson (a member of the medical party to be sure, but still a judicious individual) told a group of workers that a split within the church was coming. If the *Review and Herald* (then under Prescott's editorship) did not "fall into line" [with the Kellogg group], an alternative church paper from Battle Creek would be started.[79]

Daniells worried that his letter was too blunt. "If I have written a word that I should not, forgive me." But he wanted White to know that, unlike Israel of old—always backsliding—he was determined not to compromise the Advent movement. Perhaps nowhere else did Daniells allow his righteous indignation to flash forth as in this letter. "I am jealous for the cause." He was also jealous for White's influence being, as he saw it, perverted to an unholy end.[80]

Despite the discord, General Conference and medical leaders could not avoid working together to make important decisions about the old Battle Creek College property. Although suspicions about Kellogg's personal agenda abounded, and church leaders resisted his campaign to entice talented youth to Battle Creek, they still recognized that physicians and nurses needed to be trained. Thus, the newly styled American Medical Missionary College, an adjunct of Battle Creek Sanitarium, required support.

Providing this support ran into two difficulties emblematic of the denomination's chronic problems. First, the old Battle Creek College had a large debt, which neither removal to Berrien Springs nor the *Christ's Object Lessons* campaign effaced. Thus, the Missionary Acre Fund campaign was launched, a nationwide effort to assist what had once been Adventism's national college. Second, the revived Battle Creek school raised again the matter of denominational control. In the fall of 1903 a new association was founded as an interim owner of the campus property until the debt was paid, at which time the IMMBA would be permanent owner. (The campus classrooms, labs, dormitories, et cetera, were already occupied by some six hundred students.) Readers of the *Review and Herald* were reassured that the arrangements guaranteed that the property be "as secured *to the denomination* as any human piece of machinery or human device could make it" (italics in the original). As with so much else in these dealings, assurances proved transitory.[81]

The final attempt at reconciliation proved to be the most contentious. It came at a Lake Union Conference meeting in Berrien Springs in May 1904. Kellogg, himself worn out by the two years of struggle, considered resigning his leadership of the Association during the sessions until stalwart churchmen Butler and Haskell persuaded him otherwise. (Daniells had earlier resigned from the board, shocking E. A. Sutherland with the statement that "its dealings were so crooked" that he could not be a part of it.) Ellen White made the difficult journey east to Michigan in hopes that her presence might yet save the moment. It would prove to be a moment of great disappointment. And it displayed again the complications of prophetic advice in administrative or theological issues.[82]

Things likely would have been smoother if the word *pantheism* had never been uttered—it could only mean more contention. Prescott, who, given his past dalliance with the concept, was on shaky ground thundering against Kellogg, planned a major address on the topic. He had Ellen White's blessing to do so. But then she had second thoughts. She gave her son a note to pass on to Prescott imploring him to desist. But Willie never delivered it—and Prescott continued with his plan, giving a pointed address that so enraged Kellogg that he walked out. (If ever there was an incident that supported charges that Willie sometimes controlled the ministry of his mother, it would be at this moment.) But Kellogg's supporters remained, and they collectively gave Prescott a verbal beating, which continued a few days later with an unrelenting attack by Jones. Ellen White made desperate appeals for unity (believing that Kellogg still had a window of grace for his soul), but they went unheeded. A human tragedy struck during the meetings; Percy Magan's wife died after a long illness. Rumors had it that White held Prescott and Daniells partly to blame for her death.[83]

Kellogg felt that the Berrien Springs meetings provided, if not complete exoneration for him and his ideas, at least a show of his faction's strength. Though some Adventist leaders exhibited the now-expected confession of heart, Kellogg refused to display "a mere form intended to meet the emergency." He sought to take advantage of the moment, pushing harder for financial support for his enterprises and book. But these goals became nearly impossible when, during the meetings, he resigned from the Association, deciding that if church leaders so badly wanted control then they could have what was by now a heavily debt-laden holding company.[84]

Through this excruciating mid-May week in Berrien Springs, Daniells must have keenly perceived how even an adept, forceful leader could have events fly completely out of control. His and Prescott's reputations had taken a hit. They now seemed to some the inflexible, difficult ones. And learning the true state of financial affairs at the IMMBA could only have been a further blow.

But A. G. Daniells's resilience served him well. He (ably assisted by General Conference treasurer I. H. Evans) rolled up his sleeves and went to work on the mountain of paperwork, organizational complexity, threatened lawsuits, and debts that the Battle Creek institutions represented. It was a task that would occupy many months. Daniells, though without formal training in business or accounting, seemed at his best in these slogging endeavors. He had patience and apparent native ability to think through complicated financial and organizational matters.[85]

If the Lake Union Conference meetings witnessed the bitterest moments, in retrospect it also marked the end of the struggle. Ellen White and W. W. Prescott would have no more talk of pantheism, nor consider Kellogg's book. He made a few more changes in the text, then published it again under a different title. The legal negotiations over Battle Creek property continued, of course, with nasty moments, but the outlines of the final settlement were becoming clear. Kellogg would keep the Battle Creek Sanitarium and its college campus; the IMMBA would soon cease to exist; and all future medical work (including the new Washington Sanitarium) would come more directly under church control. The age of the stock-subscribed, quasi-independent associations was drawing to a close.[86]

When John Harvey Kellogg was disfellowshiped by the Battle Creek Church in 1907, it was a tragedy for Adventism but not a surprise. He had not attended services nor returned tithe for several years. Given his oversized presence within Adventism, the end was remarkably quiet.[87]

RETROSPECT

So was Kellogg a pantheist? Such statements as "There is a tree-maker in a tree, a flower-maker in the flower" seem hard to interpret any other way (unless one dismisses them as the shallow page-filler of a man who talked more than he thought). But Kellogg was not a theologian, and his theories of health drove his religious reflections. He may well have crossed the theological line into a notion of God's indwelling presence throughout creation. But he did so at a moment in Adventist history when there was much haziness on the subject. The 1888 righteousness by faith message—vital as it was—encouraged within the church a spirit of theological experimentation. Extreme notions about the fruits of sanctification (à la Waggoner) were bandied about the church. And although Adventists carefully distanced themselves from other Protestant groups, without question the appearance of holiness groups on the American landscape influenced fringe Adventist movements. There was much talk of Jesus' living within us. Ellen White herself penned many eloquent lines (in *Education*, notably) celebrating the ability to perceive God in nature or Christ's dwelling in man that, taken alone, could be construed as leaning toward a sort of mild pantheism. Ironically, even Prescott, the man who led the charge against Kellogg's views, had to defend himself against charges of pantheism in these years. During his period of health enthusiasm, he once wrote that "God Himself enters into our bodies in the taking of food." This was, his biographer argues, an unfortunately loose use of language rather than an ontological statement. But it illustrates how Kellogg's views were only going a step or two beyond what one found in the Adventist mainstream.[88]

As noted above, Kellogg was quick to claim that his teachings were no different from those long heard from Prescott or Ellen White. He also sent out lengthy circular letters to an array of church leaders extolling the virtues of the Adventist health movement, the contributions of a rebuilt Battle Creek Sanitarium, and evidences of divine healing, all packaged in a rhetorical mix by turn humble and boastful. For their part, most Adventist leaders gave Kellogg the benefit of the doubt for as long as they could, preferring to think he was victim of some bad judgment rather than purveying heresy.[89]

In a sense, Adventism's struggles with Kellogg, Waggoner, and Ballenger bespoke its lack of theological sophistication. Still a young church, it had no seminary, no core of trained theologians, and no clear sense of how Adventist beliefs fit into the longer tradition of Protestant thought (or even whether Adventism desired—save for identifying with a few admired reformer groups—to be part of that tradition). The church's leading scholar, J. N. Andrews, was long dead, and though there were many individuals both intelligent and astute in biblical scholarship, none had the theological grounding to carefully articulate religious thought. To be sure, Ellen White, Uriah Smith, Daniells, and other church luminaries would not have viewed this as a problem. Biblical truths were understood to be accessible to all. Sincere study by amateurs (using that term in its best sense—referring to those who love an endeavor), if blessed by God, could lead to truth. This was the tradition of William Miller, Hiram Edson, James White, and other early figures. But looking back from our vantage point, we can detect the limitations of this tradition.

Daniells viewed his struggle with Kellogg's teachings as so significant that his late-life and partially autobiographical *The Abiding Gift of Prophecy* dedicated a chapter to the incident. Though more than three decades after the events, Daniells writes of them with vividness and passion. He admitted to being responsible for suggesting that a medical book—what would become *The Living Temple*—be written as a fund-raiser for rebuilding the Battle Creek Sanitarium. Daniells focused on the early concern over pantheism in the text and the decision of the General Conference Committee not to support the book's distribution. He describes well the protracted debate (though not the early assurances given Kellogg that the project would go forward) and the agony the issue caused him. At one point, Daniells recalled, a young church worker sympathetic to Kellogg's work predicted that if Daniells persisted in opposition, he would be "rolled in the dust." Relief came in the form of two messages from Ellen White warning of the book's influence. The tide was turned against Kellogg, and, as Daniells claimed in the chapter title, the denomination was saved from pantheism. In his typical fashion, there is no boasting or self-aggrandizement in his recounting. For him the episode comprised yet another example of God's providential leading through His prophet.[90]

What Daniells does not admit in his very public retelling of the incident (though it is hard to imagine he had forgotten) was the crisis of faith to which Kellogg had subjected him. But he confided this fact to Willie White in mid-1904, shortly after the contentious Lake Union Conference meeting. By this point, Daniells had not only lost patience with Kellogg but had come to view his theology as a true threat. "He will fill these poor fellows with his ideas and spirit until they will be utterly confused and lost in the mist and fog of subtle philosophy and sophistry." Daniells was speaking from experience. Though he does not say when he felt the greatest allure, clearly at some point during the previous year or two Kellogg nearly created another disciple. "I was once on the very verge of ruin by those very subtleties," he testified. Only "God in his great mercy" saved him from "the insinuations of doubt that man had sowed in my mind." It was a remarkable moment of confession from the emotionally self-controlled and unswervingly orthodox Daniells. Which of Kellogg's many words tempted him? Pantheism? Doubtful. More likely it had to do with Ellen White's inspiration and authority. Fifteen years later he faced accusations of insufficient confidence in the Spirit of Prophecy. This would explain why in his latest recollection of this episode he could not admit to any vacillation on her inspiration. His legacy, as well as Ellen White's, was at stake.[91]

Nor does Daniells confess to any heavy-handed tactics in dealing with Kellogg and his allies. But it is clear that he could play political hardball. Daniells could assume an intimidating manner, as when (by Kellogg's account) during an argument he "straightened himself up against the wall and looked down upon me in a most imperial and kingly way." He would also take other leaders to the metaphorical woodshed via letter. "I was very sorry that you and Brother Sutherland deserted me at a critical point in my conversation with Doctor Kellogg," he scolded Magan in 1902. "You should have stayed with me and enunciated right principles." He did not hesitate to solicit help in attempts at persuasion. Daniells, Prescott, and Willie White, Magan wrote in his diary "curried me down. I am Korah, Dathan, and Abiram. A great conspirator. The maker of a mighty effort vs. administration." If arm-twisting failed, Daniells was prepared to demand resignations—which he did from the capable but independent-minded Magan. "He did not think we pounded J. H. Kellogg hard enough over the matter of his different heresies," Magan recalled decades later. Thus he was asked to step down from a clutch of positions in the General Conference.[92]

Daniells's punishing actions bespoke an administrative pressure that was taking him to the breaking point. The conflict between Arthur G. Daniells and John Harvey Kellogg was the most bitter leadership feud in Adventist Church history. Two antagonistic camps—ministerial and medical—were headed by two of the most strong-willed individuals the denomination has seen. For all of the conflict's vicissitudes, the outcome was seldom in doubt. Daniells's determination and sense of providential direction would not allow him to retreat. Further, he retained the loyalty of most church workers. Conversely, Kellogg, though certainly a formidable personality and secure in the loyalty of a legion of medical workers, was erratic and not always trustworthy. If leading churchmen respected his brilliance and ability to draw attention to the Adventist message, they nonetheless became suspicious of his motives (not to mention his theology). They understood that his primary commitment—no, his obsession—was with health, not the evangelistic mission of the church.

But the conflict, unfortunate as it was, signified no permanent breach between the official church and the "right arm" of the ministry. Neither Daniells, Prescott, Ellen or Willie White ever questioned the vital role of the medical work in Adventist outreach. Indeed, scholars of the Adventist experience have argued that church culture became even more "medicalized" in succeeding years. In 1909, the church would establish another medical school in Loma Linda, California. Care would be taken to ensure the church's control of the institution. Having given up one medical training school, Adventist leaders would be careful not to surrender another.[93]

Of course, Daniells knew nothing of the future. What he knew was that Adventism's task of warning all nations of the world's soon end was compromised by internecine struggle. And he knew that the stress of the General Conference session and the unrelenting conflicts with Kellogg and his followers beginning in 1902 had worn him down. The Oakland meetings had put him through "a heavier strain than I ever experienced before," he confided to Willie White, and he hoped he would "never have another experience like it." These were more than just the words of a tired man. Daniells reached a point—very early in his presidential tenure—when he had to reflect on his leadership philosophy. How could the pitched battles of the recent past be avoided without surrendering to principles he felt were wrong? "I am now studying very seriously the question of my attitude in the future. . . . It is very uncertain to me what course I shall pursue." His personal faith, however, in this moment of discouragement, was unwavering. "I will stop here, and let the Lord teach us all what to do as we come to our difficulties day by day."[94]

This resolve would be tested in coming years, not only as the Kellogg and Jones conflicts played out, but also in an equally difficult administrative challenge: his handling of the successful black evangelist and pastor Lewis Sheafe.

---

[1] AGD to H. W. Cottrell, April 24, 1902; AGD to A. M. Neff, August 29, 1902; AGD to W. D. Salisbury, April 11, 1902, GCPL.

[2] AGD to G. I. Butler, July 3, 1903, GCPL.

[3] AGD to A. M. Neff, August 29, 1902.

[4] AGD to WCW, August 26, 1902; AGD to W H. Thurston, August 26, 1902; AGD to R. M. Kilgore, August 26, 1902.

[5] Valentine's *The Prophet and the Presidents*, chapter 8, offers a full discussion of the background to the 1903 General Conference Session.

[6] *RH*, March 24, 1903, 7; GCCMin, February 11, 1903, February 15, 1903; *GCB*, April 6, 1903, 96.

[7] *GCB*, March 30, 1903, 16.

[8] *GCB*, March 31, 1903, 22–25.

[9] Ibid., 17–19.

[10] Ibid., 18, 20.

[11] Ibid., 18.

[12] Ibid., 21.

[13] Barry Oliver's *SDA Organizational Structure* (pp. 184–198) provides an in-depth narrative of the presidential title dispute, which I rely on heavily in my discussion. George Knight's *Organizing for Mission and Growth* (pp. 114–116) explicates the theological basis of Jones and Waggoner's position.

[14] AGD to WCW, July 1, 1901, ASTR.

[15] AGD to WCW, May 24, 1901, ASTR; Oliver, *SDA Organizational Structure*, 194.

[16] AGD to C. C. Nicola, July 30, 1906, EGW Research Center, SWAU.

[17] *GCB*, April 10, 1903, 145.

[18] Ibid., 147.

[19] Ibid., 147–149; Woodrow W. Whidden II, *E. J. Waggoner: From the Physician of Good News to the Agent of Division* (Hagerstown, MD: Review and Herald®, 2008), 243–246. Chapter 11 details Waggoner's theological basis for his views on authority.

[20] *GCB*, April 10, 1903, 150, 151.

[21] Ibid., 151–154.

[22] Ibid., 155. Jones's effectiveness as California Conference president was a subject of dispute. His early energetic work seemed to hold promise. But he could be overbearing and abrasive, and even his early champions, such as Willie White, soon changed their minds. Daniells, for example, got a scathing report on Jones's leadership from conference secretary M. H. Brown. Jones was gifted at promulgating "great principles" and "grand thoughts." But when it came to "practical work in conference affairs, he is utterly impractical because of lack of executive ability, judgment and wisdom." He verbalized a desire for counsel from others, "yet so strong and masterful is his personality and his convictions, that he brushes aside the views of others unless they agree with his views." It was "painfully apparent to brethren of experience" he was "not adapted" to the work of leadership, and it "would be an injustice" to Jones and the "cause in California" for him to be reelected. M. H. Brown to AGD, August 8, 1902, ASTR. Daniells got it about right with his observation that Jones

"will need a whole committee to keep business affairs in proper shape." Quoted by Oliver, *SDA Organizational Structure*, 192, 193.

[23] *GCB*, April 10, 1903, 151.

[24] Ibid., 157, 158.

[25] Ibid., 159, 152.

[26] Ibid., 160.

[27] Ibid., 161–163. Butler stressed that whatever the constitutional arrangements, leaders must have the right heart. In his thirteen terms as president, he recalled, "I was never reproved for any such thing [exercising imperious authority], as I can remember." If Butler forgot, a number of the veteran church leaders could have reminded him of pointed letters of advice from White about this very thing. Butler was not known for being shy about the prerogatives of leadership.

[28] Ellen White did weigh in on the matter in a letter the following year to P. T. Magan, one of the signers of the minority report. She made it clear that in 1903 a "president" needed to be chosen, a man in harmony with God's plan. That man, she felt, was Arthur Daniells. Oliver, *SDA Organizational Structure*, 200; Valentine, *Prophet and the Presidents*, 220, 221.

[29] Oliver, *SDA Organizational Structure*, 165–173.

[30] Ibid., 195, 218.

[31] On Jones and *One-Man Rule*, see George R. Knight's *From 1888 to Apostasy: The Case of A. T. Jones* (Washington, DC: Review and Herald®, 1987), 208.

[32] Richard William Schwarz, "John Harvey Kellogg," 21–43.

[33] Ibid., 170–178.

[34] Charles Landis Anderson, *Charles Landis Anderson Remembers* (Bruce Anderson, 2002), 19.

[35] On the sociology of the medical-clerical split, see Malcolm Bull and Keith Lockhart, *Seeking a Sanctuary: Seventh-day Adventism and the American Dream*, 2nd ed. (Bloomington, IN: Indiana University Press, 2007), 300–303.

[36] Ibid., chap. 17.

[37] AGD, untitled memo on Kellogg confrontation, prepared for WCW, March 6, 1903, ASTR.

[38] Ibid.

[39] On Loughborough's experience, see Brian E. Strayer, *J. N. Loughborough: The Last of the Adventist Pioneers* (Hagerstown, MD: Review and Herald®, 2014).

[40] Ibid.; A. L. White, *EGW: The Early Elmshaven Years*, 202, 203.

[41] WCW to AGD, April 9, 1902, ASTR; AGD to J. H. Kellogg, April 14, 1902, GCPL.

[42] AGD to J. H. Kellogg, April 14, 1902; AGD to WCW, April 14, 1902.

[43] AGD to W. A. Spicer, June 2, 1902; AGD to David Paulson, June 5, 1902, GCPL.

[44] AGD to ? M. Graham, December 11, 1902; AGD to L. R. Conradi, November 6, 1902; AGD to H. W. Cottrell, November 6, 1902, GCPL; Kellogg sought to assure Daniells that these policy disputes were not personal. "I judge from some of the remarks you made Thursday evening that you have in your mind the idea that I have a personal animosity

toward you, a personal dislike for you, or something of that sort. I wish to assure you that this is not the case and never has been." J. H. Kellogg to AGD, November 2, 1902, ASTR.

[45] The careful recording of Ellen White's comments in these highly charged church political battles, to be used at key moments of verbal engagement, indicates the influence she carried. "Report of a portion of a council-meeting held at Mrs. E. G. White's home, 'Elmshaven,' St. Helena, Cal., 8:00 a.m., October 19, 1902," EGW Research Center, SWAU.

[46] Ibid.; J. H. Kellogg to AGD, November 2, 1902, ASTR.

[47] GCCMin, November 11, 13, 1902; AGD, untitled memo to WCW, March 3, 1903; Moon, *W. C. White*, 282.

[48] GCCMin, November 13, November 20, 22, 1902; Valentine, *Prescott*, 173.

[49] GCCMin, November 22, 1902; Valentine, *Prescott*, 173.

[50] GCCMin, November 20, 1902.

[51] GCCMin, November 25, 1902; C. W. Flaiz to AGD, November 15, 1902, ASTR.

[52] AGD to H. W. Cottrell, August 25, 1902; AGD to N. W. Allee, December 6, 1902; November 6, 1902, GCPL.

[53] EGW to AGD, September 5, 1902; January 23, 1903; A. L. White, *EGW: The Early Elmshaven Years*, 191; Valentine, *Prescott*, 177–181. Gil Valentine also chronicles the complex relationship in his *Prophet and the Presidents*, chapter 9.

[54] AGD, *Abiding Gift of Prophecy*, 335, 336.

[55] Schwarz, "Kellogg," 380, 381, 391, 396.

[56] Schwarz and Greenleaf, *Light Bearers*, 268–270, provides an excellent discussion of issues of ownership and control; *GCB*, April 3, 1903, 67; April 22, 1903, 223.

[57] *GCB*, April 6, 1903, 73–75.

[58] Ibid.

[59] Ibid., 75, 76.

[60] Ibid., 76, 77.

[61] Ibid., 77, 78.

[62] Ibid.

[63] Ibid., 80.

[64] Ibid., 81.

[65] Moon, *W.C. White*, provides details of Kellogg's machinations to replace Daniells; P. T. Magan, diary, April 5, 1903, LLUASP.

[66] *GCB*, April 6, 1903, 87; EGW to AGD, April 12, 1903; Valentine, *Prophet and the Presidents*, chap. 9.

[67] Schwarz, "Kellogg," 398, 399.

[68] Ibid., 399, 400.

[69] AGD to H. W. Cottrell, July 30, 1903; George Watson to AGD, August 7, 1903; AGD to WCW, August 9, 1903, ASTR.

[70] J. H. Washburn to AGD, August 13, 1903; September 4, 1903; September 8, 1903; E. J. Dryer to AGD, August 25, 1903, ASTR.

[71] WCW to AGD, September 23, 1903; EGW to AGD, September 18, 1903, ASTR.

[72] A. L. White, *The Early Elmshaven Years*, 296, 297; AGD, *Abiding Gift of Prophecy*, 336, 337.

[73] AGD, *Abiding Gift of Prophecy*, 337; *RH*, October 22, 1903, 8, 9. A. L. White, *The Early Elmshaven Years*, 299, 300; Valentine, *Prescott*, 176. An elated Daniells wrote White that her message had come "at just the right time exactly." AGD to EGW, October 20, 1903, EGW Research Center, SWAU.

[74] Valentine, *Prescott*, 177, 178.

[75] AGD to WCW, January 13, 1904. EGW Research Center, SWAU.

[76] AGD to EGW, January 8, 1904. EGW Research Center, SWAU.

[77] AGD to M. E. Olsen, January 12, 1904; AGD to G. B. Starr, January 4, 1904, ASTR.

[78] AGD to EGW, January 8, 1904.

[79] Ibid.

[80] Ibid.

[81] *RH*, October 29, 1903, 20, 21; June 16, 1904, 17; AGD to I. J. Hawkins, January 17, 1902, GCPL.

[82] Schwarz, "Kellogg," 400, 401; Valentine, *Prescott*, 178–181, provides a good overview of this ill-starred meeting; E. A. Sutherland to AGD, January 4, 1904, ASTR.

[83] Valentine, *Prescott*, 179, 180; A. L. White, *The Early Elmshaven Years*, 336, 337.

[84] Schwarz, "Kellogg," 401–403.

[85] Daniells's correspondence with the church's attorney, Jesse Arthur, indicates the complexity of the Battle Creek legal issues. See, for example, Arthur to AGD, December 21, 1903, and December 31, 1903, ASTR.

[86] Schwarz and Greenleaf, *Light Bearers*, 270, 271; EGW to AGD, June 15, 1904; Valentine, *Precott*, 181.

[87] Schwarz, "Kellogg," 406–409. Kellogg did not go, however, without some self-justification. In 1907 he gave an extensive interview to A. C. Bordeau and G. W. Amadon of the Battle Creek Church, where he provided candid appraisals of his Adventist experience. He settled theological scores with Prescott and Ellen White and administrative scores with Daniells.

[88] Quoted in Valentine, *Prescott*, 172, 182. Valentine provides a complete discussion of this issue in his book, pp. 171–185. On the American religious context, see Sidney Ahlstrom's older but still serviceable survey, *A Religious History of the American People* (New Haven, CT: Yale University Press, 1972).

[89] Kellogg claimed parallels to his ideas in a chapter of her new book *Education*. Schwarz, "Kellogg," 387–390; J. H. Kellogg to L. F. Starr, December 27, 1904, ASTR.

[90] AGD, *Abiding Gift of Prophecy*, chap. 30.

[91] AGD to WCW, July 2, 1904, GCPL.

[92] Schwarz, "Kellogg," 395; AGD to P. T. Magan, September 29, 1902, GCPL; P. T. Magan, diary, March 5, 1904, LLUASP; P. T. Magan to Herbert G. Childs, July 31, 1939, CAR. Despite these measures, Magan retained his loyalty to the denomination and even reached a working relationship with Daniells. He wrote letters of apologies to certain church leaders. It is unclear if he included Daniells in this group.

[93] Bull and Lockhart, *Seeking a Sanctuary*, 312, 313.
[94] AGD to WCW, May 13, 1903.

CHAPTER VII

THE COLOR LINE

Arthur Daniells, the child of pre–Civil War Iowa, whose travels before his move to New Zealand included only Michigan and Texas, experienced an America that was racially homogenous and ethnically European. His nearly decade and a half in New Zealand and Australia offered some exposure to aboriginal peoples, but their degraded condition could hardly have elicited respect from him. Thus, when Daniells had his first serious encounters with America's African American population during his trip to the South in 1901, he had little "diversity" experience upon which to draw. Complicating matters, the Adventist Church was just then confronting the thorny issue of the color line—in society and within its own midst. Daniells would have to draw deeply upon his administrative wisdom and personal values in navigating the shoals of race.

A NEW DIVERSITY

The Adventist Church of which Daniells assumed leadership was still an overwhelmingly northern and white organization. Founded in New England and centered in Michigan, its primary growth was toward the Midwest, upper Midwest, and California, but with an increasing presence in other parts of the United States (and the wider world—a story for the next chapter). Only slowly did it establish beachheads in the South. Although the northern Adventist membership was no longer exclusively Anglo-American, diversity there meant Germans and Scandinavians.

But the South was going to be another story. Here, diversity meant polarity: blacks and whites. The American South in the 1890s and early 1900s represented the most rigidly segregated social order our nation has ever known. "Separate but equal," the Supreme Court ruled in 1896, was permissible public doctrine. In practice, separation was enforced, but equality was observed much more often in the breach. And the enforcement of separation could be brutal. These decades marked the high point of lynching (nearly all of whose victims in the South were black), a socially sanctioned form of racial control. No challenge to the prevailing customs was brooked.[1]

Adventist workers encountered these hard truths soon after entering the Southern field. Adventism's entry into the South had been fitful until the 1890s. Early work was primarily in the states of the upper South and in Texas (where Robert Kilgore, an important leader in the region's work, came in 1877). Efforts for whites and blacks advanced on separate tracks. Tradition-bound and loyal to Baptist tenets, southern whites generally found Adventist eschatology and seventh-day convictions unappealing. Work went forward slowly. Efforts for southern blacks would prove to have their own difficulties. And for some years it appeared that General Conference leaders saw them as a low priority.[2]

This began to change in 1891. Ellen White, who had said little about race or the black population since the Civil War, produced a testimony that in strong terms called for aggressive evangelism among southern blacks (America's black population was then overwhelmingly in the South). "You have no license from God to exclude the colored people from your places of worship," she counseled a General Conference session. "They should hold membership in the church with the white brethren." She went on to urge a vigorous mission effort among America's black population. Her words initially appeared to fall on deaf ears, for her influence in the church was then at a low point (she would be encouraged by leaders to travel to Australia, where she spent most of the 1890s) and her message was not a popular one. It would take several years for the church to respond, and then only because her occasionally wayward son Edson took up the challenge.[3]

Having undergone a recent spiritual conversion, Edson found an outlet for his new enthusiasm in his mother's call for black evangelism. Along with recent convert Will Palmer, he commissioned the construction of a paddle wheeler, the *Morning Star*. After establishing their work for some months in Vicksburg, the boat navigated the waters of the Yazoo River in Mississippi. It docked at landings along the river, setting up a school in one region before traveling on to Yazoo City at the border of the delta. Evangelism had to proceed carefully, especially in introducing the Sabbath to people strongly attached to a Sunday day of rest. White published a missionary tract, *The Gospel Herald.* Education and rudimentary welfare services were extended to local residents who were but a few decades removed from slavery. But local white backlash against the efforts at black advancement and the ill effects of a Deep South climate ultimately forced Edson to move further north to Nashville, where racial attitudes were less inflammatory.[4]

This was the situation when A. G. Daniells assumed church leadership. Just a couple of months into his new term, he made a June trip to Chattanooga and from there to Washington, D.C. (see chapter 4). Daniells testified that this, his first exposure to the South, immediately stimulated interest in the challenges of evangelizing its people. This was fortunate, because he had immediate challenges to face.[5]

The "colored work" issues challenged Daniells on two fronts. The first was located in the South. At Nashville and then beginning in 1896, at a new institute in north Alabama named Oakwood, organized work for southern blacks moved forward. The other front was in the nation's capital, where an urban black congregation was quickly growing. Here, the question of whether an integrated congregation could thrive—or should even be attempted—caused Daniells ongoing distress.

NEW INSTITUTIONS FOR THE SOUTH

Edson White's earlier troubles in the Mississippi Delta were not restricted to local whites. He also endured distrust and indifferent financial support from Battle Creek church headquarters. Edson's efforts in the South were a true endeavor of faith. His mission boat evangelism bordered on the audacious. He stepped into a homeland missionary field that no one else would touch. His intrepid venture risked health to climate and personal safety to mobs. When he needed money, he authored a highly successful *Gospel Primer*, royalties from which (along with small allocations from the General Conference) covered expenses. Still, money was always a problem. The blame did not invariably fall on him. The *Gospel Primer*'s success led the Review and Herald press to begin a rival paper, abruptly cutting off Edson's income. Furthermore, his and his associates' salaries seemed chronically late in arriving (this partially because of general shortfalls in church finances and the organizational disarray the church experienced in the late 1890s).

Even Edson's staunchest supporters (including family members) admitted that he occasionally lacked judgment and almost always wanted for financial acumen. Church leaders considered Edson reckless and sometimes irresponsible. He seemed untrustworthy as an institutional leader. Tensions continued even after the move to Tennessee. These followed his establishment of a third Adventist publishing house, what would become Southern Publishing. Discouraged with the Review press, he sought to publish inexpensive material for the Southern field. But the venture quickly fell hopelessly into debt. Daniells and other church leaders, despite their strong interest in the Southern work (see chapter 4), ultimately felt they must close down the press.[6]

But Ellen White's increasing interest in the Southern work could not be ignored (though her distant location throughout the 1890s attenuated the force of her admonitions). When Daniells assumed leadership in 1901—and the Whites resided much closer in California—he and she regularly discussed the Southern field. Her advocacy of black evangelism surpassed the coincidence of her elder son's involvement; she possessed a genuine burden for America's black population. This was aided by a visit to the *Morning Star* in Vicksburg. The spring visit in 1901 (shortly before the memorable General Conference session) must have been immensely satisfying for a mother who witnessed the greatest triumph of her inconstant son.[7]

Edson's original church organization was styled the Southern Missionary Society. In 1901, after the General Conference reorganization, the Southern Union Conference was established, with the existing Society now charged specifically with the African American work. Although Edson worked under veteran leader Robert Kilgore, he remained influential (and controversial) in the Southern field. Controversy came in part because he, probably before any other Adventist leader (and certainly before his mother), conceded that evangelism must bow to Southern social mores. His schools were segregated, evangelistic audiences divided by race. He had to defend himself to northern Adventist brethren. "We have done this because it is *the only way we can work.*" Edson knew of what he spoke; he and his associates faced direct threat when they gave the slightest hint of challenging prevailing racial customs. But his approach become one more thing for which some criticized him.[8]

Compounding difficulties, his new publishing venture in Nashville reinforced the image of Edson as a profligate spender. From his small printing press aboard the *Morning Star*, White grew an ambitious and immediately debt-ridden publishing house. In Daniells's early months on the job, already burdened by managing church-wide debt, he had to make hard decisions about what to do with Southern Publishing's red ink. Encouraged by Ellen White, the General Conference took over Southern Publishing in 1901, installed a new manager—and continued to run deficits. Matters appeared resolved during a meeting between leaders and Ellen White at her home in Elmshaven in the fall of 1902. In the same conversation in which Daniells described his efforts to rein in Kellogg's spendthrift ways, he raised the vexing matter of Southern Publishing. Ellen White, though bitterly disappointed, conceded that church leadership should do what it must to get the denomination on sound financial footing. Daniells returned to Michigan pleased by her approval; the Nashville facility would be scaled back to essentially a book depository for the South. But in a turn of events without parallel in her career, White received a vivid message from God. A messenger instructed her that she had made a mistake by giving in to Daniells's plea. "Let the Southern field have its own home-published books," she announced.[9]

The Southern Missionary Society continued to promote black evangelism in the South. But after a key executive meeting in Nashville in early 1902 (which included A. G. Daniells), Edson White refused any further official function. Whether it was because hard-liner G. I. Butler had assumed union presidency is not clear. Readers of the *Review* were assured that Edson's withdrawal was his choice and that he continued to preach to large and enthusiastic congregations. Indeed, the Nashville region, particularly after the founding of Madison School in 1904 by E. A. Sutherland and P. T. Magan (with Ellen White's assistance in siting the school), became well known as the birthplace of Adventist self-supporting work.[10]

The center of black education in America had in the previous decade moved to a rural farm near Hunstville, Alabama. What would be styled "Oakwood" (for its majestic trees), the 360-acre estate was purchased by the General Conference in 1895. The following spring an Iowa farmer,

S. M. Jacobs, was invited to head south and become farm superintendent of the new institution. The curriculum of the Oakwood Industrial School was influenced by Booker T. Washington's famous Tuskegee Institute in the same state. Black youth would help run a farm, through which they were to earn their board and room (tuition was initially free). Male students focused on trades such as carpentry or masonry, while females were tutored in the domestic arts. Within a few years a normal program trained teachers for the region's black schools. The educational agenda aimed at modest improvement in the lot of Southern blacks. But considering their poverty and the strident racism of the day, this represented progress. "No people in our land have been so downtrodden," the *Review* told its readers, "and from a human standpoint, the task would seem a hopeless one." But like the story of the loaves and fishes, the few workers and their limited resources would have "an uplifting influence that will be felt in all directions."[11]

Daniells found at Oakwood a growing school of some fifty students. But to thrive required strict economy on the part of students (some who literally had not a dollar to their name) and the institution. In the new spirit of Adventism, Oakwood's leaders determined on a "no-debt" policy. At the aforementioned Nashville conference in 1902, Daniells had a chance to see the products of the school, its "colored students," whom he described as "earnest, intelligent, promising young people." These were the future workers who would take "this blessed message to their race."[12]

Daniells, at this early point in his career when his chief concern was evaluating the effectiveness of the 1901 reorganization, seemed generally pleased by the results of the new Southern Union Conference. The union was given administrative oversight of Oakwood but lacked the financial means for its support. Thus, though Daniells was supportive of Oakwood, he told conference leaders that the school must do more to pay its own way (threatening the tuition-free policy). But Daniells did not pull the rug of General Conference support from under the school or union conference. Recognizing the region's relative poverty, the General Conference Committee authorized use of portions of the "second tithe" from other unions, a fund normally reserved for overseas missions. The Southern work remained, in one sense, a mission field.[13]

Thus, a pattern of segregated work for whites and blacks marked the Adventist evangelism in the mid- and Deep South from its beginnings. It could hardly have been otherwise, as Edson White and other leaders in that field grasped. Unwise challenges to the color line could only bring trouble. When R. M. Kilgore got wind of an article planned for the *Review* that challenged the South's social institutions, he prevailed upon the General Conference Committee to have the piece removed. It threatened to "do great harm in the Southern field," Kilgore warned. E. R. Palmer concurred. "Every reference calculated to arouse prejudice should be carefully eliminated." Daniells described the article (and there had been others like it) as "very offensive." Not only were the printed copies rounded up and destroyed, but the episode helped seal Uriah Smith's final removal as editor.[14]

Church leaders, including Daniells, had clearly concluded that in the South segregation could not be avoided. But it was still unclear what church policy should be elsewhere in the country. And Ellen White, though not at the center of decision making, was still officially on record as stating that racial prejudice should not sully her beloved church.

TENSION IN THE NATION'S CAPITAL

The Adventist work in the South occurred among a population highly rural and with little education. In Washington, D.C., however, the church began attracting converts from the upper end of black society. But if church leaders hoped that this would lessen racial consciousness among white churchgoers, they were soon disappointed. Indeed, the story of black-white church relations in Washington established the dynamics of future race relations in the Adventist Church. It also posed to Daniells a delicate administrative problem.

The U.S. capital held a unique place among American cities. One must first recall that it was established within the boundaries of slave territory, on the banks of the Potomac. Slavery had a long history in Washington (only abolished by Congress during the Civil War). The town's essential culture was, and long remained, Southern. Lacking the influx of European immigrants that populated other northern American cities, Washington was composed of native white residents—and many blacks. It housed a large free black population even before the Civil War, and afterwards the District became a common destination for former slaves heading north. Further, the federal government became a favored employer for those blacks who achieved a modicum of education. In an America—North and

South—that long displayed racial hostility toward them, the federal government was the least prejudicial employer (this being a matter of degree). Thus, Washington came to host a black elite, a group highly conscious of its privilege within the larger black community.[15]

But in the 1890s the status of even the relatively privileged African Americans in the nation's capital began to erode. Lines of segregation previously unknown (and even illegal) in the District began to appear. Worse, coveted federal positions diminished in number. Leaders in the still-dominant Republican Party, long the champion of free blacks, seemed less concerned about reserving for them more than a token number of civil service or politically appointive positions, and those government jobs that remained fell in the lower clerkships. Racism had come to America's capital. This bit of history is important, because the conflict within Adventist congregations there and between Lewis Sheafe and General Conference leaders was played out against its background.[16]

Daniells's first hint of trouble came during his initial visit to Washington in the summer of 1901. He spent two days there, witnessing an evangelistic effort underway on behalf of the local 200-member church. But all was not well. "The color question is a live one there," he informed Ellen White. He noted differences between the racial environment in Washington and in the Deep South, sensing that the less severe form of discrimination in Washington might actually pose a trickier situation. He learned that the tent meetings failed to have the desired outcome. Not that people were not attending, but the racial mix was undesirable. White membership was in decline while that of the black rose. The prejudice of whites against meeting with blacks was evident, and if trends continued, the Washington church would become black.[17]

Daniells did not blame black members for this. On the contrary, "the colored people have been more energetic in their missionary work. They have talked with their people about the truth, and have induced them to come to the meetings." But he regretted the imbalance in the local church. He told Willie White that he never had to think about this issue before. But his mind was now focused on the great American dilemma of race. He came to some early conclusions. First, that the Adventist Church must increase its "earnest efforts in behalf of the colored people," and in Washington particularly, since the city had the largest proportion of blacks among any American city and "as a rule they are a superior lot of people." Let this congregation become a black one headed by a minister of its own race and then bring in a "white laborer for the white people." Daniells's approach was utterly pragmatic. He did not mean to endorse white prejudice, "yet for the sake of the hundreds of unconverted people who have those prejudices," it was better to have two churches.[18]

While in Washington, Daniells also had his first encounter with Andrew Kahlstrom. A Swedish immigrant who had progressed to a position in the United States War Department, Kalstrom was an influential elder in the local Adventist church. Daniells stayed with Kahlstrom during his Washington visit. Kahlstrom was remarkably free from the racial prejudice that plagued his adopted homeland. He let Daniells know that he expected his church to be equally color blind. The Swede continued offering his insistent advice, to Daniells' consternation.[19]

Daniells reached one other consequential decision during his Washington trip: the black Adventist worker right for the job as Washington evangelist/pastor was Lewis Sheafe.

APOSTLE TO BLACK AMERICA

Lewis Sheafe, Adventism's first great black pastor-evangelist, was born three years before the beginning of the Civil War to free parents in Maryland. By contemporary standards of black Americans, he enjoyed unusual advantages of freedom and education, being raised in Massachusetts. For men of his race, no career offered more opportunities for service and position than the ministry, for which he trained at Wayland Seminary in Virginia. There is no reason to believe that he had any acquaintance with Adventism at this point in his life. At a young age Sheafe landed a pastorate in Saint Paul, Minnesota. This Baptist church, founded by runaway slaves, became a lively center of worship and social life for the local black community. He later moved to a church in Ohio, where again he enjoyed success as a spiritual leader. Although he was a Baptist, Sheafe displayed a trait that in retrospect foreshadowed his Adventist experience: he was not one to be tightly bound by denominational loyalties. He embraced both interdenominational and interracial efforts. He was a local leader of the Christian Endeavor movement, an early temperance organization. Sheafe would today be considered a progressive Christian.[20]

His introduction to Adventism remains a mystery. He had assumed the aforementioned Saint Paul pulpit the same fall as the momentous Minneapolis General Conference session, but that seems an unlikely source of conversion. However his initial attraction to Adventist belief occurred, it is clear that his experience at the Battle Creek Sanitarium in 1896 was decisive. Sheafe's talents were quickly discerned. He was even invited to preach in Adventism's leading pulpit that summer. Furthermore, John Harvey Kellogg became something of a patron. Sheafe "is an orator, a wonderfully able man," Kellogg enthused. He "can deliver a more forcible address than any other Seventh-day Adventist minister." Sheafe's commitment to health reform further endeared him to Kellogg.[21]

Sheafe was quickly put to work, first in Ohio, where he presented a series of evangelistic meetings. Despite his recognized talents, in Columbus "a big color line" arose, giving the intense but personable Sheafe a discouraging setback and intimations of things to come. Likewise, Sheafe's independent ways challenged leadership—another augury. Still, Sheafe's gifts were so obvious that leaders worked hard to find his proper niche. At the landmark 1901 General Conference Session, Sheafe (who was employed directly by the General Conference) was assigned to labor among the South's black population.[22]

But Southern Union leaders saw little merit in having a charismatic black preacher in their midst. Within two months of the General Conference session, R. M. Kilgore, president of the new Southern Union Conference, implored Daniells to take Sheafe back to the North. The issue, to Kilgore, was simple: Sheafe would not respect the need for thorough segregation in evangelistic work. Daniells, who had not yet made his initial visit to the region and did not know Sheafe well, sought to reassure all parties. He also addressed the vexatious matter of Sheafe's remuneration (the General Conference ultimately agreed to keep him on its payroll). The incident represented the first union conference–General Conference dispute since reorganization.[23]

Thus, when Kilgore informed the General Conference Committee in October that Sheafe had "widened the breach between the races in the South," and two others testified to similar problems, members yielded to regional prejudices. Sheafe's northern upbringing and education gave him ways at odds with the South. Though Kilgore and others did not use the term, Sheafe was what the region's natives would call an "uppity" black, one refusing to supinely accept conventions of segregation. They recommended that he should be transferred to a city where there was no existing Adventist work that he might endanger. Daniells would not give Sheafe a straight answer regarding his next assignment, but as it turned out the president had formulated a clear plan. He would place Sheafe squarely in the racially volatile situation in Washington, D.C.[24]

What may now appear to have been a risky strategy rested on Daniells's hopes to solve three problems at once: first, remove Sheafe from the Deep South; second, separate white and black Adventist work in the District; and finally, place Sheafe in a locale where his abundant talents could advance African American evangelism. Daniells clearly liked Sheafe. But how best to use him? A parallel in the world of sports would be a team possessing a terrific athlete, capable of changing the course of a game, but whose best position on the field was uncertain and whom teammates viewed with suspicion.[25]

Daniells unveiled his strategy at Southern Union meetings in Nashville in early 1902. Although the gathering was primarily to plan work in the South, Daniells also had Washington on his mind. Candid conversation took place behind closed doors about "the color question," fears being voiced of a looming racial war in the South "unless the Lord prevents." It was essential, leaders said, that "our people must not insist on talking about the equality of the races, and encouraging mixed congregations." This would only damage the advance of the gospel. No better expression of the traditional Adventist retreat from political or social activism can be found than in this discussion. "The time in which we live, and the message we have to give," Daniells summarized, "demand that we shall not waste our time in squabbles over the color question, but that we direct our energies to the salvation of both races." The "popular cry of elevating the colored man" was not to be the church's refrain.[26]

Daniells went on to outline his plans to a group that included Sheafe and the other black preachers. In carefully chosen words, Daniells advocated for "colored people working for their race, and the white ministers and people working for their race, and of having separate meetings wherever is seemed best." He avoided saying anything about separating the Washington congregation by force, but he felt this would be the rapid consequence of his policy. None of this was to suggest that leadership intended to "leave the colored people to themselves, nor neglect friendly counsel and cooperation." Following his talk, Daniells spoke at length to Sheafe, who, he later wrote Atlantic Union president H. W. Cottrell, "agreed with me fully."[27]

Daniells believed in consensus and sought to nurture it among his leadership team. He cherished the cooperative spirit between whites and blacks that he perceived at Nashville. "I do not think there was a dissenting voice to the arrangement; and so far as I know there was not opposition from the colored people." This apparent harmony must have added to Daniells's pain when the amicability eroded over the following years. But his future disappointment had its seeds in his failure to properly read Sheafe. He underestimated his commitment to a color-blind ministry. When Daniells spoke to Sheafe of the "folly" of black Adventists courting "trouble over the race question" and lectured him about how "the true Spirit of Christ" set a different agenda for black preachers, he spoke sincerely but with a failure to grasp the black condition. He too glibly dismissed the desire for equality (as did his other colleagues), even as he grasped the pragmatic social necessity of separate work in Jim Crow America. Daniells had great hopes that separate white and black congregations in Washington could be a model for Adventist race relations elsewhere. He did not invoke Jesus' metaphor of "city on a hill" to describe his hope, but the thought might have crossed his mind.[28]

For the moment in early 1902, Sheafe was sent to Ohio. He held efforts in various locations, while Daniells and Cottrell laid the groundwork in Washington. They needed to secure a white pastor with the abilities to labor in the difficult racial environment. That man proved to be Judson S. Washburn, recently returned from England, where he had a decade's success under his belt. Washburn was hard driving and self-confident in his ability to manage church tensions. But Daniells knew that Washburn had not yet confronted Kahlstrom, whose determination to present to the world a color-blind church would prove a formidable obstacle to the Nashville plan. Daniells's worries led him to solicit George Butler's help in prepping Washburn for his new post.[29]

Daniells, still not even a year into his presidency and as yet unscarred by the upcoming Kellogg-Jones battles, approached Sheafe in a conciliatory manner. He did not order him to Washington but asked if he would be willing to assume the post—and if he would be willing to do so under the terms agreed upon in Nashville. He confided in Sheafe the great hopes of the denomination for evangelism in Washington, the resources already poured into efforts there, and the need for him to cooperate with Washburn. "I do not believe there is another opportunity in the world like this for helping your people." Daniells never shed all doubts about Sheafe; still, he invested great hope in him. By late spring Sheafe had moved to the capital and undertook evangelistic meetings in a gospel tent. By midsummer he was attracting crowds of fifteen hundred. The effort went on into October, six days a week. Sheafe's spectacular success earned coverage not only from the city's black newspaper but even in the *Washington Post.* Importantly, the meetings were biracial.[30]

All this was to the good. Daniells assumed that Sheafe agreed to the plan of racial separation first laid out in Tennessee and later reaffirmed at meetings in Des Moines. But he soon suspected a straying from the Nashville strategy. Following the evangelistic effort, a new congregation was to be formed in Washington composed of the white converts and Caucasian members of the integrated First Church. But resistance to the plan was clear even in early June, when the First Church congregation passed a resolution that "no distinction, nor discrimination on account of race" should be attempted. Certain white laypeople, such as Kahlstrom, and prominent black congregants, like Dr. James K. Howard and Rosetta Douglass Sprague, daughter of legendary antislavery activist Frederick Douglass, called on the denomination to stand for principle. The scheduled meeting in September, where formal division was to occur, promised fireworks.[31]

In these early years of denominational reorganization, Daniells hoped the benefits of a decentralized polity would show forth in difficult moments such as these. He did not attend the Washington meeting, but he encouraged leaders from the Chesapeake Conference and Atlantic Union Conference to control the situation "with a firm hand." "The General Conference will not turn you down in any way," he promised union president H. W. Cottrell. As feared, a strong core of First Church members opposed the congregational division. W. A. Spicer, representing the General Conference as an observer, wrote Daniells that the opposing faction were in "thorough battle array." They suspected, wrongly, that the "colored folks" were going to be removed to make way for the white group. In fact, they were left with the church building, and the white members (those who wished to go—between forty and sixty) decamped for new quarters.[32]

This was a relatively satisfactory ending, it would appear, given the tense dynamics of the situation. "The Lord gave us a decided victory," Cottrell reported. The "white refugees" gathered at Washburn's tent to organize the new church. But inklings of future trouble lay in the refusal of the church board to give the property deed to the conference (the members had law on their side). Spicer, not a man to avoid confrontation, took on the task of interrogating Sheafe about why he appeared to renege on the earlier understanding. Sheafe insisted he intended no departure from the earlier plans, but Spicer was not persuaded. "I do not know that he is true and loyal to us or not," he wrote Daniells.[33]

Suspicions would remain on all parts. Daniells pointedly wrote Cottrell that Sheafe had to make a clear decision. As a direct General Conference employee (not that of the Chesapeake Conference), he must work in accordance with General Conference decisions. If Sheafe would not, then he should inform the conference and ask for an assignment other than Washington. Lacking that, he ought to labor on his own. Daniells hoped things would not come to a parting, for he genuinely liked Sheafe and respected his abilities.[34]

As if Sheafe's maverick ways were not enough, Daniells also had to contend with J. S. Washburn, who was chafing at the backseat he was taking to his black counterpart in Washington Adventism. Washburn's long and rhetorically overheated letters to Daniells and Ellen White bespoke an obsessive personality that left no room for nuance or shades of gray. As already discussed, he proved to be an effective advocate for moving denominational headquarters to Washington. And he exerted a strong influence on Daniells regarding the Washington church matter. Washburn complained that Sheafe's tent efforts were far outdistancing his own; he feared that the rapid growth of the now primarily black First Church would make it the dominant force in the Chesapeake Conference. He even reported that Sheafe was championing interracial marriage (a questionable assertion at best). Washburn's church would benefit over the years from generous General Conference funding (compared to Sheafe's). But all of Daniells's support did not prevent Washburn from ferociously turning on him years later.[35]

Washburn certainly had no cause for complaint about support from the General Conference. An aggressive fund-raising campaign in the *Review* raised money for a "Second Adventist Church" in Washington. Lewis Sheafe's mixed-race congregation at the First Church could not help noticing that none of the $10,000 raised helped them pay off their church debt. Daniells, despite his disappointment with Sheafe's interracial stance, continued expressing to Ellen White support for Sheafe and the African American work in D.C. Large in number and the best educated of American blacks, he hoped this group could be the source of Bible workers to be trained and sent into the American South.[36]

Perhaps sensing that the General Conference president could be persuaded, the First Church prepared a formal petition to church leadership asking for a portion of the funds raised for Washington's newer church and for a white minister to aid Sheafe. They based the first request on grounds of sheer equity; the second they justified on the grounds of the church's active growth (certainly among the fastest of any Adventist church in North America) and on fully one-quarter of the congregation being white (with new white members still being added). But Washburn, proud of the social pedigree possessed by some of his new congregants and fearful that a mixed-race church in town might taint Adventism's cachet, mounted an effective campaign. He lobbied Daniells, Ellen White, and no doubt others against supporting the First Church. The General Conference Committee meeting that summer concurred. No help was forthcoming.[37]

This refusal occasioned an articulate and heartfelt call for a color-blind policy. Dr. James K. Howard, an influential layman of the First Church, was a man of wisdom and eloquence. His letters to Daniells and Ellen White remain among the most impressive in church archives. In the summer of 1903, as Sheafe was in the midst of another successful evangelistic series, Howard expressed disappointment to Daniells that leadership had not provided a white preacher to labor alongside him. An opportunity to "present the pure gospel" (uncompromised by considerations of race) should not be missed. Howard sought to be tactful, but he felt compelled to tell Daniells straight up about the "terrible and growing evil of the influence of race bias in your General Conference Committee." His fellow church members expected bias from some, but had hoped that Daniells's could provide a corrective. Perhaps only Ellen White similarly spoke to Daniells in such a voice of prophetic reproof. "I tell you plainly, Brother Daniells, with all respect, that you and your Committee are grievously wrong in your course and policy on the race question. And you are wrong at a time when the world is growing more in this respect and so much needs your wise and corrective influence."[38]

Howard appealed to Daniells's principles and idealism. But Daniells's response was couched, as was often the case, in pragmatic necessity. The Adventist Church was then facing one of its most vexing moral dilemmas. A movement sympathetic to the end of slavery in its early days and with a prophet who had gone strongly on record opposing segregated churches, now faced huge pressure to conform to evolving social customs of segregation. How should it respond?

Daniells had no doubt about the church's proper priority: It was to propagate the gospel of Christ. The world is "like an old sinking ship," and the church must "rescue the people who are going down." With the world on the brink of destruction, attempts at social betterment could only be palliative, not transformative. Adventism must keep its eyes on the prize. Daniells expected black Adventists to willingly—if not cheerfully—subsume their desire for social equality to the gospel imperative. It was "folly," Daniells wrote to conference president H. W. Cottrell, for Adventists to be troubled over the "race question."[39]

But Howard would not concede Daniells's point. "The compromising plea of expediency, policy, the demands of the world and doing the thing that good may come, is too weak and unworthy of our cause," Howard powerfully argued. "The white people are injured by such a course not less than the colored people." In words that must have been calculated to cut to the heart of those striving for lives of sanctification, he wrote, "It would seem that while the people of the world will disregard each other more and more because of national differences, the people of the Savior would be all the more careful not to seem to justify the others in their wicked discriminations." Daniells—and by extension the entire white church—could not be persuaded. Evangelism must trump all other considerations.[40]

Was this moral blindness? A failure of institutional leadership? Or was Daniells's social pragmatism justified? Decades later, the church's response remains open to arguments on both sides. The case for bowing to Jim Crow laws in the Deep South seems beyond debate. Segregation was being relentlessly enforced, sometimes by lynch mobs. Could the same policy be justified, though, for the more educated and racially moderate city of Washington? Although segregation embedded itself in the nation's capital as well, it would seem that a window of opportunity presented itself for modeling a biracial worship community. Sheafe's biographer, Douglas Morgan, regrets the loss of an opportunity involving "nothing less than becoming a beacon of light for the entire nation during its darkest hour of racial oppression."[41]

If modern readers find themselves disappointed by the moral timidity of earlier Adventist leaders, mitigating factors should be considered. Despite some dalliance with abolitionist causes during its Millerite phase, Adventism lacked a vigorous reforming tradition. True, it had joined forces with the temperance movement, but the overwhelming consensus on the issue by Christian groups made that reform safe. The one political issue on which the church took unpopular stands was religious liberty. Here, denominational leaders departed from the usual stance of political quietism. But this concerned a matter of clear denominational self-interest. It proved difficult—impossible really—for the church to risk its stock of institutional influence on other controversial matters.

It did not help that Ellen White resisted giving clear counsel on the Washington church situation. By 1903 she still had not made the transition from her strong 1891 position against segregation to her influential 1909 concession to Jim Crow. In the late 1890s she began tempering her earlier statements, warning that distinctions between white and black should not be completely ignored. To Dr. Howard's appeal in 1903 she (through her secretary) could only respond that she had no more light, and they must "work this question out for themselves" until the Lord reveals more.[42]

CONGREGATIONAL INDEPENDENCE

But for several years, beginning in the fall of 1903, Daniells hoped that the vexatious race problem in Washington had been resolved. The Indian summer of race relations was facilitated by the move of General Conference headquarters to Takoma Park in August. The proximity of Daniells and his General Conference associates to District churches heightened both interest and communication. Daniells and Sheafe maintained regular contact.

Even better from Daniells's perspective, Sheafe displayed a new enthusiasm for distinctively black evangelism. In November 1903, at Daniells's urging, he established a second church, styled the People's Seventh-day Adventist Church, a black congregation. Daniells himself spoke at the dedication service, a gratifying moment for him. There were now three churches in the District, a white, a mixed-race, and a black congregation. Harmony beckoned. "As the matter now stands we can please anybody and everybody on the color question."[43]

Yet Daniells promised more than he could deliver. This was not for lack of effort. He responded to Sheafe with what seemed good-faith efforts at cooperation. Daniells showed personal interest in Sheafe's church, even appearing for special occasions such as an ordination. The two conferred about candidates to bolster the ranks of black Adventist pastors. Daniells spoke of establishing a black training school in Washington to train workers for the South. Most tantalizing, Daniells implied that there could be financial help for the People's Church building debt.[44]

But old differences resurfaced, and Daniells's conventional grasp of racial matters constrained his imagination. Further, his primary commitment was to building up the new headquarters and sanitarium in Takoma Park. The $100,000 committed to that strategic move forestalled General Conference financial support for the People's Church (though Daniells himself argued—unsuccessfully—for an appropriation). Not surprisingly, Sheafe and his parishioners grew weary of counsels for patience, particularly when the Memorial Church (Washington's white congregation) was the beneficiary of a $10,000 fund-raising campaign heavily promoted by the *Review and Herald*. By 1906 it was clear that Sheafe was considering taking his church outside the organized denomination. Daniells understood the dynamics at work, regretted them, yet seemed unable to deflect the inevitable. Sheafe had him at wit's end. Daniells and other General Conference leaders concluded that Sheafe had ambitions that trumped church loyalty. Their refusal to subsidize his church only made alienation all the more inevitable.[45]

In early 1906 the People's Church petitioned the General Conference to clarify the church's position on segregated medical and educational facilities in the Washington area. Color lines were quickly hardening even in the more moderate and cultivated upper South. Where, the petition implored, could colored members find an Adventist "hospital or sanitarium whose doors are opened" to them? Where could their youth "be educated along God's appointed lines"? Until answers to these pointed questions were provided, the petition asked "the privilege of using its tithes and offerings" for such purposes.[46]

Obviously, threats to withhold tithes called for administrative response. But circumstances dictated that a formal reply from Daniells and his associates was delayed until late spring. Before then, in April, Daniells and three associates held two meetings with People's Church members that turned acrimonious. Daniells displayed a tin ear to the concerns of his hearers when he expounded at length on the denomination's work among the colored people of "the Dark Continent." He also noted, more to the point, that the church had spent thousands on black evangelism in the South. Further, seeking understanding from Sheafe's impatient parishioners, the world church was spread terribly thin in its widespread mission efforts. His appeal for understanding was not well received. A "spirited discussion" ensued, the *Review* euphemistically reported.[47]

A second meeting was called for later in April. Again, Daniells arrived at the meeting trailing a delegation of church notables, including former General Conference president George Irwin. Church members wanted answers as to why Adventist medical and educational facilities were not available to them locally. Antagonisms quickly surfaced. Daniells and Irwin delivered long addresses, implying, as one observer commented sarcastically (and probably unfairly), that black folk should keep "out of sight, out of mind as much as possible," so as not to impede the gospel's going forward. Then Sheafe got up and unloosed a stem-winder, so that "the fire burned." Sheafe said he knew leadership was considering taking away his credentials. But he cared "that much" about the threat, as he snapped his fingers. His commission came from God. "The GC folks were real uncomfortable," a witness added with delight, "and could not conceal it." Daniells several times sought to interrupt Sheafe to correct him in some of his claims. Perhaps more upsetting to Daniells was a follow-up speech by Charles Shaffer, who as elder at the First Church (the integrated church) had taken up the departed Kahlstrom's role as the white defender of a liberal church racial policy. Shaffer lectured church leaders on the impropriety of segregation. "You have no license from God to exclude the colored people from your places of worship." He objected to Daniells's desire that the "color question" not even be brought up at the meeting. This was the heart of the matter, in his view. "It has been the scheme of the devil to get men committed to the folly of making distinctions where no differences exist." Why would leaders think that "association with our colored brethren" should imperil the gospel?[48]

Shaffer's comments may seem naïve, given the racial conditions of that day, but the well-crafted rhetoric further inflamed hearers. As Daniells and others sought to reply, Sheafe's wound-up members laughed in his face. "He got so mad that he began to quarrel with them from the desk," until he finally sat down. Daniells, the model of self-control, had reached his limit.[49]

Bruised by the experience, Daniells finally led the General Conference Committee through a discussion of the People's Church petition. In response, Daniells composed one of the most carefully crafted church position statements of his career. Given the nature of the subject, he knew his response had to be couched in delicate though straightforward terms.

"The race question is the real question at issue," Daniells admitted. But, clinging to the administrative latitude coveted by all institutions, he noted that Seventh-day Adventists had "never attempted any official action to define or settle what is commonly known as the color-line question." The testimonies, he continued, gave "explicit instructions that this should not be done." Daniells was correct that White's counsel on matters of race was undergoing change, and she would no longer decry segregated policies. In practice this meant that "every conference committee, church Board, and minister is left free to adjust the perplexities of this difficult problem according to the circumstances and the necessities" of the local situation.[50]

Daniells also wanted to assure the People's Church members that "no true Seventh-day Adventist" can cherish prejudice because of race. "The blessings of the gospel are for all alike." He was sincere in this sentiment. But Daniells cherished even more the central commitment of his presidency. "Adventists have been given the task of proclaiming to all men the everlasting gospel." Not "socialism, civic reform, and modern humanitarianism are the vital questions for them to deal with." His list did not include racial integration, but the implication was clear. These concerns were not Adventist concerns. "We have no time to get into contention over the color line"; indeed, he continued, "it is a privilege to set all such questions aside."[51]

Hoping to pacify Sheafe's congregation—and probably hoping to define a policy that could forestall problems going forward—Daniells laid out a nine-point statement that he hoped would meet with their approval "and prove a basis of union and cooperation in our work." Some of the points reiterated the need to subordinate personal rights to gospel mission. But he also included a General Conference mea culpa. General Conference members were "aware that in the past they have come far short" of doing what they wished for immigrant groups and black people. More specifically, efforts should be made to educate black Adventist youth in the Washington area and that this required General Conference funding. This was all to the good. But the final two points threatened to snatch defeat from the jaws of victory. Daniells noted that the medical and educational institutions in the area were managed by an independent board of trustees, not the General Conference. Inquiries about admission or qualifications must be addressed to them. This was technically true. But as Douglas Morgan points out, this was a "casuistic distinction," for Daniells himself presided over the Washington Training School board. Did he really think this attempt at shifting responsibility would fool Sheafe's members?[52]

Domestic unrest within Sheafe's own household—to the point that his wife began confiding to Daniells her husband's plans to take his church out of the denomination—provided Daniells with unexpected leverage in dealing with the situation. Sheafe and his wife accepted counsel from Daniells, and for a few months the possibility of an accord seemed real. But Daniells's colleagues on the General Conference Committee had no confidence in Sheafe and thus gave no support for funds.[53]

The tenuous peace ended following Sheafe's visit to Battle Creek in November of 1906. Since the removal of church headquarters three years previous, portions of Battle Creek's Adventist community had become rancorously opposed to the official church. Sheafe, whose earliest influential Adventist contacts had been there and whose interest in education and health reform appeared genuine (fueling his resentment that his own people were forbidden entrance to D.C.-area church institutions), reveled in the attention from Kellogg and Jones. Moreover, the two men, approaching the end of their Adventist affiliation, needed no prompting to encourage Sheafe to join them. They recounted to him Daniells's many sins, which now included racial discrimination. Sheafe returned to the capital city renewed in his sense of aggrievance.[54]

Sheafe's alliance with the Battle Creek faction was bad enough, but worse was his persuading his congregation of the General Conference's sins against Kellogg. Then Sheafe refused to share a testimony about the dangers in Battle Creek with his congregants. And when Daniells sought an audience with members, the church board peremptorily replied that it "did not want any more of the controversy." Daniells now had good reason to believe that Sheafe would soon take the People's Church out of the denomination. Desperate for a hearing and with his sense of office offended, he pulled rank, letting Sheafe and the People's Church board know in clear terms that such refusals were not acceptable under the governance structure.[55]

Daniells faced one of most sensitive situations of his presidency. A successful evangelist and a thriving congregation were at risk—as was the denomination's reputation in matters of race. Veteran leader George Butler urged him to take action and not let the situation fester. But Daniells's administrator's intuition told him not to appear the aggressor in driving Sheafe and his congregation away. Instead, he played a waiting game. His caution was rewarded (if such a term can be applied to this unhappy situation) when Sheafe made the first move. Despite Sheafe's repeated assurances to Daniells that he had no intention of leaving the denomination, his church unanimously voted in January 1907 to take advantage of the "rights and privileges of the individual church." In other words, they declared independence.[56]

Daniells had little hope that he could alter what appeared an inevitable course of events. But he felt he ought to appeal to the People's Church congregation at least once more. Sheafe, admitting the propriety of Daniells's request, agreed to an evening session with his members. But the February 13 meeting proved infuriating. Sheafe, determining to be in control, delayed the start until prayer meeting ended. Then he refused to allow the General Conference contingent to speak until all those not members of his congregation had left. Curiosity seekers from area Adventist churches had come, no doubt hoping for fireworks. Daniells did not care who was present, but Sheafe was adamant. After the comic-opera scene of deacons attempting to usher unwanted people away finally ended, the evening had grown late. Daniells had to abridge his presentation.[57]

He began by reminding the members that Sheafe held credentials from the General Conference, having been invited to Washington by that body. The People's Church, though never formally voted in, was from its inception considered a General Conference institution. Its withdrawing from that fellowship would be, Daniells insisted, "a terrible mistake." What has happened to other churches who decided on an independent course? None survived as Adventist churches. He cited the example of Iowa in the 1860s, when the conference president and secretary, disillusioned with Ellen White, sought to break away all the churches. Many did leave, but none survived. The lesson of history was clear.[58]

Daniells faced a group that was, in Sheafe's words, "a well-trained company of soldiers." They sat impassively as he sought to awaken them to the dangers of separation, quoting liberally from Ellen White about how God had led His church. Daniells could not understand how any hearer could fail to be moved by the clear voice of the Lord. Instead, he found "an insolent, defiant attitude . . . that I think I never witnessed before in a congregation." When he finished, there was no debate nor discussion. Members simply filed out of the church. Tithe had not been sent on to the General Conference for several months. In late February, Sheafe returned his credentials to Daniells. The end, apparently, had come.[59]

Daniells was heartsick from the ordeal. He had from the first promoted Sheafe's career against skeptics. He continued seeking money for his church even when its denominational future appeared doubtful. Now he began to get "I told you so" letters from critics. "Bombastic," "big-headed," and "self-confidant," judged Butler, who knew Sheafe in the South. "I think he is just a Baptist Sabbath keeper." Washburn was more scathing; indeed, his remarks bordered on sheer racism. He reminded Daniells of his early warnings about Sheafe. "I believe that he has been a traitor ever since I came to Washington. . . . The man looked positively venomous, and I thought if I should have met this black fellow in the depths of an African forest, and he had had his war paint on, and feathers in his wool, and a white cloth about two feet long around his waist, I should certainly have been frightened at the look on his face."[60]

Daniells's inner thoughts cannot be known, but he never expressed such overt racism. Indeed, with Sheafe on the way out, his thoughts turned to finding another black pastor to take up the Washington work. During the People's Church controversy he maintained correspondence with Sydney Scott, a young worker in the South. He wrote Scott a candid description of the Washington problems. Scott responded with professions of sympathy and profound loyalty to the organization. He clearly wanted to head north. But Butler and Washburn felt certain that if he came his head would be turned by Sheafe. Better, Washburn thought, to bring in white workers to oversee the colored work. "The colored people, as a rule, are irresponsible, and make the most cruel, tyrannical masters on earth." But Daniells would not accept such advice. He would seek the best black candidate to champion the denomination's work in Washington.[61]

Sheafe, however, did not go away. Unlike most Adventist schismatics, who denounced church doctrines and Ellen White's ministry, Sheafe's ministry continued to emphasize Adventist fundamentals (though it is unclear how much attention he gave to the Spirit of Prophecy). Judgments that he was simply a warmed-over Baptist now seemed unwarranted. Further, tantalizing prospects for his and his church's return to the fold appeared over the following year. Efforts at reconciliation were attempted by two of the other leading black workers (all Adventist workers, white or black, recognized Sheafe as the most capable and charismatic black preacher). But the efforts of Sydney Scott and William Green could not surmount lingering obstacles.

At heart, the problem was a lack of trust. Daniells had become convinced that Sheafe, under the sway of Kellogg and Jones, had thrown over loyalty to the organization (in Daniells's mind, a cardinal sin). For his part, Sheafe lost confidence that vague assurances of financial support for his church or for African American educational and health institutions in the D.C. area would ever come to fruition. Daniells conceded that General Conference leadership had perhaps not shown equitable treatment of the white and black churches. But he bridled at suggestions of systemic discrimination or of neglect of black evangelism. He never tired of the rhetorical questions: What of the generous General Conference support of Oakwood? Of black evangelism generally in the South? Of missions in Africa? He increasingly viewed Sheafe as ungrateful and imperious.

Sheafe, conversely, doubted church leadership's sincerity.

In addition, there was the matter of Ellen White. The prophet maintained hope for reclaiming Sheafe well after others had given up. She penned an exhortatory letter to him in early 1907. Its only apparent effect was to arouse Sheafe's suspicion that Daniells had been feeding White biased information. In her letter, White alluded to her conversations with "the brethren in Washington." Sheafe, no doubt informed by Kellogg that White was a tool of her son and Daniells, took her admonitions as coming secondhand from the church powers. Daniells, in a meeting with Sheafe shortly before the latter surrendered his credentials, strongly denied any communication with the prophet about him. But Daniells's denial lacked complete candor. He had had extensive communications with Willie White about Sheafe, and he explicitly authorized him to share the information with his mother. Such parsing of the facts may be no more than a necessary tactic of high-level administration. Daniells no doubt believed that Ellen White's counsel originated in her "night season representation." But Sheafe could be excused his scepticism.[62]

CONGREGATIONALISM REBUKED

What was at stake in the Sheafe affair? Church figures had left the fold before, men of greater prominence than he. And, as mentioned above, Sheafe did not repudiate Adventism.

The danger here lay in what the People's Church departure might mean for future Adventist work in black America. Affairs in Washington were watched closely by the growing black Adventist membership in the South. Concerns about unfair treatment of the General Conference toward the People's Church were widespread. "I was afraid at first that many might go," Southern Union president George Butler wrote Daniells, "and even entire congregations." Would the organizationally disaffected Sheafe spawn a general separation of black churches, much as what had happened in some mainline Protestant denominations?[63]

This prospect troubled Daniells all the more because there was concurrently a strain of congregationalism that Jones, Waggoner, and others were promoting within Adventism. These men had never become reconciled to the reorganization of the church effected in 1901 and consolidated in 1903. The struggles with Kellogg and Jones in the following years resulted in a clear victory for Daniells and Prescott for control of the denomination. But failing in that, the Battle Creek faction sought a new tactic. Built on Jones and Waggoner's extreme theology of congregational independence, they sought to alienate entire churches from the denomination. Daniells understood the stratagem. "The sanitarium leaders thought that they were strong enough to defeat the General Conference. They have found that they were mistaken. Now what they failed to do by firing a broad-side, they are attempting to do by piece-meal. Their aim is to sow disaffection among the separate churches."[64]

An example of this campaign occurred in the People's Church, where Jones gave a series of talks. Much of it was standard Adventist teaching on affairs of the day. But Jones also included unvarnished attacks on church leadership. Committees and presidents had no place in religious work. When one member sought too persistently to defend the organization, Sheafe silenced him.[65]

Jones, Kellogg, and Waggoner found ready allies. The early years of the century witnessed an unusual number of disgruntled workers. Sheafe, of course, but also New York evangelist E. E. Franke, long a thorn in church leaders' sides, took up the cause. A. F. Ballenger, who had separate theological issues, added his rhetorical talents. Then a dentist, W. L. Winner, penned *Gospel Simplicity*, a well-written tract that argued, in Daniells's summary, "Let every church be supreme in its field, and the sole custodian of its interests."[66]

Such sentiments upset Daniells profoundly. By nature he was an organization man. Order, structure, clear lines of authority—these qualities were central to his make-up. Further, he believed that the 1901–1903 reorganization of the church was ordained by God, as testified to by Ellen White. Appreciating the seriousness of the moment, Daniells undertook authorship of an ambitious fifteen-part series of articles for the *Review,* the most extensive of his presidency. Simply titled "Organization," the series reviewed in great detail the creation of the denominational structure in the 1860s. Daniells chronicled how heated debate accompanied adoption of formal organization. Millerite founders, of course, never anticipated a need for extensive structure. The historical sketch Daniells provides on the early 1860s debates remains useful today. For his purposes, he sought to illustrate that no stone was left unturned in the establishment of the denomination. "The whole question of organization received careful, serious study, and free, full, and open discussion." Moreover, Daniells reported, the very first message Ellen White delivered regarding organization "declared plainly that disorganization was Satan's method of distracting and tearing down" the church. The series' final installment gave a side-by-side comparison of Israel's earliest organization God delivered to Moses and the current Adventist denominational structure. Daniells might well have concluded to his readers, "He who has ears, let him hear."[67]

The denomination's full-court-press support for church structure and unity included soliciting help from Ellen White. In the fall of 1908 she issued a letter to "Our Churches in Washington, D. C.," which decried insistence on social equality or desire for integrated congregations. White made it clear that God was no respecter of races and that social mixing was not inherently evil. The issue was a pragmatic one (not her word); local customs ought to be respected if gospel progress is to be made. The letter had a good effect at the First Church (which had continued its advocacy of racial mixing); the influential Dr. Howard helped solidify that congregation's loyalty to the denomination. Furthermore, there was virtually no defection in the Southern field. Black pastors such as Scott, Green, and Matthew Strachan (who was brought to Washington to take up the African American work) proved both loyal and insightful in advising Daniells on the work.[68]

Indeed, Strachan kept Daniells's feet to the fire, championing certain of Sheafe's long-standing protests. When money was being raised for schools, sanitariums, and churches "for other people, how shall we excuse ourselves from the responsibility of establishing the same for the Negro in Washington?" It was a question that Daniells and other white leaders could only answer with unease.[69]

A sense that more attention should be given to black Adventism finally led to the establishment of a Negro Department in 1909. Sheafe himself had proposed such a thing at the 1901 General Conference Session. It took eight years, a steadily growing evangelistic work among blacks, and the People's Church traumatic separation in Washington to overcome white inertia. A nascent black leadership came together in support of the effort, twelve of whom affixed their names to "An Appeal on Behalf of the Work Among the Colored People." This respectful appeal, along with the precedent set four years earlier when a North American Foreign Department had been created to facilitate evangelism among the considerable northern European immigrant population, made an institutional bow to American blacks almost inevitable.

Fittingly, Daniells himself introduced the proposal at the May General Conference session. As was often his wont, he justified an innovation as necessary for carrying out the counsel of the Spirit of Prophecy. Morever, the Negro Department would allow a more "systematic effort" (charisma and order, the linchpins of Daniells's administrative world) overseeing expenditures on the range of evangelistic efforts. The 1909 General Conference was notable for the number of black delegates present. Daniells gave them all their moment to take the floor—itself a significant statement by leadership. One by one, Green, Scott, Strachan, Humphrey, and several other black workers gave heartfelt testimonies about the needs for their people. Some quibbles occurred over terminology (Is "negro" better than "colored" or Afro-American?) A more discordant note intruded when a black West Indian named W. S. Connolly objected to the notion of a special department. When American blacks shared the same language, unlike the Scandinavians or Germans, what is the need? Sydney Scott quickly took the floor and told him why. "The condition in the South regarding the negro—the color line—is stronger than language." Their exchange augured tension between Adventist West Indian and American blacks that endured for a century.[70]

But approval by delegates proved unanimous. The new Negro Department bespoke administrative recognition of the growing significance of black believers. It did not, however, signal confidence in black leaders to oversee the department. Instead, for the first nine years whites headed its executive committee. Nor did it mean that the General Conference Committee was yet ready to back up its talk with financial support of D.C. black institutions. That thorn remained in place.

But unity there would be. The threat of disabling congregationalism never materialized. Jones, Waggoner, Kellogg, and lesser schismatics drifted off, vexing the denomination no more. Indeed, 1913 brought a great moment of reconciliation. The return of Sheafe and the People's Church came following a year of tentative communications. Sheafe's second wife, a devout Adventist, may have influenced his return. In any event, a dramatic event occurred at the 1913 General Conference Session. Sheafe joined Daniells on the podium, contrite and asking to rejoin the fraternity of Adventist churches. Daniells assured delegates that he had thoroughly vetted the situation and welcomed them back. A number of black delegates rose to second the motion of readmission. With the divisive events of the past decade largely resolved, this feel-good moment must have seemed to Daniells a testament to his vision of denominational structure and unity.[71]

But in history, any final resolution of difficult issues is often elusive. Sheafe was reassigned to Los Angeles, where after a short time he again left the denomination (this time for good) over Ellen White's views on race. The People's Church likewise found new reasons for alienation (partly because it never received the financial help it thought it deserved), ultimately affiliating with the Seventh Day Baptists. Yet neither of these events seriously detracted from Adventism's steady progress in black America.[72]

Daniells's handling of Sheafe, Kellogg, Jones, and other dissidents reveals a man of great administrative capacity. His clear vision for the church enabled him to make decisions with confidence. He possessed the willpower to sustain his decisions against formidable personalities. Neither congregationalism, pantheism, nor any other variations on accepted doctrine would be tolerated. Aided by Ellen and Willie White (and other church colleagues), he piloted the church through various dangerous waters in the century's first decade. Daniells's judgment in times of conflict, though not flawless, was generally sound. For an individual of such powerful will, he also demonstrated remarkable patience and willingness to extend second and third chances to others. In modern leadership parlance, one would say he always kept his eye on the ends he sought to achieve.

But the conflicts Daniells resolved also mirrored a less pleasant face of denominational history. Adventism—then and thereafter—struggled to maintain the loyalty of talented but strong-willed individuals. Denominational culture was narrow-cast and often rigid. This had the advantage of helping maintain a consistent theological tradition over time. But it came at the cost of alienating creative individuals who were frustrated in their attempts to realize their particular vision within the institutional church. Or, as in the case of Sheafe, of becoming alienated by a sense that church leaders were unable to transcend the racism of the age. The individuals mentioned above certainly challenged traditional Adventist customs and/or beliefs—as well as its leaders. Daniells, on the other hand, felt he had to stand firm for the good of the larger church. Yet one senses that the denomination suffered in its inability to retain the presence of those "outliers" (as such people would later be styled). The range of possibilities for the church would be constrained. In a stroke of no small irony, A. G. Daniells, the great champion of Adventist orthodoxy, an utterly conventional man, would himself years later be cast as a doctrinal outlier—and pay a penalty.

---

[1] The literature on Southern race relations in the era is extensive, beginning with C. Vann Woodward's classic, *The Strange Career of Jim Crow* (1955). A more recent survey is Edward L. Ayers, *The Promise of the New South: Life After Reconstruction* (New York: Oxford University Press, 1992).

[2] On Adventism in the South, see Schwarz and Greenleaf, *Light Bearers*, chapter 15.

[3] Quoted in Ronald L. Graybill, *E. G. White and Church Race Relations* (Washington, DC: Review and Herald®, 1970), 14; Schwarz and Greenleaf, *Light Bearers*, 228.

[4] Schwarz and Greenleaf, *Light Bearers*, 225–235, contains a well-detailed survey of the beginnings of black evangelism. Ronald L. Graybill provides in narrative fashion even more description of Edson White's evangelism in *Mission to Black America* (Mountain View, CA: Pacific Press®, 1971).

[5] AGD to EGW, July 12, 1901, EGWE.

[6] Graybill, *Mission to Black America*, 51–54; A. L. White, *EGW: The Early Elmshaven Years*, 189, 190; Schwarz and Greenleaf, *Light Bearers*, 232.

[7] A. L. White, *The Early Elmshaven Years*, 63, 64.

[8] Schwarz and Greenleaf, *Light Bearers*, 234; Graybill, *E. G. White and Race Relations*, 100.

[9] A. L. White, *The Early Elmshaven Years*, 189–194; AGD, *Abiding Gift of Prophecy*, 322–327.

[10] *RH*, May 13, 1902, 19; Schwarz and Greenleaf, *Light Bearers*, 236, 237.

[11] Schwarz and Greenleaf, *Light Bearers*, 235, 236; *RH*, November 17, 1896, 11.

[12] *RH*, January 1, 1901, 13, 14; January 15, 1901, 11; February 4, 1902, 11.

[13] Ibid.; GCCmin, October 23, 29, 1901.

[14] GCCMin, October 28, 1901; AGD to G. I. Butler, April 11, 1902, GCPL.

[15] Green, *Washington: A History of the Capital, 1800–1950* provides the best history of the nation's capital.

[16] Ibid., chap. 11.

[17] AGD to EGW, July 12, 1901; AGD to WCW, July 21, 1901.

[18] AGD to WCW, July 21, 1901.

[19] This section relies heavily on Douglas Morgan's detailed and perceptive biography, *Lewis C. Sheafe: Apostle to Black America* (Hagerstown, MD: Review and Herald®, 2010); A. Kahlstrom to AGD, October 6, 1901; October 29, 1901, ASTR.

[20] Morgan, *Sheafe*, chaps. 1–8.

[21] Ibid., 113–116.

[22] Ibid., 122, 170.

[23] Ibid., 170–173; R. M. Kilgore to AGD, May 20, 1901; September 4, 1901; AGD to B. F. Gowdy, July 12, 1901; AGD to W. T. Wales, July 12, 1901.

[24] GCCMin, October 27, 1901.

[25] AGD to H. W. Cottrell, January 21, 1902, ASTR.

[26] *RH*, February 3, 1902, 11; AGD to H. W. Cottrell, January 21, 1902.

[27] AGD to H. W. Cottrell, February 3, 1902; January 21, 1902.

[28] AGD to H. W. Cottrell, January 21, 1902.

[29] Morgan, *Sheafe*, 193, 196; AGD to G. I. Butler, February 26, 1902; AGD to L. C. Sheafe, February 19, 1902, ASTR.

[30] Morgan, *Sheafe*, 194–207; AGD to L. C. Sheafe, February 19, 1902; February 26, 1902; March 21, 1902, ASTR.

[31] Morgan, *Sheafe*. 211–215.

[32] AGD to H. W. Cottrell, September 18, 1902; H. W. Cottrell to AGD, September 24, 1902; W. A. Spicer to AGD, September 25, 1902, ASTR.

[33] W. A. Spicer to AGD, September 25, 1902.

[34] AGD to H. W. Cottrell, September 18, 1902.

[35] J. S. Washburn to AGD, December 12, 1902; May 22, 1903; J. S. Washburn to EGW, June 5, 1903, ASTR.

[36] Morgan, *Sheafe*, 255–258; AGD to EGW, February 24, 1903.

[37] Morgan, *Sheafe*, 259–264; J. S. Washburn to AGD, December 12, 1902; May 22, 1903; J. S. Washburn to EGW, June 5, 1903, ASTR.

[38] J. K. Howard to AGD, July 10, 1903, ASTR; Morgan, *Sheafe*, 197, 198, 264, 265.

[39] AGD to H. W. Cottrell, January 21, 1902, ASTR.

[40] J. K. Howard to AGD, July 10, 1903.

[41] Morgan, *Sheafe*, 265, 266.

[42] Ibid., 251, 265, 266.

[43] *RH*, December 31, 1903, 5, 6; Morgan, *Sheafe*, 273, 274; AGD to WCW, December 6, 1903, ASTR.

[44] Morgan, *Sheafe*, 274–277; L. C. Sheafe to AGD, February 2, 1904; AGD to L. C. Sheafe, February 4, 1904; AGD to L. C. Sheafe, February 5, 1905; L. C. Sheafe to AGD, February 15, 1905; May 7, 1905.

[45] Morgan, *Sheafe*, 291, 294; AGD to Sydney Scott, February 4, 1907, GCPL.

[46] Petition included in GCCMin, May 28, 1906.

[47] *RH*, April 12, 1906, 18.

[48] C. Shaffer to unidentified friend in Battle Creek, April 22, 1906; C. Shaffer, report of meeting, both in CAR.

[49] C. Shaffer to unidentified friend.

[50] AGD's response to petition, quoted in Shaffer's letter.

[51] Ibid.

[52] Ibid.; Morgan, *Sheafe*, 300.

[53] Morgan, *Sheafe*, 301, 302.

[54] Ibid., 304–306.

[55] AGD to People's Church, January 16, 1907, ASTR.

[56] Morgan, *Sheafe*, 306–309; L. C. Sheafe to AGD, January 15, 1907; AGD to WCW, January 18, 1907.

[57] Morgan, *Sheafe*, 316, 317; AGD to WCW, February 14, 1907.

[58] "Remarks of Elder A. G. Daniells to the People's S.D.A. Church," February 14, 1907, ASTR.

[59] "Report by Elder Sheafe of a Meeting Held in His Church at the Request of Eld. Daniells," CAR; AGD to WCW, February 14, 1907; AGD to Sydney Scott, February 14, 1907. L. C. Sheafe to AGD, February 26, 2907, ASTR.

[60] Morgan, *Sheafe*, 320; G. I. Butler to AGD, March 3, 1907; J. S. Washburn to AGD, February 20, 1907.

[61] AGD to Sydney Scott, February 4, February 14, February 22, 1907; Sydney Scott to AGD, February 8, February 18, 1907; J. S. Washburn to AGD, February 20, 1907.

[62] Morgan, *Sheafe*, 312–315, 321–323; EGW to L. C. Sheafe, February 4, 1907; AGD to EGW, February 28, 1907.

[63] Morgan, *Sheafe*, 328, 329; G. I. Butler to AGD, July 7, 1907.

[64] George Knight presents a valuable discussion of this conflict in his *Organizing for Mission and Growth*, pp. 118–131; AGD quoted in Knight, 121.

[65] W. A. Colcord to E. W. Farnsworth, April 25, 1907, EGWE.

[66] Knight, *Organizing for Mission*, 120.

[67] "Organization," *RH*, January 31 through May 16, 1907; AGD quote in February 28, 6.

[68] Morgan, *Sheafe*, 350, 351.

[69] Quoted in Morgan, *Sheafe*, 337.

[70] Ibid., 353–356; *GCB*, May 30, 1909, 209–210; June 2, 1909, 286–288.

[71] *GCB*, June 1, 1913, 212, 213.

[72] Morgan, *Sheafe*, chap. 32.

A. G. DANIELLS'S WORLD

This photo from the 1920s is the most familiar portrait of A. G. Daniells.

A group of young Battle Creek College dandies. Taken during the 1875-76 school year. Daniells is the middle figure in the second row. The others (clockwise from Daniells's left) are I. J. Hankins, A. H. Wood, S. H. Laughhead, P. S. Kellogg, and J. T. Nicola.

Below: Arthur and Mary Daniells shortly after arriving in Auckland, New Zealand, in 1886. Mary is seated, and next to her stands a Bible worker. A portion of the gospel tent can be seen.

This portrait of Daniells, taken in Australia sometime in the 1890s, shows a church leader who cut a handsome figure.

Jessie Daniells, Arthur's sister who was three years younger, had a fraternal twin.

Daniells sits with H. E. Rogers, statistical secretary of the General Conference, in this 1906 photo.

"Leaders at work": Daniells and other GC workers, with coats off, prepare to help ready the grounds for the May, 1913 GC session in Takoma Park, Maryland. Daniells is third from the right, holding a mallet. Future GC president (1922-1930), William A. Spicer, is two figures to Daniells's right. James L. McElhany, GC president 1936-1950, stands on the far right of the second row.

A. G. Daniells, sporting a stylish derby hat, visits the campus of Walla Walla College in 1907. On Daniells's left are Ross. C. Patterson, G. A. Irwin, and Christian M. Christiansen.

Daniells addresses workers of the newly organized Asiatic Division Conference in Shanghai, China, in 1915. The mission workers appear to be a very young group.

During World War One Daniells enjoyed great evangelistic success with his public addresses and widely distributed booklets on the prophetic meaning of the war.

Daniells stands front and center before the assembled Adventist Bible and history teachers at the controversial 1919 meetings in Takoma Park.

Daniells stands at the head of a Thanksgiving dinner table in 1932 with many of James and Ellen White's descendants. Daniells's continued close relationship with the White family is evident from the photo.

This 1935 photo was the last formal portrait of the Daniellses. In the 59th year of their marriage, the couple now confronted hard facts about Arthur's final illness. Mary's face betrays the sadness enveloping her.

CHAPTER VIII

A GLOBAL VISION

By the nature of his position, Arthur Daniells dealt with difficult—sometimes intractable—problems relating to budget, personnel, or institutions. He was temperamentally well suited for these often thankless tasks. He did them at the highest church level for twenty-one years (though not without some anguish and frequent private complaint). The "American whirlpool," as he called the North American field, threatened to confine his vision. "But the Lord has blessed me in my endeavors to look far away." Foreign missions was the one part of his job in which he found transcendent joy. This affinity began early. The formative years of his career were spent in the New Zealand and Australian mission fields. He was thoroughly imprinted with the conviction that God had raised up the Adventist Church to be a missionary enterprise. If the unending search for resources and the unavoidable administrative conflicts were the spinach and parsnips of his job, then overseeing a global mission initiative was his apple pie.[1]

And without doubt, Daniells presided over a great age of Adventist missions. Certainly much had been accomplished between J. N. Andrews's auspicious departure for Switzerland in 1874 and Daniells's accession in 1901. Adventism established itself on five continents and many islands. But the scale of activity in the twenty-one years of Daniells's presidency was unprecedented. He increased the average of new workers leaving the United States for posts abroad from 60 to more than 100 per year, reaching 310 in 1920. In 1921, Daniells's last full year in the presidency, Adventists living outside America for the first time surpassed in number those residing in North America. The world church would never look back in increasing its share of membership. One scholar of Adventist missions has called Daniells "the most outstanding missionary statesman in the church."[2]

In its energetic response to the Gospel Commission, the Adventist Church partook of a much broader impulse within western Protestantism. The closing decades of the nineteenth and first of the twentieth centuries (before World War I intruded) marked the high point of European missions to the world, when the flag and the Bible went hand in hand. The culminating organizational moment came at the World Mission Conference held in Edinburgh, Scotland, in 1910. "The Evangelization of the World in this Generation" was the motto that compelled thousands of young college people to depart for Africa, India, China, and other exotic regions of their world. The Bible had by then been translated into every major language; the scourge of tropical disease was coming under control, allowing safer residence by "the white man"; and, as World Missionary Conference chair John Raleigh Mott noted, the younger Christian churches were becoming active in the mission effort. Adventists figured prominently among these younger groups.[3]

Of course, A. G. Daniells did not single-handedly champion Adventist missions. His passion was widely shared, most notably by William A. Spicer (1865–1952). Spicer, whose early childhood had been spent in a Seventh Day Baptist family, followed his parents into the Adventist Church. As a teen he worked as secretary to Dr. Kellogg at the Battle Creek Sanitarium. In 1887, he began his mission service, first in England assisting Stephen Haskell, then back in Battle Creek, where he served as secretary of the Mission Board. But after only a year stateside, Spicer and his young family were off to Africa, helping establish the first mission station in South Africa. In 1897 they moved to India, where he once again laid the foundations of Adventist work (in honor of which Spicer College would be named). He returned to church headquarters the same year that Daniells assumed leadership. Spicer first oversaw the Mission Board, then when its work was subsumed in the General Conference Executive Committee, he took up the influential post of General Conference secretary. Along with W. W. Prescott, Spicer served as the closest General Conference colleague of Daniells throughout the latter's presidency. Spicer worked tirelessly to advance the Adventist cause abroad, and he did so in a highly professional and self-effacing manner. When Daniells was replaced as president in 1922, fittingly, it would be Spicer who assumed leadership.[4]

Any complete account of Adventist foreign missions during the span of Daniells's tenure would require its own book. This chapter will attempt a more modest look at the early years of his efforts. The issue of missions will arise again in chapter 10, which discusses how in 1914–1915 Daniells especially labored to build the Asian field, only to encounter the intrusion of World War I upon missions efforts. To Daniells, whatever obstacles might present themselves, the Gospel Commission remained a defining task every year of his presidency. Without doubt, he hoped his greatest legacy would be as the champion of world missions.

LEARNING THE WORLD FIELD

A. G. Daniells was well positioned to expand world mission efforts, not only through his aforementioned time in Australasia but also by his fact-finding trips through South Africa and England during his 1900 journey from Australia to America. He was a shrewd observer of the world field. His observation regarding church conditions worldwide doubtless aided his selection at the fateful 1901 General Conference Session. Yet his first order of business as president had to be instituting the new union conference organizations. He traveled unceasingly through the United States during his early months in office, giving attention to world missions as he could.

Complex international issues came to his attention through the mails. The work in South Africa frequently occupied his thoughts. The Second Boer War (1899–1902) continued to disrupt efforts. Daniells dwelt on personnel challenges in that beautiful, if troubled, part of the world. His enthusiastic midsummer recommendations about which workers should labor where in the culturally divided regions of southern Africa succumbed in the fall to discouragement. The death of five missionaries (including two children) from malaria at Solusi Mission a few years earlier, and now Fred Mead from pneumonia, dealt "a severe blow" to the mission. "We are drenching the farm with the blood of our best workers and planting it with their graves," Daniells somberly wrote Willie White. He went on to lament that "those who remain are thin and only half alive." Further, strife over doctrine was dividing the workers. It did not help local morale that veteran leader O. A. Olsen would not after all be moving to Africa to stabilize the administration. Daniells might have found some consolation in influential layman John Wessels's affirmation that past differences "will not prejudice our hearts" in the future.[5]

Some years later at the 1913 General Conference Session a vexing cultural issue was discussed: How should missionaries deal with polygamous husbands and wives who wish to embrace Adventism? This confounding issue was encountered most frequently in African lands, but it had resonance in Asian fields as well. Missionaries generally lacked sophistication in difficult matters relating to cultural differences. The field of anthropology was still new, and missionaries had to interpret unfamiliar cultures on their own (decades later the denomination would employ anthropologists to assist mission efforts). In the inaugural "mission round tables," Adventist overseas workers caucused to tackle the matter.[6]

A committee of missionaries devised a statement that was then debated by the larger group. It strongly suggested that to join the Advent fellowship husbands must put away (but still support) all but their first wife. Plural wives, on the other hand, ought to seek permission from their husband to separate (and marry again if they desire). But if their husband refused, the church still ought to embrace them in fellowship, though not in church office. This approach was sensitive to the disadvantaged place of women in traditional societies. Nonetheless, questions of fairness versus theological correctness remained troubling. Missionaries predicated policy on the assumption that monogamy was God's plan as revealed in the Bible. Deviations ought to be avoided if possible (though they understood the troubling precedent of Old Testament polygamy), but at the least, Paul's admonition that church leaders must have only one wife should be upheld. These principles seemed clear, but as various missionaries commented, real-life situations often defied simple answers. What were they to do when the second wife was the mother of the children? Must they be made fatherless? What if a man's first wife was his father's widow? What about the practice of polygamy in the Christian churches of Greece during apostolic times, which Paul evidently did not denounce? Would it be proper if in polygamous situations the individual be granted church fellowship but not be baptized?[7]

Such questions (and more) revealed a variety of opinion among missionaries. Daniells does not appear to have taken part in the debate. It is not clear what he could have added to the discussion since he had no experience working outside European cultures. But W. A. Spicer displayed his leadership qualities in asking pertinent questions, and when it appeared consensus would fly apart, reminding everyone that they were only making recommendations for missionaries, not establishing church policy. In short, Adventist workers could return to their lands with advice on how to handle complex matters of marriage and membership, but they still had freedom to address particular situations.[8]

But of course all was not complexity or discouragement. When in Battle Creek, Daniells presided over a Foreign Mission Board that continued to send out several scores of workers to far-flung lands. As always, much of the board's work concerned locating the individuals best fit for particular assignments. And Daniells was having success in getting local conferences to sponsor missionaries abroad. The Daniells-Spicer team's enthusiasm and attention to detail augured effective days ahead for Adventist foreign missions.[9]

The Australasian field not surprisingly remained close to Daniells's heart. At some level he must have felt guilt over taking what was to be several months' leave in 1900—and then not returning. Whether he genuinely believed that deposed General Conference president George Irwin could successfully lead out in Australia (now without Ellen or Willie White in residence) we do not know. But it is clear that the Australian church needed help. Daniells received discouraging reports from down under, one giving the impression that "debts were almost all there was in Australia." Another letter, from a younger former colleague who was leaving the denomination for doctrinal reasons, detailed a litany of church faults. Daniells recognized that some Australian members were suspicious of the church reorganization at the Battle Creek General Conference in 1901 and "looked upon me with greater or less suspicion. They have been watching me like a hawk, and I have to use judgment in my work."[10]

Arthur Daniells made his first of many trips abroad in the spring of 1902. He would visit both the United Kingdom, where a European General Conference was to be held, and the Continent, where he would assess the Adventist work as well as meet with church leaders. In his usual manner, Daniells laid careful groundwork for the trip. Most notably, he exhorted various American conferences to send delegates. This met with mixed success. Travel was expensive, and conferences were not flush with extra funds. But a few conferences agreed, and their representatives joined Daniells, Kellogg, E. R. Palmer (head of denominational publishing), and

H. W. Cottrell (Atlantic Union Conference president) on trips overseas. These were no mere junkets for selected American leaders. Daniells shrewdly calculated that grassroots support for foreign missions would come only if church leaders caught the vision firsthand and then held up the needs to their constituents. "I want to see the great needs of these fields soaked into these men to such an extent that when they get home they will know how to plead most earnestly and eloquently for men and means for these fields."[11]

Daniells was gratified that certain conferences sought to become more efficient (California notably) so that they could meet Mission Board appeals with generous donations. A number of conferences were returning their "second tithe" for foreign work. But one frustration plagued him. He could not abide how certain thriving American conferences sought to use their financial resources for their own members' benefit when the world's need was so great. His home conference of Iowa particularly pained him. An Adventist membership of just three thousand was served by fifty to sixty preachers while the needs of millions abroad went begging. Daniells believed that a mature Adventist congregation should be able to function through able laymen; the paid clergy ought to serve largely evangelistic functions overseas. Obviously, the role of pastoral nurture that we today highly value was not a conviction for the General Conference president. But it also bespeaks the church's unswerving focus on evangelism. Time was short.[12]

When the *Oceanic* left from New York's Hudson River pier on April 30, the Adventist contingency, to Daniells's delight, included nine canvassers supported by various conferences to labor in England. It also included his wife and son, Mary and Grosvenor. Daniells, who traveled incessantly and who at one point considered making this a six-to-nine-month trip, prudently decided to make it a family affair. Fortunately for the family, the eight-day voyage was blessedly smooth. Daniells, a detail man, enjoyed sprinkling his letters written en route with the facts about the "splendid vessel" (including the 120 coal stokers who fed 500 tons of coal a day into the boilers). In more serious moments, he explained to a friend from Australia the unanticipated turn of events that resulted in his leaving Australia for good (a sensitive subject), but more important how he hoped that after he left the presidency in a few years he might move to England and there labor for his church. He admired that nation's churches' tremendous effort in world missions during the previous century. Of course, things did not work out as the Anglophile Daniells hoped. His career remained anchored at church headquarters.[13]

Daniells and his party landed in Liverpool and immediately traveled to London for pre-session meetings. Conradi and other European leaders met the Americans in London, where they discussed organizational matters and trouble spots, such as the acute financial distress of the Christiania, Norway, publishing house. Daniells took a high view of the occasion. "It is an unspeakable privilege for us to meet the workers on this side of the ocean, and to unite with them in planning for the more rapid advancement of the cause."[14]

But even the inveterate worker Daniells could be persuaded (no doubt helped by his family's presence) to take some time for sightseeing. They strolled about a neighborhood Dickens had described in *The Old Curiosity Shop*. They made their way to Fleet Street, Regent's Park, Buckingham Palace, Westminster Abbey, and the still new Tower Bridge. He also took the occasion to pay a visit to a tailor and order an English suit.[15]

The London conference, running from May 15 to 26, was the largest gathering of European Adventist leaders up to that time, with delegates from eleven European nations and from India and Africa. The opportunity for disparate European workers to meet face to face—something American churchmen took for granted—was treasured by them. A simple theme dominated the conference: the challenge of taking the gospel to the diverse populations of Europe with few workers and fewer resources. The Austro-Hungarian Empire, for example, encompassing some forty million people, was served by one minister. In his report to Ellen White, Daniells repeated his burden that Americans not squander their tithe on the home field but instead "share our ministers with the millions in darkness."[16]

Key discussions during the conference centered on the need to locate educational and medical institutions in England and the large debt of the Christiania publishing house in Norway. Education, medical work, publishing: these, along with evangelistic preaching, were the heart of institutional Adventism. Founding a sanitarium in England, so important to Kellogg, occasioned the most violent confrontation of Daniells's career (see chapter 6). But in May of 1902, the more crucial issue was the publishing house.

Managers of the Christiania establishment had taken out loans that burdened it with seemingly insurmountable debt in the final years of the nineteenth century. When bankers called in the loan, bankruptcy of the conference seemed a real possibility. But General Conference leaders in 1900 felt for reasons both of honor and reputation that they must stand behind Christiania. Thus, $70,000 was allocated, to be raised over the succeeding few years. By spring 1902 about $30,000 remained, still a mountain of debt for a modest denomination. But Daniells would not hear of repudiation. A renewed campaign would be mounted among members in America. Daniells appealed to members directly in the *Review* and to union presidents, asking them in turn to canvas local conference presidents, all in support of a special July offering for the cause. Daniells hated debt, and this publishing liability albatross further hardened his conviction that the church must assume no more. Kellogg soon learned the depth of that conviction.[17]

In his assessment of the conference, Arthur Daniells told slightly different stories to two of his closest confidantes. It was "in many respects, a very encouraging meeting," he wrote Ellen White. But to Prescott, a closer day-to-day associate, he complained that "this conference has not been all that I had hoped, nor all that it should have been." Daniells did not want to expend time detailing his discontents, but he alluded to another correspondent that the difficulty in managing delegates from so many countries was part of the problem. But why would he hide his true feelings with the prophet? He certainly had many moments of utter candor with her. But in this case he was not seeking her advice nor asking for any action from her. No need to upset her unnecessarily. She had sufficient church matters to fret over. It was better to share his burden with Prescott.[18]

One issue Daniells could not avoid addressing concerned the leader of the English church, O. A. Olsen. "He is wearing out mentally and physically," Daniells confided to Willie White. Olsen wanted to go to Africa, a move that seemed ill-advised given his condition. Daniells knew a change must be made. Locating an able successor was vital, for Daniells believed that a strong British church was an essential building block for worldwide missions. The only suitable candidate appeared to be Atlantic Union Conference president H. W. Cottrell. He possessed the experience and polish that might enable him to fit with British culture. But his administrative skill was much needed in America. (Olsen would surprise everyone by remaining another three years at his post.)[19]

From London Daniells traveled across the Irish Sea to Belfast. The visit was educational for Daniells. The north of Ireland was heavily Protestant, and Daniells wrongly assumed a receptiveness to the Adventist message. He attributed individuals' resistance to their embattled position in a largely Catholic land (the entire island then being still part of the United Kingdom). Conflict bred an intransigence of belief and suspicion toward rival faiths. "They are not looking for new light," Daniells concluded sadly. Even so, there was "a respectable company" of about 130 believers in the country, drawn entirely from the Protestant sector (the land's Catholics being "held by iron bands"). But if numbers were small, he took gratification in the accomplishments of some of the members. A Mr. McCreary was a prominent Irish musician who wrote a hymn that would be used in King Edward VII's coronation service. Another member of the Belfast church was a respected architect whom Daniells hoped could be persuaded to design a striking structure for the congregation. Only modest success in Ireland should be expected, Daniells concluded, and to build on this beginning, two of the colporteurs who came from America were posted there.[20]

Before Daniells headed to the Continent, he returned to Great Britain for a camp meeting and evangelistic series in the northern city of Leeds. It was, in fact, the northernmost effort in England yet attempted. The weather, unsurprisingly, was atrocious, raining virtually every day. But Daniells lived for such evangelistic occasions, and he put the best face on things. He and his English brethren had reason for optimism about the growth of Adventism in England. Christianity in general was doing well at the time. Church membership in England peaked during the first decade of the twentieth century. Daniells had a further agenda for staying by in the country for several days. He wanted to help British church leaders plan the sort of reorganization accomplished in America the previous year (a development that took place later that summer, after Daniells had returned home).[21]

Concluding his work in the United Kingdom, Daniells headed to the Continent. He followed an ambitious itinerary that would take him through Scandinavia, Germany, Switzerland, France, and Italy. Crossing the North Sea, Daniells headed first to Denmark, where he spent several days in Copenhagen conferring with Danish Conference officials. From there it was on to Christiania, Norway (today's Oslo), where he would inspect firsthand the troubled publishing house. He was delighted to find that it "looks brighter and more prosperous by far than it did when I was here before." From there he made the relatively short journey to Stockholm, Sweden. Following his usual pattern, he spent intensive time with conference leaders, hearing of the needs (for funds and workers) in that area. He found a mixed bag in Sweden. Literature sales were strong, but leadership was weak—and thus the conference struggled. Division among members over health reform and attitudes toward the Spirit of Prophecy compounded difficulties. Membership actually declined during the following year. Daniells, who had developed firm ideas about the essential nature of leadership, reflected sadly that Scandinavian leaders were "missing the mark very much."[22]

Daniells did not visit Holland, but problems there nevertheless preoccupied him. Fanaticism had reared its head. Most of the Dutch ministers had gotten "new light" on the 2,300 days, the sanctuary, Revelation 14, and the Spirit of Prophecy—in other words, virtually every doctrinal distinctive save the Sabbath. During the London conference, Daniells, Waggoner, Conradi (president of the European Division), and others had labored with the Dutch. More studies followed later. But they were set in their views. Worse, it seemed that most of the rank and file members shared their heterodoxy. "It looks as though nearly our whole work in Holland is lost," he sadly wrote Willie White. But "we shall get as many of the loyal brethren from Holland over to Friedensau as possible" and take stock as to how to "stand our ground in Holland." Daniells here faced an exemplification of Protestantism's implicit endorsement of the right to challenge doctrinal authority. As an administrator, though, he could not afford the luxury of admiring this historical tradition. His job was to preserve unity.[23]

From Scandinavia Daniells backtracked to England to aid the search for a sanitarium site. This occasioned his confrontation with Kellogg (see chapter 6). It was not surprising that after the protracted financial agony of meeting the Christiania publishing house debt that Daniells balked at any costly options. "What kind of encouragement is it to create new debts as soon as the old ones are paid off[?]" he rhetorically asked Willie White.[24]

But debts or not, Daniells never stopped looking for possible locations for future sanitariums when funds allowed. His visit to Switzerland (where presumably he and family enjoyed the land's scenic wonders) occasioned just such an endeavor. Daniells concluded that Luzern would be an ideal spot. He and his party then headed south toward Rome, stopping along the way at Lyons. He was impressed with the handful of Sabbath keepers he encountered. He acknowledged that the work in France would likely meet with more difficulties than in Switzerland but thought a "loyal body of workers will be raised up."[25]

One would love to know Daniells's thoughts as his train approached Rome. The ancient capital of the empire that put Christ to death; the seat of the great apostate, Rome held a special place in Adventist apocalyptic tradition. The city surprised Daniells in two ways. It was more modern than he expected and less dominated by the Catholic Church than he supposed. "I never saw Sunday so badly kept anywhere as in Rome," he mused. Fears of official resistance to an Adventist presence appeared groundless. "A Seventh-day Adventist missionary could work with as much liberty and boldness as anywhere else in the world." Still, so far as Daniells knew, only two Sabbath keepers resided in Rome. They were the Kellinni sisters, one of whom had learned of Adventism at the Basel sanitarium and then persuaded her sister of the truth. Daniells was very pleased with their pedigree. Their father had been a prominent figure who fought for the great Italian revolutionary, Giuseppe Garibaldi (Daniells relished converts who possessed accomplishment or social standing). The sisters were well versed in English and able to translate Adventist literature into Italian. Daniells hoped that a minister could be sent to establish a mission.[26]

After short stops at Florence, Vienna, Prague, and Dresden, Daniells proceeded to a meeting of the European General Conference at Friedensau, Germany, headquarters of Adventist work in Europe. His "grand tour" of the Continent allowed Daniells to speak intelligently of the field's needs. The council, per Daniells's wishes, made formal a request for a worker in Rome. The council also requested a $75,000 appropriation from Battle Creek, which, given Daniells's presence, had a high likelihood of success. A ten-day conference might seem excessive for a denomination numbering just a few thousand in Europe. But church leaders aspired to great things, even in a region whose people were so tightly bound to their traditional faiths. Moreover, the presence of the General Conference leader demanded that much be done now. Even in the age of steam, an Atlantic crossing could not be taken lightly.[27]

MOBILIZING SUPPORT FOR MISSIONS

The Daniells family returned to New York harbor in mid-August 1902 after sixteen weeks of travel—long, but not the six- to nine-month marathon he at one time considered. The voyage home from Cherbourg, France, was blessedly uneventful and a day shorter than the one over. Arthur was becoming enough of an international traveler to comment on the respective quality of service on various passenger lines and enough of a connoisseur to prefer the stewards and food on the *Crownprince* to others.[28]

Once home, Daniells was anxious to begin eliciting enthusiasm and funds for the European work. His passion for foreign missions was white hot. He hit the road, making the round of late-summer camp meetings. Much of his attention necessarily went to continued implementation of conference reorganization. But he stole every moment he could to devote to his beloved missions. This often entailed persuading men of "short vision" to look at needs beyond Adventism's country of origin.[29]

But his enthusiasm quickly ran up against the realities of church politics. His first stop was at the Michigan camp meeting. The conference had been in "sad condition," a problem addressed by conference reorganization (including making the Upper Peninsula a mission). Further, the camp meeting sessions were not well attended, and most of those present were elderly. In this pre-Social Security age, the elderly generally had limited means. Thus, Daniells felt he could not make the call for funds he had intended. He went next to Illinois, where again light attendance impeded successful fund-raising. Iowa camp meeting promised more. This longtime bastion of Adventism hosted well-attended gatherings. Daniells wanted to raise funds for the London treatment rooms. But a promising situation fell victim to a chronic rivalry between the Iowa Conference Committee and the Iowa Sanitarium. The controversy threatened the very existence of the conference. Daniells attended only one meeting and then avoided further controversy. "I saw that if we all abandoned ourselves to this wrangle we should lose our grip entirely on the conference." Instead, he judged that effective leadership meant appealing directly to the laypeople. Sensing it imprudent to solicit funds for an overseas medical institution in the midst of a local controversy, he instead plumped for China missions—which found a generous response. From Iowa, Daniells headed straight west to the Nebraska camp meeting in Lincoln. It had to be discouraging to find locals embroiled in similar internecine strife. Still, attendees contributed about $1,000 to Skodsborg Sanitarium, and the conference voted $2,300 for work in Scandinavia.[30]

As important as grassroots fund raising was the task of identifying individuals willing and potentially effective in evangelizing foreign fields. In this Daniells benefited from a surge of excitement among American Adventists. In part, new interest in missions was generated in the *Review* and by continued public emphasis by Daniells and other leaders. But, as mentioned above, it also followed broader national trends. America had recently completed a successful (if imperialistic) war against Spain (1898) and added territories from the Caribbean to the western Pacific. Not just geopolitical but also missionary motives were prominently forwarded in support of American action. "The White Man's Burden" (an 1899 Rudyard Kipling poem) had much currency at the time. Anglo-American culture and Christianity were to march arm in arm on a civilizing mission around the globe. Even such violent anti-Western, anti-missionary events as the Boxer Rebellion in China (1900) slowed only momentarily the surge of Christian missions. Too, the American economy was back in full swing by the new century. Adventists in the pews, Daniells never tired of mentioning, were more prosperous than ever and capable of generous offerings.[31]

Allocating funds and assigning mission posts was done from the top by the Foreign Mission Board (and later the General Conference Committee). Minutes of meetings record votes and summaries of discussions but convey little of what must have been candid conversations about individuals' fitness for various assignments. Daniells normally presided over these meetings. He would not be one to shrink from voicing firm opinions on personnel matters. Kellogg was a committee member, which, given their recent toe-to-toe in England over purchasing sanitarium property, must have made for interesting dynamics.

Daniells convened the Mission Board shortly after his return from Europe. A round of appropriations was made for mission work reaching from Britain to Scandinavia to Egypt to Latin America. By modern reckoning these were small sums. But given the modest size of the American Adventist Church, the financial investment was still impressive. Not everything could be funded at once, for Daniells resisted incurring new major debt. A $20,000 fund-raising effort for a British sanitarium, for example, was put on hold (one wonders if there was an element of showing Kellogg who was in charge in this decision). Members did approve nearly $5,000 for treatment rooms in London and Skodsborg.[32]

Allocating funds always proved challenging, but identifying the right personnel for overseas assignment was perhaps even trickier. The committee took their responsibility seriously, conferring with leaders around the country for advice. Daniells also encouraged L. R. Conradi, when he came to America, to visit Adventist colleges and collect names from faculty of likely young missionary candidates. He should then interview them so that he might make intelligent decisions about whom to request. The Mission Board was pleased when trained members offered to go abroad, such as H. L. Morse of Union College, who in the spirit of that school's golden cords, asked to enter the fledgling field of France. The Mission Board also welcomed initiatives by local conferences to sponsor missionaries. Early in his presidential tenure, Daniells attended a conference meeting in Iowa where leaders faced the encouraging problem of having more members wishing to enter the mission field than the organization could support. Vermont Conference, small though it was with only two ordained ministers, offered to pay the transportation and support of W. A. Westworth to England for one year. Best of all was the pure volunteerism exemplified by two young men from Kansas. Daniells met William Shafer and Arthur Bates at the Kansas camp meeting. They were prepared to head to England to serve at first as self-supporting canvassers and, as they became familiar with the territory, move into ministerial work. "I like that spirit very much," Daniells enthused. He saw their approach as a model for others entering foreign work, not just as an economizing measure for the church but also as a means of gradual acculturation for prospective evangelists.[33]

Missionaries were commissioned throughout the year. But December 1902 witnessed an especial flurry of activity. India was a focus of attention, and the denomination looked for workers with colonial ties to the subcontinent. Four English workers (including one with a family) received invitations. Similarly, various corners of sub-Saharan Africa merited attention: South Africa (which had been the original point of entry for African missions) gained two more workers, and missionaries were sent to Nyasaland (Malawi), Barotseland (Zambia), and the Gold Coast (Ghana). Not coincidentally, the church first entered British colonies. Adventism followed the Union Jack. Additional invitations went to workers to labor in Scotland, Wales, Central America, the West Indies, Mexico, and China. Clearly, the American Adventist Church's new prosperity sparked an ambitious missions agenda.[34]

But funds did not grow on trees, and General Conference leaders tried to discourage an annoying and costly habit of some missionaries. Some overseas workers, perhaps from homesickness or cultural discomfort, returned to the States after a relatively short period without authorization—or even prior notification. The General Conference Committee voted in spring 1903 that the denomination would not be responsible for payment or return fares if the missionaries had not been formally recalled.[35]

The new policy received an early test by none other than E. J. Waggoner. Waggoner had served in England as editor of *Present Truth* for a decade by 1902, when he was courted by Daniells and Prescott to return to America as a Bible instructor at the newly established Emmanuel Missionary College. Waggoner accepted the invitation enthusiastically. But in the process he offended school leaders Magan and Sutherland, which touched off a series of accusations and confrontations petty beyond belief among the above men. Knowing he was not wanted in Berrien Springs, Waggoner did not come immediately. But in the fall of 1903 he did—this time without explicit permission from the General Conference. When Waggoner submitted his travel expenses, Daniells responded with a letter lecturing about workers' responsibilities. "As far as I am aware, you have taken the liberty to make your own arrangements and expenses, regardless of the party you ask to pay the bills." The aggrieved Waggoner responded that no mission board would refuse to pay a worker's family's expenses after a decade abroad. Further, he was only doing now what he had been urged to do in 1902. The incident would seem to cast Daniells as the miserly Scrooge, squeezing employees for every penny. But this judgment should be tempered by the fact (mentioned by him in his letter to Waggoner) that the denomination had "been harassed with two or three expense accounts similar to yours." Daniells was a president at the end of his rope over shoddy expense reports.[36]

But such lapses into hectoring did not typify Daniells. His letters are normally filled with encouragement and hope for the Great Commission. He had a dream of securing for missions "an army of the brightest young men and women we have in our schools." "The time has come for us to take the world for Christ, and we can never do it without taking hold of our young people." Daniells allowed himself a very personal note in his letter to a young man heading to a post in England. "I left this country when I was twenty-six. . . . I would not have that experience blotted out for all the world," he wrote. "I sincerely hope that your labors abroad will be as pleasant and profitable as mine were." Daniells set a high bar. He had built up the Adventist work in New Zealand, and his decade in Australia alongside Ellen and Willie White were foundational for Adventism there. "I almost envy you the privilege you are having of going to Great Britain," he continued. "Were it not for the fact that I am detained in this country as a recruiting officer, my trunks would soon be packed for the field on the other side of the Atlantic." At heart, Arthur Daniells always remained a missionary.[37]

He took his passion to the spring 1903 General Conference Session. Seven resolutions came from the Committee on Plans pertaining to missions. At heart, they urged the local state conferences to put every ounce of available energy and resources into overseas work. Why? Because while the United States comprised only about one-twentieth of the world's population, it held roughly four-fifths of Adventist laborers and means. Thus, "a systematic and thorough campaign [must] be entered upon and kept up" to educate conference committees, ministers, and laypeople about the worldwide needs. Further, conferences should not only urge some workers to consider foreign fields but pledge to support them if they go. They encouraged conferences, as well, to set aside a percentage of tithe as appropriation for missions. The committee further recommended that all levels of church administration scrutinize their overhead costs to see if funds might be found for missions. Finally, churches were urged to keep foreign missions ever before their congregations so that offerings might be generous.[38]

As might be expected, conference administrators raised some questions about the degree to which General Conference representatives might usurp local entreaties for funds. Daniells, whose fingerprints were no doubt all over the resolutions, sought to allay concerns. Another delegate pointed out that there were needy mission fields within the United States, notably in the South. Daniells worried that these comments threatened the spirit of the resolutions. He appealed for the special status of the world work. His personal ethos returned the group to its gospel enthusiasm, and the mission resolutions found favor.[39]

INTO ALL THE WORLD

Throughout 1903 and 1904 Daniells continued to preside over an ambitious mission outreach. A detailed account of this effort would require its own volume. Space here permits only a quick survey of the world field Daniells encountered and the leadership he provided.

Though not numerically the largest foreign conference, the most institutionally advanced world region was Australia (Ellen White's decade-long presence being largely responsible). The "Down Under" was never far from Daniells's heart. "Every word you write regarding the work in Australasia is of deep interest to me," he assured E. W. Farnsworth. While important work consumed him in America, he confided, "I do not find my interest centering here." Daniells was tethered to America because of his position as denominational leader, but he served as "a recruiting officer" for the world field.[40]

As was his custom, Daniells's oversight of the Australasian Union Conference came through regular correspondence with its president, George Irwin. As Daniells's immediate predecessor at the General Conference, Irwin possessed administrative experience and a grasp of church politics (from the hard-knock perspective of someone not returned to office). Irwin kept his superior advised on the general progress of the work and, of course, on the challenges that are stock-in-trade of administration. Australia resembled every other Adventist field in its chronic financial shortfalls. The still-new sanitarium food industry was enduring rough financial weather (it eventually became highly successful). On the other hand, the *Christ's Object Lessons* campaign had wonderfully reduced Avondale's debt, and the Wahroonga Sanitarium was thriving. Australian church leaders were beginning to face complex accounting and other business issues. Men with no formal business training and limited experience in these fields had to make important decisions on the fly. Filled with enthusiasm for the cause, it was predictable that institution building would outstrip resources. Perhaps the surprise is how well the church did, on balance, to overcome shortfalls of resources and expertise.[41]

Inevitably, reports came to Daniells of disputes and personnel discontent. "Bro. Starr," Irwin lamented to Daniells, "is quite spluttering and sometimes officious, and would, if left to himself, be liable to get things in a tangle. Besides, the brethren have no confidence in him as a manager." Even more difficult, J. A. Burden, a respected administrator and board member of Australian institutions, suffered a surfeit of "conscientious convictions," to the point that he could not accept majority judgment that went against his beliefs. Irwin reported that efforts to render him accommodating failed, and he had to be dropped from union governing boards. Burden's rigidity, Daniells painfully understood, was the vice of Adventism's virtue. The denomination not only moved forward on the strength of such convictions; it was also regularly hindered by leaders unwilling to compromise their beliefs. Still, leadership was effective enough to increase by a thousand the number of Sabbath keepers in Australia over two years to nearly thirty-five hundred.[42]

Europe continued to be the focus of mission attention. Its greater human and financial resources, its colonial networks, its shared language (at least in terms of England), and the greater comfort level General Conference leaders had with its culture, explains why more resources went there and why Daniells made regular trips across the Atlantic.

Adventism confronted a culture in central and western Europe that was basking in an Indian summer of peace and prosperity. No general war had occurred since Napoleon had been captured in 1815 and no significant regional strife north of the Balkans since the Franco-Prussian War of the early 1870s. The expanding urban middle classes enjoyed widespread freedoms and new consumer delights; conversely, city dwellers were becoming more secular. An unfamiliar American religion that predicted the approaching end of time was not likely to find a warm reception. Whatever solace or ceremonial functions that religion provided could be met by familiar faiths (normally Catholic or Lutheran). Thus, instead of posing the question of why Adventism found limited success in Europe, one might as easily ask how it found as many believers as it did.

One important answer was Louis Conradi (1856–1939). A. G. Daniells never begrudged the attention or funds he secured for the European church because he had complete confidence in its leader. Conradi, who immigrated from Germany to the American Midwest as a teenager, typified the many recent immigrants who found an American-made religion congenial. After studying at Battle Creek College, he was assigned to carry the gospel to the abundant German farm population of the Midwest and Great Plains. His success led to his being sent in 1886 to Europe, where he labored among German speakers scattered across the continent. Energetic, intelligent, and shrewd, he became a natural choice to head the growing European field. He was among the best-traveled of Adventist leaders, becoming the face of the church in far-flung outposts. Conradi and Daniells shared many letters through the years, epistles that reveal a similar administrative temperament and mutual confidence.

They shared a frustration in getting the medical and pastoral arms of the church to work harmoniously. For Conradi, it was some personnel at the Skodsborg Sanitarium who proved vexatious. But he understood that his problems were not in a league with Daniells's efforts against the tectonic forces in Battle Creek.[43]

Daniells and Conradi also contended with the talented but mercurial E. J. Waggoner. As seen above, the manner of Waggoner's return to America from England vexed Daniells. Conradi, though appreciative of the former's editorial talents, was not sorry to see him leave. "I do not think this is the worst thing which could befall us," he wrote with an administrator's cautious understatement. Waggoner, besides lacking efficiency as a laborer, had stirred up animosities at the South England Conference meetings with a spirit that was "not from above."[44]

Conradi's discontent with the work in England went beyond Waggoner. "I never could agree with the manner in which my brethren in Great Britain were carrying on their work," he confided to Daniells. He only asked that leaders on the Continent be allowed the same privilege of organizing their work as they saw fit. The English field may have enjoyed various advantages over Germany, "but it has been left very much behind." In words that must have pained the Anglophile Daniells, he went on, "It is surprising how little actual progress has been made when we look over the statistics." The 1903 General Conference statistical report confirmed his sad comment. Great Britain had fewer than twelve hundred members compared to more than five thousand in the German Union. This despite favorable financial treatment from the General Conference.[45]

Conradi appreciated what funds Daniells and the General Conference Committee could provide—but he wanted more. Not that he was greedy, but he saw tremendous needs both in Europe and in the African and Middle Eastern mission fields under his purview. He had no qualms about letting Daniells know his fear about the impact of the many American church projects. The multiplying "health food restaurants, sanitariums, etc." would leave little "for the real mission fields." Conradi suspicioned that the new and much-vaunted "cash policy" of the General Conference (that is, forgoing debt in institutional development) was not in fact being followed. He had followed this conservative policy for years personally and in his oversight of the European field. But "letter after letter came from America telling us of the straitened financial circumstances of your treasury," even while other letters told of "the way in which institutions were multiplying." Americans, he heard, could not contribute more to missions because "of the demands made upon them in the home land."[46]

Daniells sensed frustration in his colleague and attempted to assure him of America's support. "I do not feel in the least discouraged about our finances," Daniells wrote, conveying the tone of optimism expected of a leader. The ambitious institutional plans for Takoma Park would not cause leadership to "forget ourselves, and pile up debts that will tax us for years to come." "We have fought and won that battle" [cash policy]. "I have a great horror of having the work in America occupy the whole attention and resources" of the church. Daniells's mission track record gave him the standing to mount a credible defense on this matter. He implored Conradi to give the Mission Board the benefit of the doubt in matters of resource allocation. "Now, Brother Conradi, be patient, and be careful what you write, and give us poor fellows over here a little chance for our lives," particularly so since they had "been pounced on by the opposition here" [meaning the Kellogg faction].[47]

Conradi expressed gratitude for Daniells's reassurances but nonetheless continued to voice concerns. "The work in the States has often moved by fits and starts." Conradi referred here to the still-recent policy of having conferences that "are better situated" earmark a "second tithe" (i.e., an additional 10 percent of their revenues) for foreign missions. Yet some of them were already backing out of the agreement. Let them meet their local needs with eight-tenths of their funds, Conradi unsympathetically advised. Further, while the Continent's churches devoted all Sabbath School offerings to missions, American churches often used as much as a half for local expenses. Conradi's remarks might be taken as unappreciative whining. But more generously viewed, they are seen as the words of a man whose passion for taking the gospel into all the world trumped polite epistolary conversation. Even Daniells desired it no other way. He told his European colleague that the American brethren "want warnings" from leaders abroad. Daniells was not one to close himself off from those of contrary opinion. Leadership in a bubble would never be effective leadership.[48]

Daniells responded with redoubled effort to increase mission offerings. He had little choice, given that contributions had not kept pace with appropriations. Weeks of Prayer, the General Conference Committee urged, should be occasions for arousing interest in world missions. Daniells pointed out that Adventists' eschewal of "harmful luxuries," such as liquor and tobacco, represent a savings of perhaps two million dollars a year. "Our people are able, if touched by the call of need, to give far more largely."[49]

If leadership meant unremitting concern for finances, it was because the Seventh-day Adventist denomination truly had a worldwide mission effort. The vast African continent, for example, demanded a king's ransom in resources. Conradi's union oversaw the incipient work in Egypt, Sudan, and Abyssinia in addition to German East Africa. But the real progress was being made far to the south, away from the difficult Islamic lands. The Dutch and British colonial outposts in South Africa provided a less exotic culture for Adventist missionaries to pursue. The South African Union Conference, headquartered in Cape Town, consisted of roughly six hundred Sabbath keepers, about three-quarters of whom were Europeans. The conference benefited from the presence of J. J. Wessels, whose family's generosity furthered church mission efforts and the white and indigenous work.[50]

Energies increasingly focused on indigenous populations. Rhodesia (Zimbabwe) had Solusi Mission, founded in the 1890s, which remained the flagship institution for indigenous work. Many other mission stations were also established, some as far north as Nyasaland (Malawi). But work had yet to start among the formidable Zulu people in Natal. Mission outposts typically were farms, where indigenous people spent part of the day tilling the soil and tending livestock and part in rudimentary schooling. Missionaries sought to emulate the industrial training schools of America. The goal, just beginning to be realized, was to train indigenous people to return to their villages and spread the gospel. But bridging the chasm between cultures was daunting. Union president W. S. Hyatt admitted that Adventist workers found the indigenous people to be a "puzzle." Further, tropical climate and accompanying disease took a heavy toll. J. H. Watson's death of "African fever" in late 1904 struck church leaders hard. Hyatt recommended to Spicer that future laborers be recruited from the American South, where the climatic "seasoning" presumably would facilitate their adjustment to Africa. He also urged that greater attention be given to the Basutoland Mission in the Cape Colony. Located in a temperate climate and populated by the relatively more educated indigenous people, it appeared suited to the strategy of building a corps of native workers.[51]

Southern East Asian countries remained Adventist missions, lightly entered, with membership numbered in the low hundreds and no formal administrative units yet established. Likewise, the great Indian subcontinent (along with Burma and Ceylon) proved one of the greatest challenges to Adventist missions. Opened in the usual way by colporteurs in the early 1890s, it took an untraditional turn in the sponsorship by the Mission Board of a female Bible worker, Georgia Burrus. Her educational efforts among young Hindu females provided an opening wedge. W. A. Spicer followed up several years later, publishing from Calcutta the *Oriental Watchman*. Discouragingly few converts, paucity of native laborers, lack of Western workers who knew native languages (Burrus being a notable exception), and insufferable heat all conspired to limit the Adventist gospel in this enormous field. Daniells apologized to mission director J. L. Shaw for the failure of the General Conference to adequately support the Indian work. Indeed, decades would pass before these Adventist sparks would kindle a true flame across India.[52]

Adventism also moved slowly on the Pacific Rim. The first Adventist missionaries entered China in 1901. The timing was either brave or foolhardy, given that they arrived hard on the heels of that land's Boxer Rebellion (1898–1900), which devastated Western missionary communities in some parts of the country. Adventist physician Harry Miller arrived in 1903, settled in Shanghai, and immediately set to work on an ambitious program of publishing, medical care, mastering the difficult language, and cultivating contacts with influential Chinese. Miller set the Adventist cause on an independent path, refusing to be kept out of other denominations' mission territory. He kept Daniells well informed of developments halfway around the world and was never shy about asking the church's leader for more help. His letters to Daniells are testaments to great faithfulness in the face of an apparently Sisyphean task.[53]

Adventist workers hit a cultural wall at least as high in Japan. As the General Conference session convened in spring 1905, Japan was involved in a major war with Russia, an event that gave concern to Adventist workers in the region. J. N. Anderson, writing from Canton, presciently warned that Japan's regional aggressions could pit it against China "as deadly enemies," delaying the proclamation of God in Asia. The incipient Adventist presence in Japan had its roots in San Francisco the previous decade, when several Japanese there responded to the Adventist message, trained at Healdsburg College, and then returned to their homeland. W. C. Grainger was the pioneer American Adventist missionary, laboring under the various restrictions that country imposed on outsiders. Grainger inadvertently discovered a mission technique that would later prove the very basis of mission work in the Orient. He opened a Bible school and was initially gratified by student interest. But, as the report to the General Conference session noted with some disappointment, the "experience has taught us that students usually attend such classes for the help they get in English language study, rather than for the Bible instruction." Ultimately, an admirable realism led Adventist workers to conclude that such English classes might prove useful for all involved.[54]

Early efforts in Korea augured the greater success that Adventism would later enjoy among that nationality ("the wonderful manner in which the truth has gone forth into Korea," as F. W. Field expressed it). Earliest Korean believers were introduced to Adventism in Japan, later taking their new faith back home. An American worker arrived in Korea only in mid-1904, holding meetings that claimed more than seventy baptisms. Christianity flourished on the Korean peninsula (particularly in the north) as in few other places in East Asia. The Philippines were among those exceptions; indeed, the islands would later become synonymous with successful Adventist missions. But when G. A. Irwin arrived there in 1904, it was purely an exploratory visit. He found a mission field that was predominantly Catholic and where the established Protestant denominations had divided up the territory to avoid competition. The many islands in the archipelago, the diverse languages, the current price inflation from the recently finished United States–Filipino war—all posed challenges. Irwin recommended starting the work in Manila through the usual canvassing channels, which, beginning in 1908, proceeded with great results.[55]

But the greatest Adventist success story of the twentieth century came in the Western Hemisphere: the Caribbean and Latin America. Initially, these lands seemed among the most difficult, despite their relative proximity to North America. They encompassed a variety of both colonial and indigenous cultures and languages. And they were predominantly Roman Catholic. It was not surprising, then, that early work in South America focused on German immigrants in Chile, Argentina, and Brazil. Conversely, Hispanic populations of northern South America at the time of the 1905 General Conference Session had seen no Adventist workers labor among them. The earliest work north of the equator came in the English-speaking areas of British Guiana. It would be 1909 before Ferdinand and Ana Stahl journeyed to Lake Titicaca in Peru to begin perhaps the most famous endeavor in Adventist mission history.[56]

In the eastern Caribbean, a vast region of islands of varying languages, Adventism moved relatively quickly. With seeds planted by itinerant Adventist colporteurs, a conference formed in 1903; by 1905 the church had twenty-nine workers and just over a thousand widely scattered members. In the western reaches of the Caribbean, Adventism showed early signs of the vitality that marked it throughout the twentieth century. Entering English-speaking territories, American workers did not have to contend with language barriers. The largest island of the Caribbean, Cuba, was entered only in 1903, when Mr. and Mrs. I. E. Moore employed their training as nurses to propagate the Adventist gospel. The Spanish-American War, only a few years previous, set the island on an uncharted independent course, but Cuba benefited from extensive infrastructure improvements by the United States. The ongoing Yankee interest in the island made it seem a propitious time for Americans (including Adventists) to renew their interest in the land.[57]

Such was the conclusion of G. H. Baber, veteran of early Adventist work in Chile, who now had interests in Cuba. He penned Daniells a letter in 1904 full of enthusiasm for the possibilities on the island. Spectacular climate, fertile land (cheaply available) with all the vegetables and fruits that a vegetarian diet could desire, awaited settlers. It would be an ideal spot for a sanitarium. Further, rural environs would satisfy Ellen White's appeal to get out of the cities. "Why not make a call for $80,000 with which to buy at least $500,000 worth of land and at the same time put a great light in Cuba, and give the people [in North America] a chance to feed all the year round on Edenic fruits and grains, and save themselves from the cold blasts of the Northern winters?" Baber's enticements appear to be another example of a common phenomenon among Protestant missionaries worldwide: some who went out to do good for others were lured by desires to do well for themselves. Baber was sensitive to how his overture might appear. "The land business may seem foreign to the work of an Adventist missionary, and no doubt does have a tendency to draw our minds from spiritual themes, . . . but we as Adventists, must stay somewhere in the earth, and live from its productions until the Lord comes." There is no record of Daniells's taking Baber's proposal to the General Conference Committee, but he was given license to pen an article for the *Review* in which he extolled the island's virtues and invited readers to contact him about investments.[58]

Not surprisingly, the American Adventist Church developed a strong mission interest in adjoining Mexico. But despite its propinquity, colporteur work did not begin there until 1891. Three years later, Dan T. Jones established a primitive medical clinic in Guadalajara, which found an overwhelming local response. A full-blown sanitarium was projected. When the General Conference could not foot the bill, Kellogg's medical association stepped in and operated the facility. Mission Board efforts now shifted to Mexico City. What followed exemplified the wisdom of the 1901 General Conference reorganization in an attempt to unify church entities. Lacking such unity in the medical work, petty squabbles erupted between

Guadalajara and Mexico City leadership that plagued mission efforts. Feelings ran so high that Daniells made his first visit to Mexico in early 1903 to resolve issues. But the thorny details of financial subsidy and control of Guadalajara between Kellogg's Medical Missionary and Benevolent Association and the General Conference defied easy solution. Although the Guadalajara sanitarium closed a few years later, Adventist medical work in Mexico thrived on a decentralized basis for at least a few years (until the Mexican Revolution made things more difficult), with more physicians in the country than all the rest of Latin America combined.[59]

In the midst of the medical work conflict and administrative dithering, one worker showed uncommon energy, scholarship, and good sense: George W. Caviness. A victim of Battle Creek College politics, Caviness found himself marooned to Mexico in 1897. Placed in Mexico City, Caviness set himself apart from most American missionaries by a determination to master the Spanish language. "Middle-aged men should never be sent to a country where they have to learn a language," he opined to Daniells, "unless they are students and have studied some language quite thoroughly in school, . . . for others it is almost a hopeless task" (a likely reference to mission director G. A. Brown, who had earlier confessed to Daniells his struggles with the language). Caviness aspired to produce Adventist literature in the native language. He did this by acquiring a small press and setting out to compose both doctrinal tracts and lengthier works on prophecies in Daniel and Revelation. Although by 1905 scarcely a hundred Mexicans professed the Sabbath, it was clear that the Adventist work was getting established on a sound footing.[60]

These early years of the twentieth century were hugely exciting ones for Adventist world missions. A. G. Daniells would have loved to be on the front lines. But like General George Marshall, who during World War II had to surrender his desire to be field commander in Europe in order to coordinate the war effort from Washington, Daniells found that his essential tasks of coordination and oversight required similar sacrifices of him.

SOUNDING THE CALL

The 1905 biannual General Conference session (the first held in Takoma Park and the last held on a two-year basis) became a great occasion for missions promotion. Delegates from around the world attended.

Daniells, who loved reviewing the history of Seventh-day Adventist organization at these gatherings, did so yet again, reminding the assembled Seventh-day Adventist leadership that a missions board was the very first committee formed. Even before the young church had crossed the Missouri River or ventured south of the Ohio, Adventist pioneers were already considering worldwide ventures. And thus the message went to "nearly every land in this world." Even tiny Pitcairn Island "was not beyond the loud voice of the third angel." This task remains "the primary work of the General Conference Committee today," he exhorted.[61]

But if delegates could "rejoice that the Lord has rewarded the efforts of his people," they must not be content. "Only a beginning has been made" in certain mission fields, and in others nothing at all. Thus, in the very first of his eight-point agenda for immediate church action, Daniells determined that leaders give "earnest, intelligent study to the unentered territory." He was thinking of places such as Greece, Sicily, Madagascar, Uganda, Persia (Iraq), and the Philippines. Furthermore, countries where Adventist work was nascent, such as China, Korea, Ceylon, Turkey, and Egypt and portions of sub-Saharan Africa, merited additional human and financial resources. Accomplishing this would require a more equal distribution of church resources, Daniells bravely announced, realizing that tinkering with accustomed budgeting patterns invited recriminations. But in his eyes this should not be a problem, for church finances need not be a zero-sum game. Rather, a campaign to "secure the payment into the Lord's treasury of a full tithe" would satisfy the needs of all fields. Tithes should be twice what they were, Daniells felt, continually telling associates that America's current run of prosperity should translate into at least double the current tithe. This would mean another half-million dollars, which would not only energize mission efforts but also provide for workers' retirement and widow's pensions, which he also called for in 1905.[62]

Daniells included two further missions initiatives in his session-opening address. He determined that experienced General Conference Committee members would travel widely in the young fields of South America, Africa, and India, helping to organize the work. He did not say so, but Daniells undoubtedly hoped that exposure to world needs would impart a broader vision to those leaders for whom local needs came first. He also called for redoubled efforts on behalf of recent immigrants to the

United States. German and Scandinavian settlers in the Midwest in particular were embracing the three angels' messages. This call met quick acceptance at the General Conference session when the Foreign Department was established. By 1908 there were thirty ordained ministers serving the thirty-five hundred German members. More Scandinavian believers were in the United States than in Scandinavian countries.[63]

It was left to W. A. Spicer, another veteran missionary whose heart for the worldwide Gospel Commission was as big as Daniells's, to sum up the session's accomplishments. "Anxious hearts were waiting in the distant fields to know if the General Conference would call for retrenchment and delay, or sound the note of advance." "Advance is the word," Spicer was delighted to report, "and the trumpet call of the conference gives the order with no uncertain sound." Workers were recommended for Europe, Africa, China, South America, and Japan. Now, Spicer concluded, it falls to the American churches to support these brave-hearts in their ventures. The July 1 offering would be dedicated to accomplishing what Ellen White requested the church to do: "belt the world" through the missionary effort.[64]

The church took another step two years later when, with obvious satisfaction, Daniells announced in the pages of the *Review and Herald* that a school for aspiring missionaries was being established in Takoma Park. Washington Training College would be refashioned into Washington Foreign Mission Seminary (and even later, Columbia Union College and then Washington Adventist University). Led by Professor Homer Salisbury (arriving from England), the school planned to create a curriculum specific to overseas mission effort. "We now want to hear from hundreds of our young people who would like to volunteer for mission fields," Daniells urged. Local conferences would later be urged to encourage promising candidates to attend. The earlier founding of Emmanuel Missionary College in 1902 made a bow toward this commitment in its name. The Washington seminary now promised to infuse the "missionary" appellation with intentionality.[65]

A. G. Daniells's determination to build on recent foreign mission successes accompanied an unsettling realization that membership growth in America was embarrassingly low. A North American membership of more than 60,000 added but 845 new members in 1904. There had been a time, Daniells was convinced, when the driving conviction of every

Adventist conference was to grow. Members largely took care of their own spiritual needs, allowing church workers to focus on evangelism. What had brought about the current evangelistic malaise? "Our vision has been shortened," he told General Conference session delegates and *Review* readers. Attention has turned from "the teeming millions abroad to ourselves at home." The recovery of domestic vitality would only come from looking abroad, renewing members' attention on "the great perishing world."[66]

Daniells shared with delegates an additional startling statistic (which he no doubt spent much time stewing over): the denomination expended $574.53 for each new member in America and only $165.14 per foreign convert. Such calculations suggest that Daniells knew but one criterion for gauging success: increased numbers of Sabbath keepers. Most of his colleagues shared this definition. E. E. Andross, for example, president of the North England Conference, wrote apologetically that membership growth there appeared slight because of the need to adjust downward previously reported figures. But, in a manner typical of midlevel administrators seeking to reassure their bosses, he hastened to add that all workers were diligently about their tasks and "our numbers will constantly be growing."[67]

Doubtless other considerations contributed to sluggish growth (including American ministers' increasing attention to the nurture of congregations—a task Daniells had yet to fully value). Still, he shrewdly grasped that a third-generation church needed a reinfusion of evangelistic vision. He was determined to accomplish just that. But at the same time he understood that however much he lived for foreign missions, most of his attention would necessarily be given to matters medical, theological, and evangelistic within America.

---

[1] AGD to E. W. Farnsworth, March 26, 1902, ASTR.

[2] Schwarz and Greenleaf, *Light Bearers*, 273, 274; quotation from Børge Schantz, "The Development of Seventh-day Adventist Missionary Thought: Contemporary Appraisal," PhD dissertation, Fuller Theological Seminary, 1983, 377.

[3] Stephen Neill, *A History of Christian Missions* (London: Penguin Books, 1964), 393–395.

[4] "Biographical Sketch of W. A. Spicer," *RH*, November 13, 1952, 14; Schwarz and Greenleaf, *Light Bearers*, 274.

[5] AGD to W. W. Prescott and O. A. Olsen, July 11, 1901; AGD to WCW, October 9, 1901; John Wessels to AGD, May 29, 1901; AGD to E. W. Farnsworth, April 3, 1901, ASTR.

[6] I appreciate veteran missiologist Russell Staples's clarifications on South African and early Solusi Mission history as well as the Mission Round Tables.

[7] Report of committee on the question of polygamy in the heathen fields, Missions Round Table, 1913 General Conference, CAR.

[8] Ibid.

[9] AGD to E. W. Farnsworth, March 25, 1902, GCPL.

[10] AGD to J. A. Burden, March 23, 1902; D. M. Stead to AGD, September 19, 1901.

[11] AGD to G. A. Irwin, March 25, 1902, GCPL.

[12] AGD to E. W. Farnsworth, March 25, 1902; Schwarz and Greenleaf, *Light Bearers*, 274.

[13] AGD to WCW, May 5, 1902; AGD to Alexander Costello, May 5, 1902, ASTR.

[14] AGD to W. L. Baker, May 8, 1902; AGD to W. W. Prescott, May 9, 1902; AGD to I. H. Evans, May 15, 1902, ASTR.

[15] AGD to Edith Graham, May 12, 1902, ASTR.

[16] AGD to EGW, June 8, 1902, ASTR.

[17] Schwarz and Greenleaf, *Light Bearers*, 285; AGD to WWP, May 20, 1902; AGD to G. G. Rupert, May 18, 1902, ASTR.

[18] AGD to EGW, June 2, 1902; AGD to W. W. Prescott, May 29, 1902; AGD to J. D. Cowell, May 26, 1902, ASTR.

[19] AGD to WCW, June 14, 1902.

[20] AGD to WCW, June 2, 1902, EGWE.

[21] AGD to WCW, August 22, 1902, EGWE; Dr. Sheridan Gilley, review of *The Death of Christian Britain: Understanding Secularisation, 1800–2000* (review no. 236), accessed August 31, 2012, http://www.history.ac.uk/reviews/review/236.

[22] AGD to W. H. Thurston, May 30, 1902, GCPL; AGD to I. H. Evans, June 15, 1902; AGD to WCW, July 4, 1902, EGWE; *RH*, August 18, 1904, 12.

[23] AGD to WCW, July 6, 1902, EGWE.

[24] Ibid.

[25] Schwarz and Greenleaf, *Light Bearers*, 276; AGD to WCW, August 1, 1902, EGWE.

[26] AGE to WCW, August 1, 1902.

[27] Ibid.

[28] AGD to Brothers Flaiz, Shultz, and Nelson, August 21, 1902; AGD to E. N. Andross, August 28, 1902, GCPL.

[29] AGD to E. W. Farnsworth, March 26, 1902.

[30] AGD to A. E. Olsen, September 16, 1902, GCPL.

[31] Neill, *History of Christian Missions*, chap. 10. John Hersey provides a fine imaginative account of the collegiate mission fervor in *The Call* (Penguin Books, 1986).

[32] Mission Board minutes, August 25, 1902.

[33] Ibid., August 25, September 18, 1902; AGD to L. R. Conradi, December 11, 1902; AGD to W. C. Sisley, September 29, 1902; "Report of last portion of Conference meeting held on the Iowa camp-ground," June 6, 1901, ASTR. General Conference Statistical Reports, 1902–1904. Details on Vermont provided in e-mail message from Floyd Greenleaf to author, December 15, 2012.

[34] Mission Board minutes, December 16, 1902.

[35] GCCMin, April 30, 1903.

[36] Valentine, *Prescott*, 158–161, on the Emmanual Missionary College brouhaha; AGD to E. J. Waggoner, January 18, 1904; E. J. Waggoner to AGD, March 6, 1904, ASTR.

[37] AGD to W. C. Sisley, September 29, 1902; AGD to W. A. Westworth, September 29, 1902, ASTR.

[38] *GCB*, April 3, 1903, 62.

[39] Ibid., Index Number, August 1903, 221, 222.

[40] AGD to E. W. Farnsworth, March 26, 1902, ASTR.

[41] G. A. Irwin to AGD, January 7, 1904; February 21, 1904; August 28, 1904, ASTR.

[42] G. A. Irwin to AGD, August 28, 1904.

[43] L. R. Conradi to AGD, June 25, 1903.

[44] L. R. Conradi to AGD, July 20, 1903, August [n.d.], 1903.

[45] L. R. Conradi to AGD, August [n.d.], 1903.

[46] L. R. Conradi to AGD, August 16, 1903; February 12, 1904.

[47] AGD to L. R. Conradi, January 17, 1904.

[48] L. R. Conradi to AGD, February 12, 1904; AGD to L. R. Conradi, January 17, 1904.

[49] GCCMin, October 11, 14, 1903.

[50] *RH*, May 25, 1905, 4; Schwarz and Greenleaf, *Light Bearers*, 282; John Wessels to AGD, February 16, 1904; W. S. Hyatt to W. A. Spicer, January 5, 1904, ASTR.

[51] W. S. Hyatt to John Wessels, August 13, 1904; W. S. Hyatt to W. A. Spicer, January 5, 1904; [Extracts from W. S. Hyatt's letter from our Nyassaland Station], August 5, 1904, ASTR.

[52] Schwarz and Greenleaf, *Light Bearers*, 223; *RH*, May 25, 1905, 13; AGD to J. L. Shaw, May 12, 1903; J. L. Shaw to AGD, December 1, 1902.

[53] Schwarz and Greenleaf, *Light Bearers*, 289, 290; H. Miller to AGD, January 24, 1904; October 20, 1904; November 2, 1904; H. Miller to W. A. Spicer, March 15, 1904, ASTR.

[54] J. N. Anderson to W. A. Spicer, March 20, 1904, ASTR; *RH*, June 1, 1905, 4.

[55] *RH*, June 1, 1905, 5, 6; June 15, 1905, 13, 14; Schwarz and Greenleaf, *Light Bearers*, 291.

[56] Schwarz and Greenleaf, *Light Bearers*, 219, 220, 283, 284; GCCMin, September 23, 1904.

[57] Floyd Greenleaf, *The Seventh-day Adventist Church in Latin America and the Caribbean* (Berrien Springs, MI: Andrews University Press, 1992), 1:12, 13; *RH*, June 1, 1905, 19; November 24, 1904, 15.

[58] G. H. Baber to AGD, June 7, 1904; *RH*, July 28, 1904, 14. Baber was soon thereafter appointed principal of Oakwood Manual Training School, apparently putting an end to his Cuban entrepreneurial schemes.

[59] Greenleaf, *SDA Church in Latin America*, 1:55–59, 61; *RH*, June 8, 1905, 14; GCCMin, May 3, 4, 7, 1903; AGD to G. H. Brown, January 7, 1903, GCPL.

[60] *RH*, June 22, 1897, 400; June 5, 1905, 14; Greenleaf, *SDA Church in Latin America*, 1:67, 68; George W. Caviness to AGD, December 9, 1904; G. H. Brown to AGD, November 21, 1904, ASTR.

[61] *RH*, May 11, 1905, 6.

[62] Ibid., 9, 10.

[63] Ibid., 10; June 8, 1905, 3; GCCMin, April 21, 1908.

[64] *RH*, June 15, 1905, 4, 5.

[65] *RH*, July 11, 1907, 5, 6; GCCMin, October 12, 1909.

[66] *RH*, May 11, 1905, 8.

[67] Ibid.; E. E. Andross to AGD, January 25, 1904. But the following November Andross had to report that though baptisms were disappointing for the most recent quarter, there was reason to believe that the next quarter he should be able to report "quite a good many." E. E. Andross to AGD, November 30, 1904, ASTR.

CHAPTER IX

ADMINISTRATOR AND URBAN EVANGELIST

The Adventist evangelistic formula was straightforward and simple in design. New fields were fertilized by literature evangelists, scattering books and pamphlets that promoted Adventist distinctives. Evangelistic meetings followed, focusing on Bible prophecies and the Sabbath. Success brought companies of believers, followed by churches. Once a beachhead was established, local publishing efforts and medical institutions followed.

But as any athletic coach will attest, even simple game plans require precise execution.

A. G. Daniells understood the need for teamwork if his beloved church were to succeed in its ordained mission. He longed for talented and selfless workers to implement the plan. But he was realistic enough to know that a worldwide effort would face setbacks. Workers would disappoint him. Bitter struggles with Kellogg and the medical arm of the church vexed leadership. And disagreements over seemingly small points of theology roiled on.

These challenges, though, seemed to energize Daniells. He maintained the denomination's commitment to medical ministry. And theological heterodoxy, distressing as it was, provoked healthy doctrinal self-examination. Further, Daniells came to appreciate that church leadership, like the military, sometimes required leading from the front. He modeled this in 1910 when, under prodding from Ellen White, he temporarily set aside other responsibilities to undertake frontline urban evangelism.

THE CHURCH IN 1910

Seventh-day Adventist history has frustrated scholars who try to place it neatly within a "sect to denomination" model. Some find the model overly simplistic. Nonetheless, the idea that religious groups tend to move through recognizable phases of development has some merit (and the sect-denomination typology was originally expressed by Max Weber and Ernst Troeltsch during these very years). The first decade of Daniells's presidency witnessed his church's continuing march toward increasing bureaucratization. Local and union conferences continued being formed around the world. The church in North America added more than fourteen hundred church employees between 1900 and 1910 without a commensurate increase in membership (resulting in a ratio of American members to workers that fell from 20:1 to 14:1). One sees bureaucratization also in the more complete statistical reports the General Conference issued each year, in the more sophisticated *Review and Herald* (which traded its earlier informal charm and candor for a more visually attractive but perhaps less revealing format), and in the management demands made upon its president.[1]

The church's 1910 *Statistical Report* happily noted that more than 100,000 people worldwide now kept Sabbath (the preferred criterion for counting) as part of the Adventist fellowship. Since 1901 the world church had grown by 25 percent under Daniells's leadership, from just over 78,000 actual church members to roughly 104,500. Church leaders took some satisfaction in this level of progress. But they could not rest content—certainly not with the rate of growth in North America, which still represented nearly two-thirds of overall membership but whose growth rate lagged. In his quiet moments, Daniells must have reflected uneasily upon the fact that significant increase in administrative overhead had not translated into membership growth. Was the evangelistic talent of the church now sitting in committees rather than hitting the sawdust trail? He was not ready to entertain the possibility of a mistake. The church, after all, had received counsel from Ellen White that it was to "enlarge the circle of administration." Better times must lie ahead. Growth was not simply an option; it was an imperative for a group persuaded that its mission had eternal consequences. Thus, Daniells pushed his church to greater efforts.[2]

If membership numbers lagged, another measure of church growth was more positive: proliferating church institutions. Adventism has always been characterized by its aggressive institution building in education, publishing, and health. In 1910, twenty-eight publishing houses produced materials in sixty-seven languages. Seventy-four sanitariums promoted the Adventist vision of health. Six hundred eighty schools, from primary grades through college, instructed more than seven thousand students. These figures reflect Adventism's paradoxical genius for putting institutional legs under an apocalyptic vision of the future. And it was Arthur Daniells's gift (one could argue his "genius") to provide highly effective leadership to this effort.

The church's annual financial reporting was more veiled than membership figures, but not income, which church publications detailed for readers. Members donated nearly $1.4 million in tithe in 1910, and another nearly half million in offerings. American members gave almost 73 percent of this total. Readers were pointedly told that per-capita giving for mission offerings was but $6.58—an unsubtle prod for more generosity. The official discretion regarded budgets, which neither Daniells nor the treasury saw reason to reveal to members.

What were the issues that most occupied Daniells in the years from 1908 through 1912? With the exception of church reorganization (which had by now became a thorough part of the warp and woof of the denomination), the matters occupying Daniells were largely those he had wrestled with from the beginning: balancing the books, debating personnel decisions, visiting camp meetings, presiding over endless conference and General Conference committees, seeking accommodation with the medical arm, and, always, promoting foreign missions.

In his 1909 presidential address at the General Conference session, Daniells focused on continued organizational growth (now 21 union conferences, 102 local conferences, and 69 mission fields). Speaking as only a dedicated organization man could, he noted that the "extension of our cause demonstrates more clearly each year the value of thorough organization." This had necessitated adding some five hundred new people to administration at various levels. Such administrative expansion, combined with tepid American membership growth rates (falling below that of the nation's population growth rate), must have raised a red flag among the more thoughtful. But Daniells, true to the presidential task of bearing primarily good news in public forums, avoided speaking uncomfortable facts. Instead, he proposed goals for the church and its leadership involving spiritual renewal, missions, improved church literature, and a new emphasis on estate planning among members to increase legacies to the denomination. Missing here was any emphasis on urban evangelism. Although most hearers probably thought little of its absence, one whose opinion mattered above all did. Ellen White was dismayed by the omission, and as will be discussed below, she soon acted to correct the oversight.[3]

Daniells also maintained an active interest in religious liberty affairs. In 1905 he led a delegation of forty that visited President Theodore Roosevelt in the White House cabinet office. Daniells read to the president a short memorial expressing the church's support for civil government. Such an affirmation might seem odd, but the church had recently suffered verbal attacks as "anarchists" and "enemies of law and order." Leaders hoped that the event, well covered by the Washington press, would be remembered as "ready refutation" against calumnies.[4]

One reason for these attacks was Adventism's vigilance against Sunday laws. From the late nineteenth century until well into the 1920s, conservative Protestant leaders sought to persuade Congress to pass Sunday closing laws in the District. The church's Religious Liberty Department (restyled the Religious Liberty Association in 1909 as a means of increasing its public influence by masking its affiliation with the church) successfully fought these proposals at every step. Daniells lent his office to the effort. He penned a strong letter to the editor of the *Christian Advocate* (a publication advocating Sunday legislation) pointing out that Adventists oppose such bills not because of their belief in a Saturday Sabbath but because of time-honored American constitutional principles of separation of church and state. He also joined religious liberty leaders on Capitol Hill, where several of them testified before a House committee considering yet another District Sunday ordinance. Prescott delivered the primary testimony, a virtuoso performance that Daniells considered "the best testimony made during the day." Concerns about religious liberty were sufficiently great to prompt the General Conference Committee to pass a series of resolutions in 1908 calling upon conferences and schools to redouble efforts to educate and advocate for America's traditional stance of unfettered religious liberty and to fight the "iniquitous traffic" in liquor.[5]

A NEW TERM, AN OLD CONTROVERSY

The 1909 session in Takoma Park was the first held on a quadrennial basis. Facing the expense and effort of including delegates from a worldwide church, the decision had been made in 1905 to extend length between sessions. Despite moments of discouragement and occasional suggestions in private correspondence that he would soon be ready to turn the reins over to another, Daniells gave no overt indication at the session that he desired to step down. In truth, the denomination was not awash in administrative talent. But did Daniells not believe that Prescott or Spicer were up to the task? Or did he think them unacceptable to other leaders? Prescott, as will be seen, had been tinged with controversy from the ongoing debates over "the daily." He was not the man for the moment. But Spicer would seem to have had no political disqualifications. More likely, Daniells had become accustomed to leadership, enjoyed it (all things considered), and perhaps even thought himself indispensable. In any event, he would continue another thirteen years in the post.[6]

A theological cloud hovered about these tented meetings (held on the grounds of what is now Washington Adventist University), and a few of the "old-timers" muttered among themselves—and to Ellen White—that the time had come for a change at the top. The discontent flowed from ongoing controversy over a point of biblical interpretation known by the brief term "the daily." It may seem today a small matter of exegesis, but it loomed very large to contemporaries.[7]

The issue dated to William Miller's interpretation of a passage in Daniel 8:11–13. The "taking away" of the *Tamid* ("the daily," the precise meaning of which scholars continue to debate) was understood by Miller as something done by Roman paganism. Neither historical nor exegetical scholarship has given support to Miller's view. This reading of a minor element in the larger prophetic understanding of Miller would not have mattered except that Uriah Smith included the exegesis in his hugely influential *Thoughts on the Book of Daniel*. Further, the young Ellen White had seemed to endorse this reading in a brief paragraph in *Early Writings*. For some veteran Adventists, that was all they needed to know about the issue. But for Prescott, the nearest thing the church had to a resident scholar, "the daily" clearly meant something else. For a number of years he had been convinced that it spoke of Christ's sanctuary ministry, which the Roman Church sought to "take away" with its focus on the earthly priestly ministrations.[8]

Prescott kept his revisionist views from the Adventist public during the difficult years with Kellogg, when the church certainly did not need another distraction. But he was encouraged by Louis Conradi's having reached the same conclusion and having published his ideas in Europe—with no fallout. Further, in 1907 Prescott had persuaded enough of the General Conference Committee that he received permission to share the new interpretation publicly. It didn't take long for friction to produce heat. A study session on the matter at Elmshaven in 1908 included Clarence Crisler (Ellen White's chief editorial assistant), Prescott, Daniells, and the leading members of the "old guard," Haskell and Loughborough, among others (though not Ellen White). Prescott presented his reasoned argument—to no avail. Haskell and Loughborough would have none of it. Historic Adventism was at risk. They responded by mounting an immediate counterattack, including use of the ultimate weapon: an appeal to Ellen White's writings to nip heresy in the bud.

Where did Daniells stand on the matter? Every administrative impulse urged caution. Moreover, he had previously shown himself a defender of orthodoxy, not only in Kellogg's matter, but also in confronting Albion Ballenger's challenge to the historic position on the sanctuary. Daniells supported the removal of Ballenger's ministerial credentials at the 1905 General Conference Session. "I think the best place for such men," he commented, "is on some farm or orchard where they can live a quiet and peaceable life, and do as little damage as possible." But the sanctuary doctrine was foundational to Adventism; "you remove that," Daniells intoned, "and everything tumbles." "The daily" did not quite rise to that level of significance (though to witness the vehemence with which some defended it might lead one to conclude otherwise).[9]

And indeed he initially appealed to Prescott to proceed slowly. There seemed little to gain from an internecine doctrinal fight. Yet the most notable thing about Daniells's role in "the daily" controversy was his willingness to become an advocate, allowing a divisive issue to move forward. Prescott had persuaded him that the new understanding constituted present truth. Daniells did not allow his conflict-avoiding administrative role to trump doctrinal integrity. Thus, he encouraged Prescott to proceed with a *Review* series on Daniel and to teach the new interpretation to Bible teachers and conference workers about the country.

The expected resistance came. As diligent as he was cunning, Haskell responded by threatening to print up and circulate an old Millerite-era prophetic chart (one Ellen White had long ago endorsed) that would remind Adventist faithful of their doctrinal roots. Dismayed by escalating developments, Willie White appealed to Prescott (begging pardon for having forgotten to deliver an earlier message of caution from his mother) to delay the already publicized series. Prescott consented, though now discouraged at the difficulty of assisting his beloved church to gain new biblical understanding. "He [Prescott] can scarcely muster the heart and courage necessary to undertake anything more," Daniells wrote Crisler.[10]

In May 1908 the General Conference Committee, more persuaded than ever by Prescott's interpretation, gave him the go-ahead on an even more ambitious *Review* series. Heartened, Prescott renewed his journalistic efforts. But Haskell's campaign against him—scarcely less than character assassination—took its toll. In Haskell's mind, a refutation of this point, as minor a doctrinal point as he admitted it to be, constituted a challenge to White's prophetic gift. She cannot have been wrong. In August, both Prescott and Daniells deemed it prudent to end the Daniel series, even before the pertinent chapter had been reached. Daniells could not fault his friend on any count. His scholarship appeared impeccable. He had followed proper procedures, been circumspect and accommodating to others' feelings. What else might he have done?[11]

Thus the issue remained vexed, even intruding itself in the 1909 General Conference Session. By this point it had clearly become a generational issue. Those pioneers such as Loughborough, Haskell, Butler, Irwin, and certain of their zealous epigones, Leon Smith (Uriah's son) and O. A. Johnson, displayed energy belying their age. The latter circulated a pamphlet on the session grounds that accused General Conference leadership of undermining the authority of Ellen White. The *Review*'s coverage of the three-week General Conference session provided little sense of the divisions. But former church president O. A. Olsen, chairing the nominating committee, dropped a hint in his report to the delegates that matters had put Daniells's job on the line. "I think that I never was a member of a committee that went more carefully into its work." Nothing was "taken for granted," he told the assembled delegates, apparently seeking to assure those who grumbled about Daniells that the committee had considered their discontent.[12]

Of course, Daniells survived. The same could not be said for Prescott.

Ellen White had made the taxing transcontinental train trip to attend the session (what she considered likely to be her last face-to-face interaction with gathered leadership). At session's end she asked to meet with selected men. As she later told son Edson, she "spoke . . . some very plain words." Prescott was to leave his post as *Review* editor and take up urban evangelism. The General Conference men were astonished and momentarily dismayed. His editorial pen would not be easily replaced. But the command was clear, and Prescott, ever the good soldier, complied.[13]

Two things seemed to have prompted White's counsel (in addition to her determination to get city evangelism moving). First, she favorably recalled Prescott's preaching during his time in Australia in the 1890s. Second, she clearly had been worn down by Haskell's unremitting criticism of him. Moving Prescott out of an influential editorial post and into the safer field of evangelism might bring the peace she desperately wanted. But she did not foresee the distress the change brought Prescott. The emotional toll the controversy took on Prescott was now compounded by his wife's rapid decline, ending in her death in June 1910. He fell into depression. In the midst of personal turmoil, the old professor had to face taking up evangelistic duties for which he was not suited.[14]

One might hope that contention over "the daily" would have ended at this point. But doctrinal controversies resist easy resolution. Too much seemed at stake for either side to let go. Thus the matter dragged on into 1910.

In part the issue continued because emboldened advocates of the "old view" mounted a campaign to reinforce their views, but also because Daniells and new *Review* editor Spicer were convinced that important principles were at stake and justified a counter campaign. The issue of "the daily" also rankled because at this time in denominational history there was no clear resolving authority—other than Ellen White herself. The church had no set of formally trained biblical scholars (such as later at the Seventh-day Adventist Theological Seminary or the Biblical Research Institute) tasked with doctrinal study. Nor had a comprehensive set of official beliefs been adopted. The *Review and Herald*'s articles on biblical and theological matters probably constituted as close an official statement of beliefs as anything in the church (which was why Prescott's removal from the editorial post was significant for his antagonists). But Daniells possessed the advantage of having direct access to conference leaders across the country. He was prepared to help dispel the confusion among them regarding the doctrinal dissension over Daniel 8. Thus, while Prescott's plans for city evangelism were still in formation, Daniells arranged for him in late 1909 to give presentations on the disputed passage to gatherings of conference leaders.[15]

Daniells displayed a side of himself during "the daily" controversy not often seen: the biblical scholar committed to truth. He was by instinct conservative in matters of belief. "I am not given to floundering around in search of new doctrines," he said, looking suspiciously on claims of "new light." Yet, as a young minister he had wondered why Uriah Smith had attributed varying meanings to the terms *host* and *sanctuary* in different verses. He had let that go and preached traditional prophetic interpretation. But, prodded by Prescott, he gave "the most careful and thorough study I have ever given any one point of our faith." He concluded that the traditional Adventist interpretation of Daniel 8 must give way to the new one. Naïvely, perhaps, Daniells believed that truth would be its own persuader. "In this I have been terribly disappointed, at least, with a few of the brethren." They "drive stakes and erect an impassible barrier against ever discarding anything that we now hold, and receiving anything that we do not hold."[16]

Daniells's blood was now up. He became positively evangelical on the issue, enthusing to Willie White (who also embraced the new interpretation) about Prescott's presentations. Daniells felt the issue spoke to the church's ability to be intellectually honest. Otherwise, he "would not waste much of my time arguing with men who persist in making claims utterly at variance with all the reliable history of the world." But the matter transcended even purely historical questions of "when paganism was taken away." It concerned "the pope, the cardinals, bishops, priests, the saints, the images, the censor, the confessional," and the rest that "have been put between the sinner and the Saviour." Daniells could not sidestep a battle when it threatened "the glorious truth the Bible teaches regarding the ministry of Christ in the heavenly sanctuary." He even researched and wrote his own paper on the subject.[17]

Daniells and Prescott understood that at the heart of Haskell and others' strenuous defense of the old position was an elemental fear. If any position that Ellen White had once endorsed was changed, such alteration would be tantamount to repudiation of her prophetic office. The rigid, literalistic definition of her words parked the denomination in a corner from which there seemed no egress. Daniells believed he had an answer to their fears. In a conversation with White about her *Early Writings* statement she seemed to say that what was revealed to her was something apart from the technical meaning of "the daily." This became the revisionist party's answer: she had endorsed the 2,300-year prophecy, not "the daily" specifically. The new interpretation did not suggest a faulty prophet. To the contrary, Daniells argued, "those who interpret that passage in 'Early Writings' as supporting the Old View are doing your mother a great wrong. They are arraying her against the plain text of the Scripture, and all the reliable history of the world."[18]

At the 1910 summer teachers' conference in Berrien Springs (the largest such gathering the church had ever held to that point), Daniells was gratified by the response of Bible teachers to Prescott's present truth, most notably by Professor C. S. Longacre (a "rather stiff-headed man," as Daniells described him). When first confronted by the new light, Longacre had been dismissive. But he had given the matter a fair hearing, and by the time of the conference could report that he had taught the revised interpretation all winter to his students. Attendees at the Berrien Springs conference wanted to hear the president's opinion. So for three evenings he read from his fifty-page manuscript on the subject and then took questions on the fourth. "These Bible teachers told me," Daniells reported to Willie, "that they had never been able to expound the eighth chapter of Daniel to their satisfaction until they got hold of this view." Daniells must have realized that persuading these shapers of young Adventist minds assured the future for the new interpretation.[19]

In his eagerness to champion the new and "correct" view, Daniells may have overstepped. At a Southern Union workers meeting in Nashville he led a discussion on "the daily." But, complained attendee J. S. Washburn, the "new view monopolized all the time. . . . No opportunity, as at Washington, was given for a statement of the old view." It seemed as though the president expected others "to hear without reply." Daniells and Washburn were still friends (at least Daniells so assumed) at this point, but the former had no inkling how sharing with Washburn his private views on the nature of White's prophetic ministry would create an implacable foe, indeed, one who contributed to his administrative downfall.[20]

Washburn, though younger than Daniells, illustrated how the interpretive old guard resisted passing the baton to the new generation. J. N. Loughborough, a self-confessed "defender of the faith," spent seven months preparing a manuscript on "the daily" that Stephen Haskell published in his *Bible Training School* periodical. Leon Smith and J. S. Washburn, unceasing, thought Daniells, in their campaign against Prescott, sought to "destroy the good name and standing of those who differ with them." They were "shockingly indiscreet" in widely reporting private conversations with Ellen White. Smith and Washburn stooped to playing the ultimate low card: they reminded people that Jones and Waggoner were sympathetic to the new view—"and look where they are." Having gotten Prescott's head, the group hoped to add Daniells's to their trophy case. His reelection in 1909 had been a setback, but the campaign to persuade the Whites of his unfitness to lead continued. Washburn had gotten from F. C. Gilbert his notes of a conversation with Ellen White in which, according to Gilbert, White seemed to repudiate Daniells as president. Washburn mimeographed Gilbert's "interview" and circulated them to eager ears. Willie sought to deflect these attacks, but it is clear that the influential voices were influencing his mother. Ellen White, of course, shared a long history with these men. They had together fought the good fight on behalf of the three angels' message. She could not help but be influenced by their persistence.[21]

These months leading into mid-1910 occasioned the most troubled moments in Daniells's relationship with the church's prophet. Complicating the situation was White's frantic desire for him to aggressively promote city evangelism. His apparent foot-dragging on urban work eroded her confidence in him and turned her ear to the intriguers on the West Coast. Relating to a prophet in declining strength proved a difficult proposition. Daniells sought her direct counsel on "the daily" issue on several occasions. In 1908 he had caught her on a good day (chronic illness had by then become her companion) and proceeded with what he thought a clear and useful discussion of Daniel 8. But when he reached the more technical aspect of the Hebrew term, she "would go into that twilight zone right away." Ellen White's inability toward the close of her life to fully grasp doctrinal questions impeded resolution of the issue.[22]

What she did know was that the General Conference president failed to heed counsel. Her unhappiness occasionally passed over to pique. Perhaps the most well-known Adventist tale of presidential comeuppance occurred in 1910, when Daniells traveled to Elmshaven for a consultation only to be rebuffed at the door. That year, her confidence in him reached its nadir. Willie reported to him that his mother was wondering out loud if Daniells had been too long in the presidency. She feared his long leadership may have brought a sense of having "superior wisdom" and becoming unresponsive to counsel of man or Holy Spirit. When both Daniells and Prescott were truly converted, she judged, they would be fit for leadership.[23]

Underlying the pleasure Haskell and others must have taken in the story of Daniells's discomfiture was a form of populist resentment many in the church felt toward the leadership elite in Washington. Church leaders in the Southern field as well as those in California resented what they considered imperious, controlling treatment from General Conference headquarters. The trend toward extensive church centralization, which would mark Adventism from the early twentieth century onward, generated a mild backlash among members. They recalled that Adventism was to be a "movement" and that resistance to organization had been a hallmark of the early, pristine days.

Although Ellen White's powers were diminishing, she was still perceptive enough to realize that contention over "the daily" had to be ended, even if not resolved. She took up her pen and wrote, "I request that my writings shall not be used as the leading argument to settle questions over which there is now so much controversy." The matter was not "to be made a test question." She took pains to be evenhanded, calling out Haskell, Loughborough, and Smith to desist from quoting her in their campaign. She also noted that there could be details in historic Adventist belief that require further study. But care must be taken not to reflect on older doctrinal positions in a manner that would undermine confidence in the church. In sum, it was best to let the matter drop for the time in the name of unity.[24]

Daniells could well appreciate the call for unity. And the habit of deference to the Spirit of Prophecy was so strongly ingrained that any question of disregarding its counsel was unthinkable. Still, he must have regretted that an opportunity to highlight the centrality of Christ's work in Adventist doctrine (which was the thrust of Prescott's interpretation) was lost. Ironically, this Christological emphasis had marked the last phase of Ellen White's career in works such as *The Desire of Ages* and *Steps to Christ*. But she was not sensing the connection.

Daniells worried to Willie White that the church faced a crucial moment on two counts. First, "that the standing and influence of your mother's work in this denomination is being imperiled" by those who possess testimonies and use them for their own purposes. He described how conference officials would come to him asking how it was that critics approached them, "their pockets full of personal testimonies" with commendations of their good work, while other hardworking men got no direction or praise. Daniells specified Sutherland, Magan, and Edson White as particularly guilty of this action. He wished they would be more modest about the compliments they received from her. Conversely, other folk would speculate about a testimony of rebuke they were sure so-and-so would be receiving soon. Leon Smith, for example, sent a note to a church worker predicting that Ellen White would soon issue a testimony that "would make the ears of the whole denomination tingle." The historic value of White's testimonies had been to correct individual, congregation, or denomination—with the purpose of binding together the church. But as now used, the testimonies were becoming a divisive, demoralizing force in the church.[25]

The second great challenge to the church regarded scholarly freedom. Daniells mused over to what extent members were "free to pursue an original investigation of the scripture, and to follow the honest conclusions at which they arrive." "Personally, I stand for liberty," he wrote. When he first entered the presidency, he faced the question of whether church leaders could follow their conscience or "whether they were to be dominated by denominational 'bosses.' " The Kellogg affair, Daniells reminisced, forced him to commit to being "true to my judgment and conscience." Now, the issue of whether "we are a free people in the matter of biblical research" had arisen. "It is idle to say that we shall not receive additional light. Both the scriptures and testimonies assure us that we will." New light came in 1888, which caused some doctrinal rethinking. By implication, Daniells was saying that more study required more rethinking.[26]

Unhappily, Daniells learned (as did earlier and would later Adventist theologians) that refining church theology was not for the faint of heart. Two steps forward and one step back is often the march of progress. "The daily" controversy represented a defeat for the ideal of careful study, rational reflection, and then change as appropriate. Not in the long run, for a Christ-centered theology would ultimately prevail in the church. But in the years 1909–1910 a spirit of dissension soured the church's atmosphere at the higher ranks. Valiant church pioneers sadly compromised their personal legacies because of their obstinate, even scurrilous actions. And Daniells had to face the melancholy and difficult matter of how to relate to a prophet whose powers were diminished but to whom the church continued to look for special guidance.

THE IMPORTANCE OF HISTORY

A. G. Daniells understood the value of history to the church. He frequently invoked denominational history during his addresses. And he appreciated the importance of Adventist publications getting their facts right.

An unpleasant incident in 1908 reinforced the need for scrupulous scholarship. In an unnamed town in New York State a church member used a popular Adventist chart purporting to show how the papacy changed the commandments. A local priest noticed it and challenged him to produce the papal document cited by the chart, threatening to expose their church to the public as frauds if proof was not forthcoming. The Latin citations were inscrutable to church members, so they contacted Prescott in a panic. Prescott did due diligence, visiting a church history scholar at Catholic University in Washington, but to no avail. The chart's claims could not be confirmed. Its citation, Daniells had to admit, might be bogus. The church's positions must be "subjected to the most rigid tests," he concluded. "If it can be demonstrated that we have based important calculations upon unreliable historical data, we shall be humiliated and the confidence of the people will be shaken in us."[27]

Daniells related this story to Clarence Crisler, Ellen White's literary assistant. The president did not need to point out the obvious: Adventism's signature text must be as historically trustworthy as possible. Since its publication in 1888, *The Great Controversy* had been subject to scrutiny. Lacking citations, certain claims it made could not be verified. There were also the inevitable infelicities and errors of fact that creep into any large work of history. The work needed an editorial update. As it happened, the opportunity came just two years later, when new printing plates would have to be made for the book. Ellen White and her staff agreed that needful changes should be made.[28]

The editorial approach was systematic and thorough. Sales people on the front lines of the publishing and canvassing work were consulted about important issues they might have faced. Prescott, with his usual diligence, submitted a thirty-eight-page letter of suggested revisions. Among the questions White's staff asked themselves, two stood out: First, what changes in wording might make the book more palatable to Catholic readers? And second, how should they deal with the many quotations that appeared originally without attribution? Willie reported to Daniells that his mother unhesitatingly agreed that sources must be cited. This would be a massive undertaking. The best English sources of church history were consulted, and what began as a project anticipated to last a few weeks extended into months. Clarence Crisler scoured libraries at Berkeley and Stanford for European history sources. People were recruited to check sources in eastern libraries and even in Europe.[29]

These changes—adding citations and revising "ambiguities and misleading terms"—all carefully accomplished by Ellen White's trusted associates, might seem unobjectionable. But the project moved forward in 1910 coincident with "the daily" controversies. And any tinkering with *The Great Controversy* raised related questions: How could the words of Ellen White need improving? People asked Willie White if Daniells and Prescott had been critical of the book and sought to have it changed to agree with their Daniel 8 interpretation. Willie was quick to answer critics that no pressure was coming from Washington, nor did "the daily" even appear in *The Great Controversy*. But more disturbing than grumbling from the usual collection of malcontents was having Ellen White express similar fears. Were Daniells and his associates in Washington seeking out errors in her work? Willie tried to assure his mother that, on the contrary, they desired to find clear evidence substantiating *The Great Controversy*. But the mistrust only added to Daniells's sense that his usefulness as General Conference president might be coming to an end.[30]

Daniells served on a committee that reviewed all changes to the text, though he generally left decisions up to those closer to the project. He had confidence that Willie would properly oversee things and—he hoped—restore the confidence of his mother in him. But Daniells took one significant action. As part of his mission to improve historical literacy within the church, he requested copies of the extensive historical sources Crisler had collected during the editorial process. Daniells then placed these at various Adventist schools where they would be readily available.[31]

Not only *The Great Controversy*'s prose but also its illustrations received attention. A number of new engravings were commissioned to update visuals and to ensure accuracy. When in 1909 illustrations for Uriah Smith's *Thoughts on Daniel and the Revelation* were also being scrutinized, a mistake was pointed out in the rendering of the pope's tiara. The cut was to be discontinued until the inscription "Vicarius Filii Dei" on the tiara could be verified.[32]

Another publication effort, one which to Daniells's dismay did not come to quick fruition, was a "complete history" of the denomination. J. N. Loughborough had earlier penned the first history of the church, *The Rise and Progress of Seventh-day Adventists* (much of it from firsthand knowledge). But Daniells wanted a history suitable for the classroom. Discussion about a history project kicked about for several years. Finally, at a teacher's council in Cleveland he met with A. W. Spalding, then principal of Bethel Academy in Wisconsin. Spalding was developing a reputation as a denominational writer, and Daniells thought he had his man. Things seemed set to go. The General Conference statistical secretary had been gathering every document that could be found pertaining to the movement since the Disappointment. Daniells took great pride in this nascent archive. He delighted in telling Spalding of having secured the first pamphlet produced by Joseph Bates. With research material gathered, it simply needed to be put in narrative form. But within a few days plans changed. A subcommittee recommended a very different approach. Uncertain that a single (and quite young) person could fully understand the complexities of the organization, the new plan had each officer and departmental secretary compile the history of their own area. The notion was impractical, as any scholar might attest. The group history never materialized, and several years later, M. E. Olsen was commissioned to do the task.[33]

A HEART FOR EDUCATION

Daniells's desire to make the Adventist heritage readily available to students bespoke his love of church, of history generally, and of the educational enterprise broadly conceived. The latter was likely nurtured by his own acute sense of limited advanced education. Largely self-educated, Daniells would have enjoyed becoming an educator.

But as an administrator Daniells could influence education more than if he moved into the classroom. His keenest passion concerned ministerial training. From the moment he took office he fretted over the lack of learning among ministers—for him an acute problem in the church. The program of weeks-long ministerial institutes, begun in the 1890s by O. A. Olsen, was expanded the next decade (when most ministers still had no college training). Daniells could scratch his pedagogical itch by teaching at these institutes. He traveled to Knoxville to attend to pastors and Bible workers in the South; to College Place, Washington, to instruct those in the Northwest; to Battle Creek, where in the old Tabernacle as many as 164 attended. Seven meetings were held per day, with presentations split among himself, Spicer, and field secretary G. B. Thompson. They were intended to reassure clergy of the biblical basis for Adventist teachings and to generally instill greater biblical and theological sophistication. Daniells assumed that attendees were as energized by the institutes as was he. "I believe it will be remembered with pleasure by all who attended," he proudly wrote E. W. Farnsworth. (Such events also allowed the president to take stock of local situations. Daniells noted that the Battle Creek Church seemed now well separated from the sanitarium and appeared in the best spiritual condition he had seen.) He participated in such institutes outside America as well, crossing the Atlantic in 1911 for one in England. If all this were not enough, Daniells the autodidact compiled a suggested reading course for pastors.[34]

By 1910, nearly every North American union conference had a college or industrial training school. None was closer to Daniells's heart than the previously mentioned Foreign Mission Seminary (operated by the General Conference). He never missed a chance when traveling about the country to scout for talent among young people, encouraging them to come east and prepare for a life of foreign service. The seminary remained in what he called an "experimental stage," but it had already begun assisting those heading to foreign service. The curriculum was not standard college fare but fashioned for its mission purpose. Sizeable numbers of students had been sent abroad, and the Mission Board decided that in the future all appointees would come to the seminary for at least a brief course in their particular area of service. In a new departure, the seminary began recruiting students planning on stateside service. Always looking for ways to extend General Conference funds, Daniells encouraged local conferences to financially support students from their region.[35]

Aiding Daniells in his oversight of education was the capable Frederick Griggs, secretary of the Education Department. His call to become president of Union College in 1910 removed from Washington a valuable administrator. Daniells expressed sincere regret at his departure, but consistent with his philosophy of administration, understood that talented leaders must go where needs are greatest. Friendships must not get in the way. The Union College call was not a demotion. The school was then the largest in the denomination, located in the "garden of the United States, if not the garden of the world; you are surrounded by wealthy conferences where there is also a wealth of young people." Naturally, Daniells asked Griggs to be on the lookout for promising youth he could send to the Foreign Mission Seminary.[36]

But one school caused Daniells grief: the Nashville Agricultural and Normal Institute (better known as Madison School). The difficulty lay on three levels: its status as an independent institution; its founders, E. A. Sutherland and P. T. Magan; and the support given to it by Ellen White. No more contentious issue faced Daniells in 1908 than how the General Conference should relate to Madison.

Sutherland and Magan remain two of the most innovative and strong-willed educational leaders in Adventist history. Heading the new Emmanuel Missionary College during its establishment in Berrien Springs, they soon left to found a school they envisioned as being more clearly patterned after Ellen White's vision. They imagined a location in the hills of east Tennessee, but Ellen White, visiting Edson in Nashville, urged them to consider a site on the Cumberland River a few miles above the city. A rundown farm was acquired, and in the fall of 1904 school opened with a handful of students and teachers. It was devoted to producing Bible workers and teachers, with minimal expense to students, and with the direct goal of evangelism. Madison became the prototype and inspiration for nearly every Adventist self-supporting institution that followed in the twentieth century. For this reason it properly deserves remembrance as among the most influential institutions ever established within Adventism. Its equalitarian, group-governed culture, celebration of rural living and agriculture, emphasis on practical skills over book learning, and high idealism about the possibilities of social transformation were the closest thing ever seen in the denomination to the earlier American communitarian groups of the nineteenth century (or of the later communes of the 1960s). Over the following decade, nearly forty groups hived off to form new units.[37]

The Madison experiment in retrospect appears innovative and healthy. But to A. G. Daniells, there were warning clouds. Madison disturbed first the recent efforts to reorganize the church's institutions. Having dismantled the troubled network of quasi-independent associations, Daniells now saw looming the ghost of independence. For Daniells's highly developed sense of propriety, this represented a deviation undermining denomination order. Making matters worse, Sutherland and Magan held Daniells in low regard, an attitude Daniells repaid through aversion. For the independent-minded founders, Daniells represented all the worst features of the organization man: small-minded and controlling, requiring all enterprises to be approved and overseen by a church committee. The gospel could not go forward with those constraints. Sutherland publically opposed Daniells's reelection in 1903. In turn, Daniells saw Sutherland as undermining gospel order. He felt their differences were nearly irreconcilable, touching as they did on the integrity of the church and on the Spirit of Prophecy. We understand today that vibrant organizations need both kinds of people—but need them to ultimately work together.[38]

The bad blood became inconvenient for the Madison founders in 1904. Although the school was to be independent and self-supporting, it still needed good relations with church administration and access to fund-raising outlets, such as the *Review and Herald*. Thus, as the two pioneers looked to head south in early 1904, Sutherland found himself writing conciliatory letters to Daniells. "I hope it will be possible to have the same cooperation in the Nashville work that we had from you when we began the work in Berrien," he implored. In a fit of compliment sharing, he added, "The Testimony which stated that you were the man for the job [General Conference president] is certainly positive, and we accept it." Daniells would "find no opposition from us at the next General Conference," Sutherland pledged, admitting that he had opposed him in the 1903 General Conference election because Daniells had changed his policy. Magan that summer began writing to church administrators, apologizing for his past spirit of ill will toward Daniells. Magan and Sutherland wanted a truce.[39]

Sutherland was placating a powerful church figure, but he held in his pocket the winning ticket: an unqualified endorsement by Ellen White. Sutherland rarely missed a chance to remind Daniells of this fact. Nor that she had counseled that Madison remain independent of the official church structure. White had warned Sutherland against a large fund-raising effort at the same time that church leaders were seeking funds for the new Takoma Park facilities. But he might properly ask for church members' help "door-to-door," so to speak.[40]

The Madison and church headquarters parties maintained a détente of sorts until September 1907, when a troubling letter from Ellen White arrived in Washington. Addressed to both Daniells and I. H. Evans, treasurer of the General Conference, it wasted no time in raising an issue of integrity. The gospel "in behalf of the colored people" is essential and deserves respect. Funds intended for the Southern field should not "be diverted to the work elsewhere." And what made White think such diversions were occurring? A church functionary in the South, Calvin Bollman, had implied to her that not all funds earmarked for the South were arriving. White scolded the men for an apparent breach of fiduciary trust. She then segued into a concern about Madison school. "The Lord has instructed me that from the first the work in Huntsville and Madison should have received adequate help." Church administration had been "standing off" from Madison "because they are not bound to the conference." "It is not the Lord's plan that means should be withheld from Madison." White went on to affirm that conference organization was generally a good thing. "But there are some enterprises under certain conditions that will produce better results if standing alone."[41]

Daniells was dumbfounded on two levels. First, he could not imagine that his or his associates' integrity would be questioned. He expressed this to the prophet with his usual deference. "We accept that counsel in its fullest, . . . and we apply it to all other fields as well."

But he went on to deny that financial irresponsibility had occurred. "It has been our fixed purpose ever since I have been connected with the General Conference treasury to never divert one dollar from the field and the particular line of work or institution for which it was intended by the donor." To defuse the seriousness of the charge, Daniells chose to interpret Bollman's comments to White as being other than what they seemed. Further, he quoted a long portion of a recent letter from the worker to Daniells that expressed gratitude for his help with funds for the region. The danger in this "misunderstanding" lay more in what other people would make of White's letter to Daniells when it became public knowledge (which private testimonies had a way of doing). It will "now be taken by some parties and used all over the country to convince the people that it is not safe to send money through the General Conference office because we divert it. . . . They will report that you have said this in Testimonies to us. I shall have to meet this everywhere I go." This may be as close to a chiding of Ellen White as Daniells ever braved.[42]

The diversion issue was upsetting; the Madison matter was both upsetting and perplexing. Ellen White had encouraged the 1901 reorganization, supported church administration (ultimately) in its struggle with the church's medical arm, and, presumably, understood the distinction between an independent ministry and a church entity. Now she advocated breaching that bright line. Did she not recall, Daniells must have wondered, the recent struggles to bring the various financially strapped ministries under institutional control?

As Daniells reviewed her earlier correspondence regarding Sutherland, Magan, and Madison, his perplexities grew. How could church leaders have known of Madison's plans or needs since there was no regular communication with the independent group? Further, Magan had said earlier that his school was not "in need of 'the necessities for existence' " and did not want to be a "burden to the General Conference Committee." Nonetheless, the church treasury did send a small sum to Madison in response to White's plea. But help would be limited. Daniells then laid before the prophet a litany of hardships missionaries endured around the world. The Andersons in China lived surrounded by fish offal because the "European quarters" were too expensive. A different Anderson family, missionaries in Africa, lived in a mud-brick house with dirt floor, living in constant danger from tropical disease. Accounts of the privation that Adventist workers labored under around the world made Daniells want to "stop my ears and run into the woods away from everything." No one in America, he reminded White, "not even Brethren Sutherland and Magan, have tasted hardships yet compared" with some of these hardworking folk in foreign lands.[43]

The point of Daniells's recital of misery? That church headquarters had severe limits to what it could do to help. "Today our treasury is ten thousand dollars overdrawn," he ruefully admitted. "I know not what to do." He reminded White that funds expended for overseas mission funds showed greater return on the dollar than those spent in America. Domestic membership growth the previous year was only 2 percent; overseas, 14 percent. This was despite having spent more than $600,000 at home compared to under $150,000 abroad. Daniells had one more thing to add (in a fit of passive-aggressive self-pity). "I have just about made up my mind that it is time for me to clear out and have some one take this place who will be able to get more means and plan better. I have tried my best, but it is too great for me."[44]

As the church's leader, Daniells correctly understood the need for following lines of responsibility and for accountability by entities that receive funds. But he was missing the human element at work here. He should have recalled Ellen White's repeated attempts to save Edson's ministry in the South—indeed her long-standing desire to develop Adventism there. Further, by this point he should have grasped that consistency was not a high virtue for her. Ellen White's prophetic ministry was pragmatic, untethered from any single philosophy of management, willing to try novel approaches. If Daniells was methodical and left-brained, White leaned toward creative responses crafted for particular situations. An individual blessed by charisma was not likely to be restricted by formulaic solutions. Differences in temperament (and function) contributed to the frustrations the two sometimes experienced with one another.

In the end, as was normally the case, Ellen White prevailed. By early 1908 the General Conference Committee (meeting in Mountain View, California) voted a $10,000 commitment to Madison. It was not a direct gift, but rather permission for the school principal to solicit funds among the conferences. Sutherland was primed to "quietly solicit the funds," a bow to the terms of self-supporting institutions.[45]

The Madison incident reflected occasional East Coast–West Coast friction within the church. In later 1908, Daniells received a note from Willie (who passed on concerns of his mother). Various workers had complained to her that Daniells was unduly influenced by close associates Prescott, Evans, and E. R. Palmer (successful head of the church's literature work). He was not blind to "the fact that my associates have weaknesses," Daniells responded. Palmer had rough edges, Daniells admitted, intending to apologize to Willie for a sharp letter Palmer had written him. But Daniells also stood squarely behind his team. "They are just as honest and true to this cause as I am." And he rejected the idea that his advisors controlled him. "I have in the fear of God tried to be on my guard and not allow any one man nor a small clique to get an influence over me so that I would become a tool." Then, paying the most direct tribute on record to his longtime friend Willie White, he added, "I think the man who has the greatest influence over me is the one I am now addressing." Daniells's testimony was heartfelt and true.[46]

This episode's primary significance is its being symptomatic of how some Adventists sought to further their personal agendas by whispering, so to speak, in Ellen White's ear. It also showed how worried she could become when possessing only partial information. We may judge such episodes to be a waste of emotional energy for White and Daniells. But in a deeper sense, such misunderstandings—and occasional true disagreements—were vital means for the two leading figures in Adventism to work out important policy matters. Charisma and order: both halves were required for the church to advance.

A RETURN TO HEALTH AND MEDICAL EDUCATION

By 1905, the contention between church and medical leadership was quieting, though certainly not resolved, and never forgotten. Kellogg and Battle Creek Sanitarium would soon go their own way. Some physicians followed. But Adventist leaders never lost the conviction that the medical work comprised the "right arm" of the gospel. Consequently, more sanitariums needed to be established, funded (until financially self-sufficient), staffed, and overseen so that they might best accomplish the work of evangelistic outreach. Within a few years the church determined it should again train Adventist physicians, believing this the best way of ensuring loyal medical workers.

In the midst of the search for the ideal way to incorporate medical work into the denomination, Ellen White reawakened the church to vegetarianism. Her newfound enthusiasm for an old teaching was a sort of "second great awakening" of health reform. In 1905, White published her last major statement on healthful living, *The Ministry of Healing*, which quickly became influential within Adventism. Her statements regarding the dangers of meat eating carried a new emphasis, influenced perhaps by the writings of muckraking journalists such as Upton Sinclair, whose exposés on the conditions in meatpacking houses worried Americans about the food on their tables. White endorsed the view that meat was a potential source of illness.[47]

In March 1908, White wrote Daniells a letter that sounded like a directive. "I am instructed to bear a message to all our people on the subject of health reform; for many have backslidden." She referred here primarily to diet: tea, coffee, rich foods generally—but especially meat. (Adventist health reform at this point still dealt more with diet than exercise or matters of a well-rounded life.) Not only could the meat supply not be trusted, but evils inherent in the product must be recognized. She stressed the need to develop habits of self-denial, which meant avoiding stimulating foods that undermined judgment and debased the appetite. Many felt, she wrote, "that they cannot get along without flesh meats." But God could help them overcome, she insisted. Then White continued her admonition with words that must have struck uncomfortably close to the church's most notorious carnivore. "Because of the example set by influential men in the indulgence of appetite, the truth has not made the impression on hearts that it might have done. I appeal to you now to set an example in self-denial." Not only was Daniells to lead by example, but she wished him to devise a temperance pledge that church members would sign. "I am sure if you will begin in Washington to do this work of reform . . . the Lord will help you to present a pledge that will help the people to return from their backslidings."[48]

Ellen White asked a difficult thing, both for Daniells's own diet and for church members generally. Indeed, the request proved too demanding.

Daniells did not respond until Willie prodded him about it. Her letter perplexed him, particularly its call for a temperance pledge requiring "abstinence from flesh food." He needed advice from his colleagues on this proposal. He recalled that several years earlier, Pastor E. P. Daniels (no relation) had proposed a similar pledge on meat, which, when attempted, "created the worst kind of heart burnings and wranglings in the churches." Members who were fanatical about abstinence "could not be happy in the Lord while others did not see it to be their duty."[49]

On this issue, Daniells had his ear closer to the ground than did either of the Whites. He understood that vegetarianism was not deeply ingrained in the membership. (The concept of "clean" and "unclean" meats based on Levitical distinctions, understood since the 1860s, did not forcefully enter Adventism until White expounded on the biblical issue in 1903.) A massive educational campaign would be needed before any sort of test could be made of the issue. The potential for internecine strife within churches was great. "We have ministers and brethren who are not well balanced. Let these men get among our Scandinavian, German and Russian brethren" who had not embraced the health message "and try to force this pledge and we shall have trouble." At a workers' meeting Daniells witnessed a man taking "a screaming position on the wickedness of eating flesh." He had no "rational explanation," simply stringing together quotes from testimonies "in an excitable manner calculated to engender controversy and division."[50]

Daniells may not have been ready to sign the meat pledge, but he wanted the Whites to know that he had made his bow to health reform. He had foresworn heavy breakfasts—an American tradition—for flakes or shredded wheat biscuits. This habit cleared his mind, he claimed, for more effective morning work. A few years earlier at a camp meeting, Daniells had been pressed by attendees about why so many church workers disregarded White's admonitions against meat eating—and why the camp meeting kitchen offered so many items she proscribed. Daniells appeared anxious to display his support for health reform. He reconciled differences between biblical permission for flesh foods and White's prohibition on the basis of greater prevalence of disease in his day. Daniells conceded that consuming flesh was not a "mortal sin," not on par with violating the Sabbath. "Yet I have been a vegetarian, what I call a vegetarian, for a quarter of a century." Daniells's carefully stated testimony suggests that he may have given up red meat but continued enjoying fish and chicken. The later testimony of others makes any other interpretation difficult.[51]

When Ellen White and A. G. Daniells differed on policy matters, the resolution normally tilted toward her position. But the meat pledge was a notable exception. Daniells's resistance caused White to rethink her stance. The two of them sat down in Elmshaven later that summer to reflect on the ramifications. Daniells pointed out that strict vegetarianism would be a problem not only in America but throughout many parts of the world. He conciliated by suggesting that an "extensive, well-balanced educational work" by physicians and ministers would prepare the field for reform. Thus, when Ellen White delivered "A Lesson in Health Reform" and "Faithfulness in Health Reform" at the 1909 General Conference, she made an emphatic statement about God's wishes for His church (including quoting language from her letter to Daniells) but gave no hint of a pledge.[52]

The church had already taken important steps at the 1905 General Conference Session when it formed the Medical Missionary Department, tasked both with promoting medical evangelism and advancing health and temperance among members. This action was no mere window dressing to placate the prophet. It called for an encompassing program of sanitariums, training rooms, food stores, and restaurants. Ministers were encouraged to make health a central part of their proclamation. The publishing work was to renew its emphasis on health materials. Nurses' training was scrutinized, and church leaders resolved to upgrade it to the standards now demanded by some states. Daniells pleaded for a "vigorous, persevering activity" by the medical department "to instruct our people and organize them for work in behalf of health and temperance." Kellogg may have left, but denominational commitment to health reform was redoubled.[53]

Committed to the medical message and with a new departmental structure in place, Daniells found himself more than ever concerned with medical work oversight. Given the crisis the medical work had gone through, Daniells reflected in 1909, "it is a wonder that there is anything left of it." But the work had shown "wonderful life and vitality." Fifty-three new sanitariums had been founded since 1901, along with other institutions staffed by a bevy of medical workers. Of course Daniells had help. Drs. W. A. Ruble and D. H. Kress, both of the Washington Sanitarium, served as departmental secretaries. As field secretary, Kress traveled the country visiting camp meetings, sanitariums, Chautauquas, temperance conventions, and the like, carrying the Adventist gospel of health. But the General Conference Committee struggled to get Ruble to pay due attention to the broader field. Thus, things had not gone smoothly in the medical department ("mismanaged and not managed," as Daniells put it), and he looked to find a physician who could provide effective leadership.[54]

Daniells admitted that he and other church leaders, being away so often, could not do justice to the hospital boards on which they served. But Daniells and the General Conference Committee could not escape the personnel issues relating to the medical work. Relocating physicians to needed fields was unending. This involved evaluating their strengths and weaknesses. "I have confidence in Doctor Hopkins," Daniells wrote Willie White. "If he can be allowed to stick close to Paradise Valley [Sanitarium], he will give good satisfaction, and develop into a splendid physician and surgeon." It could also mean dealing with strong-willed personalities. Dr. David Paulson had been a close associate of Kellogg's and continued to run a medical facility in Hinsdale, Illinois. Although Paulson had never broken ties with Adventism, he kept his institution at arm's length. Daniells dealt with him gently, hoping to warm up relations. Ultimately, Daniells confronted Paulson about revealing his true loyalties. He could not be part of the camp meeting circuit nor write for church publications until this was clear. Daniells's patience bore fruit. Paulson drew closer to the denomination, and his Hinsdale Sanitarium became a pillar of the medical work. Occasionally, Daniells had to confront moral dereliction. He advised the head of Saint Helena Sanitarium that a particular physician should not be placed there—or "conscientiously" anywhere else. No "Christian institution, exerting the highest, noblest, and purest influences for the uplifting and salvation of men and women" could employ one "who repeatedly attempts to ruin innocent girls." Daniells had no expertise in the medical field nor an unusual interest in its endeavors. Even so, he was more "in touch with the medical work" than the rest of the General Conference Committee, testified General Conference Treasurer Evans. This was true because, as in other arenas of the church, he made himself completely familiar with the work.[55]

The bottom line for medical workers, as far as Daniells was concerned, was whether they promoted the Adventist message. "It is Spirit-filled men and women alone who can use these [medical] facilities as so many tools for winning souls to Christ." Daniells constantly fretted over the imbalance between the church's resources expended in America versus those in mission fields. "Here we have scores of physicians while out in those great, needy, barren fields they have very few indeed."[56]

Daniells would have preferred to spend his time dispatching doctors to faraway missions, but he could not escape dealing with the interminable financial issues involved in operating sanitariums. Sanitariums were sometimes conference institutions (thirty-nine in 1911) and sometimes organized as independent associations (thirty-two that year). Total value of these enterprises was only slightly less than all other denominational institutions put together. Predictably, during an age of enthusiastic organization building, some institutions overextended themselves. Trouble always followed.[57]

The financial complications of medical work were epitomized by the Pennsylvania Sanitarium. Located in the urban environs of Philadelphia (ignoring Ellen White's counsel about the importance of rural settings), it struggled from its beginning in 1903. By 1909 its situation was desperate. Unable to pay its creditors as notes came due, and with the Columbia Union Conference unable (and unwilling) to assist it, its directors turned to the General Conference. But the General Conference had neither the money (it was "almost entirely out of funds," Daniells admitted) nor the inclination to extend financial guarantees. And yet, if the General Conference did nothing to prevent bankruptcy, Daniells fretted, "our depositors in other institutions" will hear of it and "feel afraid to leave their money with institutions which they know are in a hard way." "I can not tell you how weary and heart sick I am of this harassing affair," Daniells confessed to confidant Willie White. Willie White was nearly as disgusted, repeating to the president the suggestion of some that the sanitarium be allowed to fail, giving the church a chance to start over in a suitably rural location.[58]

But both men knew that planned failure was not the Adventist way. Daniells hoped to increase the patronage and somehow reduce expenses at the Pennsylvania Sanitarium. He also had bigger plans. After the fashion of the *Christ's Object Lessons* campaign for relief of the schools a few years earlier, Ellen White now volunteered the proceeds from her recent *Ministry of Healing*. In early 1910, a campaign was launched in various union conferences to promote the book. Daniells found reason for early encouragement with this "relief book." Every conference had pledged part of its proceeds to the campaign to retire sanitarium debt in Philadelphia. He had visions of nearly $50,000 raised, which would accomplish their goal. Alas, the campaign came up short. By 1911 the sanitarium was shuttered.[59]

Not all the sanitariums struggled. Paradise Valley Sanitarium in California thrived. So did the Washington Sanitarium. Daniells loved to boast about how "every room is full" and that it served "a very fine class of patients," including a Supreme Court justice and the president of the Board of Trade. Daniells dreamed of establishing a cancer hospital on its grounds to fight the affliction that most bothered him (and would ultimately claim him). When Daniells visited Florida, he was intrigued by a still-small medical institution in Orlando. "I looked the place over pretty thoroughly," he told Willie. "It appears to me that it could be made a profitable and helpful institution," he judged, in what later proved to be an understatement of large proportions. Still, the fledgling Florida Sanitarium needed an infusion of funds, and Daniells was unsure about the wisdom of the Southeastern Union Conference taking on this financial burden. He spoke from experience, as discussed above. "We do not want to be mixed up in the business management of these institutions," he vowed to an associate. So many other sanitariums had put in requests for help that the General Conference Committee following the 1909 General Conference Session took an action reminding all parties of earlier resolutions limiting the amount of loans it could authorize.[60]

Nearly as vital as healthy medical institutions was Adventist medical training. Hundreds of student nurses attended patients in sanitariums as part of their training. But physician training lagged. Kellogg's prestige within the church continued to attract some aspiring physicians to his American Medical Missionary College in Battle Creek. But that closed in 1910, and in any event, church leaders were not keen to have Kellogg influencing another generation of Adventist medical workers. Thus, young Adventists (fifty by Daniells's loose estimate) scattered across the country to many training schools during the first decade of the twentieth century.

Daniells worried that too many of these could "be lost to the cause."[61]

But what to do? The simplest and less expensive route would be to subsidize Adventists at state or private medical schools (rather as the Whites had helped John Harvey Kellogg at the University of Michigan), such as George Washington University Medical School in Washington. Daniells spent considerable time working out details for this arrangement. Administrators at the school were accommodating, even offering half tuition and promising no Sabbath class requirements. Further, George Washington's proximity to Takoma Park and Washington Sanitarium offered clear advantages. The General Conference Committee even considered the feasibility of providing housing for Adventist students attending there (three medical students graduated in summer 1908). But when new administrators assumed control at the medical school, they frowned on the generous offer to Adventists.[62]

The other path led to founding a new denominational medical school. Daniells had no illusions about the daunting nature of this task. He knew the abundant resources Kellogg had invested in equipping and running a medical school—which in the end proved insufficient. How could the denomination, which currently was seeking to put every available resource into foreign evangelism, fund a new medical school capable of preparing students to pass state medical boards and practice abroad? Further, some leaders would reason, with the memory of the Kellogg battle still fresh, why invite a new round of medical-ministerial contention.[63]

As arduous as it appeared, the latter route was chosen. The founding of a medical training school at Loma Linda, California, happened for three reasons. First, because A. G. Daniells, the man who, given his troubled history with the medical wing, might have been expected to resist such a proposal, was supportive. This support was not immediate. "I scowled at it," he confessed years later. The church was then in the midst of "the greatest foreign mission campaign we had ever known." An expensive medical school could only distract time and resources. But second, and more vitally, Daniells came onboard because Ellen White was squarely behind the idea. She had been advocating a physician training program ever since she helped found the Loma Linda Sanitarium in 1905–1906. She continued to champion the cause with her usual resolve. Finally, the school became a reality because certain individuals in the local and union conferences were willing to bear this responsibility (with help from the rest of the denomination). In spring 1908, the General Conference Committee voted to establish a committee to investigate the best means of providing medical training. Even though Daniells and White urged action, church administrators were overwhelmed with other financial demands. Thus, plans remained unfulfilled for another year, and even then moved ahead only by a large step of faith.[64]

The following summer Daniells presided over a decision that set in motion the founding of a medical training school. The action made clear that the General Conference could not assume financial responsibility; rather, the Pacific Union Conference, along with the trustees of Loma Linda Sanitarium, would attend to such important details. A small College of Evangelists was already attached to the sanitarium. In late 1909, with Daniells's encouragement, its trustees applied to the state of California and received a charter to add physicians' training.[65]

Events marched rapidly, in part because local leaders, such as E. E. Andross, president of the Southern California Conference, were willing to move ahead despite General Conference unwillingness to commit funds. At the Pacific Union Conference meetings in February 1910, where the decision would be made regarding union support for the project, resistance came from the union conference president, H. W. Cottrell. Not to be deterred, White cut the Gordian knot cleanly, reading before the assembled body a letter from herself recommending that Cottrell be replaced. With the more compliant George Irwin now in the chair, support for a college of medicine was assured. But the Pacific Union Conference did not want to carry the burden of a denomination-wide medical training school by itself. The delegates' resolution invited the General Conference and the five other union conferences to help establish and maintain the school.[66]

That spring, church leadership took up the Pacific Union Conference's action. In April, the General Conference Committee voted to join with that union in establishing a medical school. In May, a committee of delegates from all the unions as well as the General Conference (Daniells included) traveled to Loma Linda. Daniells had to be pleased with the bucolic site. Set on a prominence amidst the citrus belt of the San Bernardino Valley, it was rural and yet near the conveniences of town and rail transportation. Blissfully unaware of earthquake danger lurking beneath, Daniells was prepared to support the call for a medical school. Church transparency was in evidence. The *Review and Herald* kept Adventist readers well-informed with complete accounts of various meetings, including excerpts from White's exhortations.[67]

In the midst of these rapidly developing plans, an important question of purpose had to be answered: Was the proposed school to attempt a full medical curriculum that could meet the newly rigorous American Medical Association (AMA) standards (which were just being implemented in 1910) and prepare students to pass state board exams? Or was the school primarily to give students just enough training in medicine and nursing to enable them to adequately serve as medical missionaries abroad? The institution's name, after all, was to be College of Medical Evangelists (CME), a name implying the latter objective. The question was put directly to Ellen White. Her response was unambiguous. "The medical school at Loma Linda is to be of the highest order." Those who attend must be enabled "to pass the examinations required by law of all those who practise as regularly qualified physicians." The die was cast. The church would muster its limited resources to establish a recognized medical school.[68]

The founding of the College of Medical Evangelists (renamed Loma Linda University in 1961) represented an important first and last in the church. It was the first institution jointly created by the General Conference and the various union conferences, which all had representatives on its board of trustees; and it was the last institution that Ellen White had a role in founding. At age eighty-three, her days of travel and intensive involvement in institutional affairs were drawing to a close (though her impact on CME would continue into 1911, as she presciently insisted that more property be acquired).

Classes began in late September 1910. School leaders expected that most students would opt for the shorter medical evangelism track. Yet full theoretical, laboratory, and clinical facilities had to be provided for the regular track. The "C" rating from the AMA (its lowest level) in its initial accreditation pointed out the work still to be accomplished. Deficiencies were addressed by building a hospital alongside the sanitarium (the sanitarium quickly became a secondary auxiliary at Loma Linda) and providing clinical facilities in Los Angeles (at what would be White Memorial Hospital).[69]

By virtue of his position, Daniells was obligated to serve on the board, but he hoped that his involvement in the new enterprise would be slight. He was "glad to hear of the encouraging opening" of the school, he wrote CME president Ruble. But "I have been giving my chief attention to the city work" (this was the summer of his foray into New York City evangelism). Of course, he could not escape Loma Linda's problems—this being the nature of leadership. An acute need for funds to finance the immediate expansion inevitably came to Daniells's door. Willie White dunned him for what he understood to be promised funds. Betraying a note of impatience, Daniells suggested his friend was "not a little mistaken with regard to this question [General Conference support]." He then reviewed the history of the denomination's financial commitment and payment. Daniells had just returned from Europe to discover that the General Conference was $14,000 in arrears of debts and had to borrow to cover expenses in mission fields. Loma Linda must wait for more funds.[70]

Despite occasional grumpiness about CME's urgent supplication for funds, Daniells took pleasure in getting the denomination back on the road to medical training, particularly as a boon to mission efforts. In a sense, the renewal of physician training allowed Daniells to put to rest the Kellogg matter. As it turned out, Adventism's most prominent figure (after Ellen White) was not essential for the church's well-being. Daniells would face more challenges regarding Loma Linda's future, in 1913 and 1915. On those occasions (discussed in the following chapter) he again showed his support for the medical work.

CITY EVANGELISM

If Ellen White had been asked in 1910 her opinion of why Adventist Church growth lagged in the United States, she would have had an emphatic response: lack of evangelism in America's cities. Indeed, she did not wait to be asked. During the previous five years she had pleaded with and finally cajoled Daniells and other leaders to make urban evangelism a priority.

Why were they slow to respond? In theory, of course, no one opposed her counsel. Public evangelism had always held an honored place within the church. But one-man tent meetings that were effective in rural and small-town America failed to speak to a prospering middle-class population increasingly clustered in urban environs. Periodic efforts in cities had met with indifferent results, causing church leaders to doubt the wisdom of pouring limited resources into such efforts. And even when an evangelist came along, E. E. Franke, whose dramatic techniques found success in New York City, his egotistical ways led to friction and ultimately a break with the church, confirming suspicions about preaching stars.[71]

But White had witnessed large and successful evangelistic efforts in Australia, a country already known for its lukewarm reception to religion. Could not the same be done in America, she immediately wondered after her return stateside in 1900. Celebrated preachers such as Billy Sunday and Reuben Torrey, whose protracted city efforts attracted thousands, demonstrated the possibilities of urban evangelism. Why could not Adventist evangelists replicate that success? Moving headquarters to Takoma Park a few years earlier had been inspired in part by a desire to carry Adventist influence into the nation's capital. The time had come for more purposeful work there and in other cities.

A. G. Daniells, who himself had participated in evangelism in New Zealand and Australia, assented to White's call. But for several years little action followed, in part for excusable reasons. The church reorganization was a huge undertaking, occupying most of his considerable energies. Then in 1905 he sought to redouble church mission efforts around the world—his passion. Hearing no other voices around him calling for a concerted push for urban evangelism (save for Ellen White's—now a continent away), Daniells struggled to overcome inertial forces.

In fairness, he paid close attention to the health of the church in New York City, now in the Greater New York Conference. Membership had nearly tripled since he took office in 1901 (though still a modest 173 believers in 1908). Its various Adventist congregations reflected the melting pot of turn-of-the-century New York. Individuals representing some sixteen different nationalities attended a series of evangelistic meetings in Manhattan. Even more striking, an ethnic rainbow of ministers from other denominations embraced Adventism. Hungarian, Bohemian, Chinese, African, several Italian: these men had been taken into denominational employ. But the cost of an expanding international work meant that the shrinking American congregations in Manhattan and Brooklyn went without pastors. Daniells realized this problem needed to be addressed. The

General Conference was already spending more money there than in most places. But to move forward, even more was needed. Daniells's long epistle to Willie White, detailing the above facts, concluded with an appeal for help from the relatively prosperous Northern California Conference.[72]

Daniells's progress report failed to satisfy Ellen White. Sensing that the new frontier of Adventist evangelism must be in the major cities, she sounded a clarion call in 1909, first directly to Daniells, then before the General Conference session, and ultimately that fall in a full testimony (now part of *Testimonies for the Church* volume 9). White shared with many Progressive reformers of the age an interest in the well-being of cities. The first decade of the century witnessed an array of efforts to improve urban life. These included moral reform, which Protestant clergy (usually identified with the Social Gospel) promoted with an urgency equal to hers. White's agenda was different, of course. Social, political, or even moral reforms could only be palliative. The world needed the salvation of the Cross.

White's burden included large cities across the nation. But she always returned to the New York field. She had heard of property near the city where a sanitarium and school might be located. Adventist workers would there enjoy a quasi-rural home setting, from whence they could venture into the city to serve residents. She was persuaded that Sunday laws and other pre-apocalyptic events would soon close down opportunities for evangelism there. "Men in positions of trust will be embittered against the little handful of God's commandment-keeping people," she declared.[73]

White got action. The General Conference Committee appointed a group to plan evangelism in eastern cities. The group envisioned a mission training center on the outskirts of New York. Prescott, who had yet to find his evangelistic niche, was assigned to New York. Special funds were appropriated for New York, Baltimore, Philadelphia, Richmond, Washington, New Jersey, and Portland, Maine (recalling childhood memories, White continued thinking of it as a major city).[74]

To Daniells fell the responsibility for implementing many of the details—and for reporting to Elmshaven what was being accomplished. He worried that the attention being given to Prescott's proposed New York effort might be a recipe for disappointment if expectations were not met; better to make him part of a team of evangelists. Daniells was anxious that Ellen White appreciate not only the vigilance with which city evangelism was being undertaken but also the constraining factors of time and funds. He asked Willie to explain this "big picture" to his mother. He also wrote her back-to-back letters in early January, responding to recent missives from her. Efforts were in preparation for an ambitious series in Washington, making a "special effort for the higher classes." Local conferences began devoting more funds to their cities. "It is our determination to carry out this instruction faithfully." But Daniells also reminded her that he had broad denominational concerns to attend to in 1907 and 1908, having been away from Washington eight or nine months of the year.[75]

White was encouraged by the report, but she had witnessed too much dithering in the past to be satisfied now. Through the winter she repeatedly told her son that the end was nearer than people realized. "What can we do, what can we do" to get the brethren to enter the cities "right now!" She longed to go to Portland and mount the evangelistic platform, hoping this might rouse others.[76]

By late spring Ellen White had lost all patience with Daniells. It was not enough for him to encourage conference evangelists in their work, or even to provide special General Conference allocations. He must lead from the front. By holding his own evangelistic effort he would inspire the church in the most powerful way possible. Short of this, she felt a change at the top must be made.

Her son Willie was the bearer of this sober news in a June 1910 letter to Daniells. Willie and Daniells had seen eye-to-eye on most things through the years. Willie could normally be counted on to communicate complex issues to his mother and to assist his friend in the sensitive relationships with a prophet. But Daniells now read unsparing words from the Whites. Prescott and his active promotion of the new view of "the daily," Daniells was told, had been a mistake (a different line on this issue than Willie had taken before). Even more important (this reflecting the prophet's views), he had failed to accomplish urban evangelism to her satisfaction.[77]

To what was this failing attributed? In part, White held all church leaders accountable for "holding one man in the position of president of the General Conference for so long a time." "Prolonged power will tempt any man to consider his wisdom superior," she added. But some of the problem was specific to Daniells. Willie continued to quote liberally from his mother: "If Eld. Daniells is not so changed that he can recognize clearly the special movings of the Spirit of God, let him step aside and let another take the responsibility who will be impressed with the spiritual necessities of the church." Her testimony became more pointed. "The light has come to me decidedly that for his own soul's sake, he should not continue to occupy the position he has occupied." Daniells had not "heeded the word" in regard to the cities, which "in the east and the south, the north and the west are unworked."[78]

This letter, followed soon thereafter by the complete text of Ellen White's counsel and then by two telegrams after he had reached New York, gave even more urgent counsel. "At first I felt almost overwhelmed with perplexity and discouragement," he admitted to her. White had reproved him before but not with this intensity. "I saw your purpose of carrying things after your own devising after you were placed as president," Daniells read. "You had thought you would do wonderful things, which would be a work God had not placed in your hands to do. . . . You have very early given evidence that wisdom and sanctified judgment have not been manifested by you." "Elders Daniells and Prescott both need reconversion. . . . They are no longer to bear sway unless they show less of the ruling, dominating power. The crisis has come, for God will be dishonored."[79]

Was she saying he should step down? Daniells responded in two ways. First, as the dutiful son, he immediately detailed the further steps he had taken and would continue doing to advance urban evangelism. The General Conference Committee, sobered by her words and loyally wanting to save Daniells's job, pledged full support for evangelism. Daniells exhibited a rare display of defensiveness (both to Willie and his mother in separate letters). He noted that Adventism's presence in New York City had grown considerably during his time in office, membership doubling, workers tripling from eight to twenty-five, and tithe approaching $20,000. To Willie he was even more candid. Daniells had always assumed that his mother's exhortations had been directed at the entire General Conference Committee, not just himself. To be singled out now was dismaying. Further, "while you, Elder Irwin, and Elder Haskell are not giving your time to city work, you are as responsible as any one else on the General Conference Committee for fostering and developing that line of work."

Daniells wanted responsibility for this big task shared among leadership. Why did not "this whole question belong to the Vice-president of the North American Division [G. A. Irwin, headquartered in Mountain View, California, and closer in every regard to the West Coast faction than the Takoma Park leaders] the same as it does to me?" Daniells felt as though he was being made a scapegoat for a larger institutional problem.[80]

What did Daniells want to see happen? Two things. First, specific and creative ideas about more effective urban evangelism. "I was greatly disappointed . . . because none of the brethren seemed able to throw any special light" on the matter. Daniells was pointed with his West Coast critics. "I had earnestly hoped that Elder Irwin and yourself [Ellen White] would be able to present a comprehensive sense of some sort" that could help the Committee in its efforts. He did not mention Ellen White, but he might have wished that her admonitions had been accompanied by useful tips. Second, Daniells wanted financial help. City evangelism was expensive, and neither the local eastern conferences nor the General Conference could adequately fund it. Daniells repeatedly implored the western conferences (particularly northern California) to share their relative plenty with less well-endowed eastern conferences where the city work would occur.[81]

In a now familiar pattern, Daniells's protestations of action brought assurances of support from the Whites. He showed compliance by heading to New York to give on-site leadership to ambitious plans for the city. Mid-July weather in the city was beastly, so meetings of local workers were moved to the more bearable Bronx Park. What would be the most effective means of reaching New York's masses? workers asked themselves. They wished to establish first principles of city work. But quickly, Daniells and the others realized that the still new and largely unstudied phenomenon of mass urban culture defied simple answers (Daniells very much wanted Ellen White to understand this). "I do not know that I ever worked harder in committee," he recalled. The group decided that a massive campaign of leaflet distribution was needed, along with creative use of the local newspapers.[82]

Although he attempted to be encouraging, Daniells did not whitewash problems. The New York mission was ineffective (with the exception of the Jewish efforts) and not of much value. Laborers, he insisted, must learn how to work smarter, not harder. Indeed, many of the women were "exhausted already from the heavy work they are doing in connection with the tent effort." Evangelism was not his only worry. He became embroiled in marriage counseling for the couple running the city mission, the result of which was their separation not only from one another but also from church work, a sadness compounded by the subsequent need to temporarily close the mission. Urban evangelism thus faced difficulties of several types.[83]

Still, Daniells found gratifying responses to his plea for help. Willie reported that the Midwest Union Conference would seek to raise $10,000 for New York; support of other kinds could be expected from the West Coast. Those who had been critical of his efforts seemed now aware of their obligations. Ellen White answered the call for tactical suggestions regarding evangelism. She counseled that urban work sometimes required stealth. "We must quietly secure buildings, without defining what we intend to do. . . . On some points, silence is eloquence." She also recommended the involvement of women. "Intelligent women, if truly converted, can act a part in this work of holding Bible classes."[84]

Back in Washington in early August, Daniells still wrestled with the implications of the Whites' reproof earlier that summer. It troubled him. He had divided up his responsibilities among his associates, left his Takoma Park office, and taken a train to New York. What more could he do? Not only the Whites but also others had complained (to the Whites) of "weaknesses and imperfections in the work." The rock-solid Daniells now needed some reassurance. "At first," Daniells wrote Ellen White, "I thought it was a mild, kind way of letting me know that you believed the time had come for me to quietly resign from my official positions and take up other work." "I was sorry," he added disingenuously, that "you did not tell me who you thought should take my work and how the transfer should occur." His colleagues in New York with whom he shared the telegrams assured him they saw here no call to resign. In retrospect, it is clear that Daniells was a victim of unfortunate timing. It took four to five days for a letter to cross the continent; double that for a return. Furthermore, Ellen White's testimonies were not always promptly sent, which led to misunderstandings. In any event, Daniells repeated his determination to do his very best in whatever field he was placed. He waited now for instruction. "Whatever comes I want to take a Christian course and make no trouble nor commotion of any kind."[85]

He needn't have feared. Both Ellen and Willie White responded immediately. "Go forward as you have begun, using your position of influence as president of the General Conference for the advancement of the work we are called upon to do." Willie provided background to his mother's letter, telling Daniells how he saw her reading his letter, then every few paragraphs stopping to talk as if he were there. She reported a dream in which she was telling Daniells he should stay where he was. Willie himself was "profoundly thankful" that this difficult episode appeared over. Normal life between himself and his friend could resume. He even offered to send letters of reproof to those using his mother's testimonies against church officials. "Is there anything that we are neglecting to do here in Mother's office?" Willie asked. Charisma was returning to Daniells's service.[86]

There is no indication that Daniells's New York evangelistic series had remarkable success. Conference membership figures enjoyed no spike (indeed, North American membership actually fell in 1910). But it does appear that the Whites' prodding was successful in helping Daniells catch a vision of city evangelism that he carried forward. Over the next couple of years he gave much thought to more effective means of carrying the gospel to the cities. He understood that the usual summer campaigns of tent or hall meetings were inadequate. Rather, a "steady, continuous effort" was needed. He recalled his work in New Zealand decades earlier, where he held meetings for eighteen out of twenty-four months with considerable success. Nothing less was needed in America. An aggressive, unremitting program of evangelism was the key. The current problem was symptomatic of a larger malaise. "We are extremely lame in the evangelistic department," he sadly concluded. Evangelism itself was undervalued by many Adventists. Thus, evangelism was only part of a wider problem within the denomination.[87]

To study the issue in its broadest aspect, he convened an ambitious "Council of City Evangelists" in Washington in May of 1912. Daniells himself presided over the four-day seminar that attracted nearly fifty ministers who would be involved in urban evangelism in eastern cities. Nearly every practical consideration found its way onto the agenda: advertising and use of the press, visitation, use of Bible workers, medical missionary work, preaching and use of Scripture. Daniells would introduce a subject, then open the floor to free discussion (reported verbatim in the *Review*).

The atmosphere was sufficiently open for ministers to disagree with parts of Daniells's advice. For example, appropriate advertising by Daniells's standards would avoid featuring the evangelist (such as publishing his photograph) or "too-strong" adjectives in describing the meetings. But A. V. Cotton countered that photographs were an important aspect of newspaper advertising. People expected to see the man heading the effort. Cotton grasped in part what Daniells and other leaders may have missed: the great urban evangelists of the day were personalities. People flocked to the tent in order to see and hear Billy Sunday or other larger-than-life figures. Evangelism was entertainment. But Adventism's traditional resistance to a personality cult or too much "stage enthusiasm" (Ellen White had warned against "theatrical performance" in evangelism) inevitably compromised the church's appeal to the public. Further, Adventism's stress on doctrinal purity and on a message predicting a soon end to this world did not suit a secular, pleasure-seeking culture such as characterized urban life in the early twentieth century. The church, in short, had a difficult row to hoe in taking its gospel to the cities. Daniells, very much a traditionalist in most regards, was not likely to be the one to solve this dilemma. Nonetheless, he did what he could, and the Council of City Evangelism represented one more example of a central theme in Daniells's presidency: equipping Adventist preachers for a more professional and effective ministry.[88]

REST

By the standards of his day, A. G. Daniells enjoyed good health. Indeed, he would live to age seventy-six. But typical of Adventist leaders since the beginning of the movement, he drove himself terribly hard. He resented intrusions of ill health that slowed his brutal work pace. A serious setback occurred in the early fall of 1910 (just as he was recovering from the emotional trauma of that summer). At Florida camp meeting he contracted malaria, resulting in a month of misery. His sickness was compounded by his irritation with leaders at the camp meeting, who failed to inform him soon enough that he should take precautions against the mosquitoes. By spring of 1911 he was better. "I have had only one slight attack of fever in two months," he reported. "I have gained twenty pounds, so that now I am about as heavy as I was when I was taken sick last October."[89]

Once recovered from malaria, Daniells again threw himself into his new commitment to city evangelism. But his unremitting schedule caught up with him during the spring of 1912. He had been away from headquarters most of the previous year. Indian and Australian leaders were now begging him to visit. The General Conference Committee had given permission for him to devote his upcoming summer to city evangelism. But all that had to be put on hold. He was struck with what he feared could be a return of his malarial fever—or even worse, typhoid. "I have taxed my physical resources to about the limit this winter," he sadly concluded; "it will be necessary for me to take a little rest before going much farther." The General Conference Committee that summer ensured his taking a break. It took an action commanding him to forego his travel plans, to return home to rest, and then to attend to "the general work."[90]

Daniells's enforced rest put a period on a busy four years of leadership. If stateside growth had been disappointing, the Adventist gospel was nonetheless moving rapidly into the world (Daniells's first love). American membership would pick up during the upcoming war years. Yet the pattern had been set for the future of a world membership far outstripping the Adventist homeland. On the home front, Ellen White had but a few years to live. Seemingly pleased with his city efforts, her relationship with Daniells stabilized. She never again saw a need to give him a message of rebuke. With doctrinal and institutional conflict at a momentary subsidence, and the health work bolstered by a new medical school, Daniells could catch his breath, so to speak. This was important, because in two years a world war would break out that presented both challenges and opportunities for the Adventist Church.

---

[1] An example of Adventism's failure to fit into the sect-denomination paradigm is given in Oxford sociologist Bryan R. Wilson's "The Persistence of Sects" [first published in *Indian Missiological Review*], accessed December 27, 2012, http://www.workersect.org/2x205p.html; Bull and Lockhart, *Seeking a Sanctuary*, 119.

[2] Figures from *Statistical Report of Seventh-day Adventist Conferences, Missions, and Institutions for the Year Ending 1910*; Bull and Lockhart, *Seeking a Sanctuary*, 119.

[3] "The President's Address," *RH*, May 13, 1909, 11, 12; Howard B. Weeks, *Adventist Evangelism in the Twentieth Century* (Washington, DC: Review and Herald®, 1969), 27, 28.

[4] *RH*, June 1, 1905, 20, 21.

[5] Douglas Morgan, *Adventism and the American Republic: The Public Involvement of a Major Apocalyptic Movement* (Knoxville, TN: University of Tennessee Press, 2001), 114, 115; W. A. Colcord to AGD, August 23, 1909; AGD to Editor of *Christian Advocate* [c. May 1908]; AGD to WCW, March 9, 1910; GCCmin, April 26, 1908.

[6] In the summer of 1910 he made a casual but seeming unambiguous comment to Frederick Griggs that he would step down at the time of the next General Conference session in 1913. When the time came, he gave no indication of doing so. AGD to Frederick Griggs, June 30, 1910, ASTR.

[7] Gilbert Valentine has provided a detailed account of "the daily" controversy in his *W. W. Prescott*, chapter 13, and more recently in his *The Prophet and the Presidents*, 281–288.

[8] Arthur White also provides much detail in his *Ellen G. White: The Later Elmshaven Years* (Hagerstown, MD: Review and Herald®, 1982), chapter 19. A clear overview of the controversy is also provided by Schwarz and Greenleaf in *Light Bearers*, 608, 609. Ellen White's endorsement of the original view is in *Early Writings*, 74, 75.

[9] Calvin W. Edwards and Gary Land, *Seeker After Light; A. F. Ballenger, Adventism, and American Christianity* (Berrien Springs, MI: Andrews University Press), 133.

[10] Valentine, *Prescott*, 219–221; AGD to Clarence Crisler, March 18, 1908, EGWE.

[11] Valentine, *Prescott*, 222, 223.

[12] Valentine, *Prophet and the Presidents*, 285.

[13] EGW to Edson White, June 16, 1909; EGW, "Talk to General Conference Committee," June 11, 1909, EGWE.

[14] Valentine, *Prescott*, 230, 231, 243; AGD to WCW, January 3, 1910, EGWE.

[15] AGD to WCW, December 31, 1909, GCPL.

[16] AGD to WCW, March 30, 1910; May 28, 1910.

[17] AGD to WCW, January 3, 1910; May 28, 1910. Gilbert Valentine provides insight on the Madison controversy in *The Prophet and the Presidents*, 245, 275–277.

[18] A. L. White, *The Later Elmshaven Years*, 256, 257; AGD to WCW, February 22, 1910.

[19] AGD to WCW, June 21, 1910; August 4, 1910.

[20] J. S. Washburn to WCW, September 5, 1910.

[21] On Loughborough's activities, see Strayer, *J. N. Loughborough*, 419–421. AGD to WCW, March 31, 1910. Thirteen years after Daniells's death in 1935, Arthur White at the White Estate confronted Washburn with the full story of White's counsel to Daniells. Washburn had to admit that Daniells had indeed followed White's counsel. Arthur White, "Introductory Statement Concerning the Purported Interview with Mrs. E. G. White on June 8, 1910," EGWE.

[22] Valentine, *Prescott*, 224. The level of mistrust and confusion Ellen White experienced is suggested by a remark she made to Loughborough (understanding that he was not always a reliable reporter) to the effect that she could not champion the old interpretation of "the daily" because the Washington men "have got Willie." Quoted in Valentine, *Prescott*, 223.

[23] WCW to AGD, June 20, 1910.

[24] A. L. White, *The Later Elmshaven Years*, 257–259.

[25] AGD to WCW, August 5, 1910; August 4, 1910.

[26] AGD to WCW, August 5, 1910.

[27] AGD to Clarence Crisler, March 18, 1908, EGWE.

[28] Arthur White provides a detailed account of the preparation of the 1911 edition of *The Great Controversy* in his *The Later Elmshaven Years*, chapter 23.

[29] AGD to WCW, June 24, 1910.

[30] Ibid. "The daily" issued roiled on, though with less intensity until few members paid the matter attention. But a few felt strongly. As late as 1948 Arthur White, head of the White Estate, felt compelled to address Daniells's posthumous critics, showing them that his grandmother's statements on the doctrine did not comprise a repudiation of Daniells as church leader. Arthur L. White to Board of Trustees, September 20, 1948, EGWE.

[31] WCW to AGD, September 8, 1911.

[32] GCCMin, February 10, 1909.

[33] GCCMin, June 14, July 13, July 15, 1908; April 11, 1911; January 23, 1913; July 6, 1913; AGD to A. W. Spalding, May 14, 1908; June 19, 1908, ASTR. The task was bigger than Daniells or any on the General Conference Committee appreciated. The original plan was to have the work available for the 1913 General Conference Session. But Olsen would not complete his work, *A History of the Origin and Progress of the Seventh-day Adventists*, until 1925. Spalding would ultimately write his own denominational history, *Origin and History of the Seventh-day Adventists*, first published in 1954 and then reissued in four volumes in 1961.

[34] Schwarz and Greenleaf, *Light Bearers*, 387; AGD to A. W. Farnsworth, November 20, 1911, ASTR; AGD to WCW, March 6, 1911; October 4, 1911.

[35] *RH*, July 21, 1910, 14, 15.

[36] AGD to Frederick Griggs, June 30, 1910; September 23, 1910, ASTR.

[37] Schwarz and Greenleaf, *Light Bearers*, 236–238; Bull and Lockhart, *Seeking a Sanctuary*, 336, 337.

[38] E. A. Sutherland to AGD, May 3, 1904.

[39] E. A. Sutherland to AGD, July 11, 1904; October 16, 1904; P. T. Magan to Wm. Covert, August 9, 1904, ASTR.

[40] Gilbert Valentine in *Prophet and the Presidents* provides a thorough discussion of this conflict, pp. 245, 276–281.

[41] EGW to AGD and I. H. Evans, September 23, 1907.

[42] AGD to EGW, October 11, 1907.

[43] Ibid.

[44] Ibid.

[45] GCCMin, January 20, April 24, 1908.

[46] AGD to WCW, June 25, 1908.

[47] The two leading works on Ellen White, Adventism, and health are Ronald L. Numbers, *Prophetess of Health: Ellen G. White and the Origins of Seventh-day Adventist Health Reform*, 3rd ed. (Grand Rapids, MI: Eerdmans Publishing, 2009) and Bull and Lockhart, *Seeking a Sanctuary*, chapter 9.

[48] EGW to AGD, March 29, 1908.

[49] AGD to WCW, July 17, 1908.

[50] Ibid. This issue is discussed in Numbers, *Prophetess of Health*, 172–174; Bull and Lockhart, *Seeking a Sanctuary*, 178, 179.

[51] AGD to WCW, July 17, 1908; "Question-Box Service on the Spirit of Prophecy," August 30, 1906, EGWE.

[52] AGD quoted in A. L. White, *The Later Elmshaven Years*, 202; *GCB*, May 30, 1909, 213–215; June 2, 1909, 268–270.

[53] *RH*, June 1, 1905, 9, 10; AGD to G. A. Irwin, September 1909; AGD to WCW, December 2, 1910.

[54] AGD to H. W. Cottrell, September 8, 1909; GCCmin, January 24, 1909; October 7, 1909; AGD to WCW, October 7, 1910.

[55] AGD to Dr. Henry Harrower, March 11, 1910; AGD to WCW, October 27, 1908; AGD to Dr. George Thomason, July 31, 1912; AGD to WCW, October 23, 1908; AGD to Brother Langdon, October 1, 1912; I. H. Evans to AGD, August 8, 1909, GCPL.

[56] AGD to WCW, April 23, 1909; AGD to George Thomason, January 4, 1911; AGD to WCW, October 27, 1908, GCPL.

[57] [AGD], "Some Items of Sanitarium Work," [1911], ASTR.

[58] AGD to WCW, June 24, 1909; July 2, 1909; December 28, 1909; WCW to AGD, January 5, 1910, EGWE.

[59] *The Sanitarium Relief Campaign: History, Outline, Plan* (Takoma Park, MD: Sanitarium Relief Bureau, n.d.); WCW to AGD, January 5, 1910; AGD to WCW, March 11, 1910; February 22, 1910.

[60] AGD to WCW, November 5, 1908; AGD to G. A. Irwin, May 5, 1913; AGD to WCW, October 15, 1908; GCCMin, June 9, 1909.

[61] GCCMin, July 19, 1908.

[62] Ibid.; *RH*, June 11, 1908, 17.

[63] AGD to WCW, March 20, 1908; AGD, "Work at Loma Linda," typescript of talk at sanitarium chapel, September 11, 1931, EGWE.

[64] AGD, "Work at Loma Linda"; GCCMin, April 26, 1908.

[65] GCCMin, July 11, 1909; October 13, 1909; E. E. Andross to AGD, October 27, 1909; A. L. White, *EGW: The Later Elmshaven Years*, 270–277.

[66] E. E. Andross to AGD, November 25, 1909; December 10, 1909; A. L. White, *The Later Elmshaven Years*, 281–285. Andross, knowing of Daniells's determination to avoid new church debt, chided him that he would in this case encourage a local conference to take on such a major project without "the financial support of a single conference or union conference outside of our own territory."

[67] GCCMin, April 13, 1910; *RH*, May 19, 1910, 17, 18; June 9, 1910, 15, 16.

[68] *RH*, May 19, 1910, 17, 18.

[69] Ken McFarland, *The Impossible Dream: Railway to the Moon* (Nampa, ID: Pacific Press®, 2005), 31–34.

[70] AGD to W. A. Ruble, October 24, 1910; WCW to AGD, June 30, 1911; AGD to WCW, August 5, 1911.

[71] Weeks, *Adventist Evangelism*, 14–18.

[72] AGD to WCW, September 25, 1908.

[73] "Talk by Mrs. E. G. White before the General Conference Committee," Foreign Mission Seminary Library, Friday morning, June 11, 1909; EGW to AGD, November 1909, EGWE.

[74] GCCMin, December 19 and 27, 1909.

[75] AGD to WCW, January 3, 1910; AGD to EGW, January 2 and 3, 1910, EGWE.

[76] WCW to AGD, January 11, 1910.

[77] WCW to AGD, June 20, 1910.

[78] Ibid.

[79] AGD to WCW, July 4, 1910; "Night Letter Telegram," both July 8, 1910; EGW, "Errors and Dangers of Prescott and Daniells; The Cities to be Worked; God's Plan is 'Two by Two'; No Theatrics in Preaching," manuscript 67, [c. 1910], EGWE.

[80] AGD to WCW, July 4, 1910; AGD to EGW, July 4, 1910, EGWE.

[81] Ibid.

[82] WCW to AGD, July 11, 1910.

[83] Ibid.; AGD to WCW July 16, 1910.

[84] WCW to AGD, July 26, 1910; EGW to AGD, July 26, 1910.

[85] AGD to WCW, August 4 and 5, 1910.

[86] EGW to AGD, August 11, 1910; WCW to AGD, August 11, 1910.

[87] AGD to WCW [1912]; AGD to WCW, August 4, 1910, EGWE. Decline of membership in 1910 noted in Weeks, *Adventist Evangelism*, 61.

[88] *RH*, June 6, 1912, 13, 14; June 13, 1912, 18, 19; June 20, 1912, 15, 16; June 27, 1912, 18, 19; July 4, 1912, 19, 20; July 11, 1912, 20. Howard Weeks provides an extended discussion of new evangelistic efforts during these years in *Adventist Evangelism*, 46–60.

[89] AGD to EGW, November 24, 1910; AGD to WCW, March 24, 1911.

[90] AGD to WCW [1912]; GCCMin, July 5, 1912. In 1914, physician Harry Miller diagnosed Daniells with high blood pressure brought on by his malaria and overtaxing work. Miller thought that Daniells need not resign from his position, but he must be alert to symptoms and moderate his pace of work. Daniells would continue as president for eight more years. H. W. Miller to AGD, January 29, 1914, ASTR.

CHAPTER X

WINDS OF WAR

"This is not a day of triumph; it is a day of dedication," intoned Woodrow Wilson at his first inaugural address in March 1913. Wilson and Arthur Daniells shared many qualities, most notably a serious-minded commitment to advancing noble causes. Like Wilson, Daniells would never call his fellow believers to a shout of triumph; nothing short of the Lord's appearing would merit that response. But he did call them, repeatedly, to greater dedication. Indeed, his public statements sounded no theme more insistently than devotion to duty.

Daniells could not then have known it, but Adventism in 1913 was in the early stages of a decade of significant growth. The sluggish growth of the twentieth century's first decade gave way to impressive expansion during the second both in North America and in many parts of the world. Growth followed more aggressive evangelistic techniques in the United States. But it also benefited from the eschatological appeal of Adventism's prophetic message during World War I. The middle years of the decade also witnessed important decisions regarding the church's medical institution at Loma Linda, a denominational commitment to its success that paid dividends in the following century. Mid-decade also marked a landmark in Adventism: the loss of its prophet. With the death of Ellen White, Daniells and Adventism generally had to negotiate their future without recourse to her guidance.

The decade was bisected by war, the largest, most terrible war the world had seen. Suddenly, in late summer of 1914 General Conference leaders in Washington lost sustained contact with the church on the European continent. How the church fared across the Atlantic remained something of a mystery until 1918. For A. G. Daniells, however, the tragedy of war found partial redemption in the prophetic significance of the Ottoman Empire's decline. Daniells enjoyed his greatest success as an evangelist in explicating prophecies in Daniel 11 about the defeat of the King of the North during The Great War. Daniells also made his most ambitious international trips during these years. Two times he crossed the Pacific to visit church outposts across large portions of eastern Asia and once extended his travels to India, a world tour that lasted nearly a year.

RETHINKING STRUCTURE AND INSTITUTIONS

Spring 1913 witnessed another quadrennial General Conference session, this one held in Takoma Park. For Daniells the event meant the usual round of worry over details, railway transportation, accommodations, and the expense of bringing in scores of delegates from around the world. But the meetings would not be business as usual. The General Conference Committee was recommending to the assembled body a new level of administration: division conferences. Three divisions currently existed: North American, European, and Asiatic. These were not constitutional entities but simply geographic regions that had the benefit of General Conference vice presidents to oversee them (and in L. R. Conradi in Europe and I. H. Evans in Asia, two very capable men). With more substantial division conferences now proposed, the church reorganization begun in 1901 appeared to find its logical culmination.[1]

Initiative for the change came from Europe. Conradi and others recalled that until 1907 Europe had enjoyed for six years a parallel General Conference structure. They were never fully reconciled to being reduced to (for the sake of denominational unity) an appendage of Takoma Park's General Conference Committee. They felt that a self-supporting division conference, whose leaders were chosen by its own constituents and with true line authority to the union conferences and missions below it, was the best path forward for growth. This model should not be restricted to Europe, Conradi argued. "Europe's needs today will be the needs of South America, Asia and other parts of the world tomorrow," the memo from Europe to the General Conference read. "If the divisional system were perfected throughout the world, the General Conference president would have free hands to be fully the president of the world's General Conference, and by his presence at these divisional meetings catch his inspiration for the world-wide message."[2]

How could Daniells resist such an appeal? In fact, his endorsement represented a 180-degree reversal for him. Two years earlier, when the division idea was first being broached, he confided to Willie White that "the moment this step is taken, the world-wide unity which we now have, will be broken." Now, however, as he considered the idea, its logic appeared unassailable. He delivered to delegates an extended review of organizational development in the church. He spoke from experience in Australia, where local leaders had to wait months to get a response from Washington. From this problem came the inaugural union conference. The innovation proved a great administrative help to the denomination. Now, the proliferation of union conferences seemed to call for adding "another important piece in the great machine that is built up." He fielded questions from delegates about the new structure. An enthusiastic Daniells hoped the enabling vote—despite details of the amended constitution not fully being worked out—could occur on that day, the fiftieth anniversary of the founding of the church (which fell during the 1913 session). Spirited debate followed. Some wanted to salute the jubilee day with an action that acknowledged the marvelous spread of the message over half a century. More cautious heads, such as W. A. Spicer, counseled patience, to allow all delegates to read the consequential changes they would be asked to approve. Regular order prevailed. Division structure would wait one more day.[3]

Momentum quickly built for North America to form its own division. Some church leaders thought this premature, but the spirit of innovation had captured delegates. Adventism's embrace of bureaucratic, multileveled organizational structure continued. A vote quickly authorized North American delegates to caucus and organize a division conference. By the end of the General Conference session, I. H. Evans had been elected as North American Division president and the new entity began to lay plans. An Asiatic Division Conference composed of East Asian lands was likewise formed (and significantly enlarged in 1915). However, at the 1918 General Conference Session, after five years of experience with the new division structure, important modifications would be made. But in most regards, the Adventist Church had now assumed the form that it would carry through the century.[4]

Delegates to the 1913 General Conference Session also pondered the persistent problem of inadequate funding for the church's schools. Details regarding this problem had been worked out at a special meeting of the General Conference Committee (augmented by several score of local conference officials) at Mountain View, California, in January. Daniells, chairing the sessions, was greatly cheered by the results. He left with confidence that perhaps the most chronically vexing financial problems of the church were on the way to resolution: the debilitating debt of the denomination's medical and educational institutions.[5]

The preceding two decades had witnessed an aggressive spate of institution founding, both in health and education. But how could a modest-sized church populated by members of modest means support them all? Daniells and other leaders feared that the church had perhaps been a tad too ambitious. The problem contained two related parts. On one hand, in the schools there had been curricular inflation. Too many schools attempted twelve-grade education without the requisite teachers or financial resources; too many claimed the name "academy" without offering a complete program; and too many colleges proved unable to find qualified Adventist faculty or equip proper science labs. The solution? Following the rationalizing thrust of the Progressive Era's political philosophy, Daniells's men called for yet another General Conference committee, to be empowered to work with union and local conferences in developing a reasoned education program.[6]

The overreach problem also afflicted the denomination's postsecondary schools. Church leadership planned to endorse full college curriculum in just three schools (Union College, Pacific Union College, and Emmanuel Missionary College), to designate the other postsecondary institutions as "training schools" (junior colleges in today's parlance), and to set apart the Foreign Missionary Seminary in Takoma Park for a specialized function. This bespoke a determination to prevent ambitions from outstripping resources. They also sought a better coordination among conference secondary schools and the colleges or training schools to avoid overlap. These were noble hopes, and they marked a mature sense of limits and careful planning. But in the long run, as Daniells's successors would learn, the creation of union conferences had set up power centers that leaders in Takoma Park could not always control. Union conference constituencies owned the various colleges and training schools, and conferences owned their academies. Once financial stability was achieved, these entities would make their own decisions about their schools.[7]

The other, more pressing problem concerned institutional debt. Be it sanitariums or schools or publishing houses, acute financial distress was the bane of Daniells and earlier presidents. Daniells was determined to get control of this problem once and for all. Bolstered by financial facts supplied by General Conference treasurer W. T. Knox and a detailed report by Loma Linda leaders of the school's wide-reaching enterprises—from the dairy to the orchard to the treatment rooms—the General Conference Committee proceeded to craft an ambitious solution. The model came from the church's ministerial and evangelistic program. Church leaders asked for and generally received an average weekly offering of fifteen cents per member. These reliable offerings (in addition to the standard tithe) provided a "satisfactory basis of support" for both domestic evangelism and foreign missions. "Nowhere can there be found a system of gospel finance superior to this," boasted Daniells. The new plan, unanimously accepted by the committee, called for raising that average to twenty cents a week (Daniells pointed out that current giving fell just $12,000 shy of that average). From these enhanced offerings, 25 percent would be earmarked for institutional debt reduction (implying a small shifting of resources to North America, since nearly all previous mission offerings had gone abroad). Stringent rules applied. Funds could only be used for debt relief, and no recipient institution could accrue additional debt.[8]

Daniells must have realized that his optimistic projection of contributions depended on continued American prosperity as well as on members' devotion to the cause. Not one to leave things to chance, he ensured that the *Review and Herald* gave full coverage to this new plan. Editor F. M. Wilcox called on members to get behind the program. "The plan equalizes the burden," he enthused. "Every member, rich or poor, may share in the giving and have a part in the blessing." Daniells reminded readers of the *Review* that every cent devoted to the purpose was truly an investment, because the institutions possessed monetary value that would surpass the debt being retired. More to the point, Daniells was quick to add, the schools in need had already supplied hundreds of workers for the cause. "What should we do to-day without this great army of intelligent, consecrated workers?" he asked in a manner redolent of Ellen White.[9]

But in the midst of these efforts to economize resources and rationalize institutions, an opposite imperative was at work. Daniells and others recognized that the church needed, if not a first-rate, at least a respectable medical school. The College of Medical Evangelists had been founded several years earlier, of course, with the stipulation from the start that the college would not require General Conference funds. But financial realities intruded early, and calls for subsidies were persistent. By the time of the 1913 General Conference Session, leaders had to decide how committed the denomination would be to supporting an institution costly to properly fit, staff, and maintain.

In some ways, it was a good problem, driven by the school's growth in students, curriculum, and property. It now needed a teaching hospital. Ellen White's support added further impetus to a march of progress, costly though it was. Loma Linda supporters overturned every rock that might hide funds. But there was no avoiding asking for denominational help. Thus, at the Washington meetings, Daniells gave permission for the medical college board to make a presentation. He prefaced the discussion with the comment that he knew differences of opinion existed about the school. He hoped (in typical administrative manner) to get everyone behind the effort. Daniells was not above old-fashioned rhetorical tricks to accomplish this. "Should we endeavor to give them a medical education along the lines that we believe to be rational and right," he asked, "or should we send them out to get another kind of medical education or instruction in the worldly schools?" Further, how was the church to assure itself of a steady supply of physicians? He trusted that the answer would be self-evident.[10]

The resolutions placed before the delegates requested an empowerment of General Conference leaders to take the steps necessary to support the young medical school. They specifically solicited the North American Division Conference to advance funds from its treasury. The statement concluded by voicing the desirability of something not often heard in Adventist circles of that era: establishing an endowment fund for future operating expenses. Was there any chance the assembled church would turn down the request? Perhaps. After several years of repeated warnings about the dangers of debt, many delegates were chary of a new commitment. A special North American offering for Loma Linda just two months earlier brought disappointing results. The Adventist public might not be ready for this commitment, some feared. Might it not be advisable for

Loma Linda to provide the first two years of medical work, then have students transfer to established medical schools for their clinical intensives?[11]

Daniells was ready for objections and had lined up a formidable group of proponents. First, and most important, Elder E. E. Andross, president of the Pacific Union, reported his communication with Ellen White about Loma Linda. "The medical school at Loma Linda is to be of the highest order," she affirmed. The church's connection with the "wisest of all physicians" means that we have access to the highest knowledge about health. In short, medical students must get what they need for a first-rate education. To the notion that students could transfer elsewhere to finish their training, White countered that it "is not in harmony with the Lord's plan."[12]

Perhaps this was all delegates needed to hear. But Daniells paraded other church leaders before the session. Dr. W. A. Ruble, current head of Loma Linda, admitted he had been an early skeptic of the medical college notion. But he had been "converted to the idea," and now besought immediate support so that current students could finish a four-year program. Many of them were apt to transfer immediately if the extended training were not offered. This would be a tragedy, I. H. Evans affirmed, for they would risk "coming out crippled for life in their faith in the third angel's message." An Adventist medical college for Adventist students was essential.[13]

The context of the Loma Linda discussion was both timely and tricky. Just three years earlier the influential Flexner Report had been issued, which quickly revolutionized medical school education. Standards were elevated, so much so that in the second decade of the century the number of medical schools declined by almost half. This posed a challenge to Adventist educators. Meeting the new American Medical Association requirements (to allow graduates to sit for state board examinations) would be daunting—impossible without a hospital. But standards would also assure some credibility to the new institution. On a closer front, creation of the new North American Division added complexity to the request for funds. The General Conference session could not compel its subordinate's support; it could only request it. Further, the new entity's coffers were still empty. Where was it to get the money?[14]

The General Conference remedied that problem with an immediate appropriation to the North American Division. The North American Division in turn made a $10,000 appropriation to Loma Linda. But it would not be enough. A modest hospital constructed next to the sanitarium opened in the fall, but over the next year it failed to thrive. Loma Linda still lacked a viable venue for medical training. The medical college and denomination would face a day of reckoning in 1915. As it turned out, surmounting that challenge was linked to the death of Ellen White.[15]

THE END OF AN ERA

Ellen White did not attend the 1913 General Conference Session. Indeed, flagging energies required that she surrender involvement in wider church affairs in favor of intensive attention to her writings. Daniells sought her advice infrequently now, working almost exclusively with her son Willie. In February 1915 she fell, broke her hip, and never fully recovered. Daniells was on his long presidential tour through East Asia and India (discussed below) during her decline. He came back to America sooner than expected, arrived on the West Coast in early summer, and made his way to Elmshaven. His final meeting with the one who had fostered his leadership and corrected his missteps in Australia and America was affecting. Very weak, still she wished to see Arthur and Mary. "I am very glad to see you, but others must do the talking," she said. Daniells then gave a positive report on the work in Asia and Australia and said that people throughout the region sent their greetings and prayers. She nodded and smiled, her son Willie reported, but said no more. Daniells closed with a prayer. He and his wife soon after returned by train to Takoma Park, arriving on July 13. Three days later White died. He immediately sent telegraphic sympathies to his dear friend Willie: "All believers in Takoma Park Washington unite in expressing deep appreciation of the GREAT service our deceased sister WHITE has rendered the cause of God during her long life of toil."[16]

Planning for the most significant funeral in the history of Adventism had begun long before her passing. There would be two services in California (one at Elmshaven and one near San Francisco) and one at Battle Creek (still a major center of Adventism and the site of her burial). Daniells made clear to Willie that the family need not be concerned about funeral expenses; the General Conference, North American Division, and Pacific Press would cover them all, including travel for his family. The service at Battle Creek, in some regards the official church memorial, occurred on a Sabbath morning. Pioneer Adventist preacher, missionary, and close friend of the Whites, S. N. Haskell, delivered the sermon before some thirty-five hundred people in the Tabernacle. White's passing and service found wide notice across the country.[17]

And what of Daniells's part in the memorials? He served as historian and comforter, taking the moment to remind the Adventist public of this unique gift God had given the church. His work began a few days before her passing, while still in California, at camp meeting addresses he gave at Santa Rosa and then Oakdale. To assembled believers who understood that the end was near, he reviewed Paul's description of spiritual gifts. Through Ellen White, Adventism had been blessed with the most distinctive of these gifts. But as Daniells recently traveled throughout Asia, he heard the question repeatedly: What would happen when she was gone? Daniells knew that Americans shared this concern. "I have no fears whatever regarding the survival of the work and the products of this gift in the church," he reassured his listeners. He reminded them that the words of the Old and New Testament writers remained in demand two thousand years later. The prophet's words will likewise "become more precious than they have ever been." And what if there arises "a spurious manifestation?" "What of it?" Daniells boldly replied. Such imposters have often afflicted the church through the ages. Ellen White's influence would survive because she always lifted up Scripture and especially Jesus. Daniells's long address rambled, reviewing moments of Adventist history and current issues, drawing distinctions between his church and other denominations. And as always, he found occasion to revisit his favorite subject, missions. There was purpose in his rambling. It served to subtly take believers' minds off their anxiety about Ellen White. Life was going forward; all would be well.[18]

At the Battle Creek funeral service Daniells delivered the life sketch. This was a more formal address, suitable for the somber occasion. Here, Daniells indulged in one of his favorite rhetorical pastimes: recounting Adventist history, in this case with specific attention to Ellen Gould Harmon White's life. His thorough life sketch was interspersed with points he wished to stress. First, he reassured listeners that her special gifts had been thoroughly tested. "The evidence which supports them, internal and external, is conclusive." "They tend to the purest morality," he affirmed. "They lead us to Christ." "They lead us to the Bible." Second, he reminded people of her role as institution builder. Publishing houses, sanitariums, schools: the infrastructure of the church—all were constructed by the Whites. And she consistently held up the Bible and Christ. There was nothing cultish about her teachings, Daniells implied. Adventists could feel themselves a part—a distinctive part, to be sure—of the mainstream of Christianity. At the same time, he reminded hearers that she had advocated "broad, progressive views" in matters of health and education. In sum, Daniells used Ellen White's memorial service as an occasion to remind his community (through publication in the *Review*) of the continued meaning of Adventism.[19]

Once it became clear that White's days on earth were winding down, the issue of her estate became pressing, particularly the disposition of her writings. White had earlier directed in her will that her writings be preserved and made available to the worldwide Adventist community. A five-person board of trustees was established (including Daniells) to oversee affairs. The trustees met during Daniells's visit to Elmshaven shortly before White's death. White had sizable assets, but even more extensive debts. (Her benefactions were many, and expenses associated with publishing her books considerable.) True to Daniells's philosophy, the group determined to pay creditors every penny. The General Conference would cover current debts, counting on future royalties from her works for repayment. The consummation of her financial affairs was to be done quietly and with dignity.[20]

The passing of Ellen White had added meaning for the struggling medical school at Loma Linda. She had located the school and provided counsel and support in its nascent years. Her stilled voice would be sorely missed as the school faced a new crisis of survival in the fall of 1915. The issues were two. First, the inadequacies as a clinical facility of the new hospital at Loma Linda meant that a hospital must be established in Los Angeles (a modest clinic had opened there in 1913). Constructing and equipping a hospital to the required level was financially daunting. Second, the initial AMA "C" rating meant that graduates might not be eligible to take board examinations in many states. This was not quite a death sentence, but severely crippling.[21]

Fall Council meetings, fittingly held at Loma Linda, could not avoid debating the school's future. The outcome was in doubt. Several General

Conference leaders (including North American Division president I. H. Evans) were ready to pull the plug, sure that the institution would continue to be a money pit. Daniells was not among the naysayers, however. He had become firmly persuaded of the value of medical ministry. He made this clear in an address to medical students and staff in May 1914 just before embarking on his Asian journey. The address must certainly be among the most heartfelt of his career.

What did Daniells say? As he prepared to leave America, missions were much on his mind. "I am to visit the greatest heathen countries in the world," he boasted to students. He hoped above all to persuade them to devote their lives and talents to medical missions. The impact of medical care upon people has no equal, he believed. "It is marvelous how the news of the ministrations of our medical missionaries are spread from place to place, from house to house." Its potential surpassed literature work, long the staple of church mission work. Daniells candidly admitted that the denomination had made mistakes in some medical work abroad. The Mexican sanitarium, for example, with its "splendid furniture," catered to the well-to-do. "How many thousands of poor suffering Mexicans might we have reached if we had established" more numerous if humble dispensaries. A similar mistake had been made in India, seeking to reach the prosperous British colonials rather than the natives, who "could not get into that place."[22]

Instead, Daniells wanted students to model themselves after Dr. Riley Russell, who labored in a modest clinic in Korea. Daniells had met him at his medical school graduation in Washington several years earlier. He asked Riley if he were still willing to head to Korea. "I will be off in two hours," the young man replied. "He did not ask about his wages. He did not ask about having a sanitarium," Daniells reported. Achieving the goal was Riley's concern. A year later the mission board was astounded at the accomplishments of the young doctor, serving some fifteen thousand people in just a short time. "I love to think of that young man," Daniells mused aloud, "busy all day long for people who have no money with which to pay for his services."[23]

"You who are going through the medical school—what do you say to that?" Daniells challenged. "What are you in for? Do you want to give your lives as Livingstone gave his for Africa?" Or, he chided, was their goal "to be connected with some large and possibly, prosperous sanitarium."

Daniells envisioned "an army of three thousand medical missionaries, supported by the church on the same pay scale as preachers, Bible workers, and teachers." He called up memories of having worked for a dollar a day in his early career, then for years on nine dollars a week. It was a struggle, Daniells admitted, but he had survived with no debt.[24]

A General Conference president who possessed such passion for medical missions was not one to give a cold shoulder to requests for enhanced medical training. But could he persuade skeptical colleagues? Fall Council discussions on the topic were animated. The denomination carried a $400,000 debt on the institution. Further, applications for admissions into Loma Linda's fall 1915 class lagged. Some prospective Adventist students had questions about the school's future. Moreover, thought Percy Magan, some veteran Adventist doctors were prejudicing young minds against Loma Linda. "Worldly standards have been held altogether too high, and the real thought of sacrifice has never had its right place in their minds," sentiments Daniells agreed with. Magan, still at Madison Institute at the beginning of 1915, had earned a medical degree at the University of Tennessee. He made himself indispensable to the struggling Loma Linda, learning the ins and outs of medical accreditation and making friends in high medical circles. In autumn 1915, as the school's fate was being debated, the talented and strong-willed Magan was persuaded to become dean of CME (and later its president).[25]

A subcommittee of the Autumn Council was appointed to consider all options. The earlier idea of making CME a two-year program, from which students would transfer elsewhere for clinical training, was revived. Closing was also a possibility. But strong voices argued for not only survival but growth. Percy Magan delivered an impassioned plea. A. G. Daniells similarly weighed in. "My brethren, I am astounded and I must speak. If I do not say my mind I will be a coward and unworthy of your confidence." He then reminded delegates of Ellen White's charge that Adventist medical training be complete. "And here we are, before the prophet is hardly cold in her grave, proposing that our young men and women shall only have half of their education from us and then shall be turned loose in these worldly schools. . . . We can build up this school. We can do anything God wants us to do." But perhaps as important as the exhortations by these two forceful men was the quieter pledge by several women to lead a fund-raising effort for a new hospital. They provided delegates a practical means for pledging support of the school.[26]

Thus, on the final day of Autumn Council, church leaders voted unanimously to accept a plan adopted by the CME constituency that would both keep the school open and allow it to pursue a higher standard of accreditation. A $60,000 hospital would be built by the medical school in Los Angeles. It would go forward only as funds were available (thus preserving the "no debt" policy). It also authorized "The Women's Committee on the Los Angeles Hospital" to lead out in fund-raising (under the supervision of the North American Division Treasury Department).[27]

A collective sigh of relief was heard in Loma Linda, where "the depressing element of uncertainty that has been a real trial of faith" seemed now lifted. Likewise, P. T. Magan, who immediately began his indefatigable work for CME, told Daniells that he considered the recent controversy to be the "first big test which had come up after the death of the Prophet." Magan felt "inexpressibly thankful for your talk that Thursday morning." Magan had not always felt so kindly toward Daniells (especially during debates over reorganization in 1903). But they shared a common goal now. "Elder Daniells rallied to the support of the Spirit of Prophecy in magnificent style," he reported to Dr. David Paulson. "I think that all felt that the talks of Elder Haskell and Elder Daniells were the two which really saved the day," he confided to Haskell's wife.[28]

But fund-raising remained. A huge boon to fund-raising, one would presume, came with the decision to name the institution the Ellen G. White Memorial Hospital. Her unwavering support for Loma Linda and her recent death made the choice appealing—and seemingly inevitable. And yet, some prominent leaders opposed using her name in this way. Daniells, again, helped decide the issue with the pragmatic argument that failing to attach her name would hamper fund-raising. In a sense, the church was facing its first debate over "branding," a commercial matter complicated by the name in question being a prophet's. With that matter settled, Hetty Haskell headed the effort (along with her husband, who as a patriarch of the church carried great influence with laity in a project honoring Ellen White), but church leaders worked alongside them. As Daniells had time, he helped coordinate the effort. While in Oklahoma, for example, he sought a pledge from the conference as well as seeking out "their wealthiest folks." Efforts were successful, and White Memorial Hospital opened in 1918. With a clinical facility in hand, Magan worked hard to achieve a "B" rating from the AMA (and ultimately the coveted "A" in 1922).[29]

Adventism's commitment to medical work as "the right arm of the ministry" would never waver. This dedication would have been hard to imagine a decade earlier during the controversy with Kellogg, a time when it seemed that pastors and physicians could not harmoniously coexist in the church. A. G. Daniells repaired the rupture—or at least patched it up. He went on to serve on CME's board of trustees for a number of years. In 1931, he spoke to the medical students for a final time. He sought to instill an appreciation of the providential founding of their school, recounting crises met and overcome. He closed with another exhortation to faithfulness, reminding them that "this great medical work is going to be in the truest sense the opening wedge in the dark places of the world."[30]

INSPECTING THE CHURCH IN ASIA

A. G. Daniells continued his ambitious program to visit outposts of Adventism during the years before and during World War I. The war obviously impeded trips to Europe, and ill health prevented some other planned trips. But nothing hindered his accomplishing two extensive trips to Asia during mid-decade.

In the few years before the fateful "guns of August" brought devastation to Europe in 1914, Daniells was able to continue his nearly annual treks to Europe. His 1911 Atlantic crossing (aboard the ill-fated *Lusitania*) was his eleventh in his eleven years in office and his second that year. The visits took on a predictable pattern: meeting with leaders; inspecting publishing houses, sanitariums, and schools; holding ministerial institutes. The latter was a source of particular satisfaction for him that year in Great Britain, when almost every minister, Bible worker, and ministerial student was present, nearly a hundred in all.[31]

In 1911, Daniells also visited portions of Europe new to him, notably Russia and the Ottoman Empire's capital of Constantinople (current Istanbul). Determined to understand the people and their culture, he did "more hard tramping" over three weeks than he could ever recall, visiting Russia's impressive clutch of gardens, palaces, and museums. Daniells found some four thousand Russian Adventist believers. They contended with a powerful, established Russian Orthodox Church that tolerated no competition from other religious groups. Daniells believed himself to be under police surveillance from his arrival in the country until he reached Odessa on the Black Sea. Knowing the futility of applying for a government license to preach, he went ahead without permission and spoke across the country (fortunately without consequences). Native ministers were not always so fortunate. One Adventist brother was in prison during Daniells's visit. By contrast, in the Islamic city of Constantinople Daniells found complete freedom for his religious endeavors. A recent constitution guaranteed freedom to hold public meetings, to "say anything we pleased from cursing the old Sultan to criticizing the present ministry," he wrote facetiously to Willie White. Still, work among the Muslims went slowly, most converts being from Armenian, Greek, or other European minorities.[32]

If Daniells traveled widely in Europe, he never got to South America during his presidency. He and Latin American church leaders had made elaborate plans for him to visit all the major centers of Adventism there. Initial plans had Daniells traveling down the Pacific coast and then to Argentina and Brazil. Later, it seemed advisable for him to start in Brazil, continue to Argentina, and then move up through Bolivia, Peru, and Ecuador. But then came a complication. Daniells needed surgery before his trip. He was willing to put it off, believing he could proceed if a robust colleague accompanied him to South America. But the General Conference brethren would have none of this. They insisted on the surgery and no immediate travel. Two years of planning came to an abrupt halt. Instead, with heartfelt apologies to Westphal, Daniells announced that his friend W. W. Prescott would make the trip for him. Daniells was profuse in his expressions of gratitude to Prescott for accepting this challenge on short notice. Such trips were expensive in time and money, he admitted, but "these visits cheer the missionaries in the field, help them to pull their work together in better shape."[33]

It was not often that A. G. Daniells had to cancel a major trip, but the episode dramatically illustrated besetting health problems in these years. In 1910, he had the bout of malaria that depleted his energies. Frequently he dealt with chronic fatigue from the breakneck pace of his work. His obsessive work habits sometimes required colleagues to intervene. On a

Sabbath afternoon in the winter of 1914, Spicer and Knox informed him that after counseling with doctors they concluded he needed an extended rest far away, perhaps in Bermuda or Palm Beach. Further, the upcoming Asian trip should be dramatically shortened. Sensing a broad conspiracy afoot to keep him well, Daniells grudgingly relented. He would not go to Bermuda, however, but to Massachusetts, where he checked into the church's Melrose Sanitarium for several weeks (encouraged perhaps by son Grosvenor's attendance at nearby South Lancaster Academy). "I find it hard to stop my activity," he candidly admitted to E. E. Andross. "I am nervous, and am strongly inclined to keep in motion whether I make any progress or not." The quiet imposed by the sanitarium regimen shielded him from the incessant round of correspondence, a break which, of course, meant he had a mountain of work to face when he returned to Washington. As it turned out, his illness required more than rest. In Los Angeles, on his way to the Orient, his condition demanded surgery. The nature of his ailment is unclear, but by his own testimony the procedure "did not prove altogether successful." He soldiered on through the months and thousands of miles of travel. But need for a second operation ultimately doomed his plans for a later South American trip in 1915.[34]

Nothing, however, would keep Daniells from undertaking his much-anticipated 1914 visit to Asia. He and Mary's trip to San Francisco was something of a procession. Leaving Takoma Park on April 30, they made a detour to South Lancaster for a short visit with their teenage son. The railroad journey west included stops in Texas to visit some of Mary's family. It also occasioned a memory-filled reunion with individuals brought into the church during Daniells's earliest efforts with R. M. Kilgore in Plano. Most notably, he renewed ties with members of the Huguley family, who had become pillars of the Dallas congregation. They then proceeded through Los Angeles and Fresno (where Arthur's sister and her family resided) to Saint Helena. At this last stop, Arthur conferred with Ellen White, who was quite frail now, but still alert. "We talked over old times," Daniells reported to readers of the *Review*. Finally, on June 3, the Daniellses and Florence Shull (a Pacific Press stenographer who would volunteer her services in China) took the Matson Line's *Wilhelmina* bound for Hawaii.[35]

As denominational celebrities, the Daniells were met everywhere with fanfare by local church dignitaries. The quid pro quo for special treatment was an expectation that the General Conference president speak almost without ceasing. Daniells gladly obliged. In Honolulu, for example, he held meetings every night, preached on Sabbath, and spoke with the young people. The 3,100-mile journey to Fiji offered some respite. At the capital of Suva they met the Australasian Union president, J. E. Fulton. The size and modernity of Suva surprised Daniells, given its being so far from continental civilization. Adventism had thrived in Fiji since its introduction in the early 1890s. He preached to a church packed with some 200 islanders, sitting upon their mats. The Daniellses were touched by a ceremonial presentation of gifts from the individual congregations. Baskets, mats, oil, coins, and a whale's tooth were set before them, presents for Americans, he was told, in thanks for their bringing the message of salvation. Daniells received a further gift when he learned later that the day after his departure a spiritual revival swept over the church, including the conversion of a local chief.[36]

The Fiji stop was brief, for the Daniellses had to return to the ship for the remaining 1,600-mile passage to New Zealand. Probably no stop on their itinerary matched the emotion evoked by the return to their first mission posting twenty-eight years earlier. Their New Zealand experience had had its bumps; it was a time of learning for young missionaries. One imagines, though, that the roseate haze of time inspired largely happy memories. Upon landing at Auckland, the Daniellses enjoyed an emotional visit with Edward Hare, first New Zealand Adventist and still a pillar. Daniells spent eighteen eventful days on the North Island, where the church was strongest. Addresses, both to church groups and to the general public, including a presentation on the much-discussed issue of prohibition, filled his time. He was pleased with a prominent Adventist physician whose public esteem reflected well on the church and provided funds for the work. Overall, he found New Zealand a "brighter spot" than he had previously thought.[37]

Daniells sailed across the Tasman Sea to Sydney, Australia, where he was hardly off the boat before a reporter collared him. It seemed the arrival of the leader of the worldwide Seventh-day Adventist Church was newsworthy. This was only the first of several such interviews in the following weeks. Daniells was pleased, having become a firm believer in the power of the secular press to promote the cause. The public had become especially interested in Adventist eschatology when in early August the "Great War" broke out (Australia and New Zealand, members of the British Commonwealth, knew they would be directly affected by events). Daniells took full advantage of the new interest, delivering many addresses on "the Eastern Question" in halls and theaters. Never in his ministry had Daniells encountered such openness to Adventist commentary on contemporary events as he now found.[38]

A. G. Daniells had spent the decade of the 1890s in Australia. His early foray into administration occurred here. He had a hand in bringing scores of its current members into the church. The reunions were frequent and intense. Many of the tears were shed in Melbourne, where the Daniellses found a warm reception at the train station. Melbourne was where Adventism entered the country in 1885 (the first Adventist sermon in the Southern Hemisphere was given there) and where the denomination's first union conference was established. But he kept on the move during his three-month stay, traveling through most of the continent. He wanted a thorough connection with the Adventist community that now served as the linchpin of church work across the South Pacific. Daniells's diligence boggles the mind. Besides the usual complement of ministerial institutes and union conference meetings, he preached some 150 sermons, gave 30 Bible studies, visited 80 families, and had innumerable one-to-one encounters, contacting in some fashion most of the 5,000 members in Australia. The visit culminated with the largest camp meeting ever held in the country, 260 tents pitched and a Sabbath attendance of some 1,500. Daniells reported the Sabbath revival meeting to be "one of the most remarkable I have ever seen on a campground. Five or six hundred people, mainly the young, came forward. And this not from a general call, but for only 'the unconverted, the backslidden, and the half-hearted.' "[39]

Daniells originally planned to travel from Sydney to China, but the war intruded. German naval activity in the western Pacific made it prudent, local church leaders concluded, for him to go first to India from Australia's western port of Freemantle. The enforced change allowed Daniells to hold meetings in the Australian west (which had not been on the original agenda). Following these meetings, in early November, the Daniellses embarked from Freemantle to cross the Indian Ocean. The thirty-five-hundred-mile, nine-day passage to Colombo, Ceylon (now Sri Lanka), gave Daniells much-needed rest. These breaks also offered a chance to compose articles and his long letters home. Daniells kept up with denominational business through a correspondence with Spicer and the General Conference Committee. Even more ambitiously, he wrote extended descriptions of his travels that were published in a multipart *Review* series in 1914 and 1915. The president considered this series less travelogue than inspiration for membership support of missions.[40]

The war came suddenly nearer as they approached port. They encountered a forty-four-ship convoy carrying thirty thousand Australian soldiers on their way to Europe. The liner approached a transport close enough for passengers and soldiers to exchange greetings. It was a "remarkable sight," Daniells testified, "and it somehow made me feel peculiarly strange." He was even more unsettled when his ship cut all lights and steamed ahead through the dark. After they arrived safely, Daniells looked anxiously from the ship for a familiar face to greet him. At last he heard a voice halloing him, that of Elder M. M. Mattison, whom Daniells met years before at Keene Academy and encouraged in mission service. His cordial welcome, Daniells told *Review* readers, was "the kind a Texan gives."[41]

Daniells would like to have seen more of this far southern outpost of British India, but there was as yet no organized work in Ceylon (beyond some colporteur efforts), and church officials had him on a tight schedule. So they made a quick boat trip across the twenty-two-mile strait to Dhanushkodi. Here the Daniellses found the man they expected earlier. Elder H. H. Salisbury, head of the Indian Union Mission (and who, as a former college teacher, Daniells always referred to as "Professor"), was a veteran and well-regarded Adventist worker. He would accompany Daniells on a long circuit throughout out the subcontinent.[42]

India was an education for Daniells. The South Indian Mission, where his tour began, overwhelmed him by its size and population. Mission work had started among the English-speaking population in India. But Daniells was pleased to report that the Nazareth Mission Station (the center of Adventist work in the region) held a church complex and thriving school of 118 native students run entirely by Tamil speakers. Daniells understood that this hand-off to native leadership, still unusual in non-European regions, must become the future if Adventist missions were to thrive. He also favorably commented on something very hard for Indian girls: removal of ornate jewelry.[43]

After a week in the south, the Daniellses traveled a thousand miles by train northwest to Bombay (Mumbai). The Bombay Mission stretched along the Arabian Sea on the country's west coast. A number of American missionaries worked in a region marked by extreme poverty and broad illiteracy. The latter fact posed a challenge to Protestant missions, which depended on an individual's ability to read. After visiting a village, Daniells asked a colleague whether there was a "lower stratum of human existence" anywhere else in India. He was assured there was not. "Here we are working at the very bottom of heathen superstition and degradation," Daniells told readers in America. The church two years earlier had opened the first Christian school in the town of Kalyan, with a medical dispensary that Daniells found exemplary. But Bombay itself contained a large pocket of learning and relative prosperity. Adventism here was being promoted vigorously with modest but promising results. He saw this as a model for the rest of the country.[44]

Next came a long journey northeast to Lucknow. Daniells was fortunate in traveling in November, then only moderately hot. The heat, humidity, and monsoons of spring and summer were nearly unbearable. Fortunately, the foothills of the Himalayas were nearby, and those with means escaped to hill stations. Adventist missionaries established their own stations where they could find relief and labor for others, notably at Simla, farther into the Himalayas. This was a fortuitous choice, for it was the headquarters of the viceroy. Opportunities to witness to well-placed civil service employees were numerous. Yet cultural barriers to conversion were high. "They are fully convinced but are halting," Daniells reported. One woman of influence said she recognized the Adventist message as true but admitted she lacked the courage to take her stand. Nonetheless, a small church had been established. "Some of those who have embraced the truth," Daniells enthused, "hold important positions in government departments."[45]

His peregrination continued to the northwest, heading to the broad plain of the Punjab. With five major rivers and recent irrigation projects, this region had become a rich agricultural area. But the area was as yet lightly entered by the church, and its largely Muslim population would be difficult to persuade. Daniells's visit to one village was particularly memorable. By a local custom, twenty "bombs" were set off at intervals to welcome his party. Daniells did not know what to think, but his companions advised him to accept the custom with a smile. But the most unusual moment may have come in a village in the far northwest, near Afghanistan, where a group of some fifty Punjabis had, through influences unknown, taken the name "Seventh-day Adventist Mission." Daniells recognized some irregularity in the believers. "We are quite aware that these people have nothing approaching a clear conception of our message," he publically admitted. And "from the manner of living in the villages we visited, we could scarcely recognize them as Seventh-day Adventists." Moreover, he allowed that some might have selfish motives. Still, Daniells felt God led him to this group. He and Salisbury proceeded to explain Adventist beliefs as best they could.[46]

Daniells displayed his exhaustive investigation of mission fields in the reports he sent back to the General Conference Committee. Policy, personnel, finances, opportunity—he encompassed the range of issues facing Adventist missions. In India, for example, he noted that despite widespread illiteracy, millions of European or native residents could read English. Therefore, a more aggressive literature evangelism work should be pursued. Daniells did not simply make an observation. He followed up with a detailed eight-point plan of action.[47]

Daniells and Salisbury also took a trip far to the east. At the time of Daniells's India travels, the British Raj was at its geographic height, encompassing Burma. Rangoon, the British administrative center for Burma, was also the center of Adventist work. Here Daniells met Professor R. B. Thurber, whom five years earlier at the East Michigan camp meeting he had advised about going there. Thurber was one of twelve paid workers the church had in Burma. The limited Adventist work had gone forward primarily among Europeans and Anglo-Indians rather than with indigenous people. The Buddhist population was resistant, parents not wanting religious instruction for their children in the Adventist school. In eastern Burma, where the Karen people lived, Daniells found frustration. This was the region most influenced by Christianity. But mission work here was dominated by the Baptists, who plainly did not want interference from a rival Christian group. That, of course, would not deter Daniells. His frustration lay, rather, in workers having given years preparing themselves through intensive language study only to be delayed by a lack of funds for their housing. Daniells's answer was to gently lean on the Australian church for financial help in Burma. The eighteen-day visit to Burma was "strenuous," as the Daniellses encountered some of the most primitive conditions of the entire trip. If sobered by the obstacles here, Daniells was gratified to see a full meeting hall during an evangelistic effort, a treatment room serving many patients, and a thriving school. Thus, in typically modest fashion (particularly where low levels of literacy precluded reliance on literature evangelism) did Adventism take small steps in distant parts of the world.[48]

The Daniellses planned to head directly to Singapore from Rangoon, but the war was making havoc of ship schedules. So they returned to Calcutta, and ultimately fell eighteen days behind the original itinerary. The irenic Daniells found a silver lining, saying the extra time helped him accomplish all that needed to be done. For example, he could now contemplate the British colonial capital of Calcutta, where Georgia Burruss had introduced the Adventist message to India in 1894. Other missionaries quickly followed, and Calcutta became the center of work in Bengal and the largest Adventist presence in all the subcontinent. The potential for work among the English was greatest here, and for a time the work thrived. But efforts faltered, members fell away, and only some forty to fifty remained. But other workers focused on the educated class of Indians. Daniells spoke twice to natives at Calcutta University, relating the war to the biblical exposition on "the Eastern Question." After his talk, the school's vice chancellor engaged Daniells in extended discussion, which the latter took as a sign that Scripture had taken effect. But Daniells had no illusions about the difficulty of carrying the gospel to these lands. "Judicious, patient efforts, watered with tears," would be required.[49]

Once away, they headed to Singapore via the Bay of Bengal and through the Strait of Malacca (between the Malay Peninsula and the island of Sumatra), some sixteen hundred miles. Daniells delighted in the journey, the food, the fellowship among passengers—and not least, the smooth water—all combining to make it among the most enjoyable he had known (and Daniells had known many). But his arrival on February 19, 1915, jolted him back to the ugly reality of life. Just four days earlier a regiment of Indian soldiers had mutinied and rampaged against

Europeans. Most of the women were removed to ships in the harbor. Despite scattered gunfire in the city and martial law, a general meeting of Adventist workers in the mission went ahead. Singapore, Malaysia, and what are now the islands of Indonesia included a welter of ethnic groups, some fifty million people in all. Adventism found the greatest interest in its message among the Chinese minority in the region, a pattern of receptiveness by peoples uprooted geographically or socially, which would be seen often in the twentieth century.[50]

Daniells headed next to China via Hong Kong (still a British possession). He dreaded this leg of the journey, for he knew of the proverbially rough seas in the region. But his good fortune continued as calm waters prevailed. In Hong Kong, Daniells got word of the death of former General Conference president O. A. Olsen. "I have lost a true, dear friend," Daniells told readers of the *Review*. The Hong Kong stay was very brief, for his party had to go to Canton (Guangzhou), where a general meeting of South China workers was scheduled. Daniells was thrilled to meet two individuals in charge of literature evangelism whom he remembered as children years earlier in Australia. "It makes one's heart rejoice to see our boys and girls remain loyal to this message" and devote their lives to missions. Daniells found some satisfaction in the progress of Adventism in South China, though local church membership was generally counted in double digits. More workers and more resources comprised Daniells's prescription for growth.[51]

The Daniells party headed back to the port of Hong Kong for a visit to the Philippines. In Hong Kong they took a moment to pay homage at the grave of Adventist China pioneer "Father" Abram La Rue, who had come to Hong Kong in 1888. The Philippines trip had added significance because all the leaders of Asia and Australasia were present in Manila for a planning council. Daniells noted the geographic reach of this group: from the International Date Line on the east to Persia in the west, from New Zealand to the Arctic. Moreover, a majority of the human race resided within these boundaries. The task seemed hopeless: scarcely twelve thousand Adventist members among a population that topped a billion. Daniells admitted that workers sometimes "feel overwhelmed," and "many times depressed." But he was not a leader who dwelt on insuperable odds. God would ultimately provide.[52]

Daniells took heart at what he witnessed in the Philippines. The greatest church progress in Asia was occurring in the Philippine Islands, foretelling the church's success there throughout the twentieth century. Daniells devoted two long reports in the *Review* to his observations. "I have not met a more earnest, active, self-sacrificing body of young people," he enthused. He went out into the countryside to inspect local churches, but he did not leave the principal Philippine island of Luzon (one of more than seven thousand in the country). Alone in Daniells's travels, this visit brought him to an American possession. Just a decade and a half earlier, the United States had ousted Spain and then annexed the Philippines as a territory. An ugly suppression of a nationalist uprising followed until 1902, but America compensated for this with an administration that helped bring modernity to the islands (at least some of them). A far-reaching educational program was undertaken, with aggressive promotion of English. Hospitals, markets, and other public buildings were constructed; roads and railroads improved; the Catholic Church disestablished, and much of its vast land holdings distributed to small farmers; and a court system and a legal code were provided.[53]

Adventist missions directly benefited from the modernization of the Philippines. Work went forward more smoothly when a rule of law was in place. Further, the ability of the Catholic Church to impede missions was reduced. But most important, the advance of literacy encouraged the inroads of denominational material. Adventist missions did best when literature could be widely distributed to literate people. And Daniells was ecstatic about the colporteur work in the Philippines. Contending with second-rate facilities, nationals nevertheless produced twenty different publications of high quality and fostered an impressive colporteur network. The diligence of the Filipino people resulted in doubling the Adventist membership from two to four hundred during the year past. What might be accomplished with greater American financial support? Daniells implied to readers.[54]

Sadly, Daniells could not wax as enthusiastic about the prospects in Japan. They landed at Nagasaki, where Christianity itself had first arrived several centuries earlier. He went to Osaka and Tokyo, impressed by the beauty of the land and the caliber of church workers he encountered. Still, despite good church facilities, he had to admit that the work had not gone as well as in other Asian countries. "It is a grand disappointment to us that in that wide awake progressive country where we have had a foothold so long we are making so little headway." He conjectured several reasons that might be cited. But he put his finger on a key cultural change in Japan that clearly inhibited outreach. A nation that in the last half of the nineteenth century imbibed everything Western, in the early twentieth just as ferociously returned to its cultural roots. All gospel workers in Japan noted the difficulty of promoting Christianity, Daniells pointed out. Japan's effulgent nationalism exhibited an aggressive posture toward neighbors China and Korea. After Daniells returned home, he received a report from a Chinese worker describing the diplomatic and economic tensions between China and Japan. The upshot of these tensions (which in the 1930s would lead to Japan's invasion of China), the missionary felt, was that China would be open to American educational efforts as a counterbalance. "China will never put obstacles in the way of our educational work," he assured Daniells.[55]

It was a relatively short trip across the Sea of Japan to Fusan (now Busan), Korea. As had been true at the thirteen previous ports where they disembarked, the Daniells were met by American missionaries. The warmth of the greetings, and the local hospitality extended, prompted Daniells to enthuse to *Review* readers that Adventists were the same the world over. "National boundaries and racial peculiarities seem to be obliterated." Did Daniells believe this? Or was it harmless hyperbole, the sort of public relations language he used to build confidence in missions? Whichever, twenty-first-century church members understand better than Daniells the sad truth that doctrinal unity often does not trump ethnic or national differences. Daniells also had no way to envision the thriving industrial state that South Korea would much later become. He saw only widespread poverty and "barren, non-productive land." Still, he was gratified by the progress of the church. With an active literature evangelism effort, it boasted six hundred members and another six hundred Sabbath keepers.[56]

Daniells continued up the Korean peninsula to Manchuria. This rich agricultural region was the ancestral home of the Manchu emperors, whose dynasty ruled China from the 1640s until 1912. At this point in early 1915, two Adventist couples were the only American missionaries actually settled in Manchuria. The Petersens and Grundsets were serious about their commitment, having spent years in Shanghai learning Mandarin Chinese. Modest success had thus far been achieved; twenty or thirty nationals were attending Sabbath meetings. But Daniells heard of widespread interest in the Adventist message, and church literature was in demand. The time to strike was now, Daniells believed, for the expanding influence of Japan in Manchuria (as well as in Korea) boded ill. "It is a foregone conclusion that she [Japan] is there to stay," he wrote. Protestant missionaries might soon expect the same government regulations that they faced in Japan.[57]

Daniells then turned south to the middle region of China, holding a week's worth of morning-to-night meetings at the headquarters of the Central China Union Mission in Hankow (Wuhan). The mission served a large geographic area, but more impressively, it contained 120 million people, a population 20 percent larger than the United States. Despite these staggering figures, Daniells took courage in what workers had accomplished: twenty churches and more than a thousand people keeping the Sabbath. He detailed for *Review* readers the base condition from which individuals had been saved: sixty-six had worshiped idols; four had been opium smokers; five had practiced sorcery; two had been polygamists. Were such people reliably converted? some might ask. But anyone who had seen them, Daniells reassured, would have confidence in their conversions.[58]

The Daniellses prepared to leave Hong Kong on May 14 for the three-week voyage to San Francisco. One last set of meetings in Shanghai occupied him. These were the inaugural sessions of the Asiatic Division Conference, attracting some two hundred workers (only eighteen of whom were Asian nationals from China, the Philippines, Japan, and Korea) for two weeks. Delegates rejoiced that membership (2,743) and tithe had increased impressively, by about a third, in the past year. Daniells understood that these figures might be embarrassingly modest given the scope of the division. But the growth curve had been steep, especially given the glacial pace of the first decade's efforts. The advances in technology—steamships, railroads, and motor cars; telegraph, telephone, and printing press—enabled workers to travel widely and to communicate the gospel even more broadly. It was indeed a new age. But timeliness, Daniells insisted, was everything. There must be no delay. In an impressive display of commitment to their work, workers overwhelmingly passed a resolution ending the furlough program (foreign missionaries normally returned for an extended visit to their homeland after seven years). As Daniells bluntly summed up the action, "It expressed the conviction that they should go for life." Did Daniells suggest the change? Did he so powerfully emphasize the need to press forward now that workers felt compelled to take this radical (and perhaps unwise) step?[59]

Daniells himself claimed that he would have preferred to stay abroad. He wrote Willie that he regretted trading the mission field for work back in the United States. "I somehow dread landing in San Francisco." He felt unneeded where the church had so many members and resources "that I hardly know what service I can render after I get there." Daniells at heart was a frontline worker; he wished to be where the needs were greatest, where he could feel he made a difference. But reality set in. Daniells realized he must return to America after his yearlong travels (fourteen months away from Takoma Park and his son) in time for the summer round of camp meetings and conference sessions. In any event, the European war meant he could not return via Turkey and Europe as he had originally considered doing.[60]

It was A. G. Daniells's destiny to remain an administrator. He had a great talent for sizing up the workings of church organization and, further, of creatively imagining better structures. In the white-hot enthusiasm of his China visit, he envisioned a much-enlarged "continental" Asiatic Division, which would include India, Malaysia, the islands of what is now Indonesia, and Australia, which could provide more church resources. He addressed to the General Conference Committee a long, tightly reasoned argument for this bold move. It was necessary because Asia was "unquestionably the most difficult field in the world to evangelize," with its "great walls of Hinduism, Buddhism, Confucianism, and Mohammedanism." After years of effort, the walls had been breached. But early advances brought new problems. Financial and administrative support for the perennial backbone of Adventist missions—literature evangelism, education, and medical work—must be provided. Daniells outlined yet another plan to increase weekly giving by members. He asked that these proposals be enacted at Fall Council that year. His memo to the General Conference

Committee was among the most complete plans he ever prepared.[61]

Daniells not only could propose a change, but he knew how to close a deal. At the November meetings in Loma Linda he pursued his vision. He was aided by leaders from Asia. They recognized his gifts, appreciated his extended visit, and knew the change could help their work. H. R. Salisbury from India (himself an able leader) and J. E. Fulton of the Australasia Division made the long trip to speak in support of Daniells's plan. R. F. Cottrell, a leader in central China, reported that the training school was already at capacity, and the Chinese *Signs of the Times* had a larger circulation than the combined total of all other Christian papers. Yet stronger administration was needed to harness this growth. Predictably, the General Conference Committee voted to support Daniells's plan for organizational change.[62]

Daniells made another trip to Asia in 1916–1917 (the war still precluded a visit to Europe). This was shorter than his previous tour, leaving Vancouver in early November and returning to San Francisco in late May. He confined his travels to the fields in East Asia such as Japan, Korea, the Philippines, and China. Taking the considerable effort to make the trip reflected his conviction that now was the moment for Adventist work in that region. He had to ensure the construction of an enduring administrative framework. Daniells was particularly pleased by progress in the Philippines. Although initially skeptical of the mission's readiness for conference status, he changed his mind during the visit. He seemed pleased that this would be the first conference "organized in the non-Christian and non-Protestant part of the Asiatic Division." Daniells clearly felt a special bond with the Filipinos. "I do not see how any one with a warm, Christian heart can help falling in love with those earnest people."[63]

WAR, PROPHECY, AND EVANGELISM

A half century earlier, during the Civil War, the Seventh-day Adventist Church formally organized. Now, although America was not yet directly involved, the "Great War" (later styled World War I) served to advance the Adventist cause. An apocalyptic message that could be linked to current events was bound to arouse public interest.

But more immediate concerns for church leaders (and Daniells was in the Far East during most of the war's first year) was the impact on the European church. By early fall 1914, communication with European

Division leader Louis Conradi became intermittent. The intrepid W. A. Spicer traveled to neutral Scandinavia and Holland in early 1917 and even slipped into Germany for meetings with Conradi. His return in the spring of 1917 came after Germany instituted unrestricted submarine warfare, which in April prompted the United States to enter the war. Despite the destruction and disruption, the European Adventist Church fared better than might have been expected. Scandinavian countries (which were largely spared) enjoyed their best years ever by various criteria. Church membership in Germany grew by some 40 percent between 1914 and 1920. Whether this growth was influenced by the German church's relationship to military service cannot be ascertained. What is known is that a crisis immediately erupted within the German Adventist Church when war came in August 1914. European Division Secretary Guy Dail desperately sought counsel about military service from Ellen White through Willie. But by this point the prophet was beyond giving counsel. German church leadership had to make a quick decision, as its men were facing the firing squad. They concluded (and informed the German government) that young Adventist men need not avoid military service, even if it involved Sabbath work. At least 250 German Adventist soldiers would die in the war, not to mention a long-standing rift in the German church over the propriety of the decision.[64]

The war also claimed one of the most able overseas mission leaders, Homer R. Salisbury. A former secretary to W. W. Prescott, he had taught Hebrew at Battle Creek College and then served as principal of the Foreign Missionary Seminary in Washington (thus his title "professor") before accepting a call to head the Indian mission in 1913. He served as Daniells's host during much of the latter's Asian tour. After a trip to America, he was returning to India in late 1915 on the British liner *Persia* when it was torpedoed in the Mediterranean. For days the Adventist community hoped that word would come of his rescue on a lifeboat. But it was not to be. Salisbury's death was a blow to Daniells, who, along with others at headquarters, held him in high regard.[65]

But if the war brought inconvenience and even tragedy, it also facilitated notable growth in the church. In Germany, despite (or perhaps because of) a grinding military struggle, the church thrived in membership growth and giving. North American Adventism enjoyed a rate of growth in 1917 that surpassed any year of that century. As noted earlier, following his immersion in New York City evangelism in 1910, Daniells promoted urban evangelism vigorously. This included ministerial institutes to ready Adventist preachers for evangelism (with Daniells's blessing and involvement). Thus, even before war clouds loomed, urban outreach was underway.[66]

Adventist prophetic interpretation regarding Turkey also predated World War I. The Ottoman Empire had declined for a century or more. By the late nineteenth century it found itself struggling to hang on to its Balkan possessions. By early 1914 the Ottoman rulers found themselves stripped of most European territories. Revolt from within threatened to sunder the Turkish heartland. These events, the "Eastern Question," were followed with great interest by Adventist Bible interpreters, for Turkey had been identified by Uriah Smith as the "King of the North" mentioned in Daniel 11. The fall of "the king," which was understood to be the Turks' eviction from Europe and the establishment of a new capital in the "Holy Mountain" (Jerusalem), would mark the final days before Armageddon. As it turned out, interest in the Eastern Question existed beyond Adventist circles. In current events, Adventist evangelists found a new hook for their message.[67]

A. G. Daniells, now energized for evangelism and prophecy, wrote a twenty-five-part series for the *Review* running from early 1913 to spring 1914 entitled "Does the History of Turkey and Egypt Since 1798 Fulfill the Prophecy of Dan. 11:40-42?" In sometimes agonizing detail (the series only reached the 1840s), Daniells linked passages in Daniel and Revelation with the Ottoman Empire's changing fortunes. The series displayed Daniells's passion for history. Although many of the articles were composed primarily of direct quotations from history books strung together, he in fact did considerable research in compiling them.

This research served him well, for with the coming of the "Great War" in August 1914, public interest redoubled (although direct American involvement would wait until spring 1917). Turkey could not escape the war, and it early became evident that the remaining empire of the "King of the North" was in jeopardy from the fighting. Although Daniells was away during much of the war's first year and then, after returning, he had to catch up with denominational work, by early 1916 he hit the evangelistic sawdust trail. War and prophecy were his theme.

His first effort came in Portland, Maine, a locale carefully chosen.

Ellen White's former home remained close to her heart. In her final years she believed that a renaissance of the Adventist work in the East would start there. A revival of sorts had stirred the Maine Conference, aided by the unflagging efforts of the Haskells. A growing membership and a new church in Portland augured success. Thus, with careful preparation and ambitious advertising, in January (a month one might not consider propitious in New England) Daniells was set to deliver three talks at the spacious city auditorium. He could not have predicted that his effort would later be considered the beginning of "the modern era of large-scale Adventist evangelism." Nor could he have anticipated that 1916 would be an *annus mirabilis* for American evangelism generally.[68]

An opening crowd of some eighteen hundred—far more than Adventist evangelists typically drew—heard Daniells's discourse on the war's fulfillment of Bible prophecy. The audience appeared responsive, but more amazing to Daniells was an unexpected invitation for him to address the city's business elite the following evening on the same topic. He found the occasion unexpectedly moving. "I have felt very solemn all day," he wrote I. H. Evans, "almost sad as I have thought of those upturned faces." Daniells held a burden for souls that ran deeper than any appeal to ego the large crowds might have tempted. "There is something more than ordinary about this whole work in Portland," he judged. Indeed, he believed the effort gave every indication of fulfilling Ellen White's prediction of a general revival in the East.[69]

He had to return to church work in Washington, but interest remained so high in Portland that Daniells was persuaded to return in February. He provided an outline of his talk, with which local members papered the town. Daniells arrived at the auditorium just fifteen minutes before the program was to start; he found three thousand people seated—and hundreds more standing around the walls or waiting to get in. Police finally ordered the doors shut. Local papers chronicled the palpable excitement surrounding the meeting. Daniells's correlation of world events with Bible prophecy clearly gave people pause. Ultimately twelve meetings were held in the large auditorium, with other sessions held in smaller satellite locations about the state. Youthful evangelist Carlyle B. Haynes joined what had become a large, complex effort. The meetings were not advertised as Adventist events, but more than six hundred people turned in interest cards to learn more. "It has certainly developed into the greatest movement I have ever had on my hands in the way of public meetings," an excited Daniells wrote. But upon reflection, he was sobered to realize how unprepared the church was to handle an influx of members. By this he meant it lacked experience in dealing with large audiences, or enough trained workers to nurture new converts, or even wanted spiritual depth as a denomination. Daniells could never countenance a fly-by-night approach to things, especially at these rare moments of high church visibility.[70]

As news spread around the church, Daniells was inundated with requests to hold meetings elsewhere. Opportunity appeared white hot. Syracuse, New York, planned meetings. The Boston Adventist community rented historic Tremont Temple for meetings. For Daniells, the first half of 1916 would be devoted to the prophetic gospel—a fact he seemed not to mind at all. (Ellen White's urging voice still sounded in his mind.) He labored in Portland into April. But with others there to help, he punctuated his New England work with a trip to Pittsburgh to lecture at the Pitt Theatre. His three meetings, with little advertising for the final night, drew a packed house, some twenty-five-hundred attendees per session. These were straightforward lectures, without benefit of special music or stereopticon slides. At this grave hour of history, audiences ("a specially good class of people," Daniells testified) were prepared to devote full attention to a biblically based presentation on "The Coming of the Prince of Peace." The reluctance of mainline Protestant churches to address prophetic issues of the war opened a door for Adventist evangelism.[71]

Late spring and early summer brought Daniells to the Upper Midwest. He did double duty, wearing his administrator's hat while attending the conference camp meetings and then assuming the evangelist's role in lecturing in ten cities and towns about "The World War: Its Cause and Meaning." His lecture circuit reads like a railroad timetable of the Great Northern Railroad: Minneapolis, Saint Paul, Duluth, Superior, Jamestown, Fargo, Hutchinson, Mankato, and Cloquet. Attendance rarely disappointed. Large centers like Minneapolis brought in more than two thousand people, but even medium-sized towns such as Duluth featured fourteen-hundred-seat auditoriums. His efforts were as fruitful as those in the East. He spoke to an estimated twelve thousand people and secured some seven hundred names of those interested in hearing more. He was particularly pleased with the home missionary work of local churches, which seemed to promise effective follow-up to the lectures. Toward the tour's end, Daniells admitted that the pace had been hard on him. And more requests poured in, some of which he could accept (Columbus, Ohio) and others not (Des Moines, Iowa, among others).[72]

Yet Daniells did not limit his outreach to the lecture hall. He published his Portland address, freely distributing tens of thousands of copies. "I have worked hard to develop this subject in a way to appeal to the public," he wrote Willie White. Daniells expressed chagrin that other denominational leaders showed little interest in his writings. "So far I have not had one word of approval from any of the high officers" on the General Conference Committee. Yet this did not discourage him from proceeding with an even more ambitious project. He expanded the lecture about the war's prophetic meaning into two booklets, which were widely circulated by the Review and Herald, Southern Publishing, and Pacific Press. *The World War: Its Relation to the Eastern Question and Armageddon* appeared in 1917 and *A World in Perplexity* in 1918. While inexpensively produced, these books were full of war photographs that added to their interest.[73]

He reiterated, in all three versions, the heart of Adventism's interpretation of Daniel 11: The Ottoman Empire would fall; its capital, deprived of the last bit of Europe it held (across the Bosporus), would be moved to Jerusalem. Armageddon, the great battle of nations, would surely follow soon after. (Daniells was impressed that so many secular commentators on the war referred to it as "Armageddon," the first war so characterized, he said.) "If ever warring powers seemed to be under the control of satanic powers, getting ready for Armageddon, it is at this time." The 1918 edition added final chapters on "Signs of Christ's Coming" and "The Gospel to all Nations." In quick, popular form, these chapters made more overt the Millerite and New Testament foundations of Adventist eschatology.[74]

But as the war proceeded, events forced church leaders to reconsider. America's entry into the struggle on the Allied side in April 1917 infused a new partisanship. The *Review* had warned members earlier that year to "avoid jingoism" that might help propel the country into war. But once committed, the church found itself having to negotiate the always tricky business of relating to matters of patriotism and military service. The

Spring Council of the North American Division took up the problem of looming conscription for Adventist young men in April. It adopted a statement that simultaneously affirmed Adventists' patriotism and willingness to serve while requesting noncombatant status for its members. Church leadership backed up this statement with active advocacy for its young men and encouraging instruction in nursing to ready them for combat medic work. Although many Adventists ended up being court-martialed for failure to comply with orders, in the big picture church and government reached a working accommodation that laid the basis for World War II military service.[75]

Daniells had not yet returned from his second Asian tour when America entered the war, and thus he was not part of these negotiations. But his war-inspired prophetic evangelism came under scrutiny. Despite the welcome wartime surge in membership, emphasizing the war's apocalyptic meaning and America's expected descent into religious repression (as understood from Revelation 13) could easily arouse public suspicion now that the nation had joined the fight. Anticipation of this problem may explain the cool reception of his publication Daniells found among some of his peers. But the real problem lay with the less restrained church evangelists and with such publications as *The Watchman* and *Signs of the Times*. Wartime events were irresistible fodder to gather hearers and readership. The sensationalism finally brought rebuke in the fall of 1917 from Francis Wilcox, editor of the *Review*. "It seems strange that such admonition should be required," Wilcox wrote, but "for the sake of the influence of the movement they represent," evangelists must avoid "wild statements, fanciful interpretation of the Scriptures," or anything encouraging the "spirit of excitement and sensationalism." The editorial proved insufficient, so a Summer Council resolution in 1918 warned that church efforts to hold the attention of the public "may lead us to adopt sensational methods" not in keeping "with the sacred character and the solemnity of the message."[76]

It is understandable that at a time when the denomination was desperate to help its young men in service by professing unswerving patriotism, it would distance itself from vivid eschatology (no matter how deeply held). But the larger problem, of course, was that Daniells's widespread reiteration of Uriah Smith's "King of the North" interpretation was proven false. Turkey would not be driven completely out of Europe; and not only did it not move its capital to Jerusalem, but in December of 1917 British troops drove Ottoman troops out of "the glorious holy mountain" (Jerusalem), which reverted to Christian control. "These are days in which we do well not to hazard too much speculation regarding the trend of events in the world," the *Review* prudently noted after the event. Daniells, in his 1918 work, *A World in Perplexity*, displayed new caution ("the Turkish capital will eventually be planted in Jerusalem"). But did he ever give serious reflection to the proof-text method by which he arrived at his prophetic conclusions? There is no indication that he did. That prophecies are best understood in retrospect, an unsatisfying truth forced upon early Adventists after hard experience, remained a conclusion that Daniells's generation still resisted.[77]

As World War I finally ground to a halt in the fall of 1918, the Adventist Church felt compelled to reconsider its worldwide administrative direction. Daniells had initially opposed the new division structure, but then found himself persuaded by forceful arguments from others. The North American Division Conference, as discussed above, had come about in a fit of enthusiasm for the new divisional plan. But as early as 1915 Daniells began having severe reservations about the new structure. He had a surer grasp of administrative issues than he did prophetic exposition, and he now shared his doubts with his peers.

There were two interrelated issues. First, the divisions were organized as large conferences, that is, they had member constituencies just as local and union conferences did. This had the potential to fragment church organization. With the onset of World War I the European Division Conference hardly had a chance to prove itself. But national tensions inevitably arising from the war and some questions about certain decisions of Conradi's during the war encouraged a rethinking. Second (and the more troubling issue for Daniells), the North American Division's new autonomy threatened its support for world mission outreach. He shared his concerns bluntly with I. H. Evans (who as president of the North American Division proved a strong advocate for needs of the American church) and W. A. Spicer. "I am greatly troubled about this arrangement," he confessed. "I have been for a long time." What drove his concern? A division conference empowered to make its own decisions about financial and human resources could be an impediment to world missions. "In the important matter of securing workers and funds, and in placing returned workers it subordinates the General Conference to the Division Conference." It made the General Conference "a subordinate organization for every worker and every dollar it needs." This would not be a critical matter were it not for the inescapable fact that North America provided so much of the human and financial resources for the world church. Was this just a theoretical concern? No. Daniells recalled how recently a Fall Council action apportionment for church members was later reduced significantly. All told, current structure tended to "impair efficiency," "create uncertainty, and cause delay," all inimical to gospel work.[78]

Daniells did not have long to wait for action. With himself and Spicer present, and Evans onboard, Fall Council debated and then recommended to the next General Conference session that the North American Division Conference be discontinued. This, in order to achieve "the unity of our world-wide work."[79]

The 1918 General Conference should have occurred a year earlier (to stay on the four-year cycle). But the war interfered. Leaders hoped that a year's delay might see the war's end and allow more delegates from around the world to attend. Neither happened. The April meetings held in San Francisco (in the largest venue yet used for the sessions) were largely an American affair. In the very first recommendation of his presidential address, Daniells appealed for the need to keep North America an arsenal for missions. He left the implications of this need cryptic. But I. H. Evans spelled out in clear terms what Daniells hinted at: elimination of the North American Division Conference. If some delegates found that a surprise (not that the move had been a secret), more were caught off guard by the next step. General Conference treasurer W. T. Knox reported to the body a recommendation of an ad hoc committee on structure: that all world division conferences likewise be demoted from conference status.[80]

Why the change? Two division conferences—Asiatic and South American—had been formed since the 1913 General Conference had authorized them and had just been officially welcomed into the organization (represented in San Francisco by a handful of delegates). The ink was scarcely dry on their documents. Chairing the session when the matter came up, Daniells admitted the apparent retreat. "It will be recognized by all as retracing our steps a bit—the steps taken in the 1913 Conference." But five years' experience (at least with the European Division Conference) had resulted in "great complications thrown upon us." Delegates wanted to know more, so Evans laid out the concerns with admirable candor. "The chief purpose in doing away with the Division Conference organizations is to preserve the unity of the work; to save the possibility at any future time of having a large section of our work break away from the general body." It was not just the practice of raising world mission funds or facilitating returning missionaries; it was to avoid schism.[81]

In essence, the change meant that although divisions would remain, they would not have their own constituencies; rather, they would be administrative units of the General Conference. Vice presidents appointed by the General Conference Committee would oversee their respective division, assisted by treasurers and other necessary officers similarly appointed. The North American Division would remain even more closely held by the General Conference than the other divisions (largely in how funds were handled). This structure, which would endure through most of the twentieth century, displayed Daniells's utter commitment to maintaining a unified, worldwide Seventh-day Adventist Church. It also showed his flexibility and willingness to rethink decisions. He had originally been leery of the plan but was willing to be persuaded by Conradi and others. Now, with reports of discontent with some of Conradi's wartime leadership in Europe contributing to his change, Daniells was capable of making a quick *volte-face.*[82]

At these same meetings A. G. Daniells was elected General Conference president for the sixth time. The minutes suggest no controversy in the vote. Although he had at various times pondered aloud stepping down from the post, he gave no hint of that now. He had no reason to suspect that his 1918 reelection would be his last.

---

[1] GCCMin, January 21, 22, 1913.

[2] *GCB,* May 20, 1913, 50, 51; Knight, *Organizing for Mission and Growth*, 133–138.

[3] AGD to WCW, November 24, 1911; *GCB*, May 23 1913, 100, 101, 108, 109.

[4] *GCB*, May 24, 1913, 145; May 27, 1913, 145; June 1, 1913, 218; GCCMin, November 7, 1915; Schwarz and Greenleaf, *Light Bearers*, 314.

[5] *RH*, February 13, 1913, 152.

[6] GCCMin, January 22, 1913.

[7] *GCB*, June 8, 1913, 310; June 9, 1913, 324.

[8] GCCMin, April 13, 1913; *RH*, February 13, 1913, 152, 153.

[9] *RH*, February 13, 1913, 153, 156.

[10] McFarland, *Railway to the Moon*, 31–34; *GCB*, May 30, 1913, 193, 194.

[11] *GCB*, May 30, 1913, 194.

[12] Ibid., 195.

[13] Ibid., 195–197.

[14] Ibid., 196, 198; "The Fall and Rise of the American Medical Profession," in Hatch, *The Professions in American History*, 63.

[15] *GCB*, June 9, 1913, 333; McFarland, *Railway to the Moon*, 35, 36.

[16] A. L. White, *The Later Elmshaven Years*, 423–425, 432; WCW to "Editor," June 10, 1915, EGWE; *RH*, July 22, 1915, 24; AGD to WCW, telegram, July 17, 1915, EGWE.

[17] A. L. White, *The Later Elmshaven Years*, 432–439; AGD to WCW, July 29, 1915, EGWE.

[18] AGD, "On the Spirit of Prophecy," manuscript of talk delivered at Oakdale, CA, July 4, 1915, EGWE.

[19] *RH*, August 5, 1915, 4–8.

[20] Schwarz and Greenleaf, *Light Bearers*, 357, 358; GCCMin, November 9, 10, 1914; "Report of Conference held at Elmshaven," June 22, 1915, EGWE; GCCMin, November 17, 1915.

[21] McFarland, *Railway to the Moon*, 32–35.

[22] "Address of Elder A. G. Daniells to Loma Linda medical students and others" (typescript, May 25, 1914, EGWE).

[23] Ibid.; *RH*, May 14, 1908, 21.

[24] "Address of Elder A. G. Daniells."

[25] P. T. Magan to Newton Evans, August 9, 1915; P. T. Magan to WCW, March 3, 1915, ASTR.

[26] McFarland, *Railway to the Moon*, 38–41; Schwarz and Greenleaf, *Light Bearers*, 297.

[27] Ibid.; *RH*, December 16, 1915, 8, 9.

[28] *RH*, December 23, 1915, 18; P. T. Magan to AGD, December 12, 1915; P. T. Magan to David Paulson, December 7, 1915; P. T. Magan to Mrs. S. N. Haskell, December 9, 1915, ASTR.

[29] P. T. Magan to Dr. Newton Evans, January 9, 1916; AGD to E. E. Andross, February 16, 1916; P. T. Magan to Mrs. S. N. Haskell, December 9, 1916; WCW to P. T. Magan, February 22, 1916, ASTR; *RH*, March 28, 1918, 24; Schwarz and Greenleaf, *Light Bearers*, 297.

[30] Talk by AGD, sanitarium chapel, Loma Linda, CA, September 13, 1931, EGWE.

[31] AGD to WCW, January 2, 1912; November 24, 1911.

[32] AGD to WCW, June 23, 1911.

[33] J. W. Westphal to AGD, September 1, 1915; November 18, 1915; December 30, 1915; AGD to J. W. Westphal, October 17, 1915; AGD to W. W. Prescott, December 9, 1915, ASTR.

[34] AGD to E. E. Andross, February 19, 1914; AGD to WCW, May 6, 1914; AGD to J. W.

Westphal, October 17, 1915, ASTR.

[35] AGD to WCW, May 5, 1914; *RH*, July 9, 1914, 8; W. A. Spicer to AGD, July 27, 1914.

[36] *RH*, July 9, 1914, 8; January 7, 1915, 9; AGD to WCW, July 29, 1914, EGWE.

[37] *RH*, January 28, 1915, 10; AGD to WCW, July 29, 1914.

[38] *RH*, October 1, 1914, 15; January 28, 1915, 10.

[39] *RH*, December 24, 1914, 7, 8; February 4, 1915, 11; AGD to W. A. Spicer and W. T. Knox, September 24, 1914.

[40] AGD to G. B. Thompson, September 25, 1914; AGD to W. A. Spicer and W. T. Knox, September 24, 1914; AGD to Evans, March 7, 1915, ASTR.

[41] *RH*, April 15, 1915, 9, 10.

[42] Ibid.

[43] *RH*, April 22, 1915, 10–12.

[44] *RH*, April 29, 1915, 10, 11.

[45] *RH*, May 6, 1915, 9, 10; AGD to Brother and Sister Shaw, December 22, 1914, ASTR.

[46] *RH*, May 13, 1915, 9, 10.

[47] AGD to General Conference Committee, January 7, 1915, ASTR.

[48] *RH*, May 20, 1915, 10, 11; AGD to General Conference Committee, January 7, 1915; January 30, 1915, ASTR.

[49] *RH*, May 27, 1915, 11, 12; AGD to General Conference Committee, January 30, 1915; AGD to Evans, March 7, 1915.

[50] *RH*, June 3, 1915, 10–12.

[51] *RH*, June 10. 1915, 9, 10.

[52] Ibid.; *Annual Statistical Report, 1914*.

[53] *RH*, June 17, 1915, 9, 10; July 1, 1915, 9–11; United States Philippines Commission, 1900–1916, *Report of the Philippine Commission to the Secretary of War, 1913* (Washington, DC: Government Printing Office, 1914), 29, 30, 209, 244.

[54] *RH*, July 1, 1915, 9–11.

[55] *RH*, July 15, 1959, 9, 10; AGD to W. T. Knox, April 7, 1915; James Shultz to AGD, July 21, 1915, ASTR.

[56] *RH*, June 24, 1915, 10, 11; AGD to W. T. Knox, April 7, 1915.

[57] *RH*, July 8, 1915, 9, 10.

[58] *RH*, July 29, 1915, 9, 10.

[59] *RH*, August 26, 1915, 5–7.

[60] AGD to WCW, April 7, 1915, EGWE; AGD to Evans, March 12, 1915, ASTR.

[61] AGD to General Conference Committee, March 28, 1915, ASTR.

[62] H. R. Salisbury to AGD, June 20, 1915; GCCMin, November 7, 8, 1915.

[63] *RH*, November 2, 1915, 24; June 14, 1917, 24; AGD to Fellow Workers, November 23, 1916; AGD to General Conference Committee, December 29, 1916; AGD to WCW, January 10, 1917; AGD to Frederick Griggs, February 29, 1917, ASTR.

[64] I. H. Evans to AGD, February 5, 1917; *RH,* April 12, 1917, 24; May 17, 1917, 24; Schwarz and Greenleaf, *Light Bearers*, 372; H. Raft to AGD, October 7, 1915, ASTR; Gilbert Valentine, "They Ought to Stand to their Duty—Facing the Crisis without a Living Prophet"

(unpublished paper given at Institute of Adventist Studies Symposium, "The Impact of World War One on Seventh-day Adventism," Friedensau, Germany, May 7–12, 2014).

[65] *RH*, January 13, 1916, 24; January 20, 1916, 24; February 17, 1916, 15, 16; S. A. Wellman to AGD, January 5, 1916; AGD to S. A. Wellman, April 6, 1916; AGD to Brother Shultz, April 5, 1916, ASTR.

[66] Weeks, *Adventist Evangelism*, chapters 3–5, p. 99; AGD to Brother Shultz, April 5, 1916; regarding the need for ministerial institutes, see AGD to E. E. Andross, January 30, 1916, ASTR.

[67] Gary Land, "The Perils of Prophecy: Seventh-day Adventists Interpret World War One," *Adventist Heritage* 1, no. 1 (January 1974): 28, 29; Weeks, *Adventist Evangelism*, 77; Bull and Lockhart, *Seeking a Sanctuary*, 63.

[68] *RH*, February 24, 1916, 14; April 6, 1916, 6, 7; Weeks, *Adventist Evangelism*, 84–87.

[69] Weeks, *Adventist Evangelism*, 85–87; *RH*, April 16, 1916, 6.

[70] AGD to WCW, February 22, 1916; AGD to I. H. Evans, February 17, 1916; *RH*, April 13, 1916, 6, 7.

[71] AGD to WCW, February 22, 1916; AGD to Brother Shultz, April 5, 1916; Weeks, *Adventist Evangelism*, 89–91.

[72] *RH*, August 3, 1916, 15, 16; AGD to I. H. Evans, July 6, 1916.

[73] AGD to WCW, June 23, 1916.

[74] AGD, *The World War* (Nashville, TN: Southern Publishing Association, 1917), 80, 86; AGD, *A World in Perplexity* (Mountain View, CA: Pacific Press®, 1918).

[75] An extensive discussion of World War I and the Adventist Church can be found in Schwarz and Greenleaf, *Light Bearers*, 367–372; *RH*, February 22, 1917, 3; North American Division Committee minutes, April 18, 1917.

[76] Land, "The Perils of Prophecy," 29, 30; Weeks, *Adventist Evangelism*, 101, 102; *RH*, September 6, 1917, 3; August 1, 1918, 4; Schwarz and Greenleaf, *Light Bearers*, 371, 372.

[77] Weeks, *Adventist Evangelism*, 104; *RH*, December 20, 1917, 24; AGD, *A World in Perplexity*, 98; Land, "The Perils of Prophecy," 55, 56.

[78] Knight, *Organizing for Mission and Growth*, 137–139; Bert Haloviak, "Approaches to Church Reorganization" (unpublished paper, ASTR); Schwarz and Greenleaf, *Light Bearers*, 314, 316; AGD to W. A. Spicer, October 9, 1917, ASTR.

[79] GCCMin, October, 31, 1917.

[80] *GCB*, April 2, 1918, 28; April 3, 1918, 39; *RH*, April 4, 1918, 10.

[81] *RH*, April 4, 1918, 4; *GCB*, April 3, 1918, 39, 40.

[82] Schwarz and Greenleaf, *Light Bearers*, 314, 315.

Chapter XI

PROGRESS, CONTENTION, DISMISSAL

The November 11 armistice followed by the Versailles peace negotiations in early 1919 gave hope for a new age. In one sense, peace and prosperity were not what the Adventist Church had in mind for the world. But if the apocalyptic prospects of World War I failed to materialize, the end of war could at least remove barriers to the advance of the Advent gospel. Leadership in Washington, having endured reduced contact with the European church, was eager to learn how believers had fared during difficult times. The immediate postwar years promised to be fruitful ones for the denomination, as world mission outreach continued in high gear.

But 1919 would be significant for Daniells in a way that he could not have predicted. A much-anticipated study conference for Bible and history teachers pondered matters of prophecy and inspiration that had long troubled reflective members but which were seldom voiced. In an act of admirable administrative leadership, Daniells candidly expressed his views on controversial matters. But he learned it was far easier to define theological problems among a handful of other leaders than to devise a plan for changing the attitudes of an entire church. He learned another hard lesson of leadership: that even strong leaders are vulnerable to attacks by those willing to whip up fears among rank and file. Ultimately, the 1922 General Conference Session would be his last as president.

A NEW WORLD

"Momentous events are taking place in the world today," A. G. Daniells told readers of the *Review* in the first week of 1919. "Some of these events are startling and ominous in character. They seem to be full of danger to the world. . . . Famine and pestilence have reaped a heavy toll." (Daniells did not know the half of it. The influenza pandemic of 1918–1919 had yet to show its full horror.) “Amazing surprises,” “bewildering complications,” “wreckage of centuries of progress”—these were among the phrases being used to describe the legacy of the Great War. Indeed, the world was a new place. The European and Middle Eastern maps were radically redrawn in its wake. Monarchies ended in Russia and Germany. Likewise, empires either came to an end (Austria-Hungary and the Ottoman) or were severely curtailed. And European colonialism started down the path toward rapid decline. The playing field for missions would look very different.[1]

But the picture Daniells painted had more hope than discouragement. “Millions of our fellow men are to be delivered from the oppression of heavy-handed, despotic governments under which they have lived.” If the democratic promise, of which Woodrow Wilson spoke so eloquently, was realized, then “new freedom will come to many hitherto oppressed peoples.” The world was witnessing a new age for “man’s inalienable rights.” Not just for human rights but also for missions. “This new hour in the unfolding of divine purpose struck as far back as in 1844.” Every important world development since that date, Daniells felt, had providential meaning. “Never in its long, eventful history has the church of God stood face to face with a more definite and divinely appointed mission than it does today.”[2]

The appointed mission could now go forward more smoothly in Europe. American church leaders discovered that their worst fears about the impact of the war were unfounded. L. R. Conradi continued serving as church leader throughout the war. He reported to the General Conference Committee in 1919 that the European church not only survived four years of unrelieved conflict but actually grew in some places (including Germany). “God’s wonderful providence toward his cause has surely been evident even in this most awful struggle.” Against untold hardship, European church leaders found ways to nurture their flock and engage in some evangelism. Conradi did not mention, however, that division among German Adventists over whether young church members should fight in the army had resulted in a bitter split. Russia, reeling under the twin blows of military defeat and revolution, was even harder hit. Yet even there, pockets of encouragement were found, such as the baptism of forty-nine Russian soldiers in an Austrian prisoner-of-war camp. He estimated some forty-five thousand believers remained faithful. Conradi shared Daniells's belief that more open postwar governments would "open doors." Still, the challenge of redrawn national boundaries meant revisiting conference organization. And ongoing obstacles to travel and acute shortages of fuel interfered with any rapid return to normal conditions.[3]

In November 1919 Daniells led a delegation of American leaders across the now U-boat-free north Atlantic for a major European church gathering in Denmark. As an opening gesture of good will, Daniells announced that American conferences would double their weekly contributions for missions. He then brought European leaders up to date on recent administrative decisions, including the 1918 vote to dissolve the European Division Union. The council was not prepared to jump into the complicated matter of reorganizing European conferences and unions to reflect new national boundaries. Instead, it empowered local administrators to take action as situations might require. Daniells urged earnest effort upon his European comrades; the church could afford nothing less. "In the light of divine prophecy we know that conditions of peace will not continue to the end." Daniells could hardly have spoken truer words, given the rapid descent of Europe toward an even larger war. But for the moment, peace did prevail, and by 1922 the European church boasted some fifty-eight thousand believers, a growth of 23 percent since the war's end.[4]

The Middle East underwent even more wrenching political and boundary changes following the war. Christian missions had always struggled in the Islamic world. Now, with Ottoman oversight ended and large territorial mandates going to France and Great Britain, the possibility of new beginnings appeared. The Denmark meetings created a union mission field in the Levant. Alas, organizational tinkering was insufficient to the challenge of a resistant culture.[5]

East Asia was touched relatively lightly by the war, but ongoing instability in China provided a tenuous backdrop to ambitious Adventist efforts there. A weak central government, chronic warlordism, encroachment by Japan, and little help from Western powers (until the next war approached) contributed to the later rise of Communism. Nonetheless, the Adventist Church persevered. A spring 1919 general meeting at Hankow brought Spicer and Prescott along with most leaders from other East Asian fields. I. H. Evans, the highly competent head of the China work, detailed for Daniells its deliberations. Personnel changes always topped agendas, as did the chronic readjusting of conference and mission lines. But now matters of pay became more insistent, as inflation eroded workers' ability to sustain themselves. Better to have workers recalled from the field, Evans felt, than continue under straitened conditions. Mission schools would be improved, Evans promised, and students better supported and given longer training, as native workers currently were woefully unprepared to "preach the great message." All this would take money. "I suppose you will feel that you have done more for us than we are entitled to," Evans ruefully wrote Daniells. Nonetheless, he hoped the General Conference Committee might locate funds to help them out.[6]

The immediate postwar years brought changes to the American church as well. Leadership was energized by membership growth and an accompanying increase in funds. A surge of giving toward the end of 1918 allowed the General Conference Committee to support the mission field more generously. In 1919, giving for evangelism surpassed eight million dollars, an increase of nearly 25 percent from the previous year. Per-capita giving was also the highest in history. Leadership was never to be satisfied, however, pointing out that this represented an average gift of only eighteen cents per day for each North American member. Not mentioned publicly but a concern in committee meetings was the impact of inflation. For three years, beginning in 1917, inflation averaged more than 15 percent in the United States. Church salaries did not immediately keep pace. Administrators understood that hardships for workers had to be addressed. Although the sharp recession of 1920–1921 strained members' giving, most subsequent years of the decade were strong for the American commercial economy and enabled salary increases.[7]

The annual *Statistical Report* became ever more thorough in the information it provided, with an impressive array of data and comparisons (although membership figures were sometimes inconsistent). A member who bothered to peruse the twenty-four-page 1919 edition would be edified to learn that in the Arabic language two books totaling 208 pages, one pamphlet of 48 pages, and eight tracts of 136 pages, with a total value of $1.07, had been produced. Or that seating capacity of the Adventist Church between 1907 and 1919 had increased by 82,773. The quantitative growth of the church had to be gratifying to all involved. Denominational numeracy spoke to a long-standing Adventist predilection for hard data as the proper measure of progress.[8]

The postwar years also called for attention to overlooked needs at home. The Navajo Indian Mission in Arizona was dilapidated and lacked a reliable water supply. Only one Navajo had been persuaded to embrace the Adventist gospel, but church leadership nonetheless decided that funds must be given to upgrade the facility. At Oakwood Training School, significant funds were appropriated to acquire heavy machinery for a sawmill and to refurbish dormitories.[9]

Daniells's direct influence on church affairs continued to occur most often in the General Conference Committee meetings. During busy times these would meet daily (even twice a day during spring councils) for a week or more at a time. Attendance generally ranged from the low teens into the twenties. From the chair, Daniells could guide discussion and shape decisions. The scope of business attended to was vast, literally encompassing the world and dealing with every imaginable facet of church work. If a goal of the 1901 church reorganization was to decentralize administration, it accomplished this only in part. The denomination continued to be markedly hierarchical, with much power still at the top (exemplified by the Committee's vote authorizing Shelton Academy—later Platte Valley Academy—a Nebraska Conference school, to offer an eleventh grade).[10]

Finances were crucial, but Daniells understood that nothing was more important for organizational success than matching people's aptitudes to their post. The General Conference Committee labored over this task every meeting. Who was available? Who was qualified? Who was ill? Who was discouraged? Compounding the normal complications was the fact that the church's global reach outran its stock of talent. Thus struggles occurred among church entities to get the best people. In a set of education policies passed in spring 1919, one member implored schools to remember in the "exchange of teachers the principle of equitable distribution of talent." A few days later a subcommittee recommended to the full body protocols for transferring workers between conferences or unions and "to better avoid friction and the unsettling of workers."[11]

Education remained close to Daniells's heart. The General Conference Committee desired that denominational schools might better inculcate Adventism in their students. The Committee made pedagogical recommendations, including projects and lectures on church history topics.

It also recognized the problem of inadequate textbooks. Happily, M. E. Olsen was preparing a manuscript of denominational history that showed promise. The work would not appear until 1925, however, as *The Origin and Progress of the Seventh-day Adventist Church.* Contrarily, the church faced the problem of too many independent publications appearing under the Adventist name. Some works inaccurately reflected church positions. Thus, all books henceforth were to be vetted by publishing house book committees or executive committees of the conference. Further, church publishing houses should not print nor stock independent works. These guidelines, unobjectionable in themselves, reflected a movement that had clearly become a modern organization careful about its clarity of message and reputation.[12]

Such concerns may also have prompted the first ever editorial convention in April of 1919. The church had nearly 150 editors working in various publications throughout the world, but the gathering hosted only the 25 from the United States. Daniells presided and opened the convention with a keynote address, stressing to the attendees that their work carried the permanence of the written word. The several-day conference reflected new assumptions about the professionalization now required in Adventist publications. The meetings ended with a proposal for an Editorial Bureau in the church to coordinate publications (a suggestion not ultimately implemented).[13]

In October, a Biannual Council (between the four-year General Conference sessions) convened in Boulder, Colorado, which proved nearly as eventful for foreign missions as the 1915 General Conference Session. Delegates (with a larger international representation now that the war had ended) were inspired by the encouraging news from about the globe. That the church in Europe had grown by ten thousand souls during the grueling war years seemed miraculous. The African field had grown to the point that an African Division was established. A cable from India read, "Opportunities here unprecedented."[14]

What could the North American church do to build on these successes? Send more workers, to be sure. The Council asked that each local conference in the United States and Canada train and recommend two families to the Mission Board. But additional missionaries would need to be funded. The Council heard a recommendation for a 1920 budget of nearly $2.3

million. Daniells feared this figure "would be appalling to the brethren." But it passed. Covering this sum required the church to step out in faith. October 12, Columbus Day, marked "a remarkable day in the Council" by Daniells's testimony. H. W. Cottrell started it by announcing a $10,000 gift from the Western Oregon Conference surplus tithe. One after another, union and conference presidents arose to pledge munificent gifts for missions. By the end, more than $100,000 was pledged. This was followed up a few days later by an ambitious resolution to encourage each member to pledge fifty cents a week for missions. Full employment and inflated dollars contributed to a sense of vast possibilities for members' support.[15]

A. G. Daniells's addresses to the Adventist public in 1919 reveal both the confidence and urgency of that moment in church history. They also exemplify Daniells as rhetorician. Although his place in Adventist history did not depend on his ability to move audiences or readers, over his long career he developed skills as speaker and writer. These were evident in two sermons printed in the *Review*. The first, "Our Day, Our Message, Our Call," appeared in July; the second, "Awake! Give Light!" was printed in the *Review*'s last issue of the year.[16]

The pieces were partly sermons and partly essays—they carried characteristics of both. And they shared a similar exhortatory quality, their purpose being to inspire members to diligence and faithfulness. Daniells showed himself to be well-read in current periodicals, which he mined for indications of prophetic fulfillment. It did not take much digging. The war, still fresh in everyone's minds, offered unparalleled examples of humanity's distress. "Surely in our day we have seen the most wonderful, the most tragic fulfillment of the words of Christ that any generation has ever seen." Daniells seemed not at all perturbed by the failure of his wartime prophetic interpretations. In the bigger picture, he was sure, indications of the "time of the end" were manifest. He displayed a keen sense of timing. He could build points, utilizing excerpts from contemporary writers to illustrate how even non-Christian thinkers unwittingly supported biblical prophecy. The "perplexity" of mankind; the "bewilderment" of the world; the "moral chaos" in society—all these bespoke a world heading toward its end. Worst of all, "we are not through with war yet" (astutely sensing the next world war decades away).

Like any good preacher, Daniells understood the power of repetition.

"We cannot live to ourselves. We cannot follow our own inclinations and desires. . . . We cannot go into the world and select our own vocation and follow our own way, regardless of this day and this message." And being steeped in Adventist distinctives, he longed to renew similar convictions in his fellow believers. "We are nearer the end than any other generation has ever been." Familiar words, easily dismissed as a truism. But from Daniells they seemed more than religious boilerplate. He believed. He wished all Adventists to believe with the same white-hot intensity. As he spoke to *Review* readers at the end of 1919, he invoked a powerful mission metaphor of "people who are rapidly hurrying down the mighty river of death, flowing on to the dark abyss. In that great river, every twelve months 33,000,000 people pour over the falls into the foaming waters below." God's people, understanding their message of hope, must not delay in its delivery.

LIVING WITHOUT A PROPHET

From its beginnings, the Advent movement had known a prophet. Ellen White, as preacher, prolific writer, wife to denominational leader, and public face of the church, seemed the indispensable person. Who would provide guidance, reassurance, and occasional rebuke now that she was gone? Would God raise up another prophet? This certainly happened in Old Testament times. Furthermore, the prophet Joel (reiterated by Luke in Acts) promised that in the last days sons and daughters would prophesy.

The closest thing to Adventism's situation was found in the other major American religious movement of the 1840s, the Church of Jesus Christ of Latter-day Saints. The Mormons enjoyed a procession of prophets, with clear procedures for selecting the (always male) successor. Adventism lacked such a system. Consequently, claims to the prophetic office were unregulated. Even during White's lifetime, at least a dozen people claimed a similar calling, notably Anna Phillips. With White's death in July 1915, rank-and-file Adventists understandably hoped—in some cases perhaps expected—that God would raise up another. The heightened apocalypticism of World War I could only have reinforced this notion. F. M. Wilcox, editor of the *Review*, understood this expectation and penned a judicious editorial for the paper a few weeks after White's passing. To the inquiries the *Review* had received about a successor Wilcox stated "frankly and unequivocally that we do not know." Scripture gives "no set rule of prophetic succession." He predicted that some would come forward believing in their call. To these claims Wilcox counseled caution. "Time and circumstances and conditions, the life of the individual, the character of the message, the spirit which accompanies it, the fruit it bears, are God's great testers."[17]

As expected, pretenders to White's mantle appeared. Within two months, Daniells received a letter from Clara Resch, an American then in Vienna, Austria. "I am compelled to make a clear statement to you of something God by His Holy Spirit has revealed to me." Resch confided that since 1905 God had been preparing her through scriptural study to advise the church. "He has instructed me definitely for the succession to this sacred work and has promised to be with me always if I remain faithful." Conversely, "God has now revealed bloodguiltiness should I fail to make this known to the church."[18]

In Margaret Rowen, however, A. G. Daniells faced a more serious example of prophetic presumption, one that briefly threatened the unity of the church in Southern California.[19]

In mid-1916, Rowen, a relatively new member of a small Adventist congregation in Los Angeles, had a "vision." She told of coming world events. During her rapture, which was witnessed by a group of women, she manifested typical signs of visionaries, face upward, eyes open and fixed on an unseen object, oblivious to surroundings, and no apparent breathing. Further, her prayers appeared to restore the wife of a local physician to emotional and physical well-being. News about Rowen's gifts began to spread around the Los Angeles Adventist community and then to Adventism more widely. Believers multiplied, including some pastors and physicians. Consequently, church officials knew they had a situation on their hands. Not only Southern California Conference officials but also Daniells realized that they must investigate this "outpouring" of the Spirit.[20]

Odd predictions and unorthodox theological positions threw up early red flags. Rowen claimed, among other things, that the 144,000 would only come from America; that Jesus had originally been an angel; and that the investigative judgment of the living would begin in 1919. A conference committee decided that Rowen not be permitted to make church presentations. Earlier that summer, at a meeting in the Washington, D.C., train station, Rowen revealed to Daniells even more bizarre details about her personal life. In vision she learned that she was an illegitimate child with a birth mother she had never met. Further, she would become heir to a valuable estate in Maryland. In subsequent letters to Daniells, Rowen presumed, in the manner of Ellen White, to give him advice on how the work in Philadelphia might better go forward. Daniells visited the Southern California camp meeting in 1917, making a special point to warn members that Rowen's prophetic gift remained in question.[21]

Responding to what was becoming a splinter movement (the Reformed Seventh-day Adventists) Daniells authorized an investigation which in its thoroughness has few equals in denominational history. Legal records were scoured. Affidavits were taken from many individuals who had knowledge of Rowen's situation. Ministers in the East were dispatched to check details of her claims in the region. Contentions about her birth family received particular scrutiny. Rowen's sisters, scandalized by her claims, met with Daniells to help sort out the bizarre twists of their sister's story. Although her claims would soon be shown as fraudulent (her putative birth mother was never found), in the early stages of the investigation Daniells would not jump to conclusions. "I have gone through so many things in the world," he told the sisters, "that I don't set a thing down as true or false until I have evidence." Indeed, his correspondence with Rowen was respectful, even confiding in discussing the church's world mission.[22]

But from prophecy and fanciful autobiographical claims, Rowen modulated into outright document forgery. She sought validation for her calling from Ellen White. Rowen said she saw in vision that a letter existed in the White Estate vault in which White specifically affirmed that a prophetic successor would soon arise. "I then saw that just a little way in the future," White wrote (according to Rowen), "after my labors were finished, that God would call one to give the cry—the cry to the church of God, Repent! Repent! Lift up the standard." Many would question the new prophet, White warned, but "through all of her trials she was true to her calling. In her heart was the love." Who would this be? "I saw that the one sent of God was one of limited education, small of stature and would sign the messages, Margaret Rowen."[23]

Cloak-and-dagger escapades followed, wherein a forged copy of the alleged Ellen White letter was smuggled into the vault files. But so clumsily was it accomplished that even Rowen had to admit its bogus nature. A more skillful forgery was later mailed to Willie White, who sought to defend his mother's legacy throughout the entire affair. Multiple affidavits were collected from associates of Ellen White testifying that they never heard her allude to a prophetic successor.[24]

It is unclear how many church members Rowen enticed through her periodical *The Reform Advocate*; probably fewer than a thousand. Nor can we determine her motivation or level of conviction about her own calling. Psychiatry was then in its infancy. We can only speculate about the sort of megalomaniacal delusion she suffered from. She would not have a happy ending. Her appeal wore thin as her prophecies about the close of probation (1924) and the world's destruction (1925) to most eyes appeared unfulfilled. To forgery Rowen added misuse of donations. Ultimately, and most bizarre of all, she became involved in an apparent plot to murder a former supporter, leading to her arrest and imprisonment in 1927.[25]

The culmination of the Rowen affair came well after Daniells left office. But he had to deal with the difficult early stages, when suspicions were only in the process of being verified. Daniells's handling of the matter must be judged successful. Given the denomination's necessary openness to the possibility of a new prophet, he had to let the claim play out. It is difficult to see how he could have fully prevented the delusion from entrapping those individuals predisposed to believe Rowen's claims. In retrospect, such collateral damage seems an unavoidable cost a religious movement must incur in exchange for hosting a prophet.

A. G. Daniells's greatest leadership test regarding the Spirit of Prophecy came not from prophetic pretenders but from the challenge of understanding the proper place of Ellen White's writings in the church. This was hardly new. Questions about the nature of her inspiration and her authority accompanied Ellen White her entire prophetic life. A series of disgruntled individuals and offshoot movements beginning in the 1860s questioned her office. Some, such as Dudley Canright, made themselves synonymous with opposition to White's prophetic role. Others who had been her great champions, such as John Harvey Kellogg or Alonzo Trevier Jones (and later Louis Conradi), would in later years grow disillusioned and bitter. But dissidents and detractors, as troubling as they were, endangered the church less than an uncritical, literalistic reading of her writings. As Daniells well understood, this tendency could ultimately be more insidious than the poisons of Canright.

The problem had several parts. The first concerned what authority within a religious community a charismatic individual should possess. The relationship of that authority to organizational leadership was bound to engender friction. As noted earlier, Daniells's full acceptance of White's calling did not preclude conflict. Usually charisma prevailed. But not always, as Ellen White learned when she felt herself shuttled off to Australia in the 1890s.

A second tendency compounded the complications: interpreting White's writings without context. This became more common as her writings were compiled and published. What had been originally given to a person or group for a particular circumstance, once in print became universalized. White's voluminous writings, covering a host of topics, contained something for seemingly every aspect of life, from health to education to child rearing to forms of worship to church administration. Discerning which testimonies appropriately spoke to later situations and which did not required wisdom and a sense of denominational history. These were not available in every case. The result too often was a glib—sometimes extreme—application of her testimonies.

A third and quite vexing question to early twentieth-century Adventists was how her historical books were written. A widespread assumption existed that works such as *The Desire of Ages, Patriarchs and Prophets*, and especially *The Great Controversy* were thoroughly inspired. That is, Ellen White composed them under deep inspiration. Few Adventists believed in a mechanical form of verbal inspiration, that White was little more than a scribe recording God's words. But short of that, her words were believed completely reliable, elucidating Bible passages for believers' edification. Infallibility was never claimed for White's writings, but in practice, church members came perilously close. This assumption (as described in chapter 9) was tested in the 1911 revision of *The Great Controversy*.

A final complication resided in matters of temperament and long-term loyalty. Certain individuals had an explicit confidence in the authority and timelessness of White's writings; indeed, they seemed to need this assurance for their religious experience to be settled. Counted among these were a number of White's oldest companions. Any revisionism toward her writing they saw as tantamount to a diminution of her authority. Thus, discussions of her work quickly assumed a personal edge. Daniells faced this many times in his career.

The ongoing controversy over "the daily" raised the issue of White's inspiration quite directly. Defenders of Uriah Smith's interpretation cared less about his views than about the new position's implications for inspiration. White's endorsement of Smith's view—albeit decades earlier—stood as unyielding as Gibraltar in their eyes. When pastors or educators gathered, these controverted doctrinal matters became favorite fodder for discussion. On returning from an educational convention at Berrien Springs in 1910, Daniells confided to Willie White his conviction that "the true friends of the Spirit of Prophecy have a responsibility resting upon them to protect both the author [Ellen White] and the writings from a gross injustice." Continuing in a tone of foreboding, he asserted, "There is at work now an underground current of influence that is undermining confidence in our mother's writings. And I believe that unless we take a consistent, defensible position we shall be driven into very hard places where the cause will suffer great loss." The answer to attacks by detractors, Daniells felt, was not a retreat to an absolute, near-verbal inspiration position of Haskell and others, but rather to "claim only what your father and mother claimed in the beginning, and what you yourself believe regarding the Spirit of Prophecy."[26]

The issue of Ellen White's inspiration also simmered in Europe. During a visit there in 1911, Daniells found anxiety among pastors over views of inspiration taken by some, including the head of the European church, L. R. Conradi. Daniells was asked to speak to Conradi on the issue when he arrived at a church council in Freidensau, Germany. Some Adventists, concerned with what they perceived as insufficient support of White's authority, embraced an extreme position on the other side. After giving "careful study to the fundamental principles underlying the Spirit of Prophecy," Daniells spoke "plainly" to them. He reviewed the recent changes to *The Great Controversy*. And he admitted that "there were some things in Sister White's writings that were like those in Paul's writings, which Peter tells us about as hard to be understood."[27]

Thus, with the prophet no longer among them, but with the legacy of her writings still strong, Daniells and other church leaders sought to define her authority for the church. How could the church avoid the shoals of skepticism on the one hand and those of unwarranted literalism on the other? As always, Daniells believed in the value of educational conferences, where religious and educational leaders could study and discuss these knotty issues. Not only matters of inspiration but also various prophetic interpretations needed study. As early as 1913 Francis Wilcox had called for such a gathering, and Daniells concurred. Having dealt with hundreds of questions about the Spirit of Prophecy at camp meetings, in classrooms and ministerial conferences, he desired a forum for open discussion among the church's thought leaders. Perhaps a consensus could at last be reached. "If we could get studious, broad-minded men who stand unqualifiedly for our message," Daniells dreamed, "I believe that with such men as leaders, our Bible teachers and editors could meet with profit." But other priorities always intervened. He finally planned a conference for the summer of 1918, but wartime restrictions on travel and other complications threw up hurdles. At last, in 1919, peace having returned and the denomination at a confident moment, the time seemed propitious.[28]

1919 BIBLE CONFERENCE

Where to hold the conference? Accessibility for attendees from around the country suggested a central location, such as Michigan. But it finally landed at Washington Missionary College (WMC). Though one might argue that the convenience of General Conference officials was the deciding factor, other reasons were stated. Access to the college's library and to the records of the denomination were thought important for study. Further, at the college they could avoid holding long summer meetings in a tent. By Daniells's reckoning, nothing quite this ambitious had ever before been held. The conference was not a mere weekend affair; it ran from July 1 to 19 (with a special meeting for history teachers tacked on at the end). It was of sufficient import that the General Conference Committee decided on the VIP invitation list: members of the General Conference Committee, periodical editors, and religion and history faculty from postsecondary institutions. One important individual could not attend.

Willie White regretted that his work with the White Estate precluded his traveling across the country for the event. Given how important to the conference was clarifying the nature of his mother's inspiration, it is indeed regrettable that his voice was not heard.[29]

A committee set the agenda of topics for study. Not surprising for a church that arose through study of Bible prophecy, eight of the eleven topics concerned this area: principles of prophetic interpretation; the Eastern Question (World War I and Turkey still hearkened); the beast power in Revelation; the 1,260 days; the United States in prophecy; the Seven Trumpets; Matthew 24's prophecies of last days; and the identification of the Ten Kingdoms. One encounters in the 1919 Bible Conference a time in Adventism when scriptural prophecy still stood front and center, when believers argued passionately over historical and contemporary fulfillments of Daniel 2, 8, and 11. The conference makes sense only as one appreciates this significance—and that some traditional interpretations were up in the air. Interestingly, "the daily" did not make the list of topics, whether because leaders felt the new view was safely on the way to acceptance or because it had been sufficiently debated or that they feared reopening that can of worms (predictably, perhaps, the subject did arise during discussions). Nor was the Spirit of Prophecy a formal topic (a hot-button issue perhaps best left off the agenda). Daniells knew, however, that this troubled subject was on everyone's minds. Sure enough, inspiration came up during the open discussion periods that were scheduled almost daily.

Daniells opened the conference on July 1 with a heartfelt address to the sixty-five participants (only three of whom were women: Flora Plummer, secretary of the Sabbath School Department; Fannie Chase, editor of the *Youth's Instructor*; and Flora Williams, educational superintendent of the Eastern Michigan Conference). Daniells recognized the fears of some that the conference would engender controversy. Such concerns, Daniells admitted, gave him pause. But as he and his advisors reflected more, they realized that the need for "cooperative study of the Word of God" was essential. The sessions were not for "magnifying differences" but for identifying "the great essentials, the fundamentals." Daniells's ultimate goal for leaders, editors, and teachers was unity of belief. But he could not ignore a current of suspicion running among some church laity. "They wonder if we are going to fix up a creed for them to subscribe to. They are much disturbed about it. The secrecy alarms them." There was no secrecy about the Bible Conference, only a limited invitation list. Some who were left out asked if they could attend. But the General Conference Committee held to its original formula. Restricting participation while discussing doctrine almost ensured that conspiratorial fears would arise in the hearts of those so inclined.[30]

A. G. Daniells was a clear-minded individual. He could examine issues—administrative or theological—and arrive at conclusions based on reasoned judgment, minimally affected by emotional considerations. People with this predisposition think that others ought likewise to be so capable. Daniells was thus distressed when his brethren failed to reason clearly. A religion teacher at Pacific Union College, W. G. Wirth, had "suddenly decided that the King of the North is Rome." Daniells was nonplused. "Brother White," he wrote, "I am astonished at the conclusions men reach on this question, with very little definite and substantial evidence." Daniells must also have recalled painfully the grief his friend Prescott received for promoting biblical interpretations that Daniells thought were incontrovertible. Yet men could be persuaded. With the confidence of an Enlightenment *philosophe*, he believed that intensive study and rational discussion must inevitably lead to unified conclusions.[31]

Daniells mentioned to the attendees (Wirth included) an additional motivation for the conference. Not long before, he had visited a service in Minneapolis at the church of the notable Baptist pastor, William Bell Riley. Daniells was impressed by Riley's critique of higher criticism and of the pernicious influence of modern learning generally. Riley also headed a series of Bible conferences about America during the war years, which were the birthing places for modern Christian Fundamentalism. Prescott attended one of them in Philadelphia. For Daniells the lesson was clear: Adventism could also benefit from "a good, strong conference every year." Daniells could not have known that he was thus tying Adventism to the most powerful development within American Protestantism. Adventists shared with Fundamentalist Christians a high view of inspiration (though not verbal inspiration), fears about the acids of modernism and evolution (Adventists would shape modern creationism), and an interest in prophecy. But Daniells failed to see how the fundamentalist temper within Adventism would hamper his efforts at nurturing a nuanced understanding of the Spirit of Prophecy. And he certainly did not anticipate how creeping Fundamentalism would soon lead to his defeat.[32]

Daniells concluded his welcome to conference attendees with extensive—and very telling—passages from a Testimony. "Whenever the people of God are growing in grace, they will be constantly obtaining a clearer understanding of His word. . . . But as real spiritual life declines," Ellen White continues, "it has ever been the tendency to cease to advance in the knowledge of the truth." *Did some fear that the Bible conference might engender controversy?* was Daniells unspoken question. If so, the prophet commanded them not to over-worry about such eventualities. "The fact that there is no controversy or agitation among God's people, should not be regarded as conclusive evidence that they are holding fast to sound doctrine. There is reason to fear that they may not be clearly discriminating between truth and error. When no new questions are started by investigation of the Scriptures, when no difference of opinion arises which will set men to searching the Bible for themselves to make sure they have the truth, there will be many now, as in ancient times, who will hold to tradition and worship they know not what."[33]

Daniells laid before his colleagues White's words as their marching orders. "Agitate, agitate, agitate." Such a call to insurgency seems uncharacteristic for the administrative temperament. But it was a measure of Daniells's passion for the Advent gospel that he was prepared to override the normal risk-averse inclinations of office in order to make, as White earlier wrote, "the subjects which we present to the world a living reality." "I am much impressed with this good counsel," Daniells said in closing. It does not "stifle thought" nor "blindfold people." "It doesn't mean that we shall get a narrow creed, and stand there never stepping a foot over the line. It means greater light and intellectual advancement." Daniells hoped to lead not only a great mission effort but also an open-minded investigation of present truth. Thirteen years earlier, at a Colorado camp meeting, he had publically foresworn any attempt by the General Conference to "put a cast on anybody or to mold any conference." A "united people" did not mean uniformity in everything. "Let those diversities exist that God permits in his universe and in nature."[34]

In addition to opening the conference, Daniells gave worship talks every morning (his series on the Holy Spirit has not survived). This was regularly followed at 9:00 by a study of the "person of Christ" by W. W. Prescott (later released as a book). From 10:00 to noon, various members presented 45-minute talks on the assorted subjects of the conference. Afternoons were less structured, mostly devoted to discussion of the three morning topics (including Prescott's Christological series). But there was also time given for attendees to pursue independent research in the college library, or for more recondite historical issues, even at the Library of Congress. For the twenty-nine college teachers present from fourteen schools, the conference, in today's language, constituted in-service training. Evenings found the teachers consulting together and working on lesson plans for the upcoming school year. In the manner of official Adventist meetings in that age, organizers sought to "redeem the time" with a fully scheduled day.[35]

The individual presentations and most of the discussions were captured verbatim by a stenographer. Several gaps in the record occur when discussion became, in Daniells's eyes, private, heated, or too controversial, and he told the recording secretary to cease his work. For example, when Daniells launched into a highly personal remembrance of the 1903 Kellogg battle, he requested that recording stop. On another occasion, Prescott was being pressed on the question of Christ's having an origin in time (an Arianism he did not teach). Daniells's censorial hand suggests that he was concerned either about sensitive discussions becoming widely known or that perhaps participants would be more comfortable airing their theological questions if they did not have to worry about going on record.[36]

A detailed account of the 1919 Bible Conference goes beyond the scope of this biography. But in surveying the conference transcript, one gains an appreciation of the sophistication and the sincerity of the discussions. The leading student of the conference believes that Daniells brought together the most well-educated group ever assembled in the church up to that time. It was still an era when few Adventist teachers had advanced degrees (Daniells's belief in pursuit of truth did not extend to the pursuit of graduate degrees, which could likely serve to undermine faith). The use of Bible commentaries and original Hebrew and Greek terms was extensive. In a sense, it might have been the first scholarly conference in Adventism.[37]

Daniells felt the time was right for these open discussions. "Fifteen years ago we could not have talked what we are talking here today," he told attendees. "It would not have been safe." Although expressing confidence, Daniells's ritual appeal to his colleagues suggested an underlying concern. He knew that some workers in the field questioned his support of White's prophetic legacy. Thus, he periodically asked his colleagues "if there is a man here who has had doubt created in your mind from my attitude and the positions I have taken? . . . Or is there one of you that thinks I am shaky on the Testimonies?" The stenographer recorded supportive voices calling out "no, no."[38]

The conference focused on prophecies important to Adventists during the war, especially Daniel 11. M. C. Wilcox, for example, editor of *Signs of the Times,* delivered a detailed, even Byzantine description of how he came to abandon Uriah Smith's traditional view of the King of the North. There was no compelling reason, he concluded, to identify Turkey as that entity. Nor was there the "slightest evidence of its nearer fulfillment now than a half century ago." A key moment for Wilcox's doctrinal liberation came when he realized that Smith's interpretation was never denominational writ, only widely circulated and read interpretation. The church could alter its understanding with no repudiation of its official stance (or that of Ellen White's, from whom "we have no utterance" on the issue). A. O. Tait endorsed Wilcox's repudiation of Smith's view, arguing that the King of the North had to be a revived, dominant papacy. Daniells, in the tradition of early Adventist Bible studies, finally called for a season of prayer to help the group think through the issue.[39]

President Daniells was an active participant, insisting on always being present when any controversial issue was discussed. He welcomed advances in biblical or theological understanding as fully as he did new organizational forms. The church's grasp of the 1,260-day prophecy, for example, seemed to him now more sound, this due to study of historical detail and compiling useful sources. His comfort with the group led him toward confessional statements. He freely admitted to having held mistaken views and to his desire to learn truth (especially in regard to Bible prophecy). For example, what in the book of Daniel is symbolic and what should be viewed as literal? And despite its formal absence from the agenda, "the daily" inevitably came up. It brought out the most straightforward confession from Daniells. He could no longer accept Uriah Smith's classic interpretation. "Brother Prescott began to open up that question to me way back 19 years ago, and I hesitated, but kept looking and looking, and the facts convinced me. I accepted it, and I took my stand openly and freely."[40]

But even more than "the daily" (which was controversial primarily because of the perception that Ellen White had endorsed the earlier interpretation), Daniells weighed in on attempts to determine the proper role for White's writings in the church. The common expression "Spirit of Prophecy" suggested an authority and pertinence for ongoing church affairs. But what of situations where historical facts seemed at odds with inspiration's interpretation? Or cases where White's work received extensive editorial help? Or later revision? Confronting these issues could not be avoided for a church that wished to continue using her writings in an authoritative way.

The 1911 revision of *The Great Controversy* had raised many eyebrows at the time, and questions remained. It was inevitable then that during discussion of various prophecies the book's reliability would arise. What to do with the clear fact of mistakes of fact in the original editions? The straightforward answer was that, as Prescott summarized a comment of Willie White, Ellen White did not "claim that this book was to be an inspired authority on key facts of history." But could the matter be resolved so easily? What did the Adventist public believe about her works? "Responsibility rests upon us who know that there are serious errors in our authorized books," Prescott had written privately to Willie a few years earlier. "It seems to me that what amounts to deception, though probably not intentional, has been practiced in making some of her books, and that no serious effort has been made to disabuse the minds of the people of what was known to be their wrong view concerning her writings." But not all delegates wanted to concede the point quite so easily. Dores Robinson, former assistant to Ellen White and part of the research team for the 1911 edition, gave attendees a detailed recounting of the difficult revision process. Things needed changing, to be sure, but he also warned against accepting the conclusions of modern historians too easily. They frequently contradict one another, he reminded his hearers, and in much current history writing, ideas "are being moulded largely by the Papacy."[41]

More extended discussion of *The Great Controversy* came during the teachers' conference following the full sessions. Both religion and history teachers faced the very direct matter of having to correlate White's magnum opus with secular history. What ought they to claim for the work?

This conversation quickly passed on to the broader question of how her books were compiled and how much revision they underwent. In the 1890s Daniells was in Australia with White when she wrote *The Desire of Ages*. This had been an education for him. Chapters were written and rewritten with editorial help. But not always carefully. Daniells "wished that a different course had been taken in the compilation of the books" (meaning the acknowledgment of sources). As it was, wrong impressions (though not by White, who disclaimed any sort of verbal inspiration) were given to members about the heavenly source of her words. If members understood the process, he felt, charges of plagiarism could have been "simplified," and notions about verbal inspiration would not have become widespread. Daniells reminded his colleagues of one of White's favorite texts she applied to her gift: "We have this treasure in earthen vessels."[42]

Were people free to diverge from Ellen White on a prophetic understanding? Could they test her writings by their own study and interpretation? Speakers were hesitant to claim this freedom. But W. W. Prescott bravely admitted that his Bible study required him to do so in at least one matter. Prescott differed with an interpretation of the historical application of "Babylon" in *The Great Controversy*. When the 1911 revision was made (for which he offered research help) he got some statements corrected he felt were in error. Prescott paid a price for this, he admitted, by being suspicioned by others. Yet he, like Daniells, testified that neither the identification of occasional historical errors nor the knowledge that the book was a group effort compromised in the slightest their confidence in Ellen White's prophetic role.[43]

Daniells's only formal presentation on the subject of "The Spirit of Prophecy" came on the evening of July 16. He ventured only a few minutes into his talk before he requested the stenographer to cease recording. Did he feel he was about to tread on dangerous ground? He admitted at the start that he knew some criticized him for being "shaky" on the subject. Perhaps he wanted nothing on the record they might seize. Yet that very morning he allowed candid conversations on the same subject to be transcribed. Significantly, Daniells opened his presentation by recalling the ordeal with Kellogg in 1903. That incident, rehashed by Daniells on many occasions, was in his eyes the crucial moment of his presidency. On this occasion he impressed upon his hearers that although Kellogg wrote a nearly eighty-page missive to White complaining of Daniells's actions (not actually that long and unsent by Kellogg), Daniells refused to contact her for a half year. God was to inform the prophet of church events, not Daniells.[44]

The most thorough discussions of inspiration came after most of the attendees returned home, leaving the history and religion teachers to labor on. This smaller group had a particular stake in understanding the proper use of White's writings in the classroom. Adventist educators looked to their president for guidance; thus Daniells himself led several discussions. On the morning of July 30 and then again on August 1, Daniells engaged with the teachers in a long (and by its nature, quite rambling) question-and-answer discussion on inspiration. He opened by stating that he desired to undermine no one's faith. And although he had been occasionally perplexed by some of White's statements, he affirmed that his faith had never wavered, this despite having been on the business end of some of her harshest testimonies. One must admire Daniells's willingness to publicly recall how White indicted him for his "tendency to dominate over my brethren." Here was a leader capable of confessing weakness and public rebuke (public because his detractors made sure others knew of it).[45]

How should one test Ellen White's gift? Not by physical manifestations, asserted Daniells. He was not impressed by reports that she once held aloft a hefty Bible or that she appeared to fall into a breathless trance. "I do not know whether that was ever done or not," he said of the Bible incident, "I am not sure. I did not see it, and I do not know that I ever talked with anybody that did see it." It did not matter. Rather, he insisted, examine the fruits of her work in the church. Those tests are authenticating.[46]

What was the nature of Ellen White's inspiration? Daniells addressed this question with confidence. Having known White for decades and observed how her writings were prepared, he held informed opinions. He had, moreover, "met all the doubters," talked the issue over endlessly at ministerial institutes, and now doubted there was a "crook or a kink in it that I have not heard brought up." He also knew of "brethren who go in all over," unable to accept anything short of infallibility and verbal inspiration for Ellen White. They "make too great claims, and so we have gotten into difficulty." From his unequaled perch, knowing White and knowing the church, Daniells declared that verbal inspiration cannot be justified. "I have endeavored to ascertain the truth and then be true to the truth." "Brethren," he rhetorically asked, "are we going to evade difficulties or help out the difficulties by taking a false position? [VOICES: NO!]." Daniells perhaps unconsciously saw himself as an Adventist Luther, refusing to compromise a truth for expediency. "That is not honest and it is not Christian, and so I take my stand there."[47]

The Bible Conference transcripts suggest that a majority of attendees agreed with these sentiments. But certainly not all. M. E. Kern, for example, was baffled when he heard a man (Daniells or Prescott) express confidence in the Spirit of Prophecy only to go on to say that White's historical data cannot be trusted and other matters he does not agree with. How can one reconcile inconsistency and inspiration? Prescott, who certainly agreed with Daniells on the issue, brought up the sensitive matter that although most Adventists gave little thought to whether Scripture was verbally inspired, to deny such inspiration to White's writings invited suspicion. The interpretive bar, paradoxically, was set higher for her work. Finally, Kern pointed out the difficulty in conveying this more sophisticated, nuanced notion of inspiration to young people. "We may have confidence ourselves, but it is hard to make others believe it if we express this more liberal view." Kern identified a dilemma that remained true years later.[48]

And how should White's writings be used in the classroom? the teachers demanded to know of their president. Should they be used to settle exegetical disputes? If not, how would teachers explain this to students? These were difficult matters. A participant reminded Daniells that many students were "schooled" in a verbal inspiration model by parents or pastors. Daniells, responding with measured candor, argued that the testimonies were generally trustworthy as commentators on Scripture (although "in some very critical matters there may be some difficulties"). But the larger truth to bear in mind was that Scripture must interpret Scripture. Daniells knew that some ministers advocated the Spirit of Prophecy as interpreter of the Bible (even preached at the General Conference!), but to him this was "false doctrine."[49]

What became of the weeks of biblical and theological discussion? On a personal level, one assumes that the editors, teachers, and General Conference Committee members who attended went back to their tasks reinvigorated by the interchange, emboldened in the Adventist message, and perhaps more appreciative of complexities with prophecy and the nature of inspiration. Scholarly gatherings often have that salutary effect. But what of the transcripts? How would the discussions be communicated to the larger Adventist community? Or would they be? As noted above, Prescott's series on Christ became the basis for a book. But the very candid conversations had a different fate.

On July 16, toward the end of the full conference, the subject of what to do with the transcripts arose. Many people, especially pastors and students in the Adventist community who knew about the conference, were anxious to read the discussions. "Every minister is going to require of us at least a synopsis of what was discussed here," C. H. Branson injected. Better that they have the matter "firsthand" than get imperfect summaries from various sources. But more than a few attendees expressed concerns about their wide circulation. "I doubt the wisdom of letting immature minds get hold of this," Bible teacher Wirth asserted. N. J. Waldorf, a Bible teacher at Loma Linda College, was more accommodating, recommending that a limited number of copies be printed and distributed to each school, where professors could make use of them. Waldorf's call for limited availability, though, found no support. Publication could "sow seeds of division and discord," G. B. Thompson opined. It is worth noting that members' concerns over public disclosure had much less to do with controversial views on the Spirit of Prophecy (the major discussion of which had yet to occur) than on disagreements over prophetic interpretation, notably on the King of the North.[50]

Daniells, of course, would have the final word. He believed that the Spirit would ultimately guide them to right conclusions. "But I confess it is going to take more wisdom than we have to pilot our way through without damage to the work. As it has been stated, these [issues of prophecy] are not the fundamental things. We can all get through to heaven if we never understand all these questions." Opinions had been exchanged freely. "But now the result of such freedom which has been taken has brought us into a perplexing situation." "I sometimes think," Daniells concluded, "it would be just as well to lock this manuscript up in a vault, and have any one who wishes to do so come there for personal study and research." Daniells's musings predicted what in fact would become of the transcripts. They were shut away and virtually forgotten, recovered a half century later when the General Conference archives were established in the 1970s.[51]

In one sense, concerns over distributing the verbatim discussions were well placed. Members of a church that had long proclaimed clear understanding of Scripture—especially prophetic Scripture—were bound to be disconcerted to learn that uncertainty prevailed on certain points. Daniells and most colleagues recognized the need for frank conversations without outside scrutiny. They also understood that members wished to see a united front within leadership. Tentativeness about belief could be corrosive of faith.

But in another sense the legacy of the 1919 Bible Conference represented a failure of leadership. A. G. Daniells understood that, even more than unified prophetic interpretation, his church needed a clear grasp of Ellen White's inspiration. He was confident that a realistic view of how her writings were produced would not weaken confidence in her authority; it certainly had not for him. Daniells believed, as he told Willie White, that they should follow the prophet's counsel in "sinking the shaft deeper in the mine of truth. In doing this we must hold our minds open for clearer and larger views." But Daniells had a failure of nerve when the time came to initiate this discussion among the broad Adventist public. He knew the pushback he would receive, had seen intimations of it earlier in "the daily" debates, and had been informed several times by attendees about suspicions out in the field of Prescott's and his confidence in Ellen White. He probably remembered *Review* editor F. M. Wilcox's cautionary remark that "if we destroy faith in them [the testimonies], we are going to destroy faith in the very foundation of our work." So Daniells took the safe path. Lock the transcripts away. Leave it to a later generation to learn what he knew firsthand.[52]

A larger dilemma confronted Daniells. His opening address to the conference attendees sounded two antithetical themes. One was his confident appeal to rational study. He sought to rouse his leadership troops to follow Ellen White's call for "greater light and intellectual advancement." This embrace of openness and change eighteen years into his presidency signaled a remarkable courage (indeed, more initial bravery than he could sustain). But Daniells's other inspiration for the conference came from the Fundamentalist movement. This influential religious force was a function of fear: fear of evolution, fear of the higher criticism, fear of modernism in general. When Daniells invoked it, he could not detect its darker corners or its incompatibility with important hallmarks of Adventism. A movement based on a reflexive fear of the new could not coexist with calls to "agitate, agitate, agitate." Adventism was at a crossroads in 1919. Daniells came within an inch of being a transformational leader. But instead of insisting on the narrow path of difficult self-examination, he allowed the church to turn onto the boulevard of doctrinal complacency. This observation does not detract from his admirable hopes for change or from his shrewd analysis of what was needful for the church's well-being. It is simply to say that he faced a situation with complexities beyond his ability to solve.

CRITICISM

A. G. Daniells returned to his Takoma Park office in early August 1919 unaware, presumably, how the issues he discussed so freely at the Bible Conference would affect his career over the next few years. He had his plate full of the usual assortment of administrative tasks. But he now was less overwhelmed by correspondence, more of it being handled by General Conference colleagues. As helpful as this was, Daniells came to believe the presidential office needed further assistance. With the worldwide nature of the church, its leader "should not be under the harrow as I have been." In early 1922 he wrote Willie White of his plan after the next General Conference session ("no matter what my official position may be") to urge the furnishing of his office with a private secretary. Not simply a stenographer, this person would carry weightier duties. He would be, as Daniells foresaw him, a "Joshua" who can uphold Moses.[53]

The momentum of renewed wartime growth within American Adventism carried into the postwar years. World mission efforts moved forward. The denomination appeared to be in a good place. But rather than satisfaction, Arthur G. Daniells faced a contentious, critical spirit within the church, much of it directed at him. Faculty difficulties at Washington Missionary College in 1919 and consequent tensions with the Columbia Union Conference embroiled Daniells. The same year a book appeared by former Adventist evangelist D. M. Canright, which quickly became the most troubling challenge to Ellen White's ministry. Finally, Daniells suffered from his own critics, whose doggedness put the president on the defensive. As the 1922 General Conference Session approached, calls began to be heard for a change at the top.

The controversy at Washington Missionary College resembled similar contentions at Adventist colleges later in the twentieth century, with accusations of theological heterodoxy among faculty. In this case, three men who attended the 1919 Bible Conference had already been suspicioned for their views. E. F. Albertsworth, a professor of history (and perhaps the first teacher at an Adventist college to hold a PhD in the subject), as well as Christian Sorensen and Herbert Lacey, both professors in the Religion Department, faced accusations of promoting unsound doctrine among students. In Albertsworth's case, his advocacy of professional history methodology (which he had presented at the Conference) challenged ministerial students' naïve assumptions about historical influence and causation. Adventist higher education, still in its formative phase, was easily threatened by professors who had earned advanced degrees, brought new tools of analysis to the classroom, and who came to theological or prophetic conclusions even slightly at variance with tradition.[54]

The progressive atmosphere at Washington Missionary College disturbed some students, who complained to administrators. At a WMC board meeting in early 1919, B. G. Wilkinson, Columbia Union Conference president and a traditionalist, attempted to remove the three from the college faculty. Daniells intervened and saved their jobs—for the moment. But a year later, Wilkinson, now further unsettled by hearing his teachers' viewpoints expressed at the Bible Conference, decided changes had to be made. Albertsworth was accused by a number of his students of undermining church prophetic beliefs and of disregard of the Spirit of Prophecy. A series of emotionally charged board meetings were held, where both student accusers and defenders of Albertsworth testified. Albertsworth had greater student support, but his stubborn refusal to placate his detractors doomed him. He was relieved immediately. Sorensen and Lacey remained only one more year. Daniells, probably not wishing to worsen relations between the General Conference and Columbia Union further, stayed out of the matter. Nonetheless, he became damaged by rumors in the Adventist grapevine that he sought to protect unorthodox professors.[55]

In early 1921 Pacific Union College (PUC) was also undergoing upheaval. Efforts to oust President Irwin and replace him with Nelson from Southwestern Junior College in Keene resulted in, as Willie White phrased it, "much suspicion regarding aims, motives, and methods." "I am getting some terrible protests both from the Pacific Coast and the South Western Union," Daniells told White. A fire had recently destroyed the Keene college building, and local church officials resented the courting of their president at that difficult moment. Daniells persuaded the PUC board of the impolitic nature of their request. About this same time Daniells also met with students and faculty at Union College. There had been some contention at the school and uncertainty about the theological issues swirling about. Daniells heard later from a college official that a more positive spirit pervaded campus, including confidence in "the general men." Daniells's interventions in both campuses appear successful; but they also spoke of an atmosphere of suspicion in Adventist institutions that did not bode well for Daniells.[56]

The year 1919 would also mark the death of Adventism's greatest heretic, Dudley M. Canright. He had thirty years earlier published his infamous *Seventh-day Adventism Renounced.* Now on the heels of his death, his second broadside was issued: *Life of Mrs. E. G. White: Her Claims Refuted.* Canright was by all measures one of Adventism's most dynamic leaders in the post–Civil War decades. But his talents were compromised by emotional instability. He would be in and out of the work repeatedly. Finally, in 1887, he broke with the church for good.

Canright's posthumously published attack on the church's prophet, appearing as it did on the heels of the 1919 Bible Conference, could only serve to further inflame those people claiming that similarly unsound ideas were being promoted from within the church. Daniells could not afford to ignore the situation. The opportunity for comment came soon enough. In October 1919 he received inquiry from F. G. Duffy, a conference treasurer in Quebec, regarding Daniells's response to Canright's work. Several long letters passed between them into 1922. Daniells's lengthy response, and comments he made to others, suggested that his letters were a first draft for a future public statement on Canright (which appeared in the *Review* in 1926). But the incident likely contributed to his writing in 1935 *The Abiding Gift of Prophecy*.[57]

Daniells's original response to Duffy contained generalized indictments of Canright's reliability and purpose. Duffy pushed Daniells to provide proof for his criticisms. Daniells took nearly two years to respond, but when he did, it comprised a forty-four-page missive. His belated response, though long, was cautious. He knew that his foes were looking for any sign of wavering on the Spirit of Prophecy, and he did not know what Duffy would do with his letter. This explains but does not excuse his obfuscation or even misrepresentation on some points. Did Mrs. White, Duffy persisted in asking, promote the "shut door" view in the church's early days? Daniells could not deny that she did; but he asserted that she never claimed inspiration for the position. Does the church require belief in the prophet as a test of membership? Did it teach her infallibility? Daniells strongly denied any such test or insistence on an infallible message. Yet Duffy was familiar enough with popular Adventist belief and practice in the field that he easily refuted Daniells's protests. Daniells did admit that errors had been made in the preparation of *The Great Controversy* and *Sketches From the Life of Paul* in not attributing sources properly, an issue corrected in the former work with the 1911 edition. If Daniells appeared not quite on top of his game, it may have been because the antagonistic letters circulating within the church put him on guard. Further, the sorts of issues Duffy and others raised suggested that no response would satisfy them. They had made up their mind. Indeed, Duffy and his family soon left Adventism for another denomination. Such developments confirmed traditionalists in their resolve not to give an inch on the matter of inspiration.[58]

With intimations of trouble at the upcoming General Conference session, Daniells may have felt the need to make sure of his allies. This included Willie White. No person (perhaps other than Prescott or Spicer) would seem more staunch an ally than White. Yet, following Ellen White's death the ongoing discussions over how her writings should be handled and who would make these decisions brought unaccustomed friction between the two men. As discussed earlier, White felt that Daniells and other Washington leaders failed to support efforts to publish additional works of his mother. In the spring of 1921 Daniells tendered a direct apology for speaking "too harshly or perhaps rashly in the meetings we had regarding the manuscripts." "We have worked together in stress and storm for many years without serious misunderstandings. It is too late now for these to come in."[59]

For another longtime friend of Daniells, events had gone too far for reconciliation. Judson S. Washburn was born just five years after Daniells and grew up in the same Iowa community. His Adventist pedigree was spotless: a nephew of General Conference president George Butler and baptized by J. N. Andrews. Washburn's father served as an Iowa evangelist, one whom the youthful Daniells considered a "model preacher." The younger Washburn had been a stalwart evangelist and pastor for decades. He possessed a prodigious memory, a talent he used for memorizing much of the New Testament and long passages of Ellen White. But he had long shown unpleasant characteristics and occasionally been a thorn in Daniells's side. In the early days of Sheafe's Washington ministry, Washburn's jealousy of the African American's success caused tension.[60]

An early encounter with Ellen White had convinced Washburn of her prophetic office, and he took it upon himself to combat any attempt to reevaluate the meaning of inspiration. Washburn's crusade on behalf of a literalist/fundamentalist interpretation of Ellen White included correcting his friend and president Arthur Daniells if need be. Washburn had been concerned about certain positions of Daniells for years. During an all-night conversation at a Southern Union workers meeting in 1910, Washburn was dismayed by various Daniells positions on "the daily" and other matters. The 1919 Bible Conference, which he did not attend but whose discussions he became familiar with, was the last straw. He essentially declared war on Daniells and Prescott.[61]

Washburn had the advantage of the zealot's freedom from scruples. Even he, though, had to apologize when Daniells called him on his behavior toward Prescott. Washburn had written a letter to a friend that was widely copied, implying that Prescott's family tragedies (his wife's fatal illness and son's army death during World War I) had been judgments from God for his teachings. Washburn was the most vigorous but by no means the only critical figure; he had numerous colleagues in the ministerial and administrative ranks taking potshots at leadership. A certain level of grumbling and resentment toward authority is found in any large organization. But in the several years leading up to the 1922 General Conference, affairs turned uglier. "I am thoroughly alarmed at [the level] of criticism that has been allowed to develop among our workers," Daniells worried to White. "This has naturally led to suspicion . . . and loss of confidence. I regret to say that some of our ministers of long experience and advanced in years have been the greatest sinners along this line."[62]

Washburn's closest ally was Claude Holmes. Although a generation younger than Daniells and Washburn, he hailed from the same Iowa region as the other two. Holmes served as a linotype operator at the Review and Herald. But his passion was Ellen White's writings. He earned a reputation as perhaps the most knowledgeable authority on her words in the church. Holmes acquired an enormous collection of her books, pamphlets, and unpublished material. "These are worth more than gold to me." He solicited material from veteran Adventist workers to whom he suspected White had written. Holmes took this devotion to a fault. Through connivance he obtained access (granted by Daniells) to much unpublished White material in the Washington vault, which he proceeded to copy. These included some of White's personal testimonies to Prescott and Daniells. The matter was serious enough to merit attention by the General Conference Committee. Holmes's refusal to return the material would lead to his dismissal from the Review. Although Holmes helped stir up students against the Washington Missionary College faculty in 1919 and participated in Washburn's campaign against Daniells, one senses in his actions more a naïve and parochial earnestness than the mean-spiritedness of Washburn. In any event, both Elder and Mrs. Daniells carried on what seemed amicable correspondence with Holmes even after 1922.[63]

Holmes and Washburn both shared widely their contention that unsound doctrine was unchecked within the church. Holmes's was in the form of an open letter in the spring of 1920 to Washburn. He challenged a belief expressed at the Bible Conference (few opinions voiced there remained confidential) that Ellen White was not an authority on history. That she utilized historical authors does not detract from her inspiration, since the sources she used were vetted by the Spirit. To question this process or suggest that errors might have been made would undermine confidence in the church's prophet. If she is not an authority on history, then on what topic can she be trusted? Holmes held to an infallible prophet and message. Some accused him of making Ellen White into a pope. But no, "she is far above and superior to any Pope." White, he proclaimed, "is inspired as much as any Bible prophet, and her revelations are not limited to moral questions."[64]

Washburn replied to Holmes with an extended epistle circulated probably as widely. He targeted both Prescott and the notorious "Washington Missionary College Three" with a rhetorical style that started with pastoral concern but quickly modulated into personal invective. Washburn reported on a presentation he heard Prescott give at a recent worker's meeting. His characterization of Prescott's teaching did not rise above crude parody (his devotion to a simple proof-text hermeneutic prevented anything more). He accused Prescott—among many other things—of teaching a "combination of Christian Science and the intangible mysterious Catholic doctrine of the Trinity." Washburn then described his encounter with the leading Adventist theologian, where Prescott first asked him why he did not confront him directly with his criticisms rather than talk to others. The unpleasant meeting ended when Prescott turned on his heels and walked away, leaving Washburn as an aggrieved brother who wished to reconcile. Washburn's accounting of the Washington faculty suggested that school enrollment had fallen because of their presence, but that Daniells had given them "clear character" and were thus kept on (at least temporarily). Washburn's broadside ended by suggesting that these heresies within the church marked the advent of the "Startling Omega," an apostasy marking the last days. Based on a cryptic statement by Ellen White about an apostasy to follow that of Kellogg's, Washburn was quite sure that earlier attacks on traditional notions of "the daily" had ushered in this final apostasy centered at "our headquarters and in our principal Bible school."[65]

These sorts of criticisms flew about the church for many months in the early 1920s, nurturing distrust and hostility. Daniells, upset by Washburn's behavior to the point that he long failed to respond to the latter's apology for the Prescott attack in 1920, finally wrote him a measured missive the day after Christmas 1921. Perhaps in the spirit of the season, Daniells sought a belated reconciliation. "As I review my relationship with brethren," Daniells wrote with both sincerity and understatement, "I am conscious of a measure of estrangement between you and me." "I confess that I do not possess that confidence in, and brother love for, you that I once did, and that I desire to have again. I understand that this is your attitude toward me." Daniells reviewed their long friendship. What was the root of Washburn's disaffection? Daniells asked. He recalled their dispute of "the daily" years earlier but thought that matter could not rise to such alienation. He concluded that the heart of the estrangement must be his own well-known criticism of Washburn's behavior. He apologized for not taking up the matter with him personally. Endemic criticism of this sort had become a plague on the church. "It is a terrible evil in our midst. And the sorrow and shame of it is that ministers and conference officials of all classes take the lead. They set the example in this wicked thing."[66]

But Daniells's mea culpa was not intended to excuse Washburn's behavior. Daniells told the latter that his "Startling Omega" tract "seriously wronged a number of your brethren," and was "a bitter personal attack." Daniells denied Washburn's assertion that "infidel teachers" had been forced upon the college. Likewise, that President Wilkinson was forced to resign by Daniells and the board. "How could you dare to publish such a charge? You were never in any of the councils in which we dealt with Brother Wilkinson's retirement." Daniells had begun his letter in a spirit of reconciliation, but once his blood was up he could not restrain his antagonism. Although he closed his letter with a renewed call for reconciliation, he could hardly have believed the hatchet was buried.[67]

Indeed it was not. In early May 1922, just weeks before the San Francisco General Conference convened, Washburn issued an "Open Letter to Elder A. G. Daniells and an Appeal to the General Conference." Circulated among as many delegates to the upcoming session as he could reach, the printed thirty-page letter included Daniells's private letter to him. Apart from the impropriety of publicizing a private letter, Washburn did not reproduce the letter accurately. Notably, he omitted Daniells's offer to "make any known wrong right with my brethren." Instead, he fabricated a line that does not appear: "I consider it," Daniells supposedly said, "the worst tirade ever put in print by a Seventh-day Adventist minister against his fellow workers."[68]

Washburn had much more to say, however. If Daniells was concerned about criticism within the church, Washburn wrote, he should consider his own contribution to the problem. It was his endorsement of Prescott's new theory of "the daily" that precipitated much of the controversy. Washburn could not forgive this repudiation of the "doctrine held by the pioneers." Neither could he forgive Daniells's implying fallibility to Ellen White. In this, Washburn's powerful memory called up the fateful all-night train conversation he had with Daniells in 1910. Daniells's candor about church matters that night, encouraged no doubt by the tensions between himself and White during the year, proved fatal over a decade later. "You can never deny these terrible criticisms that strike at the very foundation of our faith," Washburn accused. "You have never been the same to me since." Washburn's discontent was partially theological. He had honest disagreements with Daniells over points of interpretation. But he also had personal resentments: that Daniells did not take his advice; that he had been taken to task by Daniells for his behavior; and that his own ministerial career seemed languishing (since "the daily" controversy he had received few calls to new posts). Washburn told *Review* editor F. M. Wilcox (who showed little sympathy for Washburn's views) that "I expect nothing but a cruel relentless, slanderous war to the death."[69]

More than theological disagreement or personal pique drove Washburn's animus. In a larger sense he spoke for the Populist/Fundamentalist fears and resentments that marked the age. Populist resentments against elites were evident in Washburn's dismissal of "Professor Prescott's" Sabbath School lessons as "shadowy, mystical, and complex." He welcomed the "simplicity" and "clearness" of the new quarter's lessons. Populism showed, too, in snide comments about the General Conference leadership's possessing "new light," which they feel is "their privilege to teach." And it informed his accusation that Daniells sought to turn Washington Missionary College into a "high class university." Washburn's fundamentalism, much in common with that of the larger American Fundamentalist community, rejected any nuance or complexity of belief. The literary product of inspiration must be understood literally. And the peculiar Adventist brand of Fundamentalism placed Ellen White's authority on a par with the Bible's. "The Testimonies," Washburn affirmed, "are the inspired word of the Lord, as truly as the Bible and on *the same level*." Thus it was no surprise that he objected to Daniells's insistence that "the Testimonies do not stand on the same level with the Bible."

As Washburn summed up, in the ultimate fundamentalist damning, "That is simply Higher Criticism."[70]

Washburn's raising the specter of an "Omega apostasy" was contrived to unsettle church leaders just as the quadrennial sessions were to begin. Daniells must have understood that he faced a serious challenge (including another open letter from Holmes, reviewing a laundry list of leadership sins). But he had weathered worse before, notably in 1903 when the more formidable array of Kellogg forces sought to unseat him. One senses that he was truly surprised when events transpired as they did. Perhaps twenty-one years in the presidency gave him a false sense of invulnerability.[71]

This campaign against Daniells and Prescott (Daniells the more important target, since he headed the General Conference and was understood to be Prescott's protector) included mailing the above letters to most Adventist leaders. They found many kindred spirits. "I am glad that you are standing for the third angel's message as given to the pioneers," responded F. H. Robbins, president of the Columbia Union Conference. A Canadian member commended Holmes for his work in exposing "the great adversary for the overthrow of God's work." Some leaders sought Washburn's and Holmes's help with their own agenda. Dr. H. S. Brown, Medical Secretary of the Columbia Union Conference, asked Holmes if he had a testimony that decried centralization of church authority. He wanted to get the union office out of the shadow of the General Conference and into Pennsylvania, a task made easier if Ellen White offered endorsement.[72]

Holmes and Washburn found many sympathetic ears, to be sure. But from the surviving letters, especially those written to Holmes after the General Conference session, one senses an element of intimidation at work. Various church officials appeared a bit too anxious to please, too complimentary of the campaign, too grateful for the material Holmes sent. They had seen what happened to Daniells. For the moment, power appeared to lie with the insurgents. Not everyone was intimidated. Frederick Griggs, one of Adventism's pioneer educators, called Holmes to task for his dismissive attitude toward Prescott. "Really, Claude, I wish that in your letters and work you did not put in the sarcastic element which you do. . . . To me that seems wrong." Griggs's courage was unusual.[73]

RECESSIONAL

The 1922 General Conference Session held in San Francisco (for the second straight time) offered the church an opportunity to showcase its four-year progress. It was the largest gathering to that point in church history. With the war now long over, opportunity again arose for a true world constituency to be present. The size of the convocation may explain the West Coast choice.

An occasion of this magnitude demanded Daniells's involvement in planning. In December he and C. H. Jones (head of Pacific Press) met to check out the San Francisco venue. The city's large Exposition Memorial Auditorium, which boasted a new voice amplifier system, would host the event (Washington had no similar venue, and General Conference sessions had outgrown any church structure in the denomination). A myriad details would have to be addressed in preparation for the most complex event the denomination had hosted. A chorister must be chosen. And an organist? A team had to be assembled to record speeches and actions for the *General Conference Daily Bulletin*. Accommodations for delegates must be arranged, a task given to each union conference. The sharp recession of the early 1920s affected the church. Budgets were tight, and foreign fields had to economize on their delegations. The Far Eastern Division named as delegates only people who were scheduled to have furloughs during the sessions (none, of course, were Asian nationals).[74]

General Conference sessions had long since assumed a repetitive pattern. Reports from world divisions and entities such as publishing, education, and religious liberty formed the backbone of the twelve-day schedule. The financial report was always received with interest. There were also regular devotionals and sermons. Election of officers and consideration of important new initiatives were accomplished during what was, after all, the church's official business meeting. For veteran church leaders, there was a comforting familiarity to the event. Enjoyable, too, was the opportunity to socialize with fellow believers not seen perhaps for years. Planners for 1922 recognized that the many reports needed to be shortened and issued directives to division presidents to that effect.[75]

New for 1922 were daily Mission Round Tables. These were intended to be very practical workshops for foreign mission workers. Topics included "Work among Catholics," "Carrying the Message to Heathen

Peoples," "Mission Finances," and perhaps most telling, "Friction Among Missionaries–How can it be Avoided?" The latter subject was assigned to veteran missionary W. B. White. "I think you will understand what we mean by this subject," wrote General Conference session organizer J. L. Shaw to White. "Every administrator in the mission field has had more or less to do with friction among missionaries. . . . Certainly it often proves detrimental to our work and workers in large and trying fields." The roundtables experiment indicated that leadership wished to move beyond the round of committees and plenary sessions to include small events with practical implications.[76]

The session convened on May 11, but Daniells was "early on the ground, counseling and advising as needed." He delivered the opening address and the sermon on the first Sabbath. His president's address was shorter than earlier ones but poised a central question: "When and how is this work going to be finished?" The question might seem the very definition of imponderable, but Adventists could not avoid it. Daniells insisted that nothing this body might do would be more worthwhile than to present church members with a clear plan for finishing the work. Where would such a plan arise? Ever the administrator, Daniells answered predictably: from a committee. A group of men "of large experience and ripe judgment" work up a statement that could be considered by the whole body (a proposal that seems to have died with his departure from the office).[77]

In most regards, the 1922 General Conference was routine. But in one respect it proved notable: the longest-serving president in the history of the denomination was not returned to office. This in itself would not be noteworthy except for the acrimony surrounding the change. Strong feelings about leadership and even politicking for change have marked other General Conference sessions. But the 1922 session commands attention for its marking a signal moment in Adventist history.

Daniells traveled to San Francisco well aware that opposition to his reelection was not confined to Washburn and Holmes. No leader, however judicious and well meaning, can exercise decisive power for as long as he did without incurring opposition. And though Daniells seems to have mellowed from earlier tendencies toward imperiousness, he remained a strong figure. It would have been remarkable if none of his colleagues suffered from the human frailty of wishing to see the strong brought low.

In any event, certain of Daniells's staunch supporters took a proactive stance, advocating for his reelection well before the session convened. The Washburn-Holmes campaign had stirred them to action. D. A. Parsons, president of the West Pennsylvania Conference, and an influential figure within the Columbia Union Conference (which had known antagonisms with Daniells), found himself the object of pressure more than a year before San Francisco. Individuals (one claiming to be part of the inner circle of "the big chief") prevailed upon Parsons not just to change his own opinion but to "quietly remold the sentiment of the Columbia Union committee." He was confidentially told at Fall Council in 1921 of the plan to reinstate Daniells for a final term and then groom J. E. Fulton to succeed him. If Parsons got on board, one said, he would "leave this meeting the happiest man in America." Even Mary Daniells joined the lobby, assuring Parsons that her husband would step down if only a qualified candidate were known. But they believed there were none at the moment. (In Mary's view, Arthur was a modern Moses, called to lead the remnant to the Promised Land.)[78]

But neither Parsons nor the other Columbia Union officials cooperated. And the tone of the entreaties darkened. If Daniells was a Moses, then those who opposed him were "openly branded as 'Korah, Dathan, and Abiram.' " More ominously, opponents were warned that a list of recalcitrants was being compiled that meant, when Daniells was elected, heads would roll. The overheated rhetoric both reflected and provoked deep division on the nominating committee. Early votes during the Sunday meeting were inconclusive. Daniells partisans, more numerous on the General Conference Committee than on the nominating committee, arranged to have the latter informally meet with the full General Conference Committee. The plan foundered when the nominating committee decided it needed no advice.[79]

For all of the verbatim reporting of formal presentations by the church's session *Bulletins*, if Adventist readers wanted a sense of church politics they would have to turn to the daily newspapers. San Francisco newspapers enjoyed the spectacle of Adventist leaders in disarray. "Veteran chief of Adventists Attacks Foes," screamed one headline; "Charges of 'Dirty Politics' Hurled by Religious Workers at Meeting," ran another subhead. The pent-up frustrations Daniells had long suffered over what he considered unfair criticisms poured out. "His voice trembled," the newspaper reported, "and the tears rolled down his cheeks as he defended his leadership." Having devoted 100 percent of his energies to the Adventist cause, Daniells could not meekly accept what he considered a campaign of vilification.[80]

Nor could his supporters. A. O. Tait, editor of the *Signs of the Times*, introduced a resolution decrying the overt politicking and spirit of criticism toward Daniells infecting the session. Most delegates agreed that matters were getting out of hand and supported the resolution. Some "pioneer" church men considered the political activism at the General Conference the worst in their memory. But Dr. George Harding (brother of sitting U.S. president Warren Harding), part of the Adventist medical establishment that still begrudged Daniells's lack of full support for health institution expansion, felt it unjust to condemn an individual who felt he was advocating the best for the church. The resolution as adopted acknowledged "unmistakable evidence that the baleful influences of political methods on the part of a comparatively small number have been at work in our midst." While each individual must have the right "to express his conviction regarding appointments of posts of responsibility," this must be done with a Christian spirit. Thus, the committee resolved to "pronounce a decided rebuke upon and repudiation of all unchristian propaganda, insinuation, vilification, and all false charges whatsoever . . . and further Resolved, That we do under God pledge ourselves to full repentance of all these unholy things."[81]

Confession of spirit and frequent calls to prayer seemed to calm the troubled waters. Before giving a dedicatory prayer early in the conference, Spicer asked that "every shadow of alienation or bitterness or grudge will be laid aside." He assured delegates that the General Conference family "are in unity of heart." Then he made a dramatic gesture. "I should like to give my hand to Brother Daniells, before you all, in token of this unity and service, with no shadow between."[82]

But a president still had to be chosen. W. A. Spicer, the front-runner in early votes, refused to accept the position as long as it implied a rebuke to his colleague. Daniells had to act. And he did. He withdrew his name from consideration. The way was open for Spicer to receive unanimous endorsement from the nominating committee. Spicer, still reluctant, surrendered to the urgings of Daniells. An executive session of the General

Conference quickly acted to endorse its choice. The following day, with gavel still in hand, Daniells gave all people present in the hall a chance to affirm Spicer. For the first time since spring of 1901 the Seventh-day Adventist Church had a president other than Arthur Grosvenor Daniells.[83]

Daniells also used the plenary session to provide his version of what had transpired. His remarks were part self-justification and part effort to reassure delegates that all was well with the General Conference ship. He acknowledged that people had been disturbed by newspaper reports. But people must recall that reporters are "fallible," they "get things a bit twisted, especially the city editors, who write the headlines to catch the eye." Daniells asserted that there was no rivalry between himself and Spicer, no contention for the presidency. Whatever contention existed came from his admittedly strong protests against "political connivance and 'wirepulling' " that had been going on for months (Daniells presumably was not referring to the actions of his own followers). Hundreds of people at the sessions, Daniells claimed, had commented on the situation. "I want our people to know that there is no such thing in our midst as a fight for office. Take it home, brethren. Tell all the people there was no fight at the General Conference to hold office."[84]

Daniells had more to say. "There was determined effort to throw me out," he admitted, but "there was solemn protest against the methods adopted to do it." He had been considering stepping down for at least ten years, he asserted, asking associates such as Spicer to consider candidates. "But at each conference, I have been elected by the people unanimously." Two years before the 1922 General Conference Session he thought even more seriously about laying down the reins. But when the campaign against him began, his supporters thought he should not go out under such implied rebuke. Daniells, not lacking in pride, agreed that he deserved the right to "go out with some kind of respect and honor." But during the contention of the previous day, against the protests of his supporters, Daniells concluded that he must take his name out of consideration. Nothing could please him more than presenting Spicer as the new president. "I feel like a bird let out of a cage."[85]

What can one conclude about the 1922 General Conference presidency election? First, the nominating committee effected a skillful compromise. Daniells's removal from office is well known in Adventist history;

often forgotten is that he remained part of the executive team as secretary of the General Conference. He and Spicer simply swapped jobs. Those who wanted Daniells gone altogether did not get their wish. Conversely, ardent supporters of Daniells lost him from the presidency but preserved him as the number-two man. Second, after twenty-one years the time had come for a new president. Daniells's insisting that he had wanted to leave the job years earlier has some truth, but he seemed quite readily persuaded to stay on. Although an immensely skillful, even visionary leader, Daniells was not the indispensable man of Adventism. The subsequent success of the detailed, self-effacing Spicer (president from 1922 to 1930) proved that. Finally, as Daniells and his followers insisted, the end of his tenure should not have happened as it did. Although his new position as secretary helped him save face (and preserve his considerable talents for the church), his presidential exit lacked dignity. Of course, had he announced a year prior to the 1922 conference that he would not be a candidate, the resulting contention would have been avoided.

Looking back from nearly a century, one might judge this but another tempest in a teapot. Leadership struggles, even nasty ones, are endemic to organizations. The church quickly put this behind it and moved on. But the spirit of criticism that plagued the denomination in these years cannot be so easily dismissed. "I will tell you one thing," Daniells told his colleagues at the 1919 Bible Conference, "a great victory will be gained if we get a liberal spirit so that we will treat brethren who differ with us on the interpretation of the Testimonies in the same Christian way we treat them when they differ on the interpretation of the Bible." However, a liberal spirit did not then permeate the church. Daniells's question, What would it take for the church to finish the work? found a partial answer here. The suspicions, the quick resort to criticism, the fundamentalist literalism: these plagues on the church would not subside easily. Daniells had identified but could not efface them. Instead, in his manner, he quietly returned to Takoma Park from the West Coast and took up his new tasks.[86]

---

[1] *RH*, January 2, 1919, 1.

[2] Ibid., 2, 3.

[3] L. R. Conradi to GC Committee, September 24, 1919; Schwarz and Greenleaf, *Light Bearers*, 372; Bull and Lockhart, *Seeking a Sanctuary*, 194.

[4] GCCMin, November 27–30, 1919; *Annual Statistical Report, 1922*, 8.

[5] GCCMin, November 30, 1919.

[6] I. H. Evans to AGD, March 20, 1919.

[7] GCCMin, February 19, 1919; *Annual Statistical Report, 1919*, 2–4.

[8] *Annual Statistical Report, 1919*, 17, 23.

[9] GCCMin, May 4, 1919; January 9, 1920.

[10] GCCMin, September 19, 1919.

[11] GCCMin, April 30, 1919; May 4, 1919.

[12] GCCMin, October 14, 1919; April 30, 1919; May 5, 1919.

[13] *RH*, May 29, 1919, 2.

[14] *RH*, November 13, 1919, 3, 4, 11.

[15] Ibid., 11, 12.

[16] *RH*, July 31, 1919, 3–7; December 25, 1919, 2, 6, 7.

[17] *RH*, August 19, 1915, 3.

[18] Clara Resch to AGD, September 19, 1915, ASTR.

[19] Roger W. Coon reviews some of these aspiring Adventist prophets in his *Heralds of New Light: Another Prophet to the Remnant?* (Nampa, ID: Pacific Press®, 1987).

[20] The most complete overview of the Rowen episode is given by Larry White, "Margaret W. Rowen, Prophetess of Reform and Doom," *Adventist Heritage* 6, no. 1 (Summer 1979): 28–40. Schwarz and Greenleaf, *Light Bearers*, 450–452, adds details.

[21] "Verbatim Report of an Interview Regarding the Experiences of Mrs. Margaret W. Rowen," February 15, 1920, ASTR; WCW to "Dear Brother," March 15, 1920; Margaret Rowen to AGD, November 26, 1917, EGWE.

[22] Documents relating to the Rowen case are held both by the General Conference archives and by the White Estate. AGD to Mrs. Rowen, December 31, 1917; J. F. Blunt, "Mrs. Rowen's Experiences," typescript manuscript, ASTR; WCW to D. A. Parsons, February 25, 1920, EGWE.

[23] "Interview Between W. C. White and Mrs. Margaret W. Rowen," December 30, 1919, ASTR.

[24] Ibid.; "Interview Between Mrs. Margaret W. Rowen and Elder J. W. Christian," January 18, 1920; "Statement by W. C. White in the office of C. H. Jones," December 28, 1919, ASTR; Schwarz and Greenleaf, *Light Bearers*, 451. An example of an affidavit is Helen Graham to WCW, January 26, 1920, ASTR. Part of Graham's statement concerned earlier prophetic pretenders: "An elderly gentleman called at the office one morning, claiming that he was to be Sister White's successor, and desiring to obtain her views on the matter. Her Secretary went to Sister White and stated his claim, returning to him with the reply that Sister White had told her to say to him that she had been given no light whatever regarding the matter of a successor in her special work."

[25] L. White, "Margaret W. Rowen," 37–40.

[26] AGD to WCW, June 21, 1910.

[27] AGD to WCW, August 3, 1911.

[28] AGD to WCW, March 20, 1917; GCCMin, April 29, 1919. For an overview of the 1919

Bible Conference see Michael W. Campbell, "The 1919 Bible Conference and Its Significance for Seventh-day Adventist History and Theology" (PhD dissertation, Andrews University, 2008).

[29] GCCMin, May 4, 23, 1919; *RH*, August 21, 1919, 1; WCW to AGD, June 6, 1919.

[30] AGD, "Opening Session of Bible Conference," in "Report of [1919] Bible Conference," transcript, July 1, pp. 9, 11, ASTR.

[31] AGD to WCW, February 14, 1919.

[32] "Report of Bible Conference," July 1, pp. 3–5.

[33] Ibid. The passage of Ellen White is from *Testimonies*, 5:706–709.

[34] AGD, "Opening Session," July 1, pp. 13, 14; AGD, "Question-Box Service on the Spirit of Prophecy," August 30, 1906, EGWE.

[35] Campbell, "1919 Bible Conference," 82, 83.

[36] "Report of Bible Conference," July 6 and 16.

[37] Campbell, "1919 Bible Conference," 86.

[38] "Report of Bible Conference," August 1, p. 1256; July 30, pp. 1209, 1211.

[39] "Report of Bible Conference," July 9, pp. 431–494.

[40] "Report of Bible Conference," July 13, pp. 670, 671; July 8, pp. 411, 412.

[41] "Report of Bible Conference," July 10, pp. 561–563; W. W. Prescott to WCW, April 6, 1915, letter reproduced in Gilbert Valentine, "The Church 'drifting toward a crisis': Prescott's 1915 Letter to William White," *Catalyst* 2 (November 2007): appendix A.

[42] "Report of Bible Conference," August 1, pp. 1241–1243.

[43] Ibid., pp. 1250, 1251.

[44] "Report of Bible Conference," July 16, p. 945.

[45] "Report of Bible Conference," July 30, pp. 1187, 1188; an early example of Daniells's willingness to publically admit to White's rebuke came at the Colorado camp meeting in 1906, "Report on Question-Box Service on the Subject of the Spirit of Prophecy," August 28, 1906, EGWE.

[46] "Report of Bible Conference," July 30, pp. 1190–1193.

[47] Ibid., p. 1189; August 1, pp. 1231–1234, 1241.

[48] "Report of Bible Conference," July 30, p. 1216; August 1, pp. 1228, 1233–1235.

[49] "Report of Bible Conference," July 30, pp. 1194–1197.

[50] "Report of Bible Conference," July 16, pp. 895–899.

[51] Ibid., pp. 899–901.

[52] "Report of Bible Conference," August 1, p. 1230; AGD to WCW, July 20, 1919.

[53] AGD to WCW, February 3, 1922.

[54] Douglas Morgan provides an overview of the contention at Washington Missionary College in his paper, "From Origins to Accreditation: Contending Values and the Shaping of Washington Missionary College, 1904–1942," 22, 23; copy provided by the author.

[55] Ibid., 24; Washington Missionary College board minutes, February 10–15, 1920, ASTR.

[56] WCW to AGD, March 8, 1921; AGD to WCW, March 4, 1921, EGWE.

[57] AGD to F. G. Duffy [late 1921].

[58] Ibid.; F. G. Duffy to AGD, January 11, 1922.

[59] AGD to WCW, March 4, 1921; Paul McGraw, "Without a Living Prophet,"

Ministry (December 2000), accessed July 17, 2013, https://www.ministrymagazine.org/archive/2000/12/without-a-living-prophet.

[60] Bert Haloviak, "In the Shadow of the Daily," accessed July 18, 2013, http://sdanet.org/atissue/books/1919bc/hal-3.htm#washburn; AGD to J. S. Washburn, December 26, 1921, ASTR.

[61] Haloviak, "In the Shadow of the Daily"; Claude Holmes to Fred Connerth, February 12, 1925; Frederick Griggs to Claude Holmes, January 18, 1922, CAR.

[62] J. S. Washburn to AGD, February 10, 1921; AGD to WCW, March 4, 1921.

[63] Haloviak, "In the Shadow of the Daily"; GCCMin, February 16 and 18, 1917.

[64] Claude Holmes, "Have we an Infallible 'Spirit of Prophecy'?"

[65] J. S. Washburn to Claude Holmes, "The Startling Omega and Its True Genealogy," April 18, 1920; the report of the White interview stated that she spoke rather than wrote her criticism of Daniells, suggesting that her comments were "very, very confidential." Paul McGraw and Gilbert Valentine, "Legacy," in *Ellen Harmon White: American Prophet*, eds. Terrie Dopp Aamodt, Gary Land, Ronald L. Numbers (New York: Oxford University Press, 2014), 312.

[66] AGD to J. S. Washburn, December 26, 1921, ASTR.

[67] Ibid.

[68] J. S. Washburn, "An Open letter to Elder A. G. Daniells and an Appeal to the General Conference," [1921].

[69] Ibid., 11–18; J. S. Washburn to F. M. Wilcox, July 3, 1921, ASTR.

[70] Ibid., 10–24.

[71] Claude Holmes to AGD, May 1, 1922.

[72] F. H. Robbins, March 19, 1922; Alex Ritchie to Claude Holmes, February 25, 1923; H. S. Brown to Claude Holmes [n. d.], CAR.

[73] Frederick Griggs to Claude Holmes, January 18, 1922, CAR.

[74] C. H. Jones to J. L.Shaw, December 1, 1921; C. C. Crisler to J. L. Shaw, November 30, 1921, ASTR.

[75] J. L. Shaw to Division Presidents, January 12, 1922.

[76] J. L. Shaw to W. B. White, March 9, 1922.

[77] *RH*, May 22, 1922, 3, 4.

[78] "Dan" [D. A. Parsons] to B. E. Beddoe, September 5, 1924, EGWE.

[79] Ibid.

[80] *San Francisco Chronicle*, May 21, 1922, 5.

[81] *San Francisco Chronicle*, May 23, 1922, 9; *San Francisco Examiner*, May 23, 1922, 4; *GCB*, May 24, 1922, 240.

[82] *RH*, June 8, 1922, 26.

[83] *GCB*, May 24, 1922, 228.

[84] Ibid.

[85] Ibid.

[86] "Report of Bible Conference," August 1, p. 1223.

Chapter XII

A SECOND ACT

What would an emotionally wounded A. G. Daniells do following his ouster? There was never any doubt in his mind. He got up the next morning and went to work, now as General Conference secretary under W. A. Spicer. Personal disappointments must be put away. It was always about the mission.

An American author once famously asserted that "there are no second acts in American lives." But of course there are. Arthur Daniells is an irrefutable example. He lived thirteen years after the 1922 General Conference Session and served in an official church capacity for nine of those. He did not simply mark time. Some of his greatest contributions came after he left the presidency: championing the new Ministerial Association, promoting righteousness by faith, chairing the boards of the Ellen White Estate and Loma Linda medical college, and authoring two notable books. These years seemed to be a time of personal spiritual fulfillment as well. Perhaps with the full burden of the denomination removed, he could now pay more attention to his own soul.

To say that Daniells climbed back on the horse that had just thrown him is not to say that he suffered no bruises. For a half year after the spring General Conference session he avoided returning to Washington headquarters by pleading the considerable work to be accomplished on the West Coast. The Pacific Union Conference needed help, he wrote almost apologetically to C. K. Meyers, his associate secretary handling the office work. He then made the rounds of the North Pacific Union camp meetings (the largest in the country), with heavy speaking duties at each. Following these, it was back to Southern California for more camp meetings and consultations.[1]

All this was legitimate. Indeed, E. R. Palmer, in his commentary to *Review* readers about the change of leadership, noted that the new General

Conference secretary was not expected to take up a desk job at headquarters. The title was almost honorific, since an associate secretary handled most of the work Spicer once did. Office manager T. E. Bowen was almost apologetic in asking Daniells to write the opening for the upcoming Harvest Ingathering appeal. Rather, Daniells would use "his broad experience and talents as a world field secretary of the Mission Board," traveling extensively and advising the Executive Committee on church matters. The wide scope made it the perfect portfolio for Daniells. At age sixty-three, he could put behind him the endless committees and personnel worries of the past decades. And he would be less subject to the politics of Takoma Park.[2]

But he could not easily put aside the concerns for a world organization that had so long occupied him. He informed Spicer of the distress of an overtaxed mission doctor in China. What could be done? More systemically, he offered reflections on how the church might encourage better use of missionary furlough time in America. Too many of them, Daniells fretted, gain little benefit from their time at home, become discouraged, then desire not to return to their posts. He suggested to Spicer a list of improvements. First, that furloughed missionaries receive full pay. Church leaders ought also to ensure that overseas workers have suitable living situations while here; that they not be burdened with speaking engagements or other tasks; in short, that they be able to rest. They should be granted "every courtesy we can extend to them, with free treatments when they are sick, and full pay" with the understanding that they must rest. Daniells's regard came with a stiff proviso: mission appointments were to be for life. "The loss of workers is something we cannot afford if we can prevent it. There should be no inducements held out to these workers other than that they return to their mission field to spend their life working for the people whose language they have acquired." Daniells expected the same dedication in others as he himself had given.[3]

DEFINING A NEW ROLE

As Daniells began the new phase of his career, a small cloud hovered over him. In September 1921 he had been involved in an automobile accident in Takoma Park. No details survive, except that the other driver, rather than Daniells, seems to have been injured. A year later Daniells faced a threatened lawsuit. Having been spared court action through most of his life, he could not assess the degree of seriousness. Daniells sought the help of his close friend Palmer (head of the Review and Herald press), a man more experienced in the legal world. Daniells was particularly concerned about stories circulating of his being issued a summons by the local sheriff. "There are some who would like to see me in trouble over this or any other misfortune," Daniells reflected sadly. The fallout from the accident preyed on his and Mary's minds; he confessed a "great dread of court proceedings." Palmer conferred with an attorney on his behalf and reassured Daniells that the summons was less serious than he had feared. Resolution of the matter is now lost, but a financial settlement may well have occurred. The accident, on top of the General Conference session disappointment, made for a stressful year. "I have had such sorrow of heart the last year that the whole aspect of things in this world has changed my confidence in the sincerity, justice and safety of mankind," he wrote Palmer.[4]

The inescapable, ineffable sadnesses of life had caught up with Arthur Daniells. But in the committed and positive manner characteristic of him, he found consolation in service. "I am praying the Lord to give me an experience that will help me to help the sorrowing, disappointed people I meet to bear their burdens. . . . I desire to give the remainder of my poor life to others." For Daniells, such service meant spiritual nurture. His postpresidential career witnessed efforts on several fronts to advance members' spiritual well-being.[5]

The first concerned spiritual revival in the church. Throughout his presidency Daniells had looked for signs of revival; indeed, he had sought to promote revival in countless evangelistic efforts. He continued the good work in the 1920s. Now free of nagging administrative duties, he could give attention to grassroots efforts. In late 1923 he returned to New York City to hold revivals in the city's churches. He detected wonderful results. Members were "confessing their sins in great earnestness." His presentations avoided sensationalism; in fact, they were only twenty minutes long, followed by a time of protracted testimonies by members. "There is no question but what a genuine work of conviction and conversion has been wrought in the hearts of hundreds."[6]

For the churches to thrive, however, Daniells had long believed that the quality of the ministry must improve. Daniells was not the first

General Conference president to observe deficiencies. O. A. Olsen in the 1890s felt likewise and had promoted the earliest ministerial institutes. But Daniells took the problem in a very personal way. His early experience with Australian workers in the 1890s had been generally positive. But in America his observations were different. "How deeply I often regret that I have been compelled to change my mind regarding this. It has hurt me terribly. It has made great scars on my soul." When Daniells was finally prompted to undertake evangelism in New York City in 1910, he quickly became discouraged by "the lack of earnest, consecrated, able ministers." The problem in part lay in a lack of education. Some Adventist clergy attended college, many did not, and all needed ongoing professional training. At the 1922 General Conference Session a dream of Daniells was realized with the creation of the Ministerial Commission (later Ministerial Association). As with the 1901 General Conference reorganization, the church drew again upon a precedent from Australia, where a ministerial association had formed in 1920. The enthusiastic and newly unencumbered Daniells took on leadership in addition to his other tasks. Although it began with a modest budget, its goals were ambitious. "The obvious need of the hour is an effective ministry to challenge the sinful conscience of a judgment-bound world," the enabling motion read. To upgrade the ministry, facts must first be gathered. What was the condition of the minister's and Bible worker's work? What problems were common? How might useful ideas and techniques be shared among the fraternity? How might young men better be encouraged and prepared for the ministry? In sum, the denomination sought to professionalize its ministry.[7]

Daniells's efforts in this direction came through a series of ministerial institutes he held from 1923 through 1925. He began in the West, then journeyed back to Takoma Park for a revival series before leading workers' meetings in the South and the Southwest. At Los Angeles's Carr Street Church in 1922, ten to twenty pastors gathered, and under Daniells's direction studied Scripture and "Testimonies" for hours. Participants experienced new conviction about their living in the final days. Not simply theological workshops, Daniells made them devotional and revivalistic. "We had one of the greatest meetings in Fresno that I have ever held with our ministers and workers," he effused after another occasion. At Fresno he held five or six meetings a day. The institutes inspired a number of young Adventist clergy. Some would go on to notable careers, such as Taylor Bunch and Carlyle B. Haynes. With leaders unwilling to sponsor a regular publication, he had to settle for mimeographed bulletins that sought to provide practical advice, not only for pastors but also for evangelists and singing evangelists, Bible teachers, and chaplains. The association's reach was worldwide, seeking to aid Adventist gospel workers everywhere. Daniells received correspondence seeking help on thorny questions faced in the field. From India, for example, came a request that a future bulletin would address the issue of how workers might judge when a convert was suitably prepared for baptism. In 1926, Daniells gave up the few duties of the secretaryship of the General Conference to devote himself fully to his writing, speaking, and championing of the Ministerial Association. He also was joined that year by LeRoy Froom, one of the bright young men of Adventism.[8]

Froom's energy and editorial skills gave a boost to the still-young organization. He took over most of the administrative oversight of the association and was not shy about letting other leaders know that. He was instrumental in replacing the low-tech bulletins with the glossier *Ministry* magazine in 1928, which developed into a model of its genre. Still facing resistance, Daniells and Froom sought to reassure Palmer and F. M. Wilcox (editor of the *Review*) that *Ministry* would not be a competitor. Its target audience was the roughly five thousand workers worldwide. "They are struggling with little help of an uplifting kind aside from what they themselves get from their efforts." The association also touted professional reading, compiling yearly a reading course for pastors. The course for 1931, for example, included Ellen White's *Patriarchs and Prophets*, but also four other books on preaching, practices, biblical studies, and theology written by non-Adventists. This ecumenical spirit suggested a willingness to learn from scholars in the broader evangelical world.[9]

The Ministerial Association established branches in the other world divisions. For the 1926 General Conference Session Daniells detailed impressive statistics regarding membership and the extent of its published material. But he asserted that the true measure of the Association transcended numbers; it should be measured in the "efficiency of all classes of workers in soul-winning endeavor." This was in fact the theme of his very first editorial in *Ministry* magazine. "A steady, growing efficiency in our ministry has been the constant aim of the Association during the five years of its existence," he observed. His invocation of efficiency as a prime measure of pastoral work was a peculiar, though not surprising, reflection of an age that elevated business values. Efficiency experts sought to help industries become as productive as possible. Daniells, ever the administrator, sought to wed a profound spirituality to a productive mentality in the pastorate. "It [efficiency] stands for the power to produce maximum results with minimum effort or cost. It aims at the elimination of waste or loss in labor, time, and money, in obtaining intended results." This sentiment could have come straight from the pen of the father of the efficiency movement, Frederick Winslow Taylor. Ministers, implicitly, were put on notice that they might be evaluated on the basis of their success in soul winning.[10]

Daniells's labors for the ministry partook of an intense personal spiritual development. Throughout his career he had chronically felt his need for a richer devotional life. He never doubted that he was doing the Lord's work, but it came at the price of his own well-being (physical as well as spiritual). He shared his regrets with his protégé Froom. "He [Daniells] called the 'peril of sheer activity for God'—the encroachment of the mechanical, the submergence of the spiritual. That, he said, was where he had erred." But his account had a happy ending. Daniells took advantage of a slightly less hectic life after 1922 to intensify his study of the Bible and the writings of Ellen White. Most significantly, he came to appreciate the beauty of righteousness by faith, not simply as a doctrine but as a living reality. Daniells's greatest regret was not for himself but for his church, which he believed had squandered the opportunity for spiritual transformation offered by the 1888 message. To call the denomination back to that moment he prepared the first of his two notable books, *Christ Our Righteousness.*[11]

The book project originated at a 1924 gathering of the Ministerial Association's advisory council in Iowa, at which time the group asked Daniells to compile Ellen White's writings on justification by faith. This initiated an ambitious search among her writings dating between 1887 and 1912. Daniells was amazed by the extent and emphatic nature of her public writings on the doctrine. The work became his passion over the next two years. He worked tirelessly in order to have the book available for workers worldwide when they assembled for the 1926 General

Conference Session. Froom was brought to the Ministerial Association that year precisely to provide editorial assistance for the project.[12]

It is hardly an exaggeration to say that Daniells experienced a Martin Luther conversion on the centrality of righteousness by faith. "It is impossible for me to believe that this vital, fundamental message has been received and proclaimed by the remnant church as the Lord intended it should be." His enthusiasm led to some overstatements that needed refining. His confidante E. R. Palmer provided a balanced perspective. Palmer valued the work and gave the manuscript high marks for careful preparation. But he made two suggestions. First, that Daniells clearly state his confidence in church organization and present activities (this caveat in light of the antiorganization stance of Jones and Waggoner, the men most closely identified with the 1888 teaching). And second, that Daniells moderate his charge that the church had virtually rejected the 1888 message. Palmer reminded him that doctrinal progress had been made. "We cannot lose sight of the blessings that have come to the movement and the extent to which it is going in a strong, unified way to the ends of the earth." Palmer worried that too great a stress on the church's failings would "have a tendency to bring discouragement rather than uplift to both people and ministry."[13]

Daniells took Palmer's advice and toned down his jeremiad. Nonetheless, *Christ Our Righteousness* remained a powerful call for the denomination to embrace fully the meaning of 1888. "Christ our righteousness is the one sublime message set forth in the Sacred Scriptures," Daniells asserted in the book's opening line. Although the book project was promoted as a compilation of Ellen White's writings on the subject—and indeed it contains an abundance of her statements—at least in the early chapters, most of the words are Daniells's. He begins with a careful biblical recounting of the doctrine, then segues to some 1887 statements of Ellen White that he sees as preparatory to the 1888 Minneapolis conference. The primary danger then facing the church—and one which would continue to haunt it in White's telling—was "formalism": substituting "forms, ceremonies, doctrines, machinery, and activities for that heart experience which comes alone through fellowship with Christ Jesus our Lord."[14]

Daniells then devotes his longest chapter to 1888. He categorized reactions to the righteousness-by-faith message into three groups. There were those who gladly received the light. There were those who were puzzled by the new teaching and could not decide what to believe. And there were others who directly opposed it or thought the message nothing new (since they believed the church's pioneers—at least in theory—had taught the same thing). Contention among church leaders, Daniells candidly admitted (a brave confession to put in print), "created controversy, and a degree of estrangement which was most unfortunate." But following Palmer's advice, he noted that over the years there "has been steadily developing the desire and hope—yes, the belief—that someday the message of Righteousness by Faith would shine forth in all its inherent worth, glory, and power, and receive full recognition." No doubt Daniells hoped his book and institutes would further his people's recognition of the great truth.[15]

For those who continued to oppose the 1888 message, however, Daniells could not restrain his reproof, or more properly, the reproofs of Ellen White. "The Lord has sent a message to arouse His people to repent, and do their first works; but how has His message been received? While some have heeded it, others have cast contempt and reproach on the message and the messenger. Spirituality deadened, humility and childlike simplicity gone, a mechanical, formal profession of faith has taken the place of love and devotion." But Daniells raised the controversy's stakes even a notch above White's, contending that "back of the opposition is revealed the shrewd plotting of that master-mind of evil, the enemy of all righteousness." In one stroke he delegitimized the position of those who opposed him.[16]

Christ Our Righteousness threw down the gauntlet in defense of Adventism's unswerving commitment to justification by faith. In a sense, Daniells cast the 1888 movement—once and for all—as the key moment in the denomination's history. He found in numerous *Review* articles by Ellen White a clear-cut rationale for this position. Early champions Jones and Waggoner may have deserted the cause, but Daniells, abetted by the legacy of White's writings and by direct allusion to Luther's work, gave the doctrine sturdier denominational legs.

And yet (as even casual students of Adventism know), the twentieth century would continue to witness tension between those committed to stressing the law and those emphasizing grace. Daniells's book found a ready reception among younger ministers, but some of the older generation had rather less enthusiasm for anything that they feared might diminish the law's significance. Palmer himself had to reassure Daniells that there was no truth to the notion that he resisted the manuscript's publication. Indeed, he wanted to see it published in several editions, including a low-cost paper binding for the widest possible circulation. (Sales were so strong within a year of its appearance that the Review and Herald press even gave Daniells a small royalty payment.)[17]

Yet the appearance of *Christ Our Righteousness* did not spare Daniells criticism. Before the 1926 General Conference Session held in Milwaukee, Wisconsin (where he played a minimal role, primarily reporting on the Ministerial Association), J. S. Washburn's critical open letter from 1922 found new life in the hands of an anonymous pastor. It was the old charge that he failed to set up "the spirit of prophecy as an infallible guide and at least equal to the Scriptures." And the self-proclaimed champion of Ellen White, Claude Holmes, though he appreciated the book's message, caustically noted to Froom, "Elder Daniells is interested in the testimonies, when they speak of righteousness by faith, but not when they refer to A. G. Daniells." The cloud of criticism lingered.[18]

ASSORTED DUTIES AND TRAVELS

From the time of the San Francisco General Conference Session in 1922, the Daniellses began spending much of their time in California. In part this reflected the great demand on Arthur's time to speak for church groups up and down the coast. Daniells was entering his late sixties, with a heart that sometimes gave him problems. Yet this did not stop him from an ambitious program of driving. In 1927, he and Mary undertook the drive from Los Angeles to Portland, Oregon. With unreliable cars and hazardous two-lane mountain roads, the trip would take five days by a direct route. But they took side trips to Fresno (where Arthur's sisters resided), Mountain View, and Saint Helena. The trip represented Daniells at his intrepid best. Automobiling became the workaholic Daniells's hobby during his later years. "Our life in our car during the last ten years has done Mary and me a world of good. It has brought needed relaxation to us just at the time in life when we could be helped." Thrifty as always, he developed a passion for buying and selling cars at a profit. He paid $900 for his first car, a Cadillac, used it for a year and a half, reconditioned it, and then resold it for $1,800. He repeated this wheeling and dealing pattern over the following years.[19]

California also beckoned because son Grosvenor and his wife, Grace, had taken up residence there. As a youth, Grosvenor had been a cause of concern for the Daniellses. During his teen years they had left him behind during their extended tours of Asia. Palmer had provided him office work at the Review office during summers and testified to his good work. Nonetheless, his parents' letters testify to an anxiety about the development of a timid youth and his early unsatisfactory experiences in teaching. But now he had entered the medical program at Loma Linda and developed into a steady if not spectacular student. He took up surgery and graduated with his MD degree in 1927. As early as 1924 they were considering a permanent move to Southern California, and with their son's medical practice located there, the Daniellses would settle down in Glendale (and later Huntington Beach).[20]

But Daniells's West Coast migration also spoke to his sense that denominational leadership felt little need for his contributions at headquarters (despite reassurances from Palmer that they missed his "steady, strong hands"). Where Takoma Park had once been the site of unending office work, now Arthur and Mary returned there during the winter months so that he could write without interruptions. The old warhorse had not been put out to pasture, but he was now seldom part of the administrative battles.[21]

After the 1926 General Conference Session Daniells no longer held the title of General Conference secretary and was unburdened with General Conference Committee work (although after 1922 his attendance had been sporadic). But this change had little effect on his activities. Still head of the Ministerial Association—and as a "grand old man" of the Advent movement—he remained a figure welcomed at every pulpit. He continued to indulge his interest in research and writing on Adventist history. And he served as "counselor-at-large" for General Conference presidents W. A. Spicer, and beginning in 1930, C. H. Watson. A. G. Daniells would never lack for things to do.

Daniells took a third and final journey across the Pacific to Australia in 1928, invited by the Australasian Union Conference to hold five ministerial institutes as well as speak at nine camp meetings. The visit must have been an emotional one for him and Mary. Many old friends were now gone, but they became reacquainted with some they had previously known as children. They arrived at Melbourne, where an institute for workers of Victoria state was planned. From there he traveled west to Perth then back to union conference headquarters at Wahroonga for Spring Council (Australian spring), and lastly camp meetings in Brisbane and New South Wales. New Zealand would not be overlooked, nor Tasmania. Activities would take them into March 1929. Having left Takoma Park in January 1928, they journeyed for more than fourteen months. Even at age seventy, Daniells found the endurance to maintain a pace that would have taxed many younger men.[22]

As if his year's work was not enough, Australian leaders implored him to stay on for a couple more years. He was gratified at being received with open arms in his old home but felt he could not remain. Daniells found himself donning his old administrator's hat while there. He promised Palmer that he would report on affairs in Australia, especially regarding Avondale School and the food business. He collected data on the church's progress, which he found generally encouraging, but which in some regards "present warning signals." Daniells felt the West Australia Institute to be particularly gratifying and instructive. Following his usual theme, he sought to emphasize the importance of an efficient ministry. "In one of the sessions of this institute there came over us all such an overwhelming conviction of inefficiency and unworthiness as to cause the whole forenoon to be spent in humble confession and importunate prayer." Daniells was not simply exhortative. A committee was formed to draw up specific plans of improvement. He was particularly touched that when the time came to vote on the recommendations, the group desired to signify its acceptance while in prayer. "Never have I witnessed a response more sincere, wholehearted, and solemn." The preamble to the recommendations bluntly stated two of Daniells's convictions: first, that Adventism was inadequately fulfilling its soul-winning commission; and second, that the "the responsibility for the state of powerlessness without and lukewarmness within" lay with the ministry. Daniells always believed that the health of the church primarily depended on its clergy.[23]

A year and a half later, Daniells (accompanied by Mary) made a final international journey: an ambitious tour of South America. By steamer and train they traversed a great arc, south from Brazil, Uruguay, and

Argentina on the continent's east, then west to Chile and north to Peru along the continent's west. He held five ministerial institutes along the way, patterned on what he had done in the United States and Australia. Workers in these countries had known few opportunities for extended training, and Daniells was gratified by their eager participation in the ten-day, seven-meetings-a-day grind. He serialized in the *Review* his travels for the Adventist laity at home, including short references to many of the American missionaries. Daniells informed readers that J. W. Westphal, a great pioneer missionary to South America, would finally be returning stateside. And he noted with satisfaction that the great majority of workers were now indigenous. A very personal moment came at South America Division headquarters in Buenos Aires, Argentina, where the Daniellses met Etta Hewgley, a secretary in the office. Fifty-two years earlier, when they helped R. M. Kilgore in a tent effort at Rockwall, Texas, Mary had led Etta's father into the church. The Daniellses were gratified and humbled at the thought of how that providential encounter led decades later to the next generation's service in the mission field.[24]

The scenic high point (quite literally) was their train passage from Buenos Aires to Chile. Daniells was struck by the lush plains of the Pampas, but then awed by the trip up the east side of the Andes and then the contorted plunge down the other into Chile. Following meetings there, they headed to Peru for two sets of institutes. He was disappointed that they would not be visiting the storied Lake Titicaca region, but concerns about its altitude prevailed. At Lima, Peru, the last stop, Daniells successfully met with several government officials. Recent developments in this Catholic country were threatening Adventist educational efforts. Yet the future looked encouraging, so he had reason for gratitude. The seventy-one-year-old Daniells also happily reported perfect health on the grueling trip.

Working for the Adventist ministry was dearest to Daniells's heart, but when necessary he could also be an effective apologist. In the mid-1920s Daniells was implored by General Conference brethren to respond to old charges of Dudley Canright against Ellen White. Canright had died in 1919, but his last book, *The Life of Mrs. E. G. White*, continued to roil the church. A complete response to Canright was made by W. H. Branson in 1933. Daniells focused on one aspect of Canright's charge: that White, under claim of inspiration, had endorsed the "Shut-Door Theory" in the years immediately following 1844. T. E. Bowen, office manager at General Conference headquarters, complained of the frequent letters they received asking about Canright's charges. What had become of the reply Daniells had been writing on this subject? Bowen asked in early 1923. Daniells admitted that the project had lapsed, but as soon as his revival work was completed he would return to it. This he did, finally, in 1926.[25]

Daniells attacked the project with his usual thoroughness. He loved researching Adventist history, and when he felt the stakes were high his energy redoubled. Building on the collection of early Adventist documents, which the denomination had accumulated decades earlier, he carefully examined the earliest published writings of Ellen White, seeking her comments on the "shut door." Daniells freely acknowledged that the disappointed band of early Adventists held that probation had closed and unbelievers had no further opportunity for salvation. By the early 1850s they had reconsidered this prophetic stance and adopted an open view of evangelism. Was it true, though, that in her prophetic office Ellen White had initially promoted this view? Daniells painstakingly established that she had not. He proved himself a careful student of the various versions of her early writings. Examining all of her earliest extant published documents, he could find no clear evidence that she had taught the "shut door." He admitted that three statements might be interpreted in such a fashion, but careful examination of their context clarified their meaning. "But this is not to be counted as strange," he added, "for we find the same perplexity in certain passages of Scripture."[26]

The key distinction Daniells strained to make was "between holding a personal belief regarding a question and declaring that this belief has been obtained by a direct revelation from the Lord." In his original 1926 *Review* article on the subject, Daniells only obliquely implied that White held the "shut-door" belief. But in the 1930 multipart *Review* reprint (its reappearance suggesting the seriousness of the matter among the Adventist public) he made a subtle but important addition. Where White's personal (though "uninspired") assent to the "shut door" was left unspoken earlier, Daniells now wrote: "Even if Mrs. E. G. White for a time shared personally this view in common with those with whom she associated, there is no evidence to show that she ever put it forth as revealed to her from the Lord."[27]

Why this later admission? Did Daniells have new evidence? Not on this point. The change probably speaks to his ongoing desire to uphold the Spirit of Prophecy while also conveying to the Adventist public a more complex appreciation of how that gift operated. That the church's prophet could change her mind, develop, progress, was a truth Daniells knew members needed. It could serve as a corrective to the rigid verbal literalism that always threatened to encompass the church's view of her. A 1932 *Review* update of his argument provided new evidence. An 1874 letter from White to J. N. Loughborough (an autographed copy of which was reproduced in the paper) made explicit her early belief that after 1844 "no more sinners would be converted." With this incontrovertible proof, Daniells could put a "case closed" stamp on his earlier argument. Advent founders had grown in their religious faith and understanding. "The pioneers in this movement never claimed infallibility, nor do we claim it for them." For Daniells, this was a truth a healthy church needed to understand.[28]

In addition to his speaking and writing, Daniells would occasionally serve as informal adviser to current General Conference presidents. He obviously could draw on immense experience. He had seen a great deal and knew virtually all of the church's leaders. He was highly regarded for his administrative skills. His long previous work with his successor, W. A. Spicer, seemed to make their new relationship smooth. Consequently, Daniells offered observations on sundry matters. During the Spicer presidency (1922–1930) most of Daniells's energy went into the Ministerial Association and championing righteousness by faith. In 1931, he laid aside leadership of the Ministerial Association, as he and Mary prepared to close their Takoma Park home and move permanently to Southern California.[29]

But Daniells continued to wield influence at church headquarters. In 1930 the first non-North American General Conference president was elected, Charles H. Watson of Australia. Watson brought unparalleled business acumen to his post (needed as the church faced the imminent economic Great Depression). Daniells had known Watson for years and was prepared to serve as his counselor. Indeed, Watson sought out Daniells, imploring him to become a general field secretary, a loosely defined post that allowed him to be a sort of adviser-at-large. Daniells kept Watson apprised of his and Mary's transcontinental car journey west in the winter of 1931 (only two flat tires along the way). In the Daniells's tradition, the trip was a procession, with stops at major Adventist institutions along the way: Southern Junior College in Collegedale, Tennessee; Southern Publishing House in Nashville, Tennessee; Southwestern Junior College in Keene, Texas; and many churches. All in all, he held twenty-one meetings in sixteen locations. "This is a bit strenuous," he wrote from Nashville, "but I am enjoying it."[30]

Daniells wished that he had more explicit instructions as to what Watson desired from him. Lacking such, he advised Watson on those church matters he deemed significant (including many at Loma Linda, discussed below). By 1931 the depression affected denominational finances. Tithes and offerings were down, so leaders spent much time worrying about how to pay the bills. Proposals were made to consolidate some conferences, including Southern California and Southeastern California. Daniells, who understood the virtues of efficient reorganization, supported their efforts. But he reported to Watson that the Southeastern California Conference president had begun a campaign against the proposal. "It was represented that this was a move to centralize authority and power in the vicinity of Los Angeles." Daniells knew about pushback. He understood that if conference leaders across the country dug in their heels "then it is going to make the work of reorganization very difficult and perhaps in some places quite impossible" (which with few exceptions is what happened).[31]

Daniells also advised (one might say meddled) on personnel issues. He was disturbed that J. L. Shaw, treasurer of the General Conference, had been away from headquarters for nearly a year because of poor health. At a time when the denomination was struggling with finances, Daniells thought it unconscionable that a worker would take off this much time for any reason. He took it upon himself to visit Shaw's doctors to check on his prognosis, then visited Shaw's wife and implored her to prevail upon her husband to resign (actions that would make modern human resource officers cringe). He also gave pointed advice about filling the presidency of the North Pacific Union. "They have had a poor weak leadership up there for years," Daniells judged. "Unless you take hold of the matter," he urged Watson, "I fear another weak man may go in." Daniells even had a name to promote.[32]

But, at least at times, Daniells found more frustration than gratification in remaining in the administrative loop. Watson had persuaded him to become a general field secretary, despite Daniells's reservations that the position represented "an easy way of shelving men." Daniells's professional ego took a blow when General Conference and union conference men ignored—or even failed to ask—his advice on important matters. "I don't like to be placed in a false light—to appear to be of some consequence, but only put on a shelf," as a general field secretary who was, in the words of another, a "dumb-bell." Thus, a wounded Daniells implored Watson to "listen to a true friend who is profoundly interested in your administrative record." He warned Watson that the administrative wheels of the General Conference were shaky. "I fear that for certain reasons your administration has lost influence since the Omaha Fall Council." Daniells then proceeded to relate the discontent of an influential layperson with the actions of some Watson associates. "I do not feel free to tell you in a letter what I would tell you in a personal conversation," Daniells confided, but these troubled affairs were certain to shake the confidence of the church's most competent men in his administration.[33]

Always thorough and conscientious, Daniells did not shy away from gathering facts and then informing Watson about a singular tragedy in the church. A church leader, a man "highly respected and truly loved," was found dead in a hotel room, having taken his own life. This was cause enough for grief—and for questions about motive. But threatened scandal was not far behind. Daniells recalled his days as president when some trouble arose and there "was a failure of men to give me full details." Thus, he provided Watson with as full a picture as possible. Despite local conference officials investigating the matter, Daniells left no stone unturned, visiting the morgue and interviewing the coroner. Daniells reported to Watson the sad background to the victim's deed: a moral lapse threatened with ignominious exposure. "We are in a hard place here," Daniells wrote with understatement. How to mitigate the damage to the reputation of individual and church? Daniells was already being hounded by ministers wanting to know the background. If church leadership says nothing and the full story leaks out, members will accuse them of attempting to "hush up a preacher's guilt." But to reveal the sordid story will mean the people "will be terribly shocked and young men will raise big questions about all of us." There was no good resolution to so awful an affair.[34]

Daniells's move to California in 1931 brought him to a new task: chairman of the Board of Trustees of the College of Medical Evangelists at Loma

Linda. The call came from CME administrators but with the cooperation of denominational leaders, particularly church treasurer J. L. Shaw. Daniells was to be a "resident representative of the General Conference Committee," a sort of liaison between the two institutions. He had been gravitating toward the West Coast for some years; this assignment solidified his move to California. Without doubt, school and church leaders had to be pleased to establish a more effective line of contact. Daniells leveraged a pledge from General Conference colleagues in Washington for frequent visits to Loma Linda to assist in medical school oversight. Given his involvement in the very founding of the institution, Daniells was a natural choice.[35]

Chairing the board was no mere preferment or sinecure. Daniells would face taxing institutional problems, particularly economic challenges from the Depression's iron grip. Indeed, some wondered if the medical school could survive. The patient census plunged at White Memorial Hospital, CME's second campus. Benevolent gifts shrank, as did the General Conference subsidy. Thus, when Daniells chaired his first meeting (and met with a "real hearty welcome" from other members) in January 1931, his plate was full. "Well Charles, I am here and realize that I am facing a most delicate and difficult undertaking," he wrote Watson. He immediately was faced with overseeing the final legal settlement of a messy property dispute with a group of individuals at Yucaipa, California. CME had gotten involved in land development (without full Board knowledge) with an eye to making a profit for the institution. But unhappiness followed—both on the part of some land purchasers and the CME Board. It became the sort of messy affair in which college attorneys insisted that the settlement included promises that no future action would be taken against any party.[36]

More grievous, however, were unforgiving income and expense balances. Maintaining two campuses (at Loma Linda and Los Angeles) was expensive. So salaries were cut, purchases kept to a minimum; nothing was too small. Travel reimbursements were reduced from eight to six cents per mile; dish washing was contracted out. Daniells was pleased to tell Watson that by the summer of 1931 they had reduced annual expenses by about $40,000. White Memorial Hospital physicians sometimes had to accept eggs or flour in place of money from some patients. But the retrenchment of personnel compromised the training program, which then threatened AMA accreditation (along with the issue of students coming from unaccredited Adventist colleges). Percy Magan, formerly dean and since 1927 president of CME, had to replicate his administrative skills of the 1910s in negotiating the shoals of medical accreditation.[37]

Given the seemingly intractable financial problems, what is most striking about these years is how the institution moved ahead with a building program. Daniells promoted the institution's needs and succeeded in squeezing some financial blood from General Conference and union conference turnips. At his arrival Daniells began championing the need for an assembly hall at the Los Angeles campus. His argument was irrefutable: students needed a place to gather for Sabbath services. Watson and the General Conference Committee concurred and allowed Daniells to approach North American union conferences for support. The result was David Paulson Hall (later White Memorial Church), dedicated in early 1932. The following fall the board asked the General Conference Committee to consider a new church for the Loma Linda campus, which was complete by 1934. Three academic buildings at the Loma Linda campus and the impressive White Memorial Hospital in Los Angeles were completed in the latter half of the 1930s, enabled by a nearly half-million-dollar authorization of borrowing and fund raising from the General Conference in 1934. The latter followed an impassioned appeal from Daniells and Magan at Fall Council.[38]

If the board chairman's attention inevitably focused on finances, he also made time to champion the spiritual well-being of medical students. For Daniells, an Adventist medical school existed for one purpose: to train workers for worldwide evangelism. But there had been concerns that CME campus religious life was not what it should be. Spiritual nurture in a professional school setting presented different challenges than at the undergraduate colleges. "We have all set our hearts on a great spiritual improvement and uplift in this college." Building adequate worship facilities at both campuses helped address an important need. Magan would later credit Daniells with a blossoming of the spiritual side of campus life. Some of the younger, more conservative students were distressed by the Sabbath work required in the clinical hospital setting. Other young men, though, were troubled by the derisive comments about their religion coming from some of the nurses. Daniells was told that most of the affected students "had been of the reckless kind before coming to the school." The answer for this, he was advised, would be "more strict standards of admission."[39]

Daniells also got involved in evaluating a creative work-study program called the "cooperative plan." This was an effort to help students finance their medical education without resort to crippling debt. Modeled on a similar concept at an engineering school, beginning in 1923 students alternated monthly traditional classes with work in a lab, as a nurse's aide, an orderly, or in a physician's office. In modern educational parlance, students benefited from regular paid practicum experience. The program continued for a number of years, winning generally favorable marks from students, who appreciated the wide range of practical exposure to medical practice it provided as well as its financial advantages. It was hard on faculty, however, who had to present all classroom material twice (one student group was in class while another labored). Daniells, Magan, and other CME leaders interviewed a sample of students and physicians about the program. Daniells was gratified with what he learned. "These young men made quite an impression upon my mind." The cooperative program would continue through the end of Daniells's tenure as chair of the Board of Trustees, discontinued in 1937 on the directive of the Council of Medical Education.[40]

Resettled on the West Coast, still busy, but with his career clearly winding down, Daniells began to worry over financial details that had not concerned him before. Having to preside over an enforced retirement of an elderly physician at CME and learning how constrained the sustentation fund was must have been sobering. Still, there were personal financial matters for which he hoped to find redress from the General Conference. He asked for reimbursement for his stenographic expenses relating to his board chairmanship. Daniells understood that his daughter-in-law Grace's being the secretary might appear an awkward conflict of interest; nonetheless, he defended her high level of competence. But Watson demurred, citing both General Conference finances and the propriety of CME's meeting his secretarial needs. Daniells also sought help with his car insurance. The General Conference Committee granted the veteran worker this perquisite. But Daniells, after thinking it over, declined. First, because he understood the straitened condition of the General Conference treasury; second, because he had never accepted any bonus for his work, just salary and expenses. "I feel a bit proud of this record covering a period of fifty-four years in my ministry, and somehow I feel that I would like to close my career without breaking the record." He had voted to approve many gifts, bonuses, or financial aid through his years, but he wanted to go to his grave with conscience undisturbed by taking more from the cause than he needed.[41]

ELLEN WHITE'S LEGACY

A. G. Daniells presided over one other board from the end of his presidency until his death: the Ellen G. White Estate. He had been intimately involved with its establishment after White's death in 1915, and he would be involved with the Estate during the final years of his presidency. Immediately after he left the presidency in 1922 he became the board's chair, and various issues involving White's writings comprised a small but significant part of his work to the end of his life. Because White's writings remained at Elmshaven (until 1938), meetings of the White Estate were often on the West Coast, convenient for Daniells as he increasingly spent time there. These were sometimes held in odd places, such as a camp ground or on a train, places where busy men could conveniently gather. Daniells, paradoxically, found himself both cautioning against further prolific publication of her writings and, ultimately, authoring one of Adventism's most important books on her vital role in the church.

Despite Daniells's repeated efforts at reassurance, Ellen White, in her final months, suffered anxiety about the future use and promotion of her writings. Indeed, there was debate over the propriety of turning her unpublished writings into books. How exactly should the voice of the prophet be heard after her death? Daniells never questioned the ongoing pertinence of White to the church. But he (and other trustees) did need to work through certain reservations before he could support an ambitious plan of publication.[42]

Ellen White's will (actually a series of wills) had authorized the creation of an estate that would own her writings and make decisions about their dissemination. Five men comprised the board, of which Daniells was one. The issues surrounding her writings and the estate were complex; meeting financial obligations of the estate was an immediate concern. This required the General Conference to purchase all the estate's assets (and assume the debts) at a court sale, then convey back to the trustees the literary rights to her works, published and unpublished. Into the early 1920s, intricacies of her final will and of later adjustments to it baffled even such knowledgeable individuals as E. R. Palmer. But under the direction of Willie White at Elmshaven, the Estate pursued an aggressive program of cataloguing and preserving her work, finishing two major works (*Life Sketches* and *Prophets and Kings,* both largely completed under her supervision), and especially undertaking translations of her major works into other major European languages. It also authorized issuance by Pacific Press of the five-volume Conflict of the Ages series, which would become the iconic heart of her work to future generations. But what about new compilations?[43]

One obvious concern about the issuance of new works under her name was that she could not be present to oversee their editing. How could one be sure that any collection of earlier articles, no matter how carefully edited, would reflect her mature thoughts on a subject? But this reservation seemed overridden by what was clearly White's wish: that her writings and sermons be made as widely available as possible. Thus, in the 1920s, with the approval of the General Conference Committee, seven books were compiled from articles previously published elsewhere, including *Counsels on Health*, *Christian Service*, and *Fundamentals of Christian Education*. Daniells was actively involved in 1923 in making selections from the earlier pamphlets, *Special Testimonies*, into the new compilation *Testimonies to Ministers and Gospel Workers*.[44]

A more serious question involved whether her unpublished writings—letters, diaries, talks, occasional writings—were properly subjects for publication. A split quickly developed between Willie White and a majority of the other trustees (as well as denominational leaders). The close friendship of White and Daniells was strained by this disagreement. At a White Estate meeting in October 1920 this division became clear. "Brethren Jones, Wilcox and Daniells spoke very clearly and forcefully stating their conviction that it ought not to be done," the minutes tersely read. Outnumbered, White resorted to the time-honored strategy of a minority position: request that any final decision be delayed until more study was given. But while no vote was taken, "it was the consensus of opinion that no unpublished Ms., even though it might have Sister White's O.K., should be published in connection with published Mss."[45]

Why the distinction? Unpublished writings were, almost by definition, rough-hewn, often intended for purposes other than publication.

They risked a serious wrenching out of their original context if compiled into a volume. In short, they were one step further removed from the prophet's ability to polish them into the final form that publication represents. Although never couched exactly in this way, one senses a feeling on the part of some (Daniells included) that the Adventist canon had closed. To perpetuate the canon's expansion through the inclusion of material not clearly intended by White for publication might be tantamount to adding to Scripture later Christian manuscripts. A practical concern held that to multiply White's books would be to devalue those already in print and possibly depress sales. And one cannot overlook the embarrassment factor: what private reproofs to various General Conference leaders lurked within the manuscript files that might see the published light of day? One could imagine Daniells's aversion to having admonitions against him find their way into print. And yet, Daniells freely and in great detail told personal stories about Ellen White's reproofs. While at a ministerial association in Australia in 1928, for example, he recounted her rebuke years earlier for his failing to take up city work. In truth, White's reproofs were so well known to church members that Daniells had little choice but to put the best face on them and testify to their salutary effect.[46]

But Willie White was on a mission on behalf of his mother. He would not easily take no for an answer. He penned a long, imploring message to the General Conference Committee in 1921 (when Daniells still presided over the committee). He told how his mother had on repeated occasions received divine messages that all her writings were valuable: "gather up the fragments; let nothing be lost." White proceeded to describe the scope and organization of her voluminous outpouring, how she would return to previous letters or statements that were carefully stored away, and emend or add to them. Her writings were a process (this, Daniells well knew), with certain themes emerging over an extended period. She anticipated that after her death two sorts of difficulties would arise regarding her writings. One group "would claim the right to print and circulate anything they chose" of hers. Another group "would demand that nothing more of her writings should be published." Both extremes should be avoided. At the moment, Willie clearly implied, the second extreme was the danger. He then quoted his mother: "W. C. White has his commission. I have instructed him to labor untiringly to secure the publication of my writings." With this endorsement in hand, he posed the central question to the General Conference Committee: "Shall we take a positive stand that nothing of Sister White's writings that were not in print before her death, shall ever be printed and given to the people?" He then laid out an agenda of publications, starting with a work on health ministry, something he said his mother much wanted in the days before her death.[47]

White's powerfully stated argument seemed to defeat all opponents. Yet his was a delayed victory. General Conference leaders were reluctant to vest in the White family heir ongoing control over the prophet's writings. Their ability to shape members' beliefs was too great to be left to one person or even a board. As indicated above, an active program of compilations and translations went forward—but only from published works and with explicit General Conference Committee approval. Reservations about use of unpublished works remained through much of the decade. Confidence in Willie White was not helped by his generous sharing of his mother's writings. In his enthusiasm to serve Adventist members who had issues they wanted resolved, Willie freely sent copies of letters and other writings. This unregulated use of her work upset Daniells and others. Further, when questions from the field came in, Elmshaven staff were assuming the role of interpreters of her words. This "manuscript correspondence problem" required Board intervention. Willie was reined in, and ultimately protocols were established for sharing his mother's writings. A companion problem came when overseas areas prepared their own abridgments of White's writings for local use. The answer seemed to be to produce authorized editions in various languages. With General Conference president Charles Watson in attendance, Willie White appealed for more cooperation by and support from the General Conference.[48]

The marginalization of the White Estate on the West Coast was reduced in 1932 with its incorporation, which further clarified its relationship to the denomination, and then ended completely in 1938, when it moved to Takoma Park. Although long frustrated, Willie won the argument over utilizing his mother's unpublished writings. Daniells, for reasons not clear, became convinced that the body of her work deserved consideration as a published resource. In 1932, *Medical Ministry*, a project Willie had promoted eleven years earlier as being close to his mother's heart, appeared as the first posthumous work compiled primarily from unpublished materials. Fittingly, Daniells wrote its introduction.[49]

Daniells's active interest in White Estate affairs continued to the end of his life. Just two months before his death he submitted to Willie a series of detailed suggestions about recent Estate publications.

THE ABIDING GIFT OF PROPHECY

A. G. Daniells's desire to promote the role of Ellen White in the church was strong. Periodic charges that he was "soft" on her inspiration surely rankled. Thus, his last major effort for the denomination culminated in one of the most important books produced on her work, *The Abiding Gift of Prophecy*.

A "comprehensive book on the Spirit of Prophecy" was authorized by the General Conference Committee in the summer of 1930. It was intended for students, teachers, and laypeople generally. It seems likely that Daniells initiated the project. He had been pondering the subject for some time and wanted to carry it through, once freed from administrative duties. His long service had earned the right to request General Conference support for a book project. The Committee voted that he be released from any foreign calls and devote most of his time to the book. It even took an action to request W. E. Howell, educational secretary of the General Conference, to assist in the research. Daniells resigned as head of the Ministerial Association and appeared ready to devote full-time to the project. The Committee desired that the book be completed within a year.[50]

But in the common nature of such things, the project took five. An important reason for the delay came from Daniells's being "commandeered" for the board chairmanship at CME. The time demands of that position—especially Daniells's hopes to effect reform at the medical school—inevitably stole research and writing time. In his first six months, only sporadic hours could be given to the book. "Writing is difficult and laborious for me," he admitted. Producing publishable quality work took much time. He also learned that being away from his sources, such as he had available at the General Conference library vault, was a great impediment. "I ought to have every hour of every day for this alone until the book is finished," he lamented to Froom. By midsummer 1931 he thought he had a plan for clearing his plate. At a planned retreat to the San Bernardino Mountains in August, Daniells would ask medical school leaders for a few months' release to finish the manuscript.[51]

His glib confidence that he could complete a big project in a short time came partly from having written his World War I prophetic booklets and *Christ Our Righteousness* in relative short order. But the former was largely commentary on contemporary journalistic literature, and with the latter, more ambitious work he had had considerable help in locating the pertinent Ellen White passages. *The Abiding Gift of Prophecy* was intended to be a more scholarly work; at more than 350 pages, it was a substantial volume.

Daniells also felt he could proceed quickly because he had a clear idea of what he wished to say. Church leaders envisioned a work on the Spirit of Prophecy, but Daniells's vision extended considerably further. He intended to illustrate how God had bestowed the prophetic gift through the ages, from patriarchal times through the Christian era, and culminating with the work of Ellen White. It was a breathtaking claim, one that paralleled a theme from White's *Great Controversy*: Just as through all times God has had a loyal band of obedient believers, so He has provided a prophetic voice for His people. "From the limited amount of research I have given this matter," he confided to Froom, "I have found enough to convince me that the Lord tried very hard to keep the gifts operating among his people." Even into the second and third centuries AD, it was clear to him "that the gifts continued in a wonderful way." Unfortunately, the apostasy of later centuries impeded the prophetic gift. Nonetheless, "down through the centuries men of deep piety and righteousness were visited by the Lord, and in a measure the gift of prophecy, discerning of spirits and healing were given to these men."[52]

It is likely that Daniells's thesis rested more on faith than research. Turning this belief into a sound historical argument would require research. Daniells was not a scholar, and he probably did not anticipate the depth of work needed. The promised help of Howell was never realized, as he was tied to his General Conference duties. Life's intrusions and the encompassing nature of the project extended the book project all the way to early 1935. Although he made steady progress, things might have dragged on even longer but for the concentrating effect of a life-threatening illness in January, which demanded that the manuscript be soon completed.[53]

News of Daniells's likely fatal illness jolted the General Conference into action. LeRoy Froom, Daniells's protégé and a budding scholar, was given leave from the Ministerial Association to join him in California. Dores Robinson, Willie White's son-in-law and a White Estate veteran assistant, joined them. The three men went to work with an urgency appropriate to the situation. Froom was presented with a manuscript not fully drafted. The early sections dealing with prophetic activity in the biblical ages was nearly—though not completely—finished. Much work had been done on the post-Apostolic Christian ages, though further research was needed to support Daniells's thesis. The final section, dealing with the Spirit of Prophecy as manifested in Ellen White, was only in outline form when Froom arrived. Since this section dealt with history that Daniells had witnessed, he felt he could complete it rather quickly. Daniells dictated these chapters to Robinson, who supplemented Daniells's memory with written material from recent Adventist history. Froom, though, dealing with the critical middle section, made treks to the impressive collection at the nearby Huntington Library in an attempt to document Daniells's assertions. He also contacted Adventist religion scholars (as well as that Adventist jack-of-all-trades, George McCready Price) for suggestions.[54]

Froom oversaw the revision of the work. Daniells admitted, as he reread what he had written, that he "was conscious of a dullness throughout." The man whose career had been spent writing functional prose never claimed to be a stylist. Froom, by contrast, had earned a reputation within the church for wielding a facile pen. The issue of maintaining a consistent stylistic tone throughout the manuscript and preserving Daniells's "voice" was one raised by some on the reading committee. This challenge was satisfactorily met. *Our Abiding Gift of Prophecy*, while not scintillating reading, possesses the virtues of clarity and force.[55]

Froom sought to follow Daniells's literary wishes as far as he could. In addition to the need to polish his prose, Daniells recognized that he had relied too much on encyclopedia entries; Froom must find more evidence of prophetic activity from primary sources and standard historical works. He entrusted Froom to write the book's introduction, which laid out the book's central thesis. Daniells also charged Froom with ensuring that his greatest fear not come to pass: that conservative voices in the church would "emasculate" his argument that God spoke to prophets even during the "Catholic" Middle Ages (more on this below). If this came to pass, he said, he did not want his name on the volume. A fading Daniells even implored General Conference president Watson not to let his manuscript be scissored. Watson reassured him that this would not happen.[56]

Froom, who carefully documented the editorial process, developed a set of guidelines for himself that reflected not only Daniells's wishes and best scholarly practices, but also the political realities of the project. For example, although they were seeking all evidence for the presence of the gift, they should make "modest assertions and not claim too much." They should not apologize for the lack of extensive evidence of the gift at certain times in history, and they should also be candid about conflicting testimony of scholars about its presence. Use the testimony of the Church Fathers, but remove any published references from earlier Adventist pioneers who had discredited them. (This would set up a jarring dissonance.) Finally the title, *The Abiding Gift of Prophecy*, should be retained. It was not Daniells's choice, but he heartily endorsed it as best expressing his thesis.[57]

Froom sought to follow Daniells's every wish, but in a few cases this was not advisable. One book chapter that was planned by Daniells but quietly dropped involved the nature of inspiration, including a discussion of prophetic infallibility versus fallibility. One wonders if inclusion of this hot-potato issue reflected Daniells's regret at not having given public airing to the discussions of the 1919 Bible Conference. At that time, prudence dictated that the transcripts be locked away. Evidently the same judgment followed here, probably at Froom's urging. Froom may have recognized that the larger point of the book would likely sink in the quicksand of this volatile issue. Nonetheless, one would like to know the discussions that preceded the decision.[58]

An important discussion of the definition of a prophet, centering on a statement of Ellen White in her book *Education*, was also omitted. Yet the matter was essential to Daniells's argument for establishing the prophetic gift through the ages. White wrote: "From the earliest times, prophets had been recognized as teachers divinely appointed. In the highest sense the prophet was one who spoke by direct inspiration, communicating to the people the messages he had received from God. But the name was given also to those who, though not so directly inspired, were divinely called to instruct the people in the works and ways of God."

Even if certain great men of God, such as Luther or Zwingli, had not received direct communication through dreams or visions, they still merited being considered prophets in the secondary sense that White uses. But Daniells's broadened use of the term was tabled by some colleagues. Was he not stretching the concept beyond its usefulness? "Sister White herself never enumerated the men who were prophets in this secondary sense," F. M. Wilcox objected, "and does it rest with us to make this classification?" *The Abiding Gift of Prophecy* utilizes Daniells's broader sense of the term. But it does not invoke White's imprimatur to do so.[59]

One other preference of Daniells was unrealized. In his author's preface he wanted to acknowledge the difficult circumstances under which he completed his book and give full recognition to his two assistants. One imagines that he did not want to replicate what he had long regretted: a lack of knowledge by the Adventist public about the editing process of Ellen White's books. Yet other heads prevailed. No mention was made of his illness and only the most general reference given to his "indebtedness to a number of my friends." The Adventist public was given no cause to speculate over which persons might have influenced the book. *The Abiding Gift of Prophecy* was to remain an A. G. Daniells work.[60]

It may have been his book, but after his death, others sought to alter it, and some perhaps to bury it altogether. Daniells understood that since the General Conference Committee had commissioned the book, a reading committee would be established to review the manuscript. But he desired some voice in selecting the committee, lest "some ultraconservative influence would 'question the advisability' of retaining the section on the Christian era." He particularly worried about who would chair the committee, offering a list of names he found acceptable. Froom's appointment was good news.[61]

With drafting and revisions on the manuscript finished literally the day before Daniells's death, Froom was next tasked with sending chapters out to members of the eight-member reading committee. Several of these offered quick endorsements with minimal changes. Froom also solicited support from others not formally involved, such as Frederick Schilling, religion professor at Walla Walla College. Willie White volunteered his sanction. But there were an influential handful who detected theological problems. Daniells may have viewed some individuals as antagonistic; in truth, they frequently raised pertinent questions about his thesis and use of evidence. Their criticisms are worth reviewing because they reflected

Adventism at an interesting moment of theological/historical reflection.[62]

Some objections reflected pragmatic concerns about not reopening denominational wounds. One felt strongly that Daniells's rehashing of the Kellogg-pantheism fracas was ill-advised (Daniells's goal was to show how crucial was Ellen White's guidance). A. O. Tait, editor of *Signs of the Times*, on the other hand, thought leaving out this recent history would be a mistake. The "thing might spring up again" if omitted; further, members might get the idea "we were afraid to mention that controversy." Daniells's chapter 30, "The Denomination Saved from Pantheistic Teaching," remained. Its inclusion suggested a maturing denomination, capable of publically retelling a difficult story in its history and doing so while many of its participants still lived.[63]

The crux of the objections, as Daniells well predicted, involved his central claim that God had provided a nearly unbroken chain of prophets throughout the Christian ages. This ran counter to perhaps the deepest historical strain in Adventism—that with the rise of the papacy, God withdrew His Spirit from the church; indeed, that the Catholic tradition could not be considered His church at all. For Daniells to hold up individuals as having the prophetic gift (relatively few in number though they were) from the post-Apostolic age—and particularly from the fourth century on—seemed almost willfully perverse. Certainly it reversed a tradition of historical interpretation stretching back to the beginnings of the denomination. A string of churchmen objected. The "endeavor to show," lamented F. M. Wilcox, editor of the *Review* and author of the 1931 statement of the church's fundamental beliefs, "that the gift of prophecy was continuous in all centuries of the church, is a weakness rather than a strength, . . . it will only serve to awaken doubt and confusion." Adventism had always taught that the gift was withdrawn during those centuries, only conferred again in the earth's final days to Ellen White. "The evidence is so meager and based so largely upon disputed testimony," Wilcox wrote in an assessment resembling that of several others, "that I question the wisdom of citing" it. Further, to accept the testimony of Church Fathers such as Tertullian or Origin runs counter to what we have said for decades, thus making the church vulnerable to its critics.[64]

M. E. Kern, secretary of the General Conference, on the other hand, did not on principle object to the idea that God might have blessed the

Medieval church with a prophet, but felt Daniells made "too labored an effort to point out many individuals who had the gift." He recognized that Daniells was an administrator, not a scholar, "not accustomed to carefully sifting historical material." His use of Ellen White's distinction between "prophets" and "prophetic men" was also without merit and that "to my mind rather cheapens the presentation." W. E. Howell also made telling points about Daniells's use of evidence and logic. Daniells was guilty of "begging the question"; that is, he was assuming proof of his point rather than actually establishing it. "Because we have every reason to believe our contention true as a general proposition, we are tempted to infer and affirm too much from evidence too meager." Here Howell struck a nerve. Daniells held an *a priori* belief in God's bestowal of the gift through the ages. This led him to see evidence where others saw only tentative possibility. "Should we not confine our presentation in the book to persons concerning whom there is clear testimony on record as possessing the spiritual gift of prophecy[?]"[65]

Froom wished to expedite the review process to get publication underway (he hoped to make the book part of the Ministerial Association's yearly reading list). He clearly viewed himself as an advocate for this final achievement of his mentor, A. G. Daniells. In early April Froom sensed danger from Wilcox's strong objections, which, in a memorandum to himself, had "set in motion influences and actions that, unless checked by countering influences and forces not now in sight, may create an ultimate blockade to the printing of the Daniells manuscript." Daniells feared this reaction from Wilcox, knowing that the respected *Review* editor's "adverse report on the historical section" might carry influence with General Conference men. "Unless there is divine intervention, this book is doomed," Froom gloomily concluded.[66]

But Froom's worries proved exaggerated. Most of the nine-member reading committee favored publication. And even those hoisting red flags added that, overall, the manuscript (properly edited) was a valuable contribution deserving publication. Still, there was enough concern about certain points that the consensus-seeking culture of church leadership required caution. "Now that our dear brother Daniells has come to his rest," Wilcox argued, "I do not see the need of this great haste" (he further stated that if this haste were pursued, he would resign from the committee). The reading committee voted to ask the General Conference officers to read the manuscript as well (since they would be perceived as implicitly endorsing the book's thesis). Watson agreed, and four General Conference leaders were selected to look over the comments and decide on necessary revisions. O. Montgomery, a General Conference vice president, chaired the group (in response, perhaps, to a desire for a more neutral figure).[67]

Through the remainder of spring and summer 1935, work proceeded. Debate continued, especially on the controversial section on prophecy in the post-Apostolic age. Were the Church Fathers—and even more troubling, the Medieval churchmen—reliable witnesses to the prophetic gift? And how should the gift of prophecy be defined? Church historians such as W. M. Landeen and N. J. Waldorf supported Daniells's more encompassing interpretation. But their view was brushed aside by one church veteran on the review committee as coming from "youngsters." A "minority committee" of the whole oversaw the project, which in turn promptly handed off editorial work to Howell. Given the sharp opinions at the beginning of the process, Montgomery was pleased to report that work went forward with "utmost good fellowship and spirit of unity." By October the manuscript was edited and ready for the printer. Montgomery urged confidentiality on the committee. "We are aware that there are those who would be very glad to get hold of any information they could concerning the Daniells book to make capital of it."[68]

Well before his death, Daniells had given detailed preferences regarding the physical appearance of his book. He had had a few pages set up in three different typefaces, to choose the one that best suited him. He designated the size of book. And he asked that there be two bindings "in dignified, dark colors" (dark red and blue cloth bindings). He also asked Froom to ensure that Pacific Press published his work. "The Pacific Press does first-class work in all that it puts out. . . . They have a lot of energy and progressiveness in the promotion of what they print."[69]

The Abiding Gift of Prophecy appeared in late 1935. Daniells would have been pleased to know that his thesis remained intact. And despite concern by some that its length might discourage readers, the book sold well. It, along with *Christ Our Righteousness*, became classics of Adventist theological literature, certainly among the most important works published by the denomination in the second quarter of the twentieth century, and both remain in print to the present.

For all the debate over parts of its argument, *The Abiding Gift of Prophecy* is a thoroughly "Adventist" work. Daniells traces the story of God's millennia-long work with humanity, culminating with the prophetic gift of Ellen White in the Seventh-day Adventist Church. It fit well as a companion piece to the Conflict of the Ages series. The book's first half, which deals primarily with Old Testament and Apostolic manifestations of the gift, is noncontroversial. All Bible believers accepted scriptural testimony to the gift. But Daniells took quite literally biblical promises that God would never leave His people without prophetic guidance. "This prophetic gift bestowed was to abide with the church from Adam to the second advent of our Lord." Thus, early reformers in the Catholic tradition, such as Montanus and Donatus, also revealed God's will. Likewise, more familiar names from the Reformation such as Luther and Zwingli should be understood as true prophets. "Just what measure of spiritual illumination they received, it is impossible for us to know and declare," Daniells admitted.[70]

The various concerns about upgrading Medieval and Reformation figures to the status of prophets seems not to have evoked an outcry among Adventist readership. A central point of the book, that Ellen White partakes of a long and distinguished tradition of prophetic vocation, may well have served to enhance a sense of Adventist distinctiveness. It made her appear less an oddity than part of God's ongoing plan. Further, for many readers the most compelling portion of the book was likely Daniells's retelling of his own experiences with White. Their labors in Australia, the publishing crises of the early twentieth century, the move from Battle Creek to Washington, the founding of Loma Linda—and most dramatically the conflict with Kellogg—became (after the Great Disappointment and along with 1888) foundations of Adventist cultural folklore. A. G. Daniells provided the church with a good share of its historical memory.

TO SLEEP WITH NO SORROW

By the early 1930s Daniells was well into his eighth decade of life. He began to experience stark reminders of the mortality of all flesh. In early 1931, E. R. Palmer fell ill with pneumonia and died suddenly. He and Daniells had been very close; the latter shared personal matters of his life with him. It was a grievous blow to Daniells. "Somehow it casts a sort of a shadow over one's mind and life. The future does not look quite so attractive." There was more. Later that year W. T. Knox, former treasurer of the General Conference, died suddenly from a stroke. Knox was but a few months older than Daniells, a pointed reminder of where in life's journey he stood. Daniells preached Knox's funeral sermon at Mountain View and wrote his obituary for the *Review*.[71]

Daniells had known his fair share of health problems through the years, in part a function of his unrelenting pace. A troubling heart issue afflicted him in the mid-1920s. In the end, though, a different scourge bested him. While at Battle Creek in the fall of 1934, he was hit with stomach problems. The troubles continued over the next couple of months, leaving doctors puzzled. He finally entered Glendale Sanitarium for more tests. In early February the bad news came. There was a spot on his stomach that meant only one thing. Judged incurable, Daniells understood that he must increase the pace of his manuscript. But he also refused to accept his fate meekly. To the end he believed in the power of intercessory healing prayer. Shortly after his diagnosis, a collection of denominational leaders visited him at his California home and held a season of prayer, "not based particularly upon friendship," Daniells wrote Willie White, "but upon a clear understanding of what the Scriptures teach about prayer for the healing of the sick." Into early March he remained convinced that he had work yet to do and "God is going to spare my life to do that work."[72]

But by the middle of March Daniells was growing noticeably weaker. He soldiered on with the manuscript project only through the grit that characterized his nature. But he had begun reflecting on even weightier matters. He was searching his heart, Froom reported to M. E. Kern, and "seeking to understand the meaning of it all." He regretted a failure to make more vivid his righteousness-by-faith message the previous decade. Opposition from some "high sources" and "indifference" on the part of others prevented, he felt, the coming of the reformation the church needed. Still, he bore some responsibility for not making a better presentation.[73]

Wanting to live, but resigned now to death, Daniells ensured that necessary details were attended to. He gave instructions to G. A. Calkins, president of Pacific Union Conference, who would help Mary through the financial issues. Daniells left a modest estate, but he had—auto enthusiast to the end—just ordered a new car from the factory. This would be sold. There was the matter of the manuscript. The day before his death he had read back to him the section dealing with the founding of Avondale School, and he was able to add some final details. He also completed a "Charge to the Advent Ministry," delivered to Froom for publication in *Ministry* magazine. This was a personal moment offered in a public forum. The burden Daniells carried for the Adventist ministry never lessened. "I speak to the aged; I address those in the prime of life; and I appeal to the young," he intoned. "I charge you all solemnly before God, to be true to your high ministerial trust." He charged them "to take up this burden, and complete the work; God expects it of you."[74]

Then followed, finally, his personal goodbyes at his home. He met with Arthur White, to whom the torch of the White Estate would soon be passed; with Leroy Froom, his faithful literary attendant and champion; with Dores Robinson; with wife Mary, son Grosvenor, daughter-in-law Grace, and sister Jesse. And two days before his death, a last meeting with Willie White, a "David and Jonathan" encounter, it seemed to Robinson. Indeed, it was heartfelt. At one point, Daniells made reference to his not having "rendered you [Willie] very good service," an allusion they both understood regarding his earlier opposition to publishing Ellen White's unpublished works. White graciously urged him not to dwell on that but rather on what they had accomplished together. Toward the end, Daniells brought the conversation around to the even greater conflict of his career with John Harvey Kellogg. The trauma of those days intruded even to his dying breath. But he also spoke of his gratitude to the prophet. When in 1903 Kellogg put on a full-court press to pry her away from Daniells, she had greeted the still-young General Conference president "just as hearty as though I were her first-born." With personal and authorial business attended to, early on Friday morning, March 22, Daniells fell into a coma and died at noon.[75]

A giant had passed, and the denomination responded accordingly. His several memorial services recalled Ellen White's passing. "With dignified simplicity, and yet with impressiveness befitting his conspicuous service to the advent movement" was how Calkins described Daniells's funeral service in Los Angeles. A student honor guard flanked his casket. The 1,100-seat Paulson Hall was supplemented with chairs in the nearby recreation hall, with speakers providing an audio feed. Police roped off surrounding streets. P. T. Magan read the life sketch, and C. H. Watson delivered the sermon. A men's quartet from CME sang at both the funeral and the graveside service at the estimable Forest Lawn Memorial Park in Glendale. Two other memorial services were also held, one in Battle Creek and the other in Takoma Park.[76]

Arthur Grosvenor Daniells labored for the Seventh-day Adventist Church for nearly fifty-seven years, fifty-three as an ordained minister, and twenty-one as General Conference president. He died still in the harness, having never retired. He was a man capable of error and imperfect judgment. But his leadership virtues far outweighed those failings. Although he spent endless hours with committees, he never became lost in the thicket of administrative details. He maintained a clear-eyed focus on the task of proclaiming the gospel worldwide. And even in moments of discouragement he clung to a transcendent optimism. "The triumph of this movement," W. A. Spicer observed at the Takoma Park service, "was to him as sure as the sure word of prophecy."[77]

---

[1] AGD to C. K. Meyers, June 22, 1922; AGD to W. A. Spicer, June 25, 1922, ASTR.

[2] *RH*, June 8, 1922, 32; T. E. Bowen to AGD, December 30, 1922, ASTR.

[3] AGD to W. A. Spicer, August 6, 1922, ASTR.

[4] E. R. Palmer to AGD, September 25, 1921; AGD to E. R. Palmer, December 11, 1922; E. R. Palmer to AGD, December 12, 1922; AGD to E. R. Palmer, December 14, 1922, ASTR.

[5] AGD to E. R. Palmer, December 14, 1922, ASTR.

[6] AGD to N. D. Quinn, December 22, 1923, ASTR.

[7] *GCB*, May 28, 1922, 292; Schwarz and Greenleaf, *Light Bearers*, 387–389; AGD to E. R. Palmer, October 28, 1928; AGD to WCW, August 3, 1911, ASTR.

[8] Leroy Edwin Froom, *Movement of Destiny* (Washington, DC: Review and Herald®, 1971), 395; *RH*, December 14, 1922, 19; AGD to WCW, January 1, 1923, EGWE; T. E. Bowen to AGD, March 27 and October 12, 1924, ASTR.

[9] AGD and L. E. Froom to F. M. Wilcox and E. R. Palmer, October 25, 1927; "Books Worth Reading: The Ministerial Reading Course for 1931," Ministerial Association pamphlet, ASTR; *GCB*, June 4, 1926, 7–11.

[10] *GCB*, June 4, 1926, 7–9; AGD, "Editorial Keynotes," *Ministry* (January 1928), accessed June 18, 2014, https://www.ministrymagazine.org/archive/1928/01/editorial-keynotes.

[11] Froom, *Movement of Destiny*, 406–408.

[12] Ibid., 398–400; AGD to "Dear Brother," March 14, 1926, ASTR.

[13] AGD to "Dear Brethren," March 14, 1926; E. R. Palmer to AGD, August 25, 1926, ASTR.

[14] AGD, *Christ Our Righteousness* (Washington, DC: Review and Herald®, 1941 [first published 1926]), 9, 28.

[15] Ibid., 41–43.

[16] Ibid., 49, 53, 54.

[17] Froom, *Movement of Destiny*, 400; AGD to "Dear Brother," August 25, 1926; E. R. Palmer to AGD, August 18, 1927, ASTR.

[18] E. R. Palmer to AGD, May 17, 1926; Claude Holmes to L. E. Froom [c. October 1927], ASTR.

[19] Mary Daniells to E. R. Palmer, May 3, 1927; AGD to E. R. Palmer, October 28, 1928, ASTR.

[20] Mary Daniells to E. R. Palmer, August 10, 1924; E. R. Palmer to Mary Daniells, August 18, 1924; E. R. Palmer to AGD, May 27, 1926, ASTR.

[21] E. R. Palmer to Mary Daniells, August 18, 1924; Mary Daniells to E. R. Palmer, August 10, 1924.

[22] AGD, "Ministerial Institutes in the Australasian Division," *Ministry* (May 1929), accessed June 19, 2014, https://www.ministrymagazine.org/archive/1929/05/ministerial-institutes-in-the-australasian-division; AGD to E. R. Palmer, July 16, 1928.

[23] AGD, "Ministerial Institutes in the Australasian Division."

[24] Daniells's South American trip was covered in *RH*, April 10, 1930, 22, 23; April 24, 1930, 23, 24; May 1, 1930, 24, 25; May 8, 1930, 24, 25; May 15, 1930, 23, 24; May 29, 1930, 22, 23.

[25] T. E. Bowen to AGD, March 22, 1923; AGD to T. E. Bowen, April 19, 1923, ASTR.

[26] *RH*, November 25, 1926, 3–8; January 14, 1932, 6–8.

[27] *RH*, February 6, 1930, 4, 5; February 13, 1930, 4–7; February 20, 1930, 6–8; February 27, 1930, 7, 8.

[28] *RH*, January 14, 1932, 6–8.

[29] AGD to C. H. Watson, May 1, 1931, ASTR.

[30] Schwarz and Greenleaf, *Light Bearers*, 404, 405; AGD to C. H. Watson, January 12, 1931; January 15, 1931; February 3, 1931, ASTR.

[31] AGD to C. H. Watson, July 7, 1931; AGD to C. H. Watson, November 12, 1931, ASTR.

[32] AGD to C. H. Watson, July 7, 1931; AGD to C. H. Watson, May 11(B), 1932, ASTR.

[33] AGD to C. H. Watson, May 11(B), 1932.

[34] AGD to C. H. Watson, May 11(A), 1932, ASTR.

[35] GCCmin, December 18, 1930; AGD to LeRoy Froom, August 13, 1931; C. H. Watson to AGD, February 9, 1931, ASTR.

[36] McFarland, *Railway to the Moon*, 61, 62; Richard A. Schaefer, Loma Linda University archives, e-mail message to author, June 25, 2014; AGD to C. H. Watson, February 3, 1931.

[37] AGD to C. H. Watson, July 9, 1931; February 9, 1931; February 16, 1931, ASTR; Merlin Neff, *For God and C.M.E.* (Mountain View, CA: Pacific Press®, 1964), 268–271.

[38] AGD to C. H. Watson, February 26, 1931; C. H. Watson to AGD, May 24, 1931, ASTR; McFarland, *Railway to the Moon*, 61–66; GCCmin., Nov 14, 1934.

[39] C. H. Watson to AGD, February 9, 1931; AGD to C. H. Watson, February 26, 1931; March 1, 1931, ASTR; Percy T. Magan, "Life Sketch of Arthur Grosvenor Daniells," *RH*, April 18, 1935, 2.

[40] Richard Schaefer, "The Cooperative Plan of Medical Education at CME," in "Glory of the Vision, Unabridged," unpublished manuscript, Loma Linda University; Neff, *For God and C.M.E.*, 224, 225; AGD to C. H. Watson, March 1, 1931.

[41] AGD to C. H. Watson, July 14, 1931; July 7, 1931; June 14, 1931; C. H. Watson to AGD, July 31, 1931.

[42] "Mrs. White's Legacy to the Trustees," statement by AGD, March 11, 1935, reprinted in Arthur White, *Ellen G. White: Messenger to the Remnant* (Washington, DC: Review and Herald®, 1969), 68; Jerry Moon and Denis Fortin, eds., *The Ellen G. White Encyclopedia* (Hagerstown, MD: Review and Herald®, 2014), s.v. "Books, Preparation of Ellen G. White's."

[43] *The Ellen G. White Encyclopedia,* s.v. "Ellen G. White Estate, Incorporated"; James R. Nix, "A Brief Look at the History and Purpose of the Ellen G. White Estate, Inc.," in "Ellen White and Current Issues," symposium proceedings, Center for Adventist Research, Andrews University, April 2, 2007; Paul McGraw and Gilbert Valentine provide a very useful overview in their chapter, "Legacy," in *Ellen Harmon White*, Aamodt, Land, Numbers, eds., 305, 321; E. R. Palmer to AGD, September 12, 1922, ASTR; EGW Estate minutes, April 22, 1918, EGWE.

[44] AGD to WCW, September 12, 1923, EGWE.

[45] EGW Estate minutes, October 26, 1920.

[46] McGraw and Valentine, "Legacy," 309–311; "First Part of the Address Given by Pastor A. G. Daniells, Monday night, June 24, 1928, at the New South Wales Workers' Institute," EGWE.

[47] WCW to GC Committee, October 3, 1921, EGWE.

[48] Tim Poirier, conversation with author, White Estate, May 28, 2014; EGW Estate minutes, June 5, 1932; November 27, 1933.

[49] AGD, "Preface to the First Edition," in EGW, *Medical Ministry* (Mountain View, CA: Pacific Press®, 1932).

[50] GCCMin, August 4, 1930.

[51] AGD to L. E. Froom, August 5, 1931; August 13, 1931, ASTR.

[52] AGD to L. E. Froom, August 5, 1931.

[53] AGD to L. E. Froom, January 29, 1935.

[54] Ibid.; L. E. Froom, "Elder Daniells' Wishes, Requests, and Charges Re. His Manuscript," memo [n.d.], ASTR; W. M. Landeen to L. E. Froom, February 17, 1935; H. A. Washburn to L. E. Froom, February 14, 1935; F. A. Schilling to L. E. Froom, February 22, 1935; G. M. Price to L. E. Froom, February 22, 1935; F. D. Nichol to L. E. Froom, February 14, 1935; February 28, 1935; L. L. Caviness to L. E. Froom, February 14, 1933; Dores Robinson to L. E. Froom, May 1, 1935, ASTR.

[55] L. E. Froom, "Elder Daniells' Wishes."

[56] Ibid.; C. H. Watson to AGD, March 22, 1935, ASTR.

[57] L. E. Froom, "Guiding Principles for Editing the Daniells Ms.," memo, ASTR.

[58] AGD to L. E. Froom, January 29, 1935.

[59] EGW, *Education*, 46; F. M. Wilcox, "Report on Manuscript 'The Abiding Gift of Prophecy,' " [n.d.], ASTR.

[60] Froom, "Guiding Principles"; AGD, *The Abiding Gift of Prophecy* (Mountain View, CA: Pacific Press®, 1935), 6.

[61] Froom, "Elder Daniells' Wishes"; C. H. Watson to AGD, March 22, 1935.

[62] Endorsements included the following: A. O. Tait to L. E. Froom, April 15, 1935; May 13, 1935; F. A. Schilling to L. E. Froom, May 5, 1935; J. E. Fulton to L. E. Froom, April 10, 1935; T. G. Bunch to L. E. Froom, April 14, 1935; WCW to L. E. Froom, May 1, 1935, ASTR.

[63] A. O. Tait to L. E. Froom, April 15, 1935.

[64] Wilcox, "Report on Manuscript."

[65] M. E. Kern, "Report on the Manuscript 'The Abiding Gift of Prophecy.' "

[66] L. E. Froom, "Memo re: Developments to Date on Daniells Manuscript"; L. E. Froom to C. H. Watson, May 14, 1935, ASTR.

[67] F. M. Wilcox to L. E. Froom, March 25, 1935; M. E. Kern to L. E. Froom, March 26, 1935.

[68] Dores Robinson to W. E. Howell, June 30, 1935; O. Montgomery to Members of the Reading Committee appointed by the General Conference Committee, July 24, 1935; O. Montgomery to Reading Committee, October 2, 1935, ASTR.

[69] AGD to L. E. Froom, February 14, 1935.

[70] AGD, *Abiding Gift of Prophecy*, 6, 220, 221.

[71] C. H. Watson to AGD, February 9, 1931; AGD to C. H. Watson, February 16, 1935; *RH*, December 17, 1931, 21.

[72] AGD to Arthur White, January 13, 1935; January 22, 1935; AGD to WCW, February 4, 1935, EGWE; *Battle Creek Moon-Journal*, March 23, 1935. No doubt certain church members judged Daniells's stomach cancer to be a fitting—if tragic—outcome to his persistent consumption of meat.

[73] L. E. Froom to Reading Committee, March 7, 1935; March 17 [27], 1935; L. E. Froom to M. E. Kern, March 3, 1935, ASTR.

[74] L. E. Froom to Reading Committee, March 17 [27], 1935; "Report of a Parting Interview Between Elder A. G. Daniells and Elder W. C. White," March 20, 1935; D. E. Robinson, "Triumphant Life Ends in Tranquil Death," manuscript prepared for *Ministry* magazine, all in ASTR. AGD, "Farewell Charge to the Advent Ministry," *Ministry* (May 1935), accessed July 8, 2014, https://www.ministrymagazine.org/archive/1935/05/farewell-charge-to-the-advent-ministry.

[75] Robinson, "Triumphant Life Ends in Tranquil Death"; "Report of Parting Interview"; L. E. Froom to Reading Committee, March 17 [27], 1935.

[76] G. H. Calkins, report on Daniells's funeral to Review and Herald Publishing, March 26, 1935; coverage of Daniells's memorial services found in *RH*, April 18, 1935.

[77] *RH*, April 18, 1935, 9.

Index

A

B

E

F

G

H

I

J

K

L

M

N

S

T

U

V

W

Y